'[A] boisterous romp . . . A loving ode to a comedy classic'

Publishers Weekly

'Mr. de Visé's book . . . races along on a whoosh of marvellous details and crackling anecdotes' *Wall Street Journal*

'A fascinating account . . . definitive telling of the making of *The Blues Brothers*' *Buzz Magazine*

'[de Visé] has compiled the definitive one-stop history of the Blues Brothers band' *Chicago Tribune*

'[A] superb social history of the 1970s in America'

Washington Independent Review of Books

'Exhaustively researched, highly informative'

Kirkus Reviews, starred review

'As fun and riveting as the comedy classic itself . . . A worthy tribute to a raucous masterpiece' Nick de Semlyen, author of *Wild and Crazy Guys*

'A lively and authoritative tribute to a comedy classic, [with] incisive biographical portraits of its two leads' *Sydney Morning Herald*

'If you're a devotee of the movie or a fan of the early *Saturday Night Live*, you'll enjoy this thorough, authoritative, and lively book'

National Review

'This thorough account of *The Blues Brothers*' origin story is as fun and riveting as the comedy classic itself . . . Daniel de Visé chronicles this unique chapter in film history like a virtuoso'

Jennifer Keishin Armstrong,
New York Times bestselling author of *Seinfeldia* and *So Fetch*

Also by Daniel de Visé

King of the Blues:
The Rise and Reign of B.B. King

The Comeback:
Greg LeMond, the True King of American Cycling,
and a Legendary Tour de France

Andy & Don:
The Making of a Friendship and a Classic American TV Show

I Forgot to Remember:
A Memoir of Amnesia (with Su Meck)

Daniel de Visé is the author of five books and journalist. He worked at the *Washington Post*, the *Miami Herald* and three other newspapers in a 23-year career. He lives in Maryland with his wife and children.

THE BLUES BROTHERS

An EPIC FRIENDSHIP, the RISE OF IMPROV, and the MAKING of an AMERICAN FILM CLASSIC

DANIEL DE VISÉ

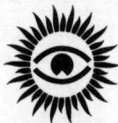

WHITE RABBIT

First published in the United States of America in 2024 by Grove Atlantic
First published in Great Britain in 2024 by White Rabbit,
This paperback edition first published in Great Britain in 2025 by White Rabbit
an imprint of The Orion Publishing Group Ltd
Carmelite House, 50 Victoria Embankment
London EC4Y 0DZ

An Hachette UK Company

The authorised representative in the EEA is Hachette Ireland, 8 Castlecourt
Centre, Dublin 15, D15 XTP3, Ireland (email: info@hbgi.ie)

1 3 5 7 9 10 8 6 4 2

A CIP catalogue record for this book is
available from the British Library.

ISBN (Paperback) 978 1 3996 2188 5
ISBN (eBook) 978 1 3996 2189 2
ISBN (Audio) 978 1 3996 2190 8

Typeset by Born Group
Printed and bound in Great Britain by Clays Ltd, Elcograf S.p.A.

MIX
Paper | Supporting
responsible forestry
FSC
www.fsc.org   FSC® C104740

www.whiterabbitbooks.co.uk
www.orionbooks.co.uk

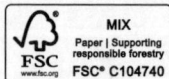

To Gene, Michiya, Phil,
and the Lincoln Park High School gang

Oh, baby, don't you want to go
to that bright-light city, sweet old Chicago

—Roosevelt Sykes, from the song
"Sweet Old Chicago"

CONTENTS

Prologue		xi
Chapter 1	*Cheesebooger*	1
Chapter 2	Rantoul Rag	16
Chapter 3	The Next Generation	31
Chapter 4	Freud, Marx, Engels, and Jung	46
Chapter 5	Welcome Back: The Death Penalty	58
Chapter 6	Change for a Quarter	63
Chapter 7	The Great Canadian Humour Test	73
Chapter 8	You're the Pits	84
Chapter 9	Saturday Night	90
Chapter 10	I'm a King Bee	102
Chapter 11	Bass-o-Matic	115
Chapter 12	Albanian Oak	123
Chapter 13	Night of the Seven Fires	132
Chapter 14	Schlock	143
Chapter 15	Little Chocolate Donuts	150
Chapter 16	Joliet Jake	164
Chapter 17	Briefcase Full of Blues	180
Chapter 18	The Phone Book	197

Chapter 19	The Mission from God	207
Chapter 20	Sweet Home Chicago	219
Chapter 21	The Blues Bar	227
Chapter 22	Get Off of That Picasso	237
Chapter 23	The Pinto Drop	251
Chapter 24	Have You Seen the Light?	263
Chapter 25	It's Never Too Late to Mend	274
Chapter 26	The Black Tower	283
Chapter 27	A $30-Million Wreck	292
Chapter 28	The 2,000 Pound Bee	299
Chapter 29	A Viking Funeral	313
Epilogue		331
Acknowledgments		341
Notes		345
Index		376

Prologue

I N THE MINUTES before *Saturday Night Live* commenced broadcast on April 22, 1978, Dan Aykroyd adjusted his thin black tie in the dressing-room mirror. He was a perfectionist, and his Elwood Blues persona was perfect: baggy black suit with narrow lapels, black trilby hat, Timex watch, crisp white shirt, and vintage black Ray-Bans.

At twenty-five, Dan was the youngest of the seven Not Ready for Prime Time Players, most of them recruited from improvisational theater troupes, who performed ninety minutes of live television on Saturday nights for a growing national audience of young hipsters, stoners, and sophisticates. *SNL* was late-night television's hottest show, and Dan and his costars, Gilda Radner, Bill Murray, and the others, were becoming household names.

Dan preferred anonymity. In the hot glare of the dressing-room mirror, he trained all his manic energy on transforming into Elwood Blues: a recidivist character, raised in a Chicago orphanage, schooled in the blues, who concealed his pallid junkie frame within the raiments of straight society, hiding bloodshot eyes behind dark shades, a Hohner Special 20 harmonica tucked in a hip pocket like a revolver.

In the next room sat Elwood's brother in blues, Jake, a role inhabited with reckless abandon by Dan's best friend, writing partner, and *SNL* costar, John Belushi. At twenty-nine, John was four years older than Dan, four inches shorter, and several inches wider. Dan was Mr. Careful. John was Mr. Fuck It. In front of his own dressing-room mirror, John assembled his Jake Blues ensemble with sloppy imprecision. His collar didn't quite fit. His hat was brown.

The cold open began with Paul Shaffer, the *Saturday Night Live* pianist, invoking his Bronx-accented impression of Don Kirshner, the music-industry kingpin whose *Rock Concert* program tapped much the same audience that watched *SNL*. Shaffer's rambling monologue parodied Kirshner's tiresome habit of thanking a long list of managers and producers as he ushered in the next act.

"So now," Shaffer concluded, "let's join 'Joliet' Jake and his silent brother Elwood. The Blues Brothers." Then Shaffer turned, or rotated, like a robot on Quaaludes, and the camera cut to the act behind him.

"I went balling the other night," John snarled. "I started drinking and got real tight." That was the opening lyrical salvo to "Hey Bartender," a 1955 blues standard popularized by Texas singer Floyd Dixon, and this was the debut performance of the Blues Brothers as musical guests on *Saturday Night Live*.

Apart from the G-man suits, everything onstage rang familiar to the audience in Studio 8H. The Blues Brothers were a thinly disguised Aykroyd and Belushi, whose partnership as writers and performers had started three years and sixty-three episodes earlier, with the *SNL* debut. They performed with the *Saturday Night Live* band, the ensemble whose roots-rock jams opened and closed every show.

Was this an elaborate skit? Was it serious? No one seemed to know. *SNL* was a comedy show that took its music seriously. Lorne Michaels, the program's creator and showrunner, had hedged his bets, presenting the Blues Brothers in the guise of a sketch rather than a musical break. He left viewers to judge whether the act was serious or satiric. After the opening bars, a round of halfhearted applause faded to awkward silence.

Undeterred, John strode to center stage, fingers snapping, hips shaking, sweat beading on his moon-pie Albanian face, that famous Belushi brow arching over the rim of his Ray-Bans. His white-guy blues growl rang shallow and shrill by comparison to the great Black blues growlers, invoking a drunkard at a karaoke bar. But John made a formidable front man, unbuttoning his suit coat, prowling around the microphone, and launching into a surprisingly agile dance during Dan's unexpectedly credible solo on his Special 20 harmonica. Cast and crew watched the performance with bemused admiration, and one of the writers had a small epiphany: "Danny knows this is a bit of a joke, but John has no idea."

John spun in circles as Dan wrung the last notes from his solo. John lurched back into the microphone to belt out the next verse. By then, everyone watching the broadcast understood that the Blues Brothers act was deadly serious, at least to the black-suited front men. Never in their three years on the *Saturday Night Live* stage had John and Dan exuded such messianic passion. The song wound down, and John barked out the final words with menace: "one, two, three, four glasses of beer!" As the musicians hung on the last note, John grabbed the microphone and loosed a primal scream. The audience exploded in applause, shaken awake and stirred to jubilation by the infectious power of the performance. John, his face glistening with sweat, nodded nonchalantly to acknowledge the cheers. He knew what he and Dan had pulled off. Was it real? Was it a joke? The audience no longer cared.

The camera cut to Paul Shaffer, still in character as Don Kirshner as he delivered the breathless line that opened every show: "Live, from New York, it's *Saturday Night!*"

That night's live broadcast would deliver a second gut-busting performance by the Blues Brothers but no real clues to their provenance. Why were *Saturday Night*'s breakout comedians masquerading as urban bluesmen? If their act was a joke, how far would it go?

For those answers, we take you now to a cramped brown-brick duplex in Chicago.

Queasimay?

Chapter 1

Cheesebooger

JOHN BELUSHI'S FATHER, Adam, was born on January 2, 1918, in the waning months of the Great War, in the Albanian village of Qytezë. Naturalization records variously give his birth name as Belliors, Beliouri, and Beloushi. The family journeyed to America in dribs and drabs. First to arrive was John's grandfather, Anastassios, in 1920. Anastassios settled within a tiny Albanian enclave in Chicago. Adam remained in Albania until 1934. At sixteen, he emigrated on the luxury liner SS *Manhattan*, traveling in third class.

After establishing a foothold in Chicago, the family simplified its surname to Belushi, which sounded Italian. In fact, the Belushis were closer to Greek; their Albanian village lay only a few miles from the Hellenic border. Either identity would serve the Belushis better in Chicago than Albanian, an ethnicity most Americans then regarded with a primal unease reserved for small eastern European nations they could not find on a map. Adam took a busboy job at the Palm Grove Inn, a white-tablecloth dining establishment on the shores of Lake Michigan in the academic enclave of Hyde Park. He worked his way up to manager.

Adam enlisted in the US Army in March 1941, months before Pearl Harbor. He served as a warrant officer in the Panama Canal Department, defending the shipping lane against an attack that never came. He struck up a wartime correspondence with a woman he had never met, Agnes Samaras, born in 1922 in Akron, Ohio, to another Albanian immigrant family. Agnes worked as a riveter at the Goodyear Aircraft

Company. She wrote to Adam at the urging of his sister, who had settled in Akron.

In 1945, at the war's end, Adam returned home and traveled to Akron, commencing a courtship with Agnes Samaras. They wed in 1946 and settled in Chicago. Postwar housing proved scarce, so the couple moved in with Adam's parents in Humboldt Park, an immigrant-rich neighborhood on the city's West Side.

Adam now managed a restaurant of his own, the Olympia Lunch, in partnership with his brother Pete. A far cry from the elegant Palm Grove, the Olympia operated as a no-frills Greek diner, a familiar and trusted species of Chicago eatery. The Belushi brothers would corral customers through a limited menu, then bark out orders.

The first Belushi child, Marian, arrived in 1947. Albanian families favored boys. Adam's parents "almost didn't let me come home," Agnes said. "Two years later, I had John, and everybody was very happy."

John Adam Belushi entered the world on January 24, 1949, a blustery Monday. The Belushis returned from the hospital to a narrow brown-brick duplex at 3114 W. Walton Street that housed three generations.

John's grandfather, Anastassios, died in the summer of 1949. His widow, Vasilo "Nena" Belushi, moved in with Adam and Agnes and became a second mother to John. By the time he entered kindergarten, John "was like a little man," Agnes said. He would walk out the front door, "wander up the street, walk into a neighbor's house, sit down and strike up a conversation." He "never really spoke like a child," so neighbors treated him like an adult. They called him Pancho, for his dark olive skin.

The Belushi home sat near Humboldt Park, the neighborhood's namesake, a two-hundred-acre sanctuary that boasted an arched boat-house overlooking a lagoon, ballfields, tennis courts, a beach, and an outdoor swimming pool. Agnes would drop John and Marian in a sand-box and leave them there, an entirely reasonable act in that era of free-range parenting. "John just took care of himself."

The Belushis welcomed a third child, Jim, in the summer of 1954. John, age five, picked up the telephone in the Belushi home and gave the operator enough information to place a call to the hospital where

Agnes lay. "Everyone thought it was very cute," he said. "I still don't know how I managed it."

A year later, Adam Belushi left the Olympia and opened a new restaurant, the Fair Oaks, five miles west of the family home. The family was outgrowing the Walton Street house. A waitress at the Fair Oaks told Adam that her brother was selling his home in Wheaton, twenty miles west of the Fair Oaks at the outer edge of Chicago's swelling suburban sprawl. She urged Adam to take a look.

Postwar suburbanization and white flight were reshaping Chicago. The city's white head count would plummet from 86 percent of the population in 1950 to 76 percent in 1960 and 66 percent in 1970. The city's overall population remained flat while the suburbs exploded, adding roughly one hundred thousand residents per year, most of them white. The Great Migration had filled Chicago neighborhoods with African Americans fleeing the state-sanctioned racism of the South. Many white communities responded by sealing their borders, working with realtors and lenders to turn away Black families, transforming Chicago into a tense checkerboard of white and Black neighborhoods. Then came the landmark *Brown v. Board of Education* decision of 1954, which decreed segregation of public schools unconstitutional. After that, the arrival of a single Black family in a historically white enclave might send white homeowners scrambling to the suburbs. Falling home prices and impoverished schools in the city drove away yet more families, feeding the cycle of flight.

In 1955, the Belushis joined the exodus, leaving the city for a home in a town so remote, it barely qualified as a suburb. Wheaton rose out of the cornfields as a vision of upscale Republican suburbia. The city's history intertwined with that of Wheaton College, a private institution founded by evangelical abolitionists. Wheaton's shops and restaurants neither sold nor served alcohol. Beyond the city's western frontier lay farmland.

"We weren't literally the last stop on the commuter train; Geneva was," said Will Greene, a family friend. "But if you looked to the west, it was Iowa."

Against Wheaton's white, Christian tableau, Blacks, Hispanics, and immigrants from impoverished communist countries stood out. Friends and neighbors assumed the Belushis were Italian, a misperception the Belushis did nothing to correct.

John and Marian Belushi enrolled at Whittier elementary school, named for the abolitionist poet John Greenleaf Whittier. The family settled into a single-story, three-bedroom wooden ranch house with an attached garage, draped in siding and shaded by pines. The dwelling sat in a working-class enclave of an upper-class town. John and Jim shared bunk beds in an alcove tucked between the kitchen and the garage. Nena slept on the sunporch. A third son, Billy, arrived in 1960. Local rumor held that Nena helped Agnes deliver him in the kitchen.

"A lot of people, and a little tiny house," said Juanita Payne, a family friend. "And they were big people."

John, broad-shouldered and barrel-chested, seemed forever hungry. He stopped frequently at the door of Jeff Moffat, a friend, to angle for food.

"Mrs. Moffat," he would beckon, nose pressed to the screen.

"Oh, hi, John," Jeff's mother would reply.

"A delectable aroma drew me to your back door as I was cruising along Pershing Avenue," he would continue, evoking Popeye's gluttonous friend J. Wellington Wimpy. Jeff's mother would invite him in.

On the first day of classes at Thomas Edison Junior High School in the autumn of 1961, Chris Sautter struck up a friendship with a fellow seventh-grader named Tom Stansfield. At lunchtime, Stansfield told Sautter, "You've gotta meet this kid, John Belushi." They headed to the cafeteria, where Sautter beheld a boy who resembled a full-grown man. The boys sat down. Tom instructed John, "Talk like Kennedy." John unfurled a familiar Boston brogue. "And so, my fellow Americans: ask not what your country can do for you—ask what you can do for your country."

John had discovered the recordings of Kennedy-era stand-ups Jonathan Winters and Bob Newhart. "John played comedy albums over and over again, a million times, until you'd go crazy," Marian Belushi remembered. "He'd imitate them in the mirror for hours, and then he'd make me listen to him act them out just to get my opinion. Sometimes he'd wake me up in the middle of the night to do this. Then he started writing little skits."

Winters was a master impressionist. "John could do all of his characters," brother Jim said: Cary Grant and John Wayne, cheeky Maude Frickert, and hayseed Elwood P. Suggins. John also developed his own impressions, targeting Kennedy; Richard J. Daley, Chicago's inarticulate mayor; and various teachers and coaches. At school, the moment a teacher left the classroom, John would launch into pitch-perfect mimicry. "When the teacher walked back in, Belushi would be sitting there like an angel, and everybody else would be laughing," Chris Sautter said.

John imitated his parents, but not to their faces. "He never actually mimicked my father in front of him. Oh, no," Jim recalled. "Of course, he probably could have done it right to my father's face, and [my father] wouldn't even have known it."

John's mother and grandmother provided most of the parenting because John's humorless father was seldom home. Agnes meted out halfhearted discipline. After one spanking, John instructed Jim, "Just laugh when she hits us." The boys kept Agnes laughing. In time, she lost interest in spankings.

At the dinner table, John would bow his head, flip up both eyelids to expose their fleshy interiors, then raise his head ghoulishly, leaving his mother breathless from laughter. Adam would go right on eating.

Adam spent weeknights in an apartment above the Fair Oaks, returning home for weekends to assign chores and enumerate rules. Adam worked through holidays. One day, his father off at work, John unfurled an impression of the patriarch at the dinner table. "Number one," he said, half rising from his seat for emphasis, as his father did. "You take out the garbage. Number two, you do the lawn. Number three, I want you to help your mother with the dishes. Number four, turn over the garden for Nena."

That act, too, left Agnes panting from laughter.

John's dark complexion drew notice in the hallways of Edison Junior High. To evade the bullies, John projected a confidence that bordered on contempt. In the fall of 1962, in eighth grade, John came upon a new student in the halls, an air force brat named George Karwoski, just arrived in Wheaton. Karwoski had completed his first class, and he could not locate the next one. He walked aimlessly down the hallway. "And here comes this guy that is the oddest-looking guy I'd seen in a long time," he recalled. "Very short legs, very long torso, and very long arms. And he had a five-o'clock shadow, hair on his knuckles, and a lot of curly hair on top of his head. And he looked kind of Italian."

Karwoski asked the boy for directions. John eyed the new student with disdain. "It's upstairs," he said coolly. "First door on that hallway when you come out of the stairway." And then he was gone.

At day's end, Karwoski encountered the long-armed boy again at basketball tryouts. John sat within a scrum of eighth-grade boys. Karwoski pegged him as the leader. As boys approached the basket with awkward leaps, the observers alternately cheered or glowered, following the lead of the olive-skinned boy. Eventually, Karwoski's turn arrived, and he leapt higher than anyone else. Silence followed. Karwoski looked over at the group and found their stocky leader, hands on his hips and a scowl on his face.

Classmates might have dismissed John as a knuckle-dragger. But time revealed the Belushi boy's complexity. At the school's annual talent show, previewing the sort of characters he would eventually perform on *Saturday Night Live*, John transformed into Soviet premier Nikita Khrushchev, holding a press conference and testily answering questions from fellow students whom he had planted in the audience. John capped the performance by banging his shoe on the podium, mimicking Khrushchev's outburst at the United Nations a few years earlier.

After the show, the principal found Adam and Agnes Belushi in a hallway. "Mr. and Mrs. Belushi," he said, "your son is incredibly talented. Compared to most of the kids that come through this school, he's really one in a million."

John's family, however, remained a source of embarrassment for him. To overcome the ethnic stigma, he grew aggressively social. "He connected with everyone—the in-crowd, the bookish types, and the greasers," Chris Sautter recalled. John entertained classmates with targeted humor, reeling off impressions of the popular kids but never the outsiders. John himself felt like an outsider.

John went out for track and football and excelled at the latter, his stumpy legs generating surprising speed on the field. Agnes brought her outsize personality to every game. John never missed an after-school activity, the better to avoid busboy shifts at his father's restaurant.

The mercurial Belushi business hovered at its prosperous peak. In 1963, Adam and brother Pete opened a second Fair Oaks restaurant. The new eatery sat in Chicago's booming northwest suburbs, with loftier pretentions than the original.

"The place had thick carpets and cloth wallpaper, oil paintings, a piano player in the bar and the best prime rib I've ever had," said the journalist Mike Royko, a family friend who attended the opening. "We toasted their success. It was a long way from tending sheep in Albania, and they had earned it."

When John was thirteen, his parents borrowed money to buy him a blue drum kit. He joined a succession of rock bands, though he could barely play.

At the end of junior high school, John took home awards for best athlete and best actor. He collected another award from the American Legion, the veterans' organization, recognizing character and classic American values. He traveled three hours south to the state capital in Springfield for a celebratory dinner. When he returned home, he told Agnes it had been the happiest day of his life.

In the fall of 1963, John entered Wheaton Community High School, renamed Wheaton Central High School the following year. Though only fourteen, he was already approaching his full height of five foot nine and his linebacker weight of 190 pounds.

He assumed the role of big brother to Marian, his older sister. "One night we were in the bleachers at a football game, and some guy called me a name," she said. "John heard him, and he got really mad, grabbed the guy and hit him. The guy dropped to the ground and tumbled all the way down the bleachers. I was really upset. I said to John, 'What did you do that for?'

"'Forget it,' he shot back. 'No one talks to you like that.'

"We went down to the bottom of the bleachers, and this guy was just lying there. I picked up his head to see if he was all right, and John goes, 'You apologize to my sister right now.' The guy's bleeding all over himself, and John's standing over him, making him apologize to me. I was a junior. John was a freshman."

After school, John practiced on his drum kit, jumping from one garage band to the next. He remained an erratic drummer and sang with a gruff, tonally challenged baritone. Once in a while, bandmates let him sing.

In the autumn of 1964, John joined his most enduring high school band, eventually known as the Ravins. The ensemble evolved from a friendship John had struck up with a fellow student named Michael Blasucci, who played guitar. Their surnames were so close, classmates thought they were brothers. The boys discovered a shared passion for Chuck Berry and the Beatles. They talked music in class until the teacher separated them. They gathered after school for jam sessions, guitar and drums pounding away until they ran out of songs or police shut them down. John liked to sing "Bad Boy," the old Larry Williams song repopularized by the Beatles, with a shredding faux-Lennon vocal. A classmate joined on keyboard. Michael's brother Dick learned bass.

The Ravins performed in Belushi's garage, in school hallways, and at the local youth center. Michael handled most of the vocals. John was "a little shy at first, but then he would come out front and sing," Blasucci said. "He actually accused me of upstaging him because the drums were always set up in the back."

Blasucci remembered Nena, John's grandmother, as the woman who would answer the phone and apprise him, in her limited English, "Johnny no home." He remembered Agnes Belushi as irrepressible.

"She would do some things that would really embarrass John," Blasucci said. Once, the Ravins threw a party for some friends in the Belushi basement. Before long, Agnes appeared in the basement and started dancing. John shooed her away.

In the summer after John's sophomore year, the Rolling Stones released "(I Can't Get No) Satisfaction," their first number-one hit in the United States. John learned to sing it. When the Stones toured America that fall, John persuaded some bandmates to go into the city for the concert, staged on November 28, 1965, at the Arie Crown Theater.

Inspired by the Beatles and the Stones, the Ravins found matching red-and-black uniforms, topped with black, removable turtleneck collars. That winter, they traveled downtown to a studio owned by a Blasucci family friend and recorded a single, penned by the band, titled "Listen to Me Now." Michael Blasucci sang lead. They pressed one hundred copies and dispatched some to local deejays, to no avail. The boys gave some away, painted the rest ironical gold and repurposed them as Frisbees.

The Ravins impressed everyone at Wheaton Central but the football coach. By his junior year, John had earned a starting position on the varsity football team. Coach didn't like his star linebacker moonlighting in a rock 'n' roll band.

For John, football was performance. "He didn't like to practice or do the drills," recalled Howard Barnes, the coach. "But as soon as you turned the lights on, he was super." John worked up a devastating impression of Coach Barnes using gym-teacher math to break down the grading policy for phys-ed class: "One-fifth for wrestling, one-fifth for basketball, one-fifth on calisthenics, one-fifth on volleyball and one-fifth on football. And one-half on attitude." In another bit, John portrayed Coach delivering a pregame pep talk and then reluctantly turning it over to his inebriated assistant, who wobbled and waved his arms as he slurred, "All right! How many of you guys beat off last night? How many times do I have to tell you? Don't masturbate. It saps your strength. Did any of you touch yourself before the game? I bet you did."

Agnes shared her son's impulse to lean into Wheaton social life, leveraging her big personality to counter the stigma of otherness.

"That's where John got all that. She was funny and charming," said family friend Juanita Payne. "She was not very tall but very, very fat. She worked at the drugstore, and people would go into the drugstore just to see Mrs. Belushi. She was a wonderful person. They would have football dinners. She was the one who organized them. She was a little pushy, so some of the other mothers shied away from her."

Agnes Belushi worked so hard, in part, to compensate for the social shortcomings of her dour and elusive husband. The American economy of the middle 1960s was booming. But Chicago was enduring an exodus of affluent families of all races to the suburbs. Adam Belushi found that he could not support his family on his earnings at the Fair Oaks. Agnes worked at a pharmacy. John took shifts as a dishwasher at an iconic Wheaton diner called the Seven Dwarfs, next to the drugstore. Agnes sometimes came in for lunch.

Much of the time, John's outward persona was decidedly unfunny. He stalked the halls of Wheaton Central, glaring with intense eyes framed by heavy, arched brows. He did not drink or smoke or take drugs. He did not really date. He was home in bed by ten. He lectured team-mates to follow his puritanical lead. At the start of his junior year, he threatened to turn in Chuck Kelley, the star quarterback, for drinking beer over the summer. "And we needed Kelley," said Tom Stansfield, a teammate. "Because we only had one quarterback who was any good." Friends dissuaded him.

John won election as sergeant at arms in the school's mock Congress, a job he took all too seriously. In a meeting with school administrators, John learned that students had been marking up lockers. "I'll take care of it," he told the principal. After school the next day, the principal found John with the offending students, standing guard like a warden while they scrubbed lockers.

John's impulse for caveman violence usually found a righteous outlet. At times, he meted out cruelty for no apparent reason, like a brute in the showers snapping others with a twisted-up towel. Once, during the sadistic gym-class ritual of dodgeball, John cornered Tom Stansfield against the bleachers with his shirt off. "He's gonna throw this dodge-ball at me," Stansfield recalled. "I said, 'Belushi, don't do that.' He did it anyway. Put a welt on me. Consequently, I punched him in the face. We went to the athletic director's office. I got kicked out of school for three days. He wasn't being funny at all. He was being an asshole. I've still got a scar on a finger of my right hand from where I cut the finger on his tooth."

John's glowering presence made the funny stuff funnier. In one variety-show sketch, he took the stage in football pants, a whistle around his neck and a clipboard in his hand. He blew the whistle.

"All right, campers," he growled. "Gather round. First, I want to welcome you to Camp Concentration. And I want to introduce you to your counselors: Igor. Frankenstein. Now, I want to let you all know that there are things you can buy at the camp canteen. You can buy a Camp Concentration T-shirt, and for an extra three bucks, they will brand Camp Concentration on your chest.

"Now, I'm sure you're wondering why you're all handcuffed together," he continued, in a Newhart deadpan, to riotous laughter. "Well, we're going on our opening hike, and I want you to know, we've never had one accident or one fatality on this hike. Well, would you believe two accidents? Would you believe one fatality? Well, we're hoping this will be the first one that we make it through OK. Igor? Where are you going? You're heading off the cliff! And they're all handcuffed together! Igor! Igor!"

In another sketch, John and some friends dressed as acrobats and lined up onstage. They leapt into motion, crisscrossing the stage, running past each other and yelling "Hey!" but never performing any actual acrobatics.

At the end of his junior year, John upgraded from a bicycle to a BMW motorcycle. He bought it with his own earnings from a departing football teammate. John persuaded some friends to procure their own motorcycles.

The last Friday night of school found John and his football buddies riding around Wheaton on their motorcycles, weighing which party to crash. "Hey, listen," John beckoned to Mark Carlson. "Come on over to my house. I want to watch this thing on TV." The boys arrived at the Belushi home. John went to the television and turned on WTTW, the public broadcasting station. "It was some kind of *Playhouse 90* thing, you know, *Masterpiece Theater* or something like that," Carlson recalled. John wanted to spend the last Friday night of the school year watching a televised play. Minutes ticked away. Carlson pleaded, "John, this is *terrible*. This is really, really boring. Let's get out of here."

"Oh, no way," John replied. "I gotta see this, I gotta watch this. This is really good. I'll catch up with you later." Carlson sighed and departed.

John's football teammates never warmed to his theatrical impulses, but other classmates did. His Camp Concentration sketch intrigued Judy Jacklin, a freshman of fifteen with aqua eyes, chestnut hair, and a rebellious streak. She hailed from a WASP family in an upscale section of Wheaton. She first spotted John at a party, singing the dirty version of "Louie Louie" and enunciating the words. She admired his mischievous wit.

One summer day, Judy attended a baseball game with friends, trolling for boys. The girls encountered a group of older students, one of whom she recognized as the variety-show boy with the expressive brown eyes. John was leaning against a car and talking to his friends, dressed in jeans and a V-neck sweater, "hands stuffed in his front pockets, thumbs out, James Dean style," she remembered. The boys offered the girls a ride home.

"When we got to my house," Judy said, "John stepped out of the car to let me out. Goofing around, I shut the door, waved to the driver and said, 'Thanks for the ride!' They just drove off and left us there. We were both a little surprised and embarrassed, because we'd hardly ever spoken." They stood and talked until the car returned, John reticent and tongue-tied, drawing Judy's attention to his eyes. When his gaze accidentally caught hers, both conversants recoiled as if from shock.

A few days later, Judy and her girlfriends went to Herrick Lake, a forest preserve outside town. They found some older boys, and Judy spotted John among them. The group rented boats. John and Judy wound up in the same craft. A water fight erupted. On a backswing with his oar, John struck Judy in the arm. He dropped the oar in horror, grabbed Judy's arm and rubbed it gently, anguished that he might have hurt her. He apologized, again and again. That night, he telephoned her at home to ask, "How's your arm?" She said it was fine. He telephoned again the next night: "How's your arm?" Judy laughed. They talked some more. He called again every night for a week. On the fourth or fifth night, he changed his question and asked if Judy would accompany him to the homecoming dance. She said yes.

Judy had penned a list of traits for the perfect boyfriend: "Good at sports, smart, musical, and funny," she recalled. "And he was all those things. And, of course, I thought he was Italian, as most people did."

Over the summer, John spent two weeks in Lansing, the capital of Michigan, four hours away. A Michigan State University program offered sessions in debate, a discipline in which John excelled. But he spent his two weeks studying theater, his new passion. A photograph in the *Lansing State Journal* pictured him sitting beside three costumed princesses.

One steamy morning in August, George Karwoski sat with some football teammates at the A&W stand after a sweat-soaked preseason practice, chugging root beer. They watched as John appeared on the horizon, leading a squadron of boys on motorcycles, sneering like Brando in *The Wild One*. "These are white-bread, west-suburban kids," Karwoski remembered. But the display unnerved the restaurant manager, who emerged from the stand. Pegging John as the ringleader, the manager walked up to him and asked him to leave. John gazed at the restaurateur for a long moment, impassive. Then he shrugged. "OK." He twirled a forefinger in the air, and he and his friends started their engines en masse. He twirled the finger again and steered his bike into a tight circle around the A&W stand. His friends followed. They circled, five, six times, drawing smiles from surrounded teammates as the poor manager looked on in horror. Then, they revved their engines and rode off.

Football season arrived. One Friday night that fall, the team faced a worthy opponent, featuring an all-state offensive back named Al Lettow. "He was fast and big," said Bob Haeger, a teammate. "And we were getting pumped at stopping this guy." The opposing team got the ball. In the silence before the first play, John bellowed, "Give it to Lettow! I want Lettow!" Every time the fullback got the ball, John tried to bring him down. At halftime, the opposing school announced that Lettow had been named homecoming king. John's eyes widened. "So, the first time they get the ball in the second half," Haeger recalled, John screamed, "GIVE THE BALL TO THE KING! I WANT THE KING!"

The next weekend was homecoming at Wheaton Central. The dance would be John's first real date with Judy. He wore a tuxedo with a white jacket. She wore an ankle-length white dress with a ruffled front. John drove her to the dance in the Jacklin family car; Judy wasn't allowed on a motorcycle. Wheaton students named John the homecoming king. Judy settled for a seat in the queen's court. The tin crown sat too small on John's bulbous head, and he looked uncomfortable posing for pictures and dancing with the queen. When the ceremony was over, he told Judy he wanted to leave.

The first time Judy arrived at the Belushi home for dinner, she felt she had entered another world—and this was why John usually met friends at the curb. "Most of the activity took place in the disproportionately large kitchen," Judy said. Nena, John's grandmother, struck Judy as a stereotypical immigrant woman, wearing a housedress, apron, hairnet, and slippers, and communicating with John in Albanian phrases that he somehow understood. "It was clear from the beginning that she was the one who held the family together," Judy said. Nena set the table with massive platters of food, enough for two or three families. When the Belushis sat down, the table erupted in movement, diners racing to fill their plates, everyone talking at once.

Dinner at the Jacklin home, by contrast, unfolded in silence, save for the clinking of silver on china. Judy's mother served tiny portions. John went home hungry.

In his senior year, John co-captained his football team. The *Chicago Tribune* named him an all-star. Yet, his days as a five-foot-nine linebacker were numbered, and it was punishing work. John led the team in tackles. "He got his bell rung a lot. There were a lot of concussions," Jim Belushi recalled, though none was ever diagnosed. One day, Jim walked into the laundry room of the family home and found John "holding onto the cement sink, and he was shaking," gripped by some sort of seizure. "And then he fell." Paramedics rushed him to the hospital. "He had spinal taps, X-rays. They couldn't find out what it was." John returned home and carried on as if nothing had happened, reprising his role as human battering ram on the football field.

* * *

Increasingly, John gravitated toward his speech teacher, Dan Payne. John was the star debater at Wheaton Central, and Payne directed the annual spring variety show, with John playing an ever-greater role. "Whenever John walked out from the curtains, the audience was already laughing before he was even halfway to the microphone," Payne remembered. "By his senior year, we'd just tell him, 'Okay, we need a comedy routine here, here and here. John, you got two minutes, five minutes and four minutes.' We never knew what he was going to do. We just knew it was going to be funny."

For one senior-year sketch, John trotted out a jug band called the Mountain Men, one student on banjo, another on guitar, a third on kazoo, and serenaded the crowd with a version of Tex Ritter's "I Dreamed of a Hill-Billy Heaven" that seemed "somewhat serious," Bob Haeger said. John didn't joke about music.

John and his motorcycle had appeared one day at the home of Dan and Juanita Payne. Soon he was doing odd jobs for the couple and their neighbors for extra cash, washing windows poorly, sometimes sleeping in an extra bedroom the couple outfitted as an escape from the Belushi home. When John started dating Judy, he told Juanita, "She's the one for me."

"How can you tell so soon?" she asked.

"I just know," he replied.

Judy wasn't so sure. She was sixteen. They traveled in different circles. John abhorred drugs and drink. Judy feared drugs but was already drinking when she and John became a couple. When alcohol ran scarce, Judy and her friends turned to cough syrup. John disapproved. The couple sparred. Judy declined dates with John to drink with friends. Six months into the relationship, spatting over a house party, they broke up. She was glad—she didn't want to miss the party. Within hours, though, she regretted the split. "And there was something else," she said, "something I couldn't quite put my finger on. A feeling in the pit of my stomach." The next day, Judy wrote John a note and confessed her feelings. He told Judy he loved her, too. They resolved to go steady, and soon they were spending every free hour together.

Chapter 2

Rantoul Rag

A S JOHN'S HIGH SCHOOL CAREER neared its end, he fretted over how to finance a future. Both of his father's restaurants were struggling. Marian, his older sister, was soon to wed, an event for which John's parents were planning a lavish party with meager funds. If John wished to avoid the draft and a ticket to Vietnam, he had to start college. He would need some kind of scholarship, football or theater. During senior year, he took a drama class, and Dan Payne cast him in a prominent role in a production titled *My Three Angels*, about a trio of convicts in South America. It was John's first serious role, performed to considerable fanfare.

As summer approached, Payne pestered John to audition for stock theater. One of Payne's Chicago friends, Adrian Rehner, operated a summer program in rural Indiana, five hours south. Rehner mostly hired college theater majors and twenty-something actors. Payne persuaded him to consider John, who reluctantly agreed. Payne picked him up one rainy Saturday for a trip into the city for the audition. John emerged from his house in a suit and tie, as dressy as Payne had ever seen him. He climbed into Payne's Ford station wagon, and they drove off.

"I'm not sure I really want to do this," John said softly, peering out the passenger window. "I can't be in shows if I play football." They pulled into the parking lot beside the football field, a symbol of John's conflict, and stopped to talk. John explained his fear of the draft, his family's profligate spending, and his need for scholarship funds. John had to choose football or acting. Slow down, Payne urged. He wasn't talking about a career, just a summer job.

They drove on. As they reached the city, John asked to stop again. Payne pulled up to a White Hen Pantry convenience store. John purchased a soda and again unburdened himself, complaining bitterly about his father's failing business and reckless spending and absentee parenting, and his sister's impending nuptials. "If they can pay for the wedding," he seethed, "why can't they pay for my college?"

Payne patiently talked John back into the car, telling him he had nothing to lose by auditioning.

They arrived at Adrian Rehner's home. John walked inside, joining fifty other actors reading for a dozen jobs at Shawnee Summer Theatre. Payne waited in the car. When John emerged, he told Payne, "I wasn't very good." Payne suspected otherwise. John sometimes sleepwalked through rehearsal or practice, but when the lights went up, he went all out, always.

When the auditions were over, Payne and John entered the Rehner house together. The director had several auditioners perform additional scenes. When John's turn came, he lit up the room, reducing fellow actors to peals of laughter. Rehner motioned Payne to join him in the kitchen.

"Does he have problems memorizing lines?" Rehner asked.

"No, no," Payne replied. "He can learn lines very well." In truth, John didn't so much memorize lines as intentionally forget them. He was always improvising, trying to improve on the script. He struggled to stay in his assigned spot onstage. He tended toward overacting. In one high school variety show, John had revealed a dead-on Marlon Brando impression. At each performance that day, John had ripped his shirt, then ripped it a little more. By the final skit, the shirt barely hung from his back. Payne shared none of this. Rehner told Payne he would call that night with his decision.

Back in the car, John's mood had transformed. "That's what I want to do," he beamed. The other actors had all been older and more experienced, but John had commanded the room, had gotten the laughs. He peppered Payne with questions: Would the gig pay fifty dollars a week? That was how much his father demanded from a summer job. Who was Adrian Rehner? Did Payne think John would get the gig? He seemed to have forgotten football.

Payne dropped John off and returned home. A half hour later, Rehner called.

"He's the most talented son of a bitch I've ever seen," Rehner said. John had the job. "It's forty-five dollars a week," he said. "That's all we can afford."

Payne explained that John's parents expected fifty. The Paynes would cover the difference.

John graduated in the Wheaton Central High School class of 1967 with a C average and the "Most Humorous" award. He packed up his motorcycle for the drive to Indiana.

Adrian Rehner and his brother had launched the Shawnee theater in 1960 in Bloomfield, Indiana, a lonely prairie town not far from Indiana University. John roared into the camp on his motorcycle, all eyes upon him. He dismounted theatrically, as if he were already onstage.

The presumptive star of Shawnee that summer was Vic Caroli, a working actor of twenty-five who had served in the army. Caroli promptly hooked up with Lynn Lowry, a cat-eyed beauty of nineteen.

"Well, John had a real hard-on for Lynn," Caroli recalled. "He wanted to be shacked up with Lynn, but I was. And this did not sit well with John." Caroli didn't know his romantic rival had a steady girlfriend back in Illinois.

John was too far from Wheaton for weekly visits, so he sent Judy letters. "I can't believe it here," he wrote on June 25, in the first week of rehearsal. "There is no supervision at all. At night, every time I do something, I always expect some adult to say, 'Hey kid, you can't do that!' But no one cares."

John had arrived in Indiana a clean-cut, teetotaling jock. The other actors took him out drinking. They introduced him to pot. Toking remained taboo, even in theater circles, so John and his castmates retreated with their stash to a mysterious spot they called Strawberry

Fields. Beer outings, too, took planning. Bloomfield had one stoplight and one bar. The only other action lay at the Naval Surface Warfare Center, ten miles away.

"Strangely enough, there was a naval base," said Mark Kurlansky, a theater major from Butler University, destined for fame as a best-selling author. "I say 'strangely enough' because you couldn't be more inland than southern Indiana. They invited us all to go to their officers' club." They journeyed there, John and Kurlansky joined by Tommy Long, a friend from Chicago.

"And we had a drink. One drink." John gulped his down like root beer. "And suddenly, John just got this wide-eyed look and made some kind of noise, like *o-ye-o-ye-o*, and he went out of the bar, and he jumped onto the grass and started rolling down the hill. He was completely blotto from this one drink. And I remember Tommy and me saying to him, 'You ought to stay away from alcohol.' That was the next day, because he was too blotto; we had to take him home. This was a guy who couldn't deal with substances. I'd never seen anybody react that way to one drink."

The Shawnee company continued rehearsals. As a theatrical performer, John revealed himself as remarkable, and remarkably raw.

"He wasn't very big, but he had this big personality," Vic Caroli said. "There was a fire about him, and he wanted all eyes to be on him. You kind of knew right away he wasn't an actor." No: Belushi was a comedian. He would go off script, improvising new lines that sounded funnier. "You just didn't know what he was gonna do. But he did the best Marlon Brando I ever heard in my life."

Backstage, John picked up where he had left off at Wheaton Central, breaking up his castmates with impressions, enlisting them in impromptu sketches.

"He'd have somebody put a ping-pong ball in his mouth," Mark Kurlansky said. "And he'd walk into the room, and he'd do a voice-over, 'Suzy Creamcheese, what's got into you?'" riffing on a song by the anarchic Mothers of Invention. "And then you'd spit out the ping-pong ball. He got all of us to do bits. And he said this was his career, this was what he was going to go on to do. And I remember thinking, I don't know how he's going to make a career out of this."

The Shawnee Summer Theatre launched its season in July 1967 with a production of *John Loves Mary*, a wartime romantic comedy. John played a general. "Some special word should be given about this last performer," a reporter opined in the *Linton Daily Citizen* of July 6. "Belushi has a lot of possibility, but he seemed to have either been directed to be too big, or else he simply ran away with the part and made it too unreal." John was overacting.

John didn't mention the review in his letter to Judy, two days later. He did say he had bought a copy of the new Beatles album, *Sgt. Pepper's Lonely Hearts Club Band*, and had played it over and over for the other actors. He thought of Judy when he heard Ringo sing "With a Little Help from My Friends." That thought led to another.

"Well, I guess I better tell you now, Judy," he confessed. "I smoked pot the other night. It's really something. It is better than being drunk and doesn't do any physical harm to you. I might take it again, but I don't know." John did not want his beer-drinking, drug-fearing girlfriend to know he was toking every night.

Castmates had told John about an improvisational comedy troupe in Chicago that sounded like a perfect fit for his skills. "When I get back," John wrote, "we'll have to go to Second City once to see a show."

John learned quickly. Rehner, the director, taught him how to stay in the scene, even if his character wasn't doing anything, and not to shuffle around or ad-lib or create his own little scene. "It's not about you," he instructed.

John couldn't really act, castmates observed, but he could imitate. Cast as Cardinal Wolsey in *Anne of the Thousand Days*, the British costume drama, John voiced his part as Rod Steiger, the combustible character actor. The audience loved it.

Dan and Juanita Payne and Judy drove down to southern Indiana in August to watch John in *Harvey*, his final production at Shawnee. Six plays in seven weeks had sharpened his skills. "I just couldn't believe that it was John," Dan Payne recalled. "I was amazed."

On the final night, John walked up to Vic Caroli, who had snagged the lead in the final show. "You know, Caroli," John said, "I don't like you very much."

"Yeah, John," Caroli replied, "you made that pretty plain." John still resented his costar for hooking up with lovely Lynn Lowry.

"But you know what?" John continued. "One day I'd like to be half the actor that you are." He stalked away.

The next day, John climbed onto his motorcycle and caravanned back to Wheaton behind Judy and the Paynes in their station wagon.

Over the summer, John had evolved from clean-shaven jock to hirsute hippie stoner. He was done with football. He wanted to act. "You should leave me now," he told Judy, "because it's not going to be easy. I'll probably never make any money, so you'll have to support us." Judy told John she didn't care. John pledged that if he couldn't make a living as an actor by age thirty, he would find a real job.

The Belushis had no money for college tuition, so John chased scholarship dollars. One local school, Illinois Wesleyan University, recruited him for drama and football, only to reject him for grades. He settled for the University of Wisconsin campus in Whitewater, two hours north, a public institution with relaxed admissions and a serviceable drama department.

Tommy Long, the fellow Shawnee performer, ran into Dan Payne and congratulated him on the splendid work the Albanian had done in summer stock.

"The Albanian?" Payne replied, perplexed. John had told the Paynes his parents were Italian and Greek. Why would he have made that up?

Long explained that John had gotten loaded and confided his secret identity. Sometime later, Payne confronted John on the lie.

"The people in Wheaton . . ." John explained haltingly. "There was enough trouble around here without telling anyone."

The revelation drew them closer. As a belated graduation present, just before John departed for college, the Paynes drove John and Judy into the city to watch a performance at Second City, Chicago's famed improvisational comedy troupe. On the way, Dan Payne told John the theater's story.

At the turn of the 1950s, some University of Chicago students produced a series of erudite plays for the school's University Theater. They experimented with breaking the fourth wall—interacting with the audience rather than pretending it wasn't there. In 1955, those efforts spawned the Compass Players, an ensemble that more or less launched the genre of modern improvisational theater. The Compass Players had no scripts. They crafted scenes from brief outlines, performing on a bare stage. In 1959, some Compass Players alumni formed a new group in the Old Town section of Chicago's North Side. The ensemble started each show with prepared scenes, then staged an improvisation inspired by audience suggestions. They took their name from a pretentious *New Yorker* series about Chicago titled "Second City."

By the time John and Judy walked into the theater in August 1967, Second City and its antecedents had launched the careers of Ed Asner, Mike Nichols, Elaine May, Alan Arkin, Barbara Harris, Alan Alda, and Joan Rivers. One month earlier, the theater had moved into an ambitious new entertainment complex at 1616 North Wells Street. The inaugural revue, *From the Second City*, comprised a greatest-hits package of reliable scenes from past shows. For John and Judy, the performance provided a Second City primer: sketches about a pedestrian transformed into a mannequin in a store window, a sadistic dentist and his fretful patient, a couple at a Catholic high school dance, and a klatch of Irishmen recounting ghastly good old days.

As the show unfolded, John sat mesmerized, looking as if he might leap from his seat and join the action. Leaving the theater, he stopped, turned to Judy, and said, "This, this is what I want to do." On the way home, John offered an animated commentary for Judy and the Paynes, replaying some scenes from memory, passionately critiquing others, thrashing wildly in his seat.

After the summer adventures, John's first year of college in Wisconsin rang anticlimactic. He nearly flunked speech class. He barely registered in student drama productions. He grew his hair. He hitchhiked home on weekends to visit Judy. He sometimes worked weekends as an usher at an improv theater in Chicago—not Second City but a revival of the Compass Players, the original Hyde Park troupe.

"Dear Judy," John wrote in a letter.

I guess I'm going through what they call an identity crisis. You know, who am I, who do I want to be. Any way you look at it, we're going to suffer in life. The only thing we can do is choose which way we will suffer. Sure, I've got big plans for us, but what if I fall on my face and we're miserable? Being a basically happy person, prone to occasional melancholy despair, I'm not sure of anything right now in this whole damn fucked-up world. The only thing I am sure of is that if it wasn't for you, I'd be a mental and physical wreck, and you're the most wonderful thing that's ever happened to me.

Judy's parents grew increasingly wary of her hippie boyfriend. John and Judy argued over politics and war. John told Judy he supported the Vietnam protesters even when they rioted. "Democracy is no good unless it is dangerous," he wrote. Judy responded with patriotic platitudes parroted from her parents.

Over the winter holiday, at a social gathering, Judy overheard John in covert conversation with a friend, hissing, "Did you get it?" The only contraband she could imagine John chasing was condoms. She winced at the thought of John telling someone they were sleeping together. On the car ride home, she sulked. John asked what was wrong. She admitted overhearing the conversation.

"I just got a little pot," John said.

Judy and her friends had raided their parents' liquor cabinets since the start of high school, but of cannabis culture, she remained oblivious and afraid. She stared out the window in silent shock as John explained that lots of kids on campus smoked dope, that it was as common on the quad as beer.

After many more arguments, Judy agreed to try marijuana. "One night at a drive-in," she remembered, "he pulled out a joint and lit it, reminding me of a pusher in a movie I'd seen at school." Judy felt nothing—until she realized she could no longer follow the plot of the film. They went for a soda, and Judy marveled at how brightly the snack bar glowed. They waited at a table for service, wondering why the waitresses ignored them.

Then they realized they had to order at the counter, and they burst out laughing. Back in the car, they kissed. Judy felt giddy and warm.

As John's first year of college drew to a close, it became clear his family would not fund a second year. He returned to Wheaton, unsure of his next step. Adam Belushi had always expected his oldest son to inherit the family business, however meager. He pressed the issue that summer.

"I'll give you my business," Adam said. "I'll sign it over to you right now." That was the immigrant way: son helped father.

No, John replied. That was not the life he wanted. He was going to act. To support his education, John found a job delivering furniture in the city. "On payday," Judy recalled, "he would keep some of the cash for spending and give me the rest to save for him—his entire life's savings was in my piggy bank."

John's orbit drew ever closer to Chicago. One summer evening, he turned up on his motorcycle at a noisy town house on Orchard Street, near the Second City theater. He was looking for Warren Leming, cofounder of a locally famous band named Wilderness Road.

Leming's pot-scented house parties were legendary. "A bluegrass band in one room, and there'd be someone banging on a drum and doing a beatnik rap in another," Leming recalled. John introduced himself, telling Leming he was torn about his future and needed someone to advise him whether to return to Wisconsin and study or stay in Chicago and act. Friends had referred him to Leming, as if the guitarist were some kind of seer.

Leming regarded the visitor, attired in a battered army jacket beneath shoulder-length hair. "Look," he said. "You drive back to Wisconsin State, or whatever it's called, and you quit, and you come back to Chicago, and you start a theater group."

Assassins' bullets killed Dr. Martin Luther King Jr. and Robert F. Kennedy in April and June of 1968. On the August day when the Democratic Party met in Chicago to nominate Hubert Humphrey for president, Mayor Richard J. Daley vowed all-out war against the hippies who had gathered to protest the nation's deepening military commitment in Vietnam. Rob Jacklin, Judy's older brother, watched the coverage live from his home, noting "huge crowds on TV as they headed down Halsted Street. The National Guardsmen had jeeps covered with barbed wire and flamethrowers rigged to fire liquid tear gas. When the crowd wouldn't budge, they started firing the gas, and it hit the crowd like water shooting out of a fire hose. I saw the first blast just topple this guy, and I thought, 'Whew, they nailed *him* all right.'"

An hour later, Jacklin's doorbell rang. He answered it and beheld the man the police had toppled on Halsted Street. It was John, barely conscious and reeking of tear gas. Jacklin helped John out of his clothes and into the shower. "I can't believe how much tear gas hurts," John told Judy on the phone.

That fall, John enrolled at College of DuPage, a new two-year institution that had opened near Wheaton. The campus provided him a far cheaper means to maintain his deferment from the draft, and his separation from Judy was over.

At the Belushi home, however, the fiscal turmoil roiled on. Adam reluctantly shut down the original Fair Oaks restaurant, leaving him the second, more prosperous eatery to the north. In 1970, the last Fair Oaks would close. An auction listing for the shuttered restaurant in the *Chicago Tribune* featured a four-foot bronze statue of a horse and a painting titled *Amazon Attacked by Panther*.

Adam's financial duress had compelled him to borrow against John's beloved motorcycle. That seemed the very height of parental irresponsibility. Some months after John's return home, Adam defaulted on the loan, and John lost his ride. Disgusted, John moved out.

He stayed with friends and amassed the funds to buy a battered old Volvo, securing loose fenders and broken door handles with gaffer tape. "It had a coat-hanger antenna, and you could only go in or out through the passenger door," Judy recalled. The vehicle's disrepair only amplified the unease of any passenger who dared to ride with John, whose eyes, when he drove, seemed to dart in every direction but toward the road.

Around Christmas, John visited his childhood home and found Jim, his younger brother, in his pajamas in the alcove where both boys had slept. A religious icon hung in a corner. A sixty-watt bulb burned in a wall lamp John had built in a woodshop class.

"Look. Mom and Dad are irresponsible parents," John told Jim, fixing his intense gaze on his brother and pointing a finger. "Just use this place to sleep. Go to school all day, go to football, come back here and eat and go out all night and come here and sleep. Go out for football, wrestling. Go out for the speech team. Go out for dramatics. Do whatever you want to, but just do it. And stay out of here."

Jim was starting high school. With the newfound perspective of adulthood, John explained to his brother why Adam and Agnes Belushi would surely drag him down. "They weren't like parents," Jim recalled. "They were like siblings, very immature and competitive." Adam and Agnes made impulsive decisions, oblivious to how those choices might affect their children. Agnes "actually ran away once and did a play, left home, no one knew where she was," Judy said. "And then she came home, and that was the end of that."

At the College of DuPage, John courted two new friends. Steve Beshekas and Tino Insana were fellow ethnic suburbanites. After weeks of couch surfing, John and Insana moved into an apartment carved out of a barn, next door to cows, for forty dollars a month. When that lodging fell through, they pitched a tent in the Insana family's backyard.

The three friends found an immediate comedic chemistry. "John started fooling around, creating these funny bits," Steve Beshekas said. "We didn't know what we were doing, really. We just did whatever John told us."

John proposed that the friends form a comedy troupe, thus fulfilling the prophesy of Warren Leming that smoky night in Old Town. In homage to the Hyde Park ensemble that had spawned Second City, John named his group the West Compass Players. The trio debuted at a "hootenanny night" on the DuPage college campus. "Most of the sketches we did that first night were about cops beating up hippies," Insana said. By year's end, the three were performing at the student union and suburban coffeehouses. Most of their bits turned on rudimentary sight gags and antiwar politics. John honed his impression of Mayor Daley, who never uttered a grammatically correct sentence.

Driving around in his broken-down Volvo, John would crank up the radio whenever a favorite song came on. By singing along, he developed a killer impression of Joe Cocker, whose cover of the Beatles song "She Came In through the Bathroom Window" spun in heavy rotation. One night, the West Compass Players challenged the audience and themselves with a first line/last line routine, with audience members feeding them lines to start and end an improvisational scene. One proffered line was, "She came in through the bathroom window." Seemingly out of nowhere, John unveiled his Joe Cocker impression. The room exploded. John had been making people laugh since elementary school, but never like this.

In the autumn of 1969, Judy went downstate to attend the flagship University of Illinois campus at Urbana-Champaign, a move that underscored the class divide that separated her from her working-class boyfriend. John had neither the grades nor the funds to join her. The night before her departure, she and John embraced in her driveway, holding tight, neither partner wanting to say goodbye. Judy began to cry. John held her face and wiped her tears.

"I'll come see you almost every weekend," he vowed, "and I'll phone whenever I can. We both have things we have to do right now, so work hard and do well. That's what I'm going to do." He lifted her chin and gazed into her eyes. "Come on now, say you love me and it will be all right." They lingered in embrace. "We'll be OK, honey, I promise."

John's brave romantic resolve didn't last.

"You've only been gone 4 days and I'm almost out of my mind with misery," he soon confessed in a letter. "It's strange, much stranger than when we've been apart before. I've dreaded the thought of you going away to college for three years and now you are really gone. When you left you took a part of me with you, so will you please send my right foot back?"

Leaving home liberated Judy from her family's suburban conventions. True to his word, John hitchhiked down almost every weekend. Judy began smoking pot regularly with John in the women's dormitory, stuffing wet towels beneath the door to trap the skunky smell, blasting the Beatles and Rolling Stones and Led Zeppelin.

"We had no money," Judy recalled, "but fortunately college life com-plements that. We didn't drink, and movies on campus were cheap. Our only real expense was pot." To pad their supply, John and Judy located a notorious field of cannabis growing wild among the cornstalks. Students called it Rantoul Rag, after a nearby town. It made them more dizzy than high. They collected enough to fill a few pillowcases, which they stashed in the dorm closet, sufficient buds to last the year.

College allowed Judy and John to sleep together more regularly. She needed birth control pills, but she kept postponing a trip to the campus health clinic for fear someone there would call her parents. Then she missed a period. Braving a visit to the clinic, she learned she was preg-nant. She telephoned John.

"Whatever you decide, honey, I'll be there," he told her. John thought it might be smarter to get an abortion or give the child up for adoption. But if Judy wanted to keep it, he vowed, "I'll marry you tomorrow."

Abortion was illegal. The couple dithered for weeks. Finally, John hazarded an opinion: abortion was their best choice. Judy agreed.

A month later, a fresh crisis descended. On December 1, 1969, the Selective Service held a lottery draft, the first since 1942, to fill the ranks in Vietnam. The drawing ranked draftees by month and date of birth. The fifty-ninth date drawn was January 24, John's birthday. With draft-ees called up at a rate of about one date per day, John had a couple of months. The order arrived in February.

John was "definitely not fit for military anything," Judy remembered, "but getting a determination to that effect was becoming difficult. There was a time you could just say you were homosexual or drop some acid during your physical and you'd be rejected, but those days were over." He gathered intel from leftist groups and decided his best chance lay in playing up the mysterious seizure that had sent him to the hospital in high school. In the end, his physical revealed high blood pressure, and the military granted him a coveted 1-Y classifica-tion, designating him as unfit for service.

In the spring of 1970, the West Compass Players graduated from the College of DuPage with associate degrees. Staying in school offered further insulation from the draft, so all three friends applied to the University of Illinois at Chicago Circle, an urban campus well below Urbana-Champaign in the academic food chain.

The campus had opened in 1965, the nation's only college named for a freeway interchange, a poured-concrete nightmare. Construction had displaced thousands of residents in Chicago's Little Italy, bulldozing historic homes.

John and his West Compass Players found a dirt-cheap apartment on Taylor Street, across from Al's #1 Italian Beef. They went scouting for performance space and found a storefront on Polk Street. They called it the Universal Life Coffee House, leveraging a connection with the church upstairs to secure a $100 monthly rent.

The West Compass Players developed dozens of new sketches, many of them culled from the daily newspaper. Insana's father, a conductor at the city's outdoor Grant Park symphony orchestra, sometimes joined the group on piano. John stood at the coffeehouse entrance every night, beckoning to passersby with a promise to refund their one-dollar admission if they weren't completely satisfied.

On Saturday nights, the performers would collect the nightly take and head to Diana's in nearby Greektown, bringing much of the audience along, buying them dinner with the money they had just spent on the show. "There'd be a table of twenty-five or thirty people, and we'd eat shish kebab and drink ouzo and dance and smash plates until the sun came up," Insana said.

The players made occasional pilgrimages to Champaign, a two-hour journey, allowing the group to perform on campus, and John to see Judy, and the friends to fill their pockets with Rantoul Rag.

Back in Chicago, John performed for an audience of one—anyone, that is, from Second City, which he saw as the next stop on his comedic journey.

John took his West Compass Players to a Second City workshop for new talent. "He had a leather jacket on and maybe a beret or something," said Roberta Maguire, a cast member who attended. "And he was playing a movie director, and he pulled out of his jacket a roll of film, a full roll of film. And then he said, 'Roll film,' and he held the end, and he threw it out into the audience. And then, very, very slowly, with that one eyebrow up, he pulled it back in. And he probably took several minutes doing that. And we couldn't take our eyes off him. And there aren't very many comics in the world who could get away with just pulling that film back. And I saw him, and I thought, *Wow*."

Chapter 3

The Next Generation

I N THE SPRING OF 1970, Joyce Sloane drove out from her office
at Second City in Chicago to the College of DuPage in the western
suburbs. She found the activities director and asked if he might want
to hire the Second City touring company—the B team, essentially, a
troupe of mostly younger, less experienced performers who played
college campuses and waited in the wings for an opening in the main
cast.

"We don't need Second City," the activities director replied. "We've
got a student who goes to see your shows and comes back and does the
whole thing for us."

"Oh, really?" Sloane said. "I'd like to meet him."

"Well, as a matter of fact," the director said, "he's right over there."
He pointed across the student center to a stocky young man playing
foosball.

The activities director walked Sloane over to John, who arched an
eyebrow at her approach.

"I understand you're doing our material," Sloane said.

"Well, you know," John replied, "I've got my own group, and we're
working on a lot of stuff. Why don't you come see us sometime?"

She did not. A few months later, John came bounding up the stairs
at Second City. He found Sloane and handed her a flyer. "We're playing
the church tonight," he said. "Come and see us?"

Again, she passed. And then, in February 1971, John answered the
phone in his Taylor Street apartment. It was Joyce Sloane. She still

hadn't seen him perform, but she invited him to audition. John had made an impression.

In the waning years of the 1960s, the politics of race and war were transforming Chicago, polarizing the city's law-and-order Mayor Daley and his mostly white police force against rising resistance from many Chicagoans who were young, Black, or liberal.

Second City patrons, most of them young, white, and liberal, no longer resembled the Second City cast, which comprised mostly thirty-something men in suits, hair slick with Brylcreem, weaned on the buttoned-down stand-up comedy of Newhart and Shelley Berman and Johnny Carson.

To solve this generational problem, in the autumn of 1969, Second City owner Bernie Sahlins sent the entire main-stage cast to New York for an extended residency. He promoted the younger touring company—the B team—to take its place in Chicago. When the residency ended, Sahlins quietly sacked his A team. They no longer fit the zeitgeist.

The touring company played around town and out of town, reprising classic Second City material and polishing its members' improvisational skills. The troupe had a regular gig on Second City's main stage on Monday nights, working out new material for the college circuit. By 1969, "we were drawing our own crowd, younger folks," said Jim Fisher, a member of the touring cast.

The new cast comprised five men and two women, most in their early twenties. They swore. Many of them smoked pot. They took the stage in blue jeans and long hair. Producers titled the new revue *The Next Generation*.

The age gap between the old and new casts "made a difference," recalled Judy Morgan, one of the newcomers, who was twenty-two. "I picture us as never being without a TV set, where I think they were more radio. They were Korea, and we were Vietnam."

The Next Generation cast was as strong as any in Second City's ten-year history. Brian Murray, twenty-three, came from a large Irish Catholic family in the northern suburbs, and played comedic mentor to his wildman younger brother Bill. Joe Flaherty, twenty-eight, was a classically trained actor from Pittsburgh, lured to Second City as stage manager. Harold Ramis, twenty-four, was a North Side hippie intellectual sporting a towering Jewfro, who came to Second City after writing jokes for *Playboy*. Roberta Maguire and Judy Morgan, the troupe's two women, easily matched the men for improvisational chops. They fell into natural roles: Joe Flaherty as the archetypal dad, Ward Cleaver on mescaline; Harold Ramis, the hippie; Brian Murray, the wiseacre; Roberta Maguire, the mom; Judy Morgan, the daughter; Jim Fisher, the son.

The battle over Second City's future mirrored a larger generational brawl on Chicago's streets. William Leonard, the fifty-something *Tribune* entertainment columnist, warmed only slowly to the new cast.

"Remember when all the boys used to dress in solid black?" he asked in a column in March 1970. "Now the five guys are decked out in wide trousers, wider ties, gaudy shirts, glaring jackets, and haircuts of every length." But the new cast was filling seats, and the new stuff was electric, a production built around the Chicago Seven trial and titled *Justice Is Done or, Oh, Calcoolidge!*

Joyce Sloane summoned Belushi to audition just as her main-stage troupe was departing for another residency in New York, although this time, Bernie Sahlins would bring them back. She needed people to populate a temporary replacement cast. In the back of their minds, Sahlins and Sloane were probably thinking of Harold Ramis, the card-carrying hippie of Second City, with his wild hair, striped pants, John Lennon glasses, and army jacket. Ramis was leaving for a sabbatical. The producers needed a new freak.

On the day of John's audition, Sahlins left his apartment and walked to the Second City theater, filled with enough round bar tables to seat more than three hundred customers at three or four dollars a head. He headed to the back of the room, took a seat, and unwrapped a cigar. A short while later, Joyce Sloane entered the theater, joined by a few members of the cast. Sahlins generally auditioned performers on cold material, but he knew John was bringing his own little trio. He wanted to see what they came up with.

John and his West Compass Players took the stage in pin-drop silence, just as Sahlins liked it. John wore an oversize trench coat, carrying a stack of books and looking frightened and shy, channeling Jonathan Winters, playing against type. Tino Insana walked onstage as a bully, shouting, "Hey, you!" John turned and opened his mouth, but nothing came out. Insana began a tirade of mockery, knocking the books to the floor. Then John stepped back, transforming into a figure of confidence and resolve, throwing open his coat to reveal his linebacker frame. He arched his brow, summoned a Shakespearean lilt, and asked, "Is this a greaser that I see before me?" He produced a pair of swords, throwing one to Insana. The two launched into a cinematic duel, trading blows and lines of pidgin Shakespeare. With a final lunge, John cried, "And thee I thrust," as Insana fell dead.

Sahlins hired John on the spot. "I want you to come to work," he said. "I should put you in the touring company," the B team, "but I'm not. I hope that you vindicate my judgment." John would start in the replacement cast. After a month, he'd join Joe Flaherty and the others on the main stage. At twenty-two, John would be the young troupe's youngest member. The gig paid $150 a week.

John accepted his dream job without a trace of surprise. He asked Sahlins to hire his friends. Tino Insana showed promise, the Second City founder deemed, and could take a spot in the touring company. Steve Beshekas did not. The West Compass Players were no more.

Sahlins explained to John that Second City worked as a team. He would have to support the other performers and retreat from the starring role he played in the West Compass Players. John said he understood. He went off and called Judy, then his parents and the Paynes, telling them in turn that he was going to quit school and seize his destiny.

Both Brian Murray and Joe Flaherty had adopted stage names—Brian Doyle-Murray and Joe O'Flaherty—to distinguish themselves from same-named actors. Sahlins told John he should change his surname to something more memorable and less ethnic. John spent the next few weeks trying out new ones. He telephoned Judy and asked, "Belwish? John Belwish?" He considered John Bell. Judy offered, "How about John Chadworth?" For the next few days, John answered the phone as Chad Bumforth. In the end, John told Judy, "Fuck it. I'll just make sure they remember my name."

John had promised Sahlins he wouldn't hog the stage. The choice wasn't always his. His mere presence on any stage—his sheer bulk, the Jackie Gleason–on–speed gleam in his eyes, that devilishly arched brow—seemed to create its own gravitational field.

"Something about him would just connect with the audience," Jim Fisher said. "You could be out there working, and all of a sudden, people's heads would turn. John's making an entrance."

The first time Joe Flaherty saw John, he thought an auto mechanic had wandered onstage. Flaherty pushed Sahlins and Sloane to promote John to the main cast. Then he watched the newcomer disrupt the ensemble's delicate equilibrium.

"We'd get an idea for a scene, and we'd go out and start to perform," Flaherty said. "And I noticed that the audience was only looking at John. That's the only person they were concentrating on. And everything he did got laughs. I thought, *Holy hell.* And I guess I thought at some point, *This kid's a star.*"

But Second City's new star seemed incapable of following the first rule of improvisation, which Roberta Maguire remembered as, "You take whatever somebody gives you, and you build on it."

Maguire's very first scene with John illustrated this deficit to metaphorical perfection. She took the stage, alone, to pantomime a ballerina on a tightrope. She built the scene for a minute or two. Then John walked onstage, cocked his eyebrow, and deadpanned, "Why don't you use a rope the next time?" The audience exploded in laughter. "He wiped me right offstage," she recalled.

Backstage, Maguire fumed: "If you ever do that to me again, John, I'll rip your heart out." John apologized profusely, sounding truly contrite. "He was the only person who could really get away with that," Maguire said, "and still have people love him."

In the spring of 1971, Bernie Sahlins sent the cast on a tour of California university campuses. One of the best new bits had the troupe pantomime a football play, first forward, then backward, and lastly in slow motion, the final sequence revealing "a medley of eye-gouges, karate chops, jabs, kicks and other dirty tricks," by one account. Students gathered after each show to marvel at John's Joe Cocker impression. No one enjoyed the trip more than John. "We'd be down on the beach," Maguire remembered, "and he'd be conducting the waves: 'Now you guys. OK, now you guys.'"

John watched Marlon Brando portray a bisexual army major in the film *Reflections in a Golden Eye*. It struck him that Brando was channeling Truman Capote, the author. In an epiphany of logical equivalence, John realized that if he could do Brando, he could do Capote. John brought the impression to Second City, playing off Joe Flaherty's take on the erudite conservative writer William F. Buckley.

Flaherty did a brilliant Buckley, but it was hard work. "We would take questions from the audience," he said, "and I would have to answer them as Buckley would." Buckley peppered his pronouncements with Latin phrases and obscure literary references. "Talk about playing to the top of your intelligence. In the meantime, John comes out there as Truman Capote, 'Hell-*owe*,' and the audience just went crazy. They loved John. They loved him."

Agnes Belushi, ever drawn to her son's pursuits, began turning up in the Second City audience, although never with her dour husband. "She was always dressed in skirts with high leather boots, a blousy blouse, and some kind of hat. Beret, maybe," Roberta Maguire remembered. "The word I would use for her is 'Bohemian.'"

Maguire and Brian Murray left Second City in 1971. The new hire was Eugenie Ross-Leming, twenty-four, a Chicago native who had done a previous stint on the main stage. Her husband, musician Warren Leming, had counseled John to quit college and start a comedy troupe one hazy night back in 1968.

Ross-Leming immediately recognized John as an outlier. "He would just eat everything up. He would just throw himself into things. He would hurt himself. He would also hurt other people," including Ross-Leming herself, who nearly matched John in height but not in weight, and who occasionally went home black and blue. "He didn't feel the pain. He just felt the joy," she said. She ended up doing most of her scenes with John. "Nothing was too humiliating for him to try, and he would humiliate anyone, including himself, if he thought there was a joke at the end."

John had promised Sahlins he would play for the team. Once onstage, though, he seldom summoned the discipline to leave. He would retreat to the rear, a position of power, where the audience could see him but fellow performers could not. Other cast members would drop hints about his overbearing presence. He ignored them.

The final affront came during an improvisation. John wasn't saying much. As the other performers traded lines, "I started hearing these huge laughs from the audience, and I knew it wasn't coming from me," Joe Flaherty said. "And I look over at John in the corner, and he's lying down on the floor, shooting up," or pretending to. "And that's who the audience was looking at."

After the show, Flaherty took John aside. "John," he said, "you can't do that. You're upstaging us. You can't go off and do your own thing. This is a group. We work as a group."

"I know, I know," John replied. "It's just that I'm having so much fun up there that I get carried away." John adjusted his approach. After that, Flaherty said, "we had all kinds of fun with him onstage."

The new cast triumphed with a biblical scene that imagined Mary explaining to Joseph that she was a pregnant virgin. Jim Fisher brought the idea to a rehearsal. John arrived late that day, as he often did. His castmates had grabbed all the best parts, leaving him to play the angel who delivers the news of Mary's blessed event, a one-joke role.

John disappeared backstage and returned wearing "this red flying helmet that we'd had for years as a prop," Fisher remembered, "and also this pair of wings that we had from a parody of *Swan Lake* called *Swine Lake*." In rehearsal, John learned that if he walked very slowly across the stage, he could make the little wings flap. In performance, John savored every slow step toward Judy Morgan's Mary. The audience howled.

John lived in an apartment around the corner from the theater that he shared with Paul Flaherty, Joe's brother, and a rotating cast of visitors, including Tino Insana and Jim Belushi, now a taciturn teen. With the October opening of Second City's new revue *Cum Granus Salis*, Paul and John and the rest of the cast celebrated till dawn. Paul went to bed. Hours later, John's voice awoke him. Paul peeked out his bedroom door and beheld John at a window, silhouetted in the soft midday light, reading aloud from a newspaper article.

"We all have our personal favorites," John recited, "and mine was John Belushi, who has only to step out on the stage to start me tittering like a schoolboy. Whether he is being a fatuous expatriate, an inarticulate rock singer, a flunking college student, or an angel of God, Belushi has that ineffable comedic quality glimpsed only rarely. Many comedians have a wide range of expressions; Belushi has more different kinds of lack of expression than I've ever seen before—and each lack, paradoxically, has some positive attribute of its own. Real magic."

John was reading a review penned by *Chicago Daily News* columnist Sydney J. Harris. "And what he was saying, in essence, was that John was a genius, and a star is born," Paul Flaherty remembered. He watched as John read and reread the piece, "two or three times. He was like a little kid. He kept repeating it to himself. I felt like an interloper in a very private moment. At the same time, I was fascinated at how great the review was, and how happy John was."

John tucked the review into his wallet. When the cast visited a local television talk show to promote the new revue, John walked up to Dick Cavett, host of a much bigger talk show, who was the main guest. He produced his wallet, fished out the review, and handed it to Cavett like a business card. "This is me," he said.

Sydney J. Harris had praised the entire cast, but he singled out Belushi, further disrupting the delicate balance of talents and egos in a nominally democratic ensemble. Joe Flaherty and the others teasingly confronted John about the article in his wallet, asking if he had a clipping service and whether he carried the column wherever he went.

"Yes," John said, "I carry that article around."

"John," Flaherty replied, "you really want to make it big in this business, don't you?"

"Damn right I do."

John dragged Paul Flaherty to a neighborhood bar that employed some of the same women who worked as servers at Second City. John had his eye on one. He commenced a round of flirting but got nowhere.

They left the bar with John shaking his head, saying, "I don't get it. I just don't get it."

John didn't date other women or bring them home to the apartment. He loved Judy. But he seemed to crave female attention. John had attracted a measure of celebrity. He was getting noticed, at least by Second City patrons and *Daily News* critics. "But it didn't translate into chicks wanting to have sex with him, or even flirt with him," Flaherty recalled, "and that's what he didn't understand."

Second City thrived on a heady spirit of Hyde Park erudition and grad-school pretension. The more esoteric the reference, the better. Second City patrons laughed lest they be revealed as rubes.

"I think there were a lot of people in the audience in the early days who probably didn't get it as much as they pretended to," Harold Ramis said. "Not everyone read *Steppenwolf*."

From the day of his Second City audition, with his pidgin Shakespeare, John seemed more intent on mocking the intellectuals. One of his first ideas for a sketch turned on his impression of "the grossest date in the world," said Ross-Leming, who played the unfortunate girlfriend. John probably drew inspiration from his discomfort at meeting Judy Jacklin's buttoned-down family in Wheaton for a dinner of clinking silverware.

The sketch began with Ross-Leming arriving at her parents' home with her new boyfriend, who abruptly announced, "Hey, I've gotta take a shit," and fled to the bathroom. She tried to reassure her aghast parents: "He's not that bad, he's just a little rough around the edges." John returned, holding his hands apart like a fisherman exaggerating the size of his catch, announcing, "I just laid the biggest shit I ever had." The laughter that followed was part shock. Second City players seldom swore. John dialed up the grotesquerie in subsequent performances, as was his habit, telling the speechless parents that he'd saved the specimen in the bowl in case they wished to see. After that, Bernie Sahlins reinforced a house rule: only one "shit" per show.

The battle over profanity at Second City soon escalated. One evening, John, playing a lout in an improvisation, instructed Ross-Leming to "eat a bowl of fuck." The line drew a huge laugh, so John said it again. Sahlins accused John of playing to the gutter. John shot back that the line had worked: the audience had laughed.

"I don't give a damn if it's a success with the audience," Sahlins replied. John wasn't playing to the top of his intelligence. He was trolling for laughs. After that, John loosed his vulgar catchphrase when Sahlins wasn't around.

Sahlins complained about John's wardrobe, a fragrant ensemble of torn jeans and shredded shirts. One day, he told John to get new clothes if he wanted to perform again. John returned to the theater wearing red platform shoes and checkered pants, his uncultured idea of dress-up. When he walked onstage that night, Joe Flaherty howled like a vampire cringing from the sun. John discarded the clothes.

More than anything else, Sahlins bristled at John's voracious intake of drugs. By 1971, John had developed an appetite for pot that distressed even Paul Flaherty, his roommate, who played guitar in a rock band. Judy spent several weeks living with John that summer. She told her parents she was taking summer classes. She did not tell them she and John were cohabitating. During those months, a brief crisis descended when police jailed John over unpaid parking tickets. The couple could not scrape together twenty-five dollars for bail. Judy dared not approach her parents, so she tapped an affluent roommate from Champaign for the funds. John repaid the loan with comp tickets to Second City.

John craved discipline; Judy supplied it. "Judy had a practical side to her," Paul Flaherty said. "Very un-hippie. That was very good for John. She would always go, 'John, you can't do that. You can't just leave five toilet-paper rolls on the floor. You've got to throw them away.' And he would snap to."

When Judy was absent, John seemed adrift. Flaherty worried when his roommate wandered up North Avenue alone in the middle of the night to score weed or worse. John's drug intake seemed to be moving beyond weed. He was trying everything, from speed and acid to mushrooms and peyote. Nearly everyone in the cast dabbled in drugs, but John feasted. One night, during a group mescaline trip, houseguests ribbed John about his hippie pad, poking fun at the industrial spool he and Flaherty employed as a coffee table and the Peter Max–style illustration painted on the wall at the entrance. When Flaherty good-naturedly joined in, John turned on his roommate and snapped, "If you don't like this place, you don't have to live here." Conversation froze. "Whoa, John," Flaherty pleaded, "we're just joking." John forgot it all by the next day.

Second City performers of that era sometimes smoked joints before the show. John could do a show high on just about anything and get away with it. One evening, though, he took a little too much of whatever hallucinogen he had procured from a local dealer known to the cast as Dr. Psychedelic. Onstage, his masterful comic timing faltered. When he made his entrance as Gabriel, the winged angel, he walked too slowly, allowing the laughs to fade to awkward puzzlement.

Joe Flaherty, the cast's agent provocateur, called John out onstage, glaring into his glassy eyes and announcing, with mock reproach, "You're high on marijuana." The line got a laugh, but after the show, John was livid. "Don't tell people I'm high," he fumed.

Sahlins put his foot down: "Enough with the drugs." John had to clean up or he was out. John thanked Sahlins and vowed to stop using. John needed a disciplinarian to curb his excesses, and Sahlins became that character at work, echoing the role Judy played at home. John went cold turkey.

"And he was noticeably different," Paul Flaherty said. "He was sharper. He was more present. He was completely there." His work with Second City took on a new urgency. He confided to Flaherty, "I am sooo much better onstage." Flaherty thought, *So that's it. John's off the drugs.* A month later, he was on again.

One Saturday, John and Eugenie Ross-Leming tried a new drug, angel dust, procured from Dr. Psychedelic. "It was amazing," she remembered. "The top of my skull unzipped, opened up and pieces of my brain floated away." Then it dawned on her that they had to go onstage that night and perform two full shows. Somehow, they muddled through.

After the final show, John and Ross-Leming tumbled out onto the Chicago streets. They wandered aimlessly, still too buzzed to go home. When they tired of walking, they sat down on a curb. At length, a van slowed on the street. The rig belonged to Wilderness Road. Warren

Leming's bandmates had spotted his wife on the corner. The van stopped, and a roadie loaded the two friends in the back, with the amplifiers. He dropped them at someone's house. They sat for hours, drinking tea, coming down.

John asked, "How do you feel?"

"Not so great." Ross-Leming wondered if she'd ever assemble a sentence again.

John turned to her, ashen, and asked, "Do you think I'll ever be funny again?" For John, that was all that mattered.

John and Ross-Leming had grown close. After some shows, they would meet Paul Flaherty at an old warehouse where Wilderness Road rehearsed. Flaherty would lead the trio in a loose jam—John on drums, Ross-Leming on bass—through the Allman Brothers, Grateful Dead, a little Zeppelin. "That heavy-metal vibe was definitely a John vibe," Ross-Leming said. "I suppose his fantasy was being John Bonham," the Led Zeppelin drummer.

John's platonic friendships with castmates may have lessened the sting of missing Judy. At year's end, she resolved to join John in Chicago for good, transferring from the flagship university campus in Champaign to the lesser one in the city. In January, a few days after her twenty-first birthday, the couple went to visit the elder Jacklins in their Wheaton home. Given the gravity of the moment, the Jacklins assumed John was about to announce an impending marriage. Instead, John somberly advised, "Mr. and Mrs. Jacklin, Judy and I would like to live together." That news wasn't much better. Judy still had three semesters of college. When Judy saw her parents' stricken faces, she began to cry. John took her hand.

"Judy and I love each other and want to live together," he continued. "I'm making good money now, and I can take care of us."

"Why don't you get married?" Judy's mother asked.

"It's not the right time, and we don't need a piece of paper to prove we love each other," John replied, paraphrasing Joni Mitchell.

Now Mrs. Jacklin started to cry. John said their minds were made up. Judy marveled at John's strength in confronting her parents and his chivalry in seeking their blessing. Her parents were less impressed. Judy moved into John's hippie pad. Paul Flaherty moved out.

Harold Ramis returned from his sabbatical for the forty-third Second City revue, which opened in March 1972 as *43rd Parallel or Macabre and Mrs. Miller*. Critics hailed it as the best show in years. The cast, now a sextet, was as strong an ensemble as anyone could remember. The troupe had a new director, Del Close. He had started at Second City in 1961 and revealed a genius for improv, as well as a habit for heroin, which eventually got him fired. The cast delighted in his return. Close loved improv, risk-taking, and boundary pushing, all things Bernie Sahlins seemed to detest.

Del Close and John became instant friends. Close endorsed casual drug use. "My work's better on drugs," he would tell John, who hardly needed such encouragement. The director marveled at John's native comedic timing and sensed a larger gift. When John took the stage with the cast, he seemed the only performer who wasn't acting, a real person among comedians. "Del," John said once, "you know why I'm so comfortable onstage? It's because that's the only place in the world where I know what I'm doing."

John's typical workday began around eleven with rehearsals. The cast would break and retreat to Lums, an Old Town diner whose menu featured beer-steamed hot dogs and sherry-flavored sauerkraut. The performers would hold court for hours, drinking coffee or beer, eating fried clam strips, and scanning the papers for news worthy of parodic comment. Characters and scenes would take shape as Harold Ramis worked the crossword in pen.

John loved his castmates. He loved the city. He bought a bicycle and rode it through Lincoln Park in warm weather, sometimes after dropping acid. He would stop at a favorite spot near the zoo to gaze across the lagoon at the statue of Ulysses S. Grant, taking in the trees, boats, and ducks, an Impressionist landscape come to life.

Not long before the opening of *43rd Parallel*, the young cast had attended a funeral. Perhaps inevitably, something struck someone as funny, leaving everyone struggling to suppress laughter through the service.

Back at the theater, Joe Flaherty suggested the performers write a scene about a group of mourners fighting laughter. Del Close offered, "You know, I've always wanted to do a sketch about a guy who dies with a gallon can of Van Camp's beans on his head." The funeral scene was born.

The sketch opened with Judy Morgan as the grieving widow, John as her son. One by one, mourners arrived at the church service, asking the widow how her husband had met his end. Each time, Judy explained, "He got his head stuck in a gallon can of Van Camp's beans." At every retelling, the mourners concealed fresh spasms of laughter. John, the aggrieved son, would squirm and rage, banging his fist, pulling his hair, pacing around the room, pretending to hang himself. Judy Morgan closed the scene with a wistful eulogy. "I can still remember his last words: 'I think there's a little bit more at the bottom,'" she deadpanned. At that, John's simmering rage exploded. The funeral would become perhaps the best-known sketch from John's tenure at Second City.

Late one night in April 1972, John climbed onstage with folk singer Ed Holstein at the Earl of Old Town pub, guzzled beer, and launched into his Brando impression: "I coulda been a contendah, Charlie . . ." He was performing for another audience of one, Marshall Rosenthal of the *Chicago Daily News*, who had tapped the Second City star for a full profile. John leavened his comments with modesty, crediting castmates with showing him "the difference between schtick and entertainment" and teaching him subtlety.

"But a funny thing happens at Second City," John said. "A year after you're there, you start to get this fear that you'll die there, and you start wondering when you'll leave." John had been at Second City for fourteen months.

The star treatment, coupled with surging ambition, began to distance John from the rest of the cast members, all of whom harbored ample ambitions.

Veteran actor Cliff Robertson attended a show. Harold Ramis hatched a practical joke. He approached John after the show and told him Robertson had savored John's performance, adding, "Boy, John, you've really got a fan there." Ramis planted a phony message at the Second City box office that read, "John, call me at once, have a movie I want you to be in. Cliff Robertson." John took it to heart, telling everyone who would listen that Cliff Robertson wanted to work with him.

The Cliff Robertson call never panned out, but John didn't have to wait long for a genuine lead to arrive. It came by telephone from Peter Elbling, a comedian who had joined John briefly in the Second City replacement cast. Peter told John of a new off-Broadway show taking shape in New York. It was the brainchild of *National Lampoon*, the highborn humor magazine. Its working title was *Lemmings*. A brutal parody of Woodstock, the epic music festival, occupied the entire second act. With his devastating Joe Cocker impression, John would be perfect for the cast. John leapt at the opportunity. Elbling made more phone calls. Soon, an emissary from *Lemmings* was on his way to Chicago.

Chapter 4

Freud, Marx, Engels, and Jung

B Y 1965, the satirical *Harvard Lampoon* had spawned a succession of great wits, notably John Updike, author of the landmark 1960 novel *Rabbit, Run*, and George Plimpton, famed sportswriter and cofounder of the *Paris Review*. Yet, off the Harvard campus, the *Lampoon* barely registered. That changed in 1966 when a group of *Lampoon* editors dreamed up a full-issue parody of *Playboy* as a commercial venture. *Pl*yb*y*, the parody, sold a half million copies in five days, putting *Lampoon* on the map.

In the summer of 1968, a group of *Lampoon* writers inked a deal with New York publishers to pursue further parodic projects. Two Harvard boys, Doug Kenney and Henry Beard, collaborated on *Bored of the Rings*, a send-up of the Tolkien classic that sold 750,000 copies. Buoyed by success, the students created a national humor magazine. They pitched *National Lampoon* to the nation's young adults with content that blended high-concept satire and lowbrow smut, part *Playboy*, part *New Yorker*, part *Mad*. The first issue appeared in April 1970. Its writers delighted in pushing the boundaries of taste, as with a mock advertisement for the erotic drawings of Norman Rockwell.

Two Harvard wits drove the early success of *National Lampoon*: Kenney, a long-haired, fast-living Ohioan who could insert his entire fist into his mouth; and Beard, a pipe-smoking, patrician New Yorker. The typical *National Lampoon* reader resembled the typical *National*

Lampoon writer: young, white, and male, much the same audience that devoured the rock-music bible *Rolling Stone*. In 1972, the *Lampoon* editors took the next logical step and entered the record business.

National Lampoon's multimedia era brought new voices to the fore. One was Michael O'Donoghue, an upstate New Yorker, older than the Harvard boys, with a theater background and a nihilistic streak. One of O'Donoghue's early *Lampoon* stories was "Vietnamese Baby Book," a dark commentary on the lingering war. *National Lampoon*'s other resident dramatist was Tony Hendra, a Brit who had attended Cambridge and performed in the university's Footlights revue alongside future Monty Pythons Graham Chapman and John Cleese.

After a tentative first long-playing record (LP), a scattershot series of sketches titled *Radio Dinner*, the cynical minds at *National Lampoon* mapped out an elaborate Woodstock parody. Ostensibly a utopian gathering, a hippie world's fair, Woodstock had degenerated into a purgatory of mud, overdose, and anarchy. Producers drew inspiration from a *New York Times* editorial that suggested the festival "had little more sanity than the impulses that drive the lemmings to march to their deaths in the sea."

Lemmings was born.

Re-creating Woodstock as the "Woodshuck Festival, Three Days of Peace, Love, and Death," required not just performers but patrons. The producers considered employing canned crowd sounds, then reasoned they could perform *Lemmings* live, netting a record and ticket sales.

In the autumn of 1972, the producers set about recruiting a cast. They needed performers who could sing, play, and act. They recruited Christopher Guest, a New Yorker who had studied at the High School of Music and Art and performed on Broadway. He possessed several vintage guitars and a killer Dylan impression. Guest looked up an old classmate from Bard College named Cornelius "Chevy" Chase. Born in 1943 to an aristocratic New York family, Chase played piano and drums. He was tall, dark, handsome, and undisciplined.

To fill out the *Lemmings* band, Hendra contacted Peter Elbling, the folk singer and comedian. Elbling remembered Belushi from Second

City. He told Hendra that John would be perfect and then telephoned
John.

"If there was anything John had ever wanted in his life," Judy recalled,
"this was it."

John and Judy didn't know much about *National Lampoon*, but John
savored the thought of realizing his musical ambitions. He didn't want
to sit by the phone and wait for Tony Hendra to call, so he borrowed a
friend's reel-to-reel recorder, made an audition tape, and mailed it to
New York.

"The tape contained a series of impressions," Hendra remembered,
"mostly of Brando and Truman Capote, all very tedious, and an absolutely brilliant takeoff of Joe Cocker." Hendra told John he loved the
Cocker and cared little for the rest. John urged Hendra to fly to Chicago
and watch him perform.

John told his Second City castmates someone from *National Lampoon*
was flying in to scout him for a role in *Lemmings*. The group pledged
to abandon the veneer of democracy that night and put John at center
stage. John worked with the Flaherty brothers on freshening up an old
musical sketch based on John's theatrical mash-up of Elton John and
James Taylor. They trotted out another musical bit that parodied Sérgio
Mendes, with John singing "a hard dazz night." The troupe worked John
into every scene, leveraging his Brando and Capote and, of course, his
Cocker. "Our mission that night was to make John look good," Eugenie
Ross-Leming said.

Their motives were not entirely selfless. Some in the Second City cast
wanted Belushi out. He stole attention and adulation from the rest of
the troupe, even when he wasn't trying.

That evening, "John inserted himself into practically every sketch in
a two-hour show," Hendra said. "If he felt like entering a scene, he did it
without rhyme or reason, with irrelevant characters, listening to no one,
taking the action wherever it would leave him front and center. After a
while I stopped trying to gauge his talent, which was clearly enormous,
and just sat back to enjoy the audacity of what he was doing."

After the show, John urged Hendra, "Come on back to my place.
We'll do some drugs, have some drinks and talk." Hendra telephoned

Matty Simmons, the chairman of *National Lampoon*'s publishing company, and told him he had found his Joe Cocker. "Make sure he can play music," Simmons advised. Much of the cast repaired to John's apartment. Hendra said he had liked some of John's bits but not others, echoing his lukewarm response to the audition tape. He asked John to prove he was a musician. John grabbed a guitar and performed a competent "Louie Louie," a three-chord song Paul Flaherty had hurriedly taught him. "Good," Hendra said. "Can you play anything else?" John played "Louie Louie" again. It was the only song he knew.

Hendra returned to New York. Days ticked by without a word. Hendra's critique rang ever louder in John's ears. John told Judy he had bombed the audition. Yet, two weeks later, Hendra telephoned and offered John the job. John departed for New York around Thanksgiving, taking up temporary residence on a castmate's couch.

John arrived in the offices of *National Lampoon* in a green army jacket, his face framed by his wavy, shoulder-length hair and a Fidel Castro beard. He found a kindred spirit in castmate Paul Jacobs, who looked like a hippie despite his Juilliard training. And John loved Alice Playten, a diminutive Broadway actress best known for her work on Alka-Seltzer commercials, who brought a remarkable Mick Jagger impression to *Lemmings*. John "had a very sad, puppy dog quality about him that made us all think we needed to take care of him," Playten recalled.

Judy shortly followed John to New York. Matty Simmons put them up at the Roosevelt Hotel on East Forty-Fifth Street. John had telephoned Judy every night during their separation, going on and on about all his heroes who had made it in New York, the Dylans, the Brandos. But when Judy arrived, she realized John was struggling with the *Lemmings* troupe.

"There wasn't a feeling of camaraderie like there'd been at Second City," she said. "Second City provided a home for the cast. Here, it was cold and impersonal."

John was butting heads with two other alpha males. Chevy Chase could be just as physical as John, and he shared John's uncanny ability to create his own gravity when he entered a room. John's conflict with Christopher Guest ran deeper. Detached and methodical, Guest "was a stickler for professionalism to the point of being an asshole sometimes," said Michael Simmons, Matty's son, who worked on *Lemmings* as a teenager. "And John was the opposite. He always delivered, but he delivered his way. John was more improvisational. John was more in the moment."

Guest favored tightly scripted scenes and always took the stage in character, while John and Chevy Chase mostly played themselves. John had tired of improv. Chase's first impulse was toward sabotage.

In the end, the three men found a common language in music. The songs scripted for *Lemmings* mocked some of the most venerated musical artists of the Woodstock era, exploiting idiosyncrasies that would register with knowing fans. In a song titled "Lemmings Lament" and credited, in erudite *National Lampoon* style, to Freud, Marx, Engels, and Jung, Paul Jacobs aped David Crosby's goofy falsetto and Neil Young's overloud guitar in the celebrated quartet of Crosby, Stills, Nash & Young. In "Positively Wall Street," Christopher Guest took the mighty Bob Dylan down a peg by hounding on his mercenary reputation. Guest returned as James Taylor for "Highway Toes," cruelly referencing the singer's heroin use with "Shootin' up the highway on the road map of my wrist." On "Colorado," Chase channeled John Denver, wasting away in a dystopian cabin where "we ran out of things to smoke and say and eat and wear."

John, laboring against stiff competition, wrote lyrics to "Lonely at the Bottom," a song that would ensconce his Joe Cocker impression in the show. Studying Cocker's palsied style, John amplified his impression into a quivering spastic fit, a performance that climaxed with John spinning around and collapsing like a floundering fish.

A decade earlier, rock 'n' roll had dwelt in the pop-cultural gutter, ridiculed by intellectuals, rebuffed by artistes, ignored by aging music critics at legacy newspapers. All that had changed with the Beatles and *Sgt. Pepper* and Woodstock. At the close of the 1960s, rock artists and fans took themselves almost as seriously as they took the war. By and large, "the rock 'n' roll generation had not made fun of rock 'n' roll," recalled Anne Beatts, a *National Lampoon* writer who contributed to *Lemmings*. "And that was what was so startling about *Lemmings*."

Between songs on the *Lemmings* script, the stage notes said simply, "Emcee." John studied the script of the actual Woodstock festival and wrote up some bits, reworking the famous hipster stage announcements to sinister purpose. Instead of warning patrons not to take the brown acid because it might be laced with strychnine, John would warn the *Lemmings* throngs not to take the brown strychnine because it might be laced with acid. Instead of preaching that your neighbor was your friend, John would instruct that your neighbor was your dinner. Instead of begging fans to climb down from the speaker towers for their own safety, John would encourage them to climb up.

The musical numbers populated the second act of *Lemmings*. The shorter first act stitched together unrelated sketches. The writers took potshots at *National Lampoon*'s usual targets—drug culture, religion, and President Nixon, reviled by much of young America for the lengthening Vietnam War. One scene had a group of doctors attempting surgery while tripping on acid. Another had Christopher Guest playing Jesus Christ as Borscht Belt comic Jackie Christ: "Thank you very much. You've been a beautiful multitude." John and Chase performed a scene only they could have attempted, colliding head-on while wearing motorcycle helmets and then reveling in the resulting "high."

Judy still needed to find a job. John waited until late January, a few days before *Lemmings* was to open, a moment when Matty Simmons would be powerless to replace him. Then he appeared at Simmons's office and said, "I've gotta leave. I've gotta go back to Chicago."

"Why are you leaving?" Simmons asked, incredulous.

"Judy," John replied. "Judy hates it here. She's got no friends, no job. She's goin' nuts. She wants to go back to Chicago, and I can't let her go alone."

After a long pause, Simmons asked, "What does Judy do?"

"She's an artist."

Simmons nodded. "She can't leave. Neither one of you can leave. Judy's got a job working in the *Lampoon* art department."

Simmons telephoned the art department and barked out instructions. When he hung up, John was grinning impishly.

"Oh, by the way," John said, "Judy just got a new job and needs some clothes. Can I borrow a couple hundred?"

Lemmings opened on January 25 at the Village Gate, the Greenwich Village nightclub, to a packed house. Producers recognized several reviewers in the audience. Predictably, the scattershot first act inspired scattershot laughter, even through "Jackie Christ, Superstar," a sketch whose writers had harbored high hopes. "The audience never got it," recalled Sean Kelly, a *National Lampoon* writer. "Half of them didn't know what the hell we were doing, and the other half were deeply, deeply offended. It was the definition of a bomb."

At intermission, Matty Simmons walked by the table where *Lampoon* editors sat. Henry Beard glared at him and mouthed, "I hate it."

The second act began. John took the stage in a tie-dyed T-shirt and grabbed a microphone. "Can I have your attention please? CAN I HAVE YOUR ATTENTION? I got an announcement. I got an announcement. From now on, this is a FREE CONCERT."

The audience stirred. The stage announcement sounded real, as if the actors had rebelled against their own inferior material. The man at the mic looked unhinged.

"OK," John instructed, "we all know why we came here. A million of us. We came here to off ourselves."

Lemmings took flight. Christopher Guest unveiled his Dylan and James Taylor. Paul Jacobs did his David Crosby and Neil Young. Chase debuted his John Denver. Alice Playten nailed Mick Jagger. John did Joe Cocker. Then he introduced the All-Star Dead Band, a roll call of expired pop stars that underscored the self-destructive impulse of the Woodstock generation: Janis Joplin and Jim Morrison on vocals; Brian Jones, Jimi Hendrix, and Duane Allman on guitar. John took center stage, fronting a silver-faced metal band for the finale, "Megadeath": "Life's an antidotal gyp / Freedom is a lie / Dying is a total trip / Die, baby, die!"

John and his bullying, badgering emcee electrified the second act of *Lemmings*. The laughter never really stopped. At the end, patrons leapt to their feet with deafening cheers. John and Chase and the others returned for curtain calls, bowing and smiling as they basked in the hot glow of newfound celebrity.

The cast retreated to Minetta Tavern, a literary hangout on MacDougal Street, to await the reviews. Shortly after midnight, someone rushed in with the first edition of the *New York Times*. Matty Simmons glanced at the review and, judging it to be reasonably positive, climbed on a chair to read it aloud.

"'Lemmings' Fails Early, Recovers Later," the headline announced. "The first act, a headlong, supposedly comic assault on sex and politics, suffers from a serious case of the puerilities," Simmons read. "But in the second act the show mercifully finds its wits for a wicked parody of the world of rock, spoofing the talented along with the pretenders, their absurdities, conceits and affectations." The reviewer moved on to praise individual *Lemmings* performers, applauding Christopher Guest as "an extremely deft verbal and visual mimic," and hailing Alice Playten's "devastating" Jagger. And then, just like the Chicago critics before him, the writer singled out John for a higher order of praise.

"The discovery of 'Lemmings' is John Belushi," Simmons read, "a bushy-bearded clown with a deceptively offhanded manner." The reviewer noted John's "brief, perfect" Brando impression as a highlight of the weaker first act.

The *New York Daily News* weighed in the next day: "Friendly and self-effacing, Belushi is marvelous." A few days later, the *New Yorker* termed John "invaluable," a credit to his Second City pedigree, "a real discovery."

Matty Simmons had planned an eight-week run for *Lemmings*, plenty of time to record the concert for vinyl release and test the market for a longer run. The show grossed $11,000 in its first week, four times what the production cost. Simmons extended *Lemmings* indefinitely.

One by one, stars filed in to watch *Lemmings* portray them in parody. James Taylor buried his head in Carly Simon's lap as the couple heard Guest croon about "the road map of my wrist." Joe Cocker showed up one night and wound up joining John onstage.

As *Lemmings* stretched on, John kept trying to top himself. Every night, his Joe Cocker grew a little more spastic, the spins a little tighter, the falls a little harder. Sometimes John would spit beer in the air and let it rain down on his hair and tie-dyed shirt. Once, John fell so hard he knocked himself out. All the while, Christopher Guest watched in horror from the wings, terrified John would collide into one of his $10,000 guitars.

Watching *Lemmings* night after night "was sort of like seeing the Grateful Dead," Michael Simmons said. "The beauty was in its liveness, in its mutability. And the audience could read when something was fresh and John had just come up with it, and every night there was something new."

Back in Chicago, John had performed hundreds of improvisational sets while high on one recreational compound or another. In *Lemmings*, he doubled down. John told Judy the *Lemmings* cast introduced him to cocaine, although she suspected he had snorted surreptitiously in Chicago. Tony Hendra periodically rewarded the performers with coke procured with petty cash from the *National Lampoon* vaults. John countered the coke with Quaaludes, whose sedative effects he likened to drinking an entire six-pack. Most of the *Lemmings* cast did drugs; John did more.

Popular culture in 1973 regarded cocaine as a safe, nonaddictive buzz. Only John's salary hindered his intake. He cleared roughly $200 a week in *Lampoon* pay, and he and Judy paid $375 in monthly rent for the apartment they found on Bleecker Street in the Village. "That left him with about $400 a month to live, buy groceries, take the subway and so forth, and on top of that, buy all of these drugs," Paul Jacobs said. "A gram of coke in those days was about $85, so you can do the math."

John could still stage a convincing performance after ingesting a quantity of drugs that would have put tiny Alice Playten in a coma. Some nights, 'ludes left him so wobbly that someone had to revive him with a pot of coffee and a brisk walk around the block or, on occasion, a sobering punch to the kidneys. Those remedies didn't always work. During one performance, John fell from the stage while holding one of Chris's guitars, this one worth $20,000. Somehow, he landed on his feet.

In March, John made a pilgrimage with the *Lemmings* band to see the Grateful Dead at the Nassau Coliseum on Long Island. They took mescaline before the show, high-end stuff. "Everybody did a hit, and John did four," said Michael Simmons, who accompanied them. "So, I'm wandering around, I'm tripping, the Dead are playing, and I look up and I see John, and he's surrounded by five cops. And I go, 'Oh, shit, this is not good,' because I know how high John is.

"John's talking, but I can't hear what he's saying, because he's too far away. And suddenly all the cops start laughing, and I realize that John is doing schtick, and he's charming them. And then he looks down, and he sees me looking up at him with this wide-eyed grin, and he gives me the Belushi eyebrow, like, *You know and I know, but these guys have no idea.*"

In the spring of 1973, Jim Belushi hitchhiked to New York to visit his older brother and see *Lemmings*. Jim was eighteen. After the performance, John took his awestruck sibling to the White Horse, the historic tavern at Eleventh and Hudson Streets. They found a table. John pointed to a spot near the end of the bar. "Right over there is where Dylan Thomas died," he told Jim, "in that very seat, after he'd had eighteen straight whiskeys."

Jim asked John to remind him who Dylan Thomas was. A great poet, John said, who died at thirty-nine. Old Grand-Dad was his favorite whiskey, the White Horse his favorite tavern.

At twenty-four, John sat on top of the world, but he seemed drawn to death. He recited a few lines of Thomas's poetry to his brother: "The force that through the green fuse drives the flower / Drives my green age; that blasts the roots of trees / Is my destroyer . . ."

"He died right there," John said again. "He died right fucking there."

That summer, John and Judy escaped the stinky sweat bath of the city to Tony Hendra's home in rural New Jersey. Hendra and John spent a happy day floating in inner tubes in the stream behind the house. After an evening of drink, they awoke around lunchtime to find the stream swollen from rain. "It was incredibly dangerous," Hendra recalled. Before Hendra could stop him, John wandered blearily down to the stream, pulled an inner tube into the water, jumped in, and disappeared. "I mean, within seconds he was gone," Hendra said. "It would have been madness to go in after him." He and Judy ran downstream, trying to spot John in the swift current, to no avail. Hendra feared he had drowned. And then they spotted him, about a mile downstream, crawling onto the bank.

"Wow," he said. "Man, that was great." They asked what had happened.

"I don't know," John replied. "I guess I must have banged my head on the bank and passed out for a second. Hendra, you chickenshit, why didn't you follow me?"

The *Lemmings* album emerged in the summer of 1973 to warm reviews. The *Lemmings* cast members found themselves flirting with real fame, at least in the city. They lobbied Matty Simmons for more pay. Sensing a mutiny, Simmons summoned Chase, John, and Guest into his office. "You guys are a dime a dozen," he told them. "Stop making trouble or you're out."

Instead of firing John, Simmons created a second job for him. John would assemble a new *Lemmings* cast and take the show on the road, boosting his pay to about $700 a week. Chase joined the road company as musical director. John recruited performers to round out the cast. Christopher Guest and the others remained in New York. Rhonda Coullet, twenty-seven, a former Miss Arkansas who had performed in *Hair*, became the sole woman in the touring company. The writers cut weaker material from act one of *Lemmings* and added new content, most of it political.

On June 17, 1972, police had arrested burglars inside the Democratic National Committee offices at the Watergate complex in Washington, DC. *Washington Post* reporters linked the burglars to sources inside the Nixon White House. Televised Watergate hearings dominated the summer of 1973. On November 17, in a press conference at Walt Disney World, Nixon would utter the historic words "I am not a crook."

All through that summer and fall, someone from *Lemmings* would monitor the day's news to see whether "there was anything we could fit into the evening's events," Sean Kelly said.

The *Lemmings* touring company crisscrossed the nation by airplane, staying in Howard Johnsons. "I was always in the back of the cab," Coullet said, "with Chevy on one side, John on the other, these incredible comics trying to one-up each other, and I'm laughing my ass off."

The rivalry between John and Chase raged on, much of it now focused on trying to make Rhonda Coullet laugh. John missed Judy. He would hang out in Coullet's hotel room, lying on the floor and watching television. John and Chase would burst into her room at odd hours, clad in underwear, and strike a series of poses, mimicking the ads in Montgomery Ward catalogs, a knee propped on the bed, hands on hips, eyes focused on some distant spot, Chase sometimes holding a briefcase, all for the benefit of the beautiful blonde. The performance never turned sexual, which somehow made it funnier.

Chase missed his girlfriend. He kept a framed eight-by-ten-inch photo of her on the nightstand in his hotel room. John wandered in one evening, beheld the picture, and said, "Oh. You got that picture too? I got the one with the donkey dick in it."

Chapter 5

Welcome Back:
The Death Penalty

I F THE MULTIMEDIA EVOLUTION of *National Lampoon* had a
next logical step, it was radio. By the autumn of 1973, *Lampoon* had
released two full-length comedy albums. Michael O'Donoghue, hungry
to put his stamp on a new project, persuaded Matty Simmons that the
magazine should launch a syndicated weekly radio show, which, naturally, he would lead.

O'Donoghue approached the *National Lampoon Radio Hour* with typical perfectionist zeal. Bob Tischler, a music producer, supervised construction of the Radio Ranch, a state-of-the-art studio built to meet
O'Donoghue's exacting standards, both technical and aesthetic. An
artist painted shadows of the furniture on the walls, creating the illusion
of a setting sun pouring in through the Madison Avenue windows and
ensuring that no one could ever move the furniture.

Simmons assigned two women from the *National Lampoon* offices,
Janis Hirsch and Judy Jacklin, to find radio stations to broadcast
Radio Hour. Neither had any radio experience. Hirsch, twenty-three,
used crutches because of childhood polio, an affliction that inspired
O'Donoghue to call her Wobbles the Goose. She took his jests in good
humor, just as she did the time Chevy Chase seized her crutches and
repurposed them as stilts.

Hirsch cold-called dozens of stations, asking, "Would you like a free
hour of radio?" The broadcast left room for eight commercial spots,

four for *Lampoon*, four for the station. Judy schlepped giant reel-to-reel tapes to the post office for shipment to the stations, often at astronomical cost, because O'Donoghue had delivered them so close to the Saturday air date.

With the *Lemmings* production winding down, John became consumed with the universal actor's fear that he might not work again. Judy lobbied O'Donoghue to audition John for the radio show, but his answer was always an abrupt "no." Yet, as the show's November debut approached, O'Donoghue found the available talent spread thin, and Judy found her opening one day during recording sessions.

One scene called for a Peter O'Toole impression, but the voice actor had canceled at the last minute. Judy told O'Donoghue, "John does a great Peter O'Toole." John did a bit from *Lawrence of Arabia* in which O'Toole's character walks defiantly into a segregated tavern with an Arab comrade and announces, "We want two large glasses of lemonade."

O'Donoghue looked at her for a long moment. "OK," he said. "If he can come in today, he's hired."

John hurried to the studio and did his "two large glasses of lemonade" line. O'Donoghue loved it. He asked for more. As it turned out, John could do only the one line. "But Michael was in good humor that day," Judy said, "and John turned the session into a personal audition," reeling off impressions of Capote and Brando. O'Donoghue hired him.

The *National Lampoon Radio Hour* debuted on November 17, 1973, sponsored by the nation's 7 Up bottlers. Roughly sixty radio stations carried the broadcast.

The *Radio Hour* alternated between spoofs of old-timey game shows and vaudeville and contemporary political commentary. In one segment, an announcer challenged contestants to identify a celebrity based on a primal scream. John and his castmates reimagined the Samuel Beckett play *Waiting for Godot*, with Godot arriving in the very first scene, complaining that he couldn't find a cab. A mock newsreel covered the world tricycle championships and flooding in Mississippi set off by an overflowing bathtub.

In another bit, a vintage-sounding radio announcer intoned, "Once again it's time for the familiar *tap tap tap* and *quack quack quack* of

No-Eyes Hooligan, blind detective, and his seeing-eye duck, tapping and quacking for truth and justice." The detective summoned fire-fighters to extinguish a blaze. When they arrived, a firefighter chided, "No-Eyes, that's a man crinkling cellophane." Clever and cruel, the blind detective scene was classic O'Donoghue. However, after three or four weeks of *Radio Hour*, O'Donoghue was running out of ideas.

"It seemed like a bottomless pit of brilliance," Sean Kelly recalled. "But he was only human, and eventually he would reach the bottom of the pit."

At the start of 1974, producers cut the *Radio Hour* to thirty minutes. They impishly neglected to change the name or inform the listening audience; after a half hour, the program went to commercials and didn't return.

On Easter Sunday, O'Donoghue stopped by the Radio Ranch with his girlfriend, *National Lampoon* writer Anne Beatts, who found that someone else was using her desk. That affront touched a nerve. The few female *Lampoon* writers and performers struggled daily for sim-ple recognition as employees, let alone equal pay and status. Beatts told O'Donoghue she wanted her work taken off the next *Radio Hour*. O'Donoghue called Simmons. They argued. O'Donoghue quit.

John stepped in to direct the *Radio Hour*. Under his lead, the pro-gram became gradually looser and more improvisational, though still tethered to scripted scenes. "We would run tape for as long as we wanted to, and then I would cut an hour of tape down to five minutes," Bob Tischler said.

With the *Radio Hour* now short-staffed, John reached out to his old Second City pals and convinced one of them, Brian Murray, to move east. They collaborated on the *Radio Hour* episode "Welcome Back: The Death Penalty," inspired by a 1972 Supreme Court ruling that declared capital punishment unconstitutional. Dozens of states defied the deci-sion by enacting new death penalty laws. The episode, broadcast on May 4, 1974, mocked their embrace of state-sanctioned murder. In one bit, a condemned man poignantly stalled for time on his execution day by laboriously brushing his teeth, cleaning his cell, writing a note to his mother, and losing a shoe. The episode closed with the electrocution of Wobbles the Goose.

Nearly two hundred stations now carried the *Radio Hour*, including dozens of college stations, making it the most popular radio program among young listeners and one of the first radio variety shows to find broad success since the medium's golden era. Many stations refused to air the "Death Penalty" episode, earning the writers a round of congratulations from the *National Lampoon* editors.

In the summer of 1974, Matty Simmons asked John to assemble a new *National Lampoon* touring show. Against all odds, the most hedonistic, least disciplined performer in *Lemmings* had emerged as a leader.

In the months since John's departure from Chicago, most of his Second City castmates had remained close to the fold. Joe Flaherty and Brian Murray had traveled to Canada in 1973 to help Bernie Sahlins launch a satellite operation in Toronto. Harold Ramis remained in Chicago, along with Brian Murray's younger brother Bill, who had joined the main Second City cast.

By the summer of 1974, the Second City operations in Chicago and Toronto were operating a vigorous exchange program. The Toronto cast traveled to Chicago in August to perform a revue titled *The Canadian Show 1 or, Upper U.S.A.* Largely unknown outside Canada, the Toronto troupe included a rotund, sandy-haired performer named John Candy; a versatile, wiry-haired Ontarian named Eugene Levy; a glamorous, rubber-faced blonde, Catherine O'Hara; a lovable Michigander, Gilda Radner; and a mysterious, mustachioed Ottawan named Dan Aykroyd.

Feeling increasingly confident in his recruiting skills, John traveled to Toronto in September 1974 to scout the celebrated Second City satellite troupe, just returned from Chicago. He worked his way downtown and found the Second City venue, the Old Fire Hall.

"We were backstage there, and the door flew open," Dan Aykroyd recalled, "and there was a silhouette there. He had a hexagonal driver's cap on, and he had a white cable-knit sweater and a white scarf and a pack of cigarettes and a butt going, and sneakers."

At John's appearance, Dan felt an instant warmth, "the jump you get when you see a beautiful girl. It was that pit-of-the-stomach feeling."

John needed no introduction. He was Second City royalty. He joined the cast for the nightly improvisation. "I think he hit the wall for us that night," Dan said, speaking literally. "That was his famous thing, running from the front of the stage, hitting the wall, and sliding down."

After an evening embedded with the Second City cast, John decided to offer *National Lampoon* jobs to two of the six performers: Gilda Radner, the Detroit-born comedienne who could pivot from vulgar to adorable and back again within a single scene; and Dan, the tall, tightly wound Ottawan, who came off like a cop in one moment, a criminal in the next.

Chapter 6

Change for a Quarter

D ANIEL EDWARD AYKROYD was born on July 1, 1952—Dominion Day, a national holiday—in Ottawa, the Canadian capital city. His eyes were different colors, one brown, one green. A thin membrane connected his second and third toes on each foot, a condition known as syndactyly. His mother, Lorraine, was French Canadian, his father British Canadian. The Aykroyd family patriarch, Samuel Aykroyd, had settled in Ontario in 1810. In subsequent generations, the Aykroyds had amassed property and names. Dan's great-grandfather, Samuel Augustus Aykroyd, dabbled as a medium, penning breathless accounts of the paranormal. Dan's father, Samuel Cuthbert Peter Hugh Aykroyd, was born in 1922. He went by Peter and worked for Canada's National Film Board, directing footage of Princess Elizabeth on her 1951 visit to Canada. He lost that job and joined the National Capital Commission, overseeing construction of a roadway in Gatineau Park, a wedge of picturesque wilderness north of the capital that conveniently ended outside the family home.

The Aykroyds welcomed a second son, also named Peter, in 1955. The family lived in a succession of little apartments, then a house in the capital city, then a nicer house across the Ottawa River in Quebec, a region distinct in language and culture.

By age three, Dan had learned to imitate the announcers on the family television. Dan's father fashioned a toy microphone from a hockey stick and electrical tape. In later childhood, Dan spent hours performing for himself and his family, reeling off impressions of comedians

Phil Silvers, Desi Arnaz, and Danny Thomas and variety-show host Ed Sullivan. The parents encouraged Dan's antics at dinner, a nightly ritual of laughter and song.

Peter Aykroyd prized independence in his sons. By age seven, Dan endured a nearly three-mile trek from his home to his Catholic grammar school across terrain that sounds lifted from a Jack London story. "My mother would send me out the back door," he recalled, "into the woods, into the Gatineau Park. I would go down a path where the timber wolves were howling a half mile away, go up under the hydro lines, down this steep, steep, rocky cliff to this creek. I'd go down in the snow, and then I'd try to get across . . . but inevitably I'd fall in to my waist. Then I'd go across this busy highway into this neighborhood where the French Canadian kids picked on me because I was English. They'd try to grab my books. They'd try to attack me. By the time I'd get to school, I was soaking wet. I was traumatized." As a final indignity, Dan sometimes had to remove his sodden clothes in front of the class and lay them atop a radiator to dry. Then he faced a daily torrent of physical abuse from a teacher who had singled him out for thrashings with a ruler, a pointer stick, or bare knuckles. When the school day ended, Dan trekked home.

Perhaps as a consequence of those stresses, Dan developed an ensemble of tics. He blinked his eyes repeatedly, goggled them cartoonishly, and emitted barking and grunting noises. Dressing up like a fireman or soldier or police officer, affectations for other children, became obsessions for Dan. One childhood snapshot shows him wearing a cowboy hat and carrying a toy machine gun as he sits astride a motorcycle. "Even then," brother Peter remembered, "he had at least three characters going at once." Dan's facile mind cataloged weaponry and fighting ships in encyclopedic detail. The first record he owned was a collection of Canadian military marches.

Dan's parents sent him to therapy. A doctor diagnosed Tourette syndrome. Testing revealed a genius-level IQ, which, coupled with the Tourette, created the impression, when he spoke, that Dan's mind moved faster than everyone else's.

In school, Dan learned to distract the bullies by entertaining them. He did pitch-perfect impressions of teachers and classmates. At a school assembly in third grade, he sang an a cappella version of "McNamara's Band," the Bing Crosby standard, picked up from his father's record collection. When he finished, the audience exploded in applause. Dan felt an affirmation he had not known before.

Dan took full advantage of the freedom his father afforded him. By age nine, he recalled, "I was running around with older kids, smoking cigarettes, drinking beer. I had this room in the basement with the window near the driveway, so I'd just climb out and be gone." Peter grounded Dan when he learned of his son's excursions. Then he built the boys a clubhouse and outfitted it with cots and a camp stove, hoping to at least keep them close.

Dan was not particularly athletic. He compensated with boundless energy and industry. At age eleven, he won an award as best camper at the Archdiocese of Ottawa Catholic Camp for Boys. A photograph in the *Ottawa Journal* of March 2, 1964, shows him hugging an enormous trophy and smiling serenely. Dan was handsome, in a regular-guy sort of way, with arched eyebrows and too-large ears framing a long face, warm eyes set a little too close, and a ski-slope nose. Brother Peter had the movie-star looks.

At age twelve, Dan started acting classes at the Ottawa Little Theatre, a renowned community playhouse. Traveling by bus across the Ottawa River "gave me a sense of independence," he recalled. "I was pretty nerdy, geeky and shy, withdrawn and not that confident. It helped hugely." Dan's acting teacher, Brian Gordon, "was aware of commedia dell'arte, Pirandello, all the absurdist playwrights and also of the American improvisation movement that emerged in the late 1950s," at Second City in Chicago. "He was teaching us this stuff in the classes: sharing and giving, not to take too much, how to overcome fear and build self-confidence onstage, how to not be afraid of flying, dying and trying." Dan savored a new sense of purpose.

In the autumn of 1964, Peter Sr. and Lorraine took twelve-year-old Dan to meet Father Leonard Lunney at St. Pius X Preparatory Seminary, a new Catholic high school charged with preparing Ottawa boys for the clergy. Dan's father had converted to Catholicism upon marrying into Lorraine's Catholic family. Perhaps they thought seminary school would tame their older son. Both brothers had endured many belt whippings. "We deserved it," Dan recalled. Though Dan had not yet entered his teens, the priests thought him ready for high school in Ottawa, a calculus that reflected both his superior intellect and a swifter curriculum across the river in Quebec, where high school began in grade seven.

"Well, Dan," Father Lunney greeted the boy. "So, you feel you've got a calling for the priesthood. You feel this is something you'd like to do."

"Aaaaaaaaa-hummmmmmm, welllllll, yeah," Dan stammered in reply.

"So, you'd like to be a priest."

"Yowwwww," he yelped, as if the priest had stabbed him with a pencil.

Dan did not feel a calling to the cloth. But his mother wanted him in the seminary, and the campus lay near his father's office, so he assented.

St. Pius X Preparatory occupied a stern, tan-brick complex southwest of downtown Ottawa. Many students boarded on campus, dropped by their parents on Sunday nights and held captive by the priests until Friday. Through the week, the austere grounds felt a bit like an orphanage. Years later, Dan would bring those memories to life in his *Blues Brothers* script.

Pius X students hewed to a rigid daily schedule that the priests oversaw with military zeal. "We were up at seven o'clock and we had chapel at seven thirty, breakfast at eight," said Gary O'Dwyer, Dan's classmate and friend. After breakfast, students returned to their dorms, which they termed "cells," as in jail. "You made sure you made your bed, your cell was all clean, and then you went to class."

Dan fell in with a group of Pius X students drawn together through shared suffering. He arrived at the school still afflicted with a pronounced facial tic, expressed in spasms of uncontrollable blinking, an open invitation to bullying. Dan was two years younger than most of his classmates, another grave disadvantage in the world of adolescent boys. But he was tall, approaching six feet, and he won over potential adversaries with his wit. He poked fun at his tic. He channeled his verbal outbursts into an endless soundtrack of explosions and airplane sounds and machine-gun bursts that buoyed the spirits of his incarcerated friends.

Dan learned to mimic every teacher at Pius X, replicating not just voices but facial expressions and body language. At quiet moments in the dorm, he would reel off impressions and hold his classmates in thrall, ever mindful that the priests remained out of earshot.

One miserable winter day at Pius X, the dormitory roof sprang a massive leak. Dan stood up in his cell and launched into a routine, bellowing, "Abandon ship! Abandon ship! Women and children first!" The water turned to ice on the outdoor walkways. Dan and his friends skated to the cafeteria for their meals.

That scene would harden into school legend. But Dan's defining moment at Pius X arrived the following year, in grade ten. One night, at a school variety show, Dan performed a sketch he called "A Day in the Life of the School," mimicking the entire faculty for an audience peppered with priests. "He made a lot of enemies that night," a classmate remembered.

One of Dan's favorite targets was Father Paul Baxter, a math and science teacher with a working-class background and a short fuse, fond of hurling chalk. The kids called him Quasimodo behind his back. One day, Father Baxter walked up on Dan as he entertained his friends with his Quasimodo impression, interrupting it with "Well, aren't you a comedian, Mr. Aykroyd."

Father Baxter became a cinematic foil to Dan's pranks, failing him in math and supervising him in many nights of study hall, a mandatory two-hour work session for boarders. At the conclusion of one session, Dan leapt up with the ironic exclamation "To the fun and games!" Father Baxter exploded: "Everybody but you, Aykroyd! Everybody but you! Siddown!" Dan endured two more hours of study hall. Years later, in *The Blues Brothers*, Dan would reimagine Father Baxter as a sadistic nun.

In May 1966, near the end of Dan's tenth grade, an emotionally disturbed man detonated a bomb inside Canada's House of Commons. Not long after, Dan arrived with his class for a tour of the Parliament building, filled with extra police amid heightened security. He was carrying a briefcase. He told the officers he hoped no one would discover the bomb inside. Guards and Mounties piled on top of him. Finding no bomb, they allowed the odd-humored boy to depart with his class.

That summer, Dan and six friends packed into a Vauxhall Viva sedan and drove eighty miles across the US border to Massena, a town along the St. Lawrence River in neighboring New York. Dan had just turned fourteen. Others in his party were eighteen, old enough to buy liquor in 1960s New York. The group procured a bottle of Fanta and a jug of vodka, mixed them into a ghastly punch, and settled into a field to drink. Their noise attracted the farmer, who drove the group off his property with a barrage of rock-salt pellets from his shotgun. The boys weaved back into town, found a diner, and sat down to eat, "throwing hamburgers around and laughing and putting up a display of terrible drunken behavior," Dan recalled. Someone called police. An officer arrived and took the students to jail. He balked at incarcerating Dan, because of his age. Instead, the officer drew Dan aside and lectured him on the wisdom of moderation. Back home, Peter Aykroyd sentenced his son to spend the rest of the summer mowing neighborhood lawns.

Beyond the forbidding walls of Pius X, the 1960s were breaking out all over Ottawa. A few blocks from campus, the Auto-Sky Drive-In pushed the envelope of cinematic taste with features such as *Women of the World*, a leering Italian "shockumentary" that showed women in various climes and states of undress. Dan and his sex-starved classmates would sneak out of their cells on Wednesday nights, climb the fence, and settle in among the cars to watch.

The boys fancied themselves rebels. "We were all supposed to be little angels, little priests," Dan said. "But we'd put on our polka-dot mod shirts, Wildroot Cream-Oil, Beatle boots, and cut loose." Even more than the clean-scrubbed Beatles, Dan and his friends embraced the pimply bad boys of Britain, the Rolling Stones and the Animals. When the Animals visited Ottawa in March 1967 for a concert at the Coliseum, the boys set out to attend, only to be swept up in a near-riot when the band refused to play. Angry concertgoers smashed windows and set fires in trash cans. Dan made off with a tire valve cap from an Ottawa police car, a thimble-size crime.

The strictures of life at Pius X drove Dan and his classmates deeper into rebellion, plotting ever-wilder excursions into the Ottawa streets. "There was always some police force to run from," he said. "There were

Mounties, Quebec police, there were Ontario police, Ottawa police, Hull police, military police. If you wanted to get in trouble, have some fun and get the adrenaline going, boy, there was a lot of opportunity for it there."

Most Ottawa boys avoided police as a matter of primal adolescent instinct. Dan sought them out, chatted them up, called them "sir."

Dan and friends went out marauding one night in a tidy suburban neighborhood, hooting and knocking over garbage cans. When word reached the priests, they ordered everyone involved out of the dorm, a step short of expulsion. Dan finished his third year of high school as a day student, returning home after classes. At year's end, the priests told the Aykroyds that perhaps Dan wasn't suited to the priesthood.

For all his troubles at school, Dan loved to work, and he loved to earn. That summer, at fourteen, he took a job unloading railroad boxcars. "I worked all kinds of overtime, came home with a real paycheck," he recalled.

For his final years of Canadian high school, grades twelve and thirteen, Dan transferred to St. Patrick's, a traditional Catholic school. The Aykroyds had crossed the river back into Ottawa, purchasing a lovely old row house in town. St. Patrick's had a theater program. Dan threw himself into theater, driven by twin passions for the dramatic arts and meeting girls.

A production of *Stardust*, the Walter Kerr comedy, gained Dan entrée to Immaculata High School, a girl's school. Dan won one of two male roles in a mostly female cast. He felt like he'd won the lottery.

"We had to walk through the halls, with the Catholic girls all at their lockers," said castmate Geoff Winter. "With the nuns not around, they were very vocal with catcalls. Kind of a reverse role of girls walking by a construction site. And I think Dan and I, being so young and só naive at that point, we'd never heard girls say such things."

Brady Long, the St. Patrick's theater director, became Dan's next artistic mentor. Unlike the priests at Pius X, Long didn't view Dan's overactive mind as a threat. He steered Dan into acting roles in productions with neighboring schools. Dan played Schlegel, the grumpy ringmaster, in a March 1968 production of David Merrick's *Carnival!*

His costars included Valri Bromfield, a student from Notre Dame High School, three years older, who shared his irreverent wit. She had grown up in the Toronto suburbs before moving to Ottawa with her family. Like Dan, Bromfield excelled at mimicry. They met in a tunnel beneath her school and became instant friends, writing and improvising comedy sketches. She could perform male or female roles with equal fluency.

By the time Dan entered St. Patrick's High School, he was approaching his full height of six foot one and had largely conquered his Tourette tics. He still loved to mimic his teachers. After one impression too many, a teacher tried to get him expelled. Brady Long negotiated terms for his return.

Off campus, Dan crafted an edgy persona to distance himself from the jacket-and-tie conformity of Catholic school. Dan's father had amassed a vast record collection, centered on British swing-jazz bandleaders such as Jack Hylton and Ray Noble. Dan loved the horns, but his own tastes favored the British invaders.

The Stones and Animals populated their sets with cover versions of songs by John Lee Hooker, Jimmy Reed, and Willie Dixon, American rhythm-and-blues icons. Few white Americans had heard the originals. Institutionalized segregation and racism had siloed Black R & B into the "chitlin circuit," a network of venues and radio stations that offered Black music to Black patrons, while America's white pop bands mostly played white music for white fans. A few Black artists managed to break through: Ray Charles, a brilliant, blind performer with an unearthly baritone who had single-handedly bridged the genres of soul, country, and orchestral pop; and Berry Gordy's roster of pop-soul crossover stars at Motown. But they weren't blues acts. And thus, British pop bands largely introduced white Americans to the foundational music of Black America.

At least one American band could play the blues. Paul Butterfield, a harmonica virtuoso from the same Hyde Park enclave that had spawned Second City, formed an ensemble to play Black blues in 1963. Butterfield recruited a Black rhythm section, creating one of a very few integrated bands in American pop music. Their music reached Dan in

Ottawa, plotting a new course for his musical endeavors. He took up the harmonica.

Dan visited Expo 67, the world's fair, in Montreal, where he witnessed a performance by Sam Moore and Dave Prater, the Memphis soul duo, who performed their number-one R & B hit, "Hold On, I'm Coming," dressed in smart suits, looking like hipster hitmen.

"I came back," Dan recalled, "and I said, 'This is the music I want to know about.'"

Dan scoured record bins for rhythm-and-blues LPs. He tuned his short-wave radio to Black stations in Detroit and Boston and New York. He fell in with a group of older boys, some of whom had committed actual crimes. They gave him his first joint and introduced him to "this whole underworld I never knew existed. The most profound night of my life, the turning point, was the night we went out in a stolen Cadillac with this guy called Ray the Green Beret. Ray was an ex–Green Beret who'd ripped this Cadillac off in Wisconsin and driven it north. I got high that night and met George the Thief, a crazy French Canadian," dealer in fenced goods.

Dan greased his hair back, hid his eyes behind sunglasses, and concealed his lean frame within a billowing trench coat. He learned to play the drums; proficiency on two instruments doubled his chances to sit in with local bands. He haunted Le Hibou, an Ottawa coffeehouse that hosted blues legends. One night in January 1968, he saw Muddy Waters. Muddy couldn't find his drummer and asked into the microphone, "Anybody play drums in the house?" Dan stepped forward. The band began to play, and Dan managed to keep time. Muddy turned and said, "Keep that beat going, boy. You make Muddy feel good." A few bars later, the drummer returned and shooed Dan away.

Ottawans rolled up the sidewalks at six. Most of the action lay across the river in Quebec, in an area known as Little Chicago for its abundance of drinking and dancing, gambling and smoky jazz. Louis Armstrong, Duke Ellington, and Sarah Vaughan all had passed through. "The most notorious spot," one friend said, "was the Chaudière country club, where you could drink and dance until three a.m. and score weed in the carpark. They sold beer only in quart bottles, which rowdy patrons would throw at the stage if they didn't like the band." Years later, elements of the Chaudière would find their way into *The Blues Brothers.*

Dan made regular pilgrimages into Little Chicago, looking for bar bands that would allow him onstage with his harmonica, always ready in his coat pocket. He fell in with an act called Top Hat and the Downtowners.

Valri Bromfield shared Dan's impulse to escape Ottawa for good. In early 1969, the friends spent four days together, trapped inside the Bromfield family home, first by a blizzard and then by Bromfield, who wouldn't let Dan leave until they had a serious talk about their act. "You're not going to be a cop or a prison guard," she pleaded. By the time plows cleared the roads, they had resolved to leave town.

The partners created a fifteen-minute sketch comedy program titled *Change for a Quarter* and talked their way onto Ottawa public-access television, launching their broadcast careers.

That spring, Dan graduated from St. Patrick's High School. He and Valri Bromfield compiled a videotape of material from their public-access show. They drove to Toronto, the nation's English-speaking capital for everything but government, like New York and Los Angeles rolled into one. They found the offices of the Canadian Broadcasting Corporation, Canada's BBC. Bromfield was twenty, with intense eyes and a wild mane of dirty-blond hair. Dan was not quite seventeen, slender and tall. They carried "a full-inch videotape, a foot across, with a handle on it," Dan recalled. "We brought it in and showed it to a few executives." The executives referred them to a pair of young producers, whom they described as "a couple of guys putting together a comedy thing."

The couple of guys were Hart Pomerantz and Lorne Michaels.

Chapter 7

The Great Canadian Humour Test

L ORNE DAVID LIPOWITZ had grown up in an affluent Toronto suburb, the son of a furrier. Like Dan, he showed a prodigious talent for comedy. At summer camp, he assembled weekly Saturday-night performances with two friends, Rosie Shuster and Howard Shore. "It was kind of a variety show," Shore said. "Lorne and I and a few of our friends would do sketches, lip-synch songs, read poems, do a lot of silly things to attract girls."

Lorne attended University College in Toronto. He met Hart Pomerantz, a Mel Brooks–style funnyman and lawyer-to-be. They formed a stand-up act in 1965, with Lorne playing the straight man. They wrote for Canadian radio, and for a short-lived Phyllis Diller show on NBC, and for *Rowan & Martin's Laugh-In*, America's dominant sketch comedy show of the late 1960s. In 1969, the CBC offered them a contract to make a series of television specials, which would air under such titles as *Today Makes Me Nervous* and *I Am Curious (Maple)*. The specials would evolve into a regular series, *The Hart and Lorne Terrific Hour.*

On the day he met the young Ottawans, Michaels wore shoulder-length hair and a Zapata mustache. He liked their tape and offered them a job, to write and act in one of his specials, *The Great Canadian Humour Test.*

That summer, Dan and Bromfield plied their Nichols-and-May act in Toronto and built a modest following. "We played in the gay bars on

Yonge Street," Dan said. When fall arrived, Dan returned to Ottawa and enrolled at Carleton University, a public campus south of downtown. He studied criminology, with a focus on deviant behavior. He drove a mail truck for extra cash and mulled a career in Canada's prison system.

Paradoxically, the criminology student moved in with a group of self-styled criminals, including Ray the Green Beret and George the Thief. They roared around town in a purple school bus and called themselves the Black Top Vamps. They took stylistic cues from the same Hollywood biker clichés that had motivated John Belushi in Wheaton, although these toughs lacked motorcycles. Dan, or "Rocco," evidently committed no actual crime more sinister than shoplifting steaks from Loblaws supermarket. Beneath the leather, "they were sons of Parliament members," said Marcus O'Hara, Dan's friend and fellow traveler. Flirting with the law by day and lawlessness by night, Dan seemed unable to decide whether his destiny lay as cop or criminal. His ultimate fantasy, a friend once observed, was to rob a bank and then arrest himself.

Dan immersed himself in the Carleton theater scene. He joined the Sock 'n' Buskin troupe, the university's oldest club, starting as a stagehand, progressing from walk-on parts to meatier roles. No one seemed to regard him as leading-man material. He performed in *Servants of the People*, a short, experimental play by San Francisco beat icon Lawrence Ferlinghetti; and *Gods*, a contemporary take on the Greek myth of Iphigenia, adapted by Carleton student William Lane, the group's artistic director.

Many on the Carleton theater scene dismissed Dan "as a prankster," Lane said. "I always maintained he was impressively gifted and a truly original actor."

Dan was every bit a prankster. He skulked around the Carleton campus with a marker and decorated the walls of the subterranean tunnels with renderings of Dr. Al Kazali, a sort of "Turkish underground character with a cigar," said Gay Hauser, a classmate. Dan drew inspiration from Gahan Wilson, the *New Yorker* horror-fantasy cartoonist. His drawings plotted Al Kazali's story in geographical sequence, "so you could follow along as you walked to class."

Onstage, in the middle of a scripted speech, Dan would suddenly veer off and "just start creating text, which was enormously funny, and the audience was just roaring," Hauser said. "Of course, the rest of us didn't know what our cue was."

Most Sock 'n' Buskin players stuck to the script. Dan could not resist the urge to improvise. Directors and castmates learned to work around him. "And there might be this slight hint of resentment, because he's not following the text, and he's not doing what he's told," said Elizabeth Hanna, a fellow performer. "But it's cool, and it's genius-ish."

After a show, Dan would unfurl stream-of-consciousness monologues at pot-scented cast parties. "He could go for two hours," Gay Hauser said, "starting and ending at the same point, and everything would connect."

In social settings, Dan radiated "a rootedness and a familiarity and a comfort with the world," Elizabeth Hanna said. He liked to drink and smoke pot and drive at excessive speed along the old streetcar tracks, always retaining a suave, upper-class gentility.

The Aykroyds occupied a Victorian row house brimming with books, paintings, and Peter Sr.'s records. Unlike Belushi, Dan had no reservations about inviting friends inside his family home.

"There was one evening when we all went over to Dan's house, went up to the attic, and smoked dope," Hanna said. "There was a genuine politeness to Dan: 'How lovely you're here. Thank you for coming. Here, have a toke.'"

Dan remained in contact with the Ottawa Little Theatre and his high school drama teacher, Brady Long. In the autumn of 1969, he played the wicked gnome in Long's production of the Grimm fairy tale *Snow-White and Rose-Red*. On the day of dress rehearsal, he struck up a conversation with the makeup assistant, a lovely girl of sixteen named Lauren Drewery.

"I wondered how this tall, lanky, kind of nerdy-looking guy could possibly play a creepy old ogre," Drewery said. But when the rehearsal commenced, "Dan emerged from his ogre's hut onstage channeling a dark, grotesque creature from the Grimms' twisted imagination. I, and the other watchers from the crew and cast, were dumbstruck. . . . He took control of the stage as if he'd been on it for years."

Dan and Drewery became a couple, joining hands in odd nocturnal outings. "If we had nothing much on or no money on a Saturday night," she said, "he would borrow his dad's car and take us on a tour of the city's funeral homes. He knew a lot about them: who owned them, what the interiors looked like, and what kind of hearses they had."

Between semesters, Dan worked a procession of jobs that fed his everyman persona: stock worker, warehouseman, penitentiary clerk. As a student project, he wrote a manual for prison guards.

"The best job," he said, "was one I took at seventeen in the Northwest Territories, surveying a road. We were up in an isolation camp. It was heavy work, but you could really enjoy the territory: the crows, white wolves, bears. We used to skin and roast ground squirrels on a stick."

During summer breaks, Dan made periodic expeditions to Toronto, reprising his comedy partnership with Valri Bromfield. In the summer of 1971, they took their act to a Toronto theater called Global Village, where a young producer named Andrew Alexander staged late-night shows. "Danny and I went up at midnight," Bromfield said. "When the people who ran Global Village's regular shows had gone home, we would ask them to leave the lights on." The show would start with Bromfield onstage and Dan in the audience, heckling her. Bromfield would heckle back, launching into a street-theater squabble. Their work attracted a loyal collegiate following, much of it centered on Bromfield, who was openly gay and embraced by the young and hip within Toronto's queer community. They took their characters everywhere, breaking into spontaneous improvisation as a bickering, middle-aged couple from hell on random Toronto sidewalks and in the back seats of cars.

Gilda Radner worked the Global Village box office. When Dan and Bromfield accompanied Radner to parties, they sometimes fell into roles as her wealthy Detroit parents. They once carried on for an entire car trip across Toronto, with Radner and Martin Short, another struggling actor, as their audience. Short told friends it was the funniest improv bit he had ever seen.

"They were like machine guns," said Dan's friend Marcus O'Hara.

By the spring of 1972, Dan had earned good-enough grades at Carleton University but lacked the credits to graduate. He was restless and, like every ambitious teen in Canada, dreamed of seeking his fortune in Toronto. Dan soon took up residence there. He and Bromfield played gay bars and coffeehouses and rented theaters, posting flyers on sidewalks. Dan landed a summer gig in a vaudeville act called The Pickle, joining two other young actors, Stu Gillard and Rosemary Radcliffe. For reasons long forgotten, someone decided the show should be performed in Montreal.

"It involved singing, dancing with a cane, 'Putting On the Ritz' kind of stuff," Stu Gillard said. "You can imagine how stupid this was. We were playing Noël Coward, this very English comedy, in Montreal. And first of all, Montreal hates Toronto. It was probably the dumbest booking ever. I think we did two shows a night, and it was a total disaster. Danny and I would end up doing soft-shoe, me not being able to sing. I think the only people in the audience were Danny's relatives. Them and a couple of mob guys."

After The Pickle, Dan took a job as a postal carrier to pay the bills. He and Bromfield found broadcasting work on City-TV, one of Canada's first UHF stations. His rapid-fire delivery style made him a natural announcer, voicing breathless commercials for cars and beer and working regularly on a game show called *Greed*. His boss was a struggling Czech-born filmmaker and producer named Ivan Reitman.

Dan and Bromfield fell in with the insular Toronto theater scene. The big show in 1972 was *Godspell*, a Canadian spin-off of the 1971 off-Broadway smash, a hippie musical based on the Gospel of Saint Matthew. Producers cast a troupe of talented unknowns: Andrea Martin from Maine, Gilda Radner from Detroit, and Canadians Martin Short and Eugene Levy. Paul Shaffer, a talented pianist from Thunder Bay, served as music director. Dave Thomas, Canadian by way of North Carolina, joined a short time later. The performers grew close. They spent Friday evenings drinking beer and wondering who among them would be first to make it big.

In early 1973, word spread among the *Godspell* cast that Second City would launch a satellite troupe in Toronto. Two veterans of the

Chicago cast, Joe Flaherty and Brian Murray, volunteered to assemble the new group. Dan and Bromfield petitioned Joyce Sloane, the Second City producer who had hired Belushi. "They arranged a performance at the Variety Club in Toronto so I could get a look at them," Sloane said.

She invited them to the Second City auditions, held in a rented church. Several *Godspell* players turned up. Dan and Bromfield performed material from their act, including a bit about a mother and father telling their son his first joke. Dan revealed "the mind of a calculator, the metabolism of a hummingbird," one observer recalled. The producers were sufficiently impressed to offer them jobs. They tapped Radner and two other *Godspell* players. With Flaherty and Brian Murray, that made seven.

At last, Dan and Bromfield had top-drawer acting jobs. Dan ditched his backup plan, to join the Mounties.

Second City Toronto opened on June 11, 1973, "in a welter of champagne, perspiration and talent," by one account. The theater sat in a former photography studio on Adelaide Street, in a quiet section of town, across from a thrift store. In a revue winkingly titled *Tippecanoe and Déjà Vu*, the Toronto players reprised several successful sketches Joe Flaherty had developed with the Chicago cast, including the Bible scene (with Radner as Mary and Dan as Joseph), the slow-motion football scene, and the funeral scene. The *Globe and Mail* singled out Dan for delivering "some of the top monologues of the evening."

The troupe developed original content in a Canadian vein, steering clear of Watergate and Vietnam, nonstarters in Toronto. Dan and Bromfield created an enduring sketch called "Hotel," about a teacher leading English lessons with an immigrant student who struggles to mouth the words. ("Hello." "He-yow." "Come in." "Coe-wee.") Dan wrote an impression of William Shatner as Captain Kirk, imagining the *Star Trek* actor performing a commercial for Loblaws, the Canadian supermarket chain, something the Canadian-born Shatner had actually done. Dan's dead-on Shatner dazzled Joe Flaherty, who served as both actor and director. He reckoned the young Ottawan might be as sharp as Harold Ramis, the top idea man in Chicago.

"Especially, and this is weird, his knowledge of weaponry. Rifles. He knew a ton about armaments," Flaherty said.

Only one thing about Dan bothered Flaherty: onstage, Dan wouldn't look him in the eye. Eye contact mattered in improv, and Flaherty never learned why his castmate avoided it. When Dan posed for photographs with the Second City troupe, he often wore sunglasses.

The theater on Adelaide Street lacked air-conditioning. It baked like a sauna in Toronto's summer swelter. It lacked a liquor license and a kitchen. When a customer ordered food, someone would run across the street to a crêperie to get it. The troupe sometimes played to an empty house. Attendance would pick up for the improvisational session that closed the evening; those sets were free. "We would do the show for an audience of six or seven people," Joe Flaherty said, "and then when the improvs came on, the show would fill up, *boom*, with these young people."

Valri Bromfield emerged as the first breakout star of Second City Toronto. The troupe's only openly gay cast member had a massive following in Toronto's LGBTQ community, built over many months of midnight shows with Dan. "If Valri came out to start any scene, she'd get a huge round of applause," Joe Flaherty said, bringing the improv to a disconcerting halt.

Fame bred resentment. Radner, in particular, "had a hard time with Valri getting so much attention," Flaherty said. He also noticed Bromfield growing increasingly critical of Dan, like a domineering older sister. "He would do something in a scene that she didn't like. She would really berate Danny afterwards, backstage. She would really chew him out, and he would just take it."

The performers hummed with adrenaline at the end of each show. They needed to unwind, and last call was one a.m. in Toronto. Dan opened an illicit tavern with his housemates at 505 Queen Street, a glass-walled space outfitted with a glass bar, antique couches, fish tank, and barber's chair. The 505 Club operated outside Toronto's liquor laws. Dan lived above the club with Marcus O'Hara and another friend. Brother Peter sometimes slept beneath a pinball machine. The club opened when the law-abiding bars closed. Dan served his theatrical friends, visiting celebrities, and the occasional patrolman, a paradox that more or less ensured Dan's speakeasy would never see a raid.

"Street-car drivers, dancers, waiters and waitresses, cops off-duty," Dan said. "Buck a beer, two bucks a shot, and great music and great times. It enabled me and my partners to basically live free. I bought a motorcycle, a car, and I had all this cash all around, and I had a great life."

Few who entered the 505 Club would have guessed that the twenty-one-year-old college dropout tending bar hailed from an old Canadian family, his father a high-placed civil servant in the Ottawa government. Dan's adolescence had played out like one long rebellion against his patrician upbringing and Catholic schooling. He had plunged into blue-collar toil like a method actor, steering trucks, loading boxcars, driving rail spikes. He surrounded himself with a menagerie of actors, roughnecks, and punks. He exuded an everyman authenticity, even a touch of danger. Off-duty cops, bikers, and ex-cons all embraced him with an improbable kinship.

Marcus O'Hara remembered Dan as a walking class contradiction, with "greasy hair, a chain wallet, the dirty fingernails of a guy who worked in a garage, and glasses with a bandage in the middle, like a nerd." He dressed like a punk and talked like a mechanic, or an aerospace engineer, or a feed salesman. Once, Dan raced O'Hara through a moving Toronto subway train. When they reached the last car, Dan leaned over the guard chain and dangled inches above the blur of track, arms extended as if in flight. Pushing himself abruptly upright, Dan yelled, "Marcus, get off at the next stop." He leapt from the car and vanished down the dark tunnel. Thirty minutes later, Dan found O'Hara at the station. "I dropped my glasses," he explained.

Joe Flaherty and Brian Murray left Toronto at summer's end, driven out by an odd and insistent drumbeat about Canadian actors and Canadian content. Eugene Levy from *Godspell* replaced them, the company trimmed to six. Shortly after his arrival, the show abruptly folded, doomed by sparse attendance. Performers arrived to find a padlock on the door.

"We were hugging each other and crying," Dan said. "We felt like the gypsy theater group that had been shut down by the mean old sheriff."

Andrew Alexander, the theater producer, was sitting at the bar at Second City in Chicago when Bernie Sahlins told him of the Toronto company's demise. "License me the rights," Alexander offered, "and I will take over the debts you have there, and I will try and make a go of it." Alexander and Sahlins sealed a licensing agreement in a contract written on a napkin. Alexander found a new venue: the Old Fire Hall, a former fire station on Lombard Street that housed a theater and restaurant.

The *Hello Dali* revue opened in March 1974, featuring John Candy, Eugene Levy, Radner, Rosemary Radcliffe, and Joe Flaherty, lured back from Chicago. Dan rejoined the group a few months later, after making the rounds of Canadian variety shows. He replaced Flaherty, who went back to Chicago. Some months later, producers added a sixth player: twenty-year-old Catherine O'Hara, Marcus's younger sister, promoted from a waitress job in the Second City restaurant.

Valri Bromfield did not return. She and Dan had plenty of work elsewhere in the Toronto theater scene.

The new Second City production parodied a wave of Canadian theater exploring essential Canadianness. In a sketch entitled *We're Gonna Be All Right, You Creep, Leaving Home and All, Eh?*, Joe Flaherty played a tyrannical father, Rosemary Radcliffe the submissive mom who bemoaned, "Angus is always a little hard on me when he gets to drinking. Still, I know he loves me, eight times a day sometimes."

The lure of food and copious booze filled the seats. Drunken patrons hurled ice cubes at the stage.

Offstage, the Second City players inhabited a spirited social circle. Martin Short and Eugene Levy rented a brick house on the confusingly named Avenue Road. "You'd go down to the basement," Dan recalled. "The piano would be there, drinks would be served, and then somebody would start to sing, and then somebody would start to do charades, and then somebody would start to do improv."

Short did a great Bette Davis and an uncanny Katharine Hepburn, and Dave Thomas, a frequent guest, did a killer Bob Hope. Thomas had worked in *Godspell* and dreamed of a theatrical career, but he was making good money in advertising. One night, he caught a performance at Second City. Dan's work enthralled him.

"There was a change in comedy at that time, and Danny, I thought, was kind of in the vanguard," Thomas said. "Prior to Danny's arrival on the scene, if the sketch player was doing a plumber, he would do the plumber as a stupid guy, because the sketch artists looked down on plumbers. Well, when Danny started doing plumbers, he had this amazing reference level that he brought to the table. Different types of PVC pipes that you could do. He was informed, and giving the audience all kinds of information. And he'd do the same if he was a priest or if he was an airline pilot."

In one memorable bit, Dan walked onstage and Eugene Levy greeted him and asked him to sit down.

"No thanks," Dan replied. "I've been testing ejection seats all morning."

"I see. And how has that been going?"

"Not too good. I get in them, and here's what happens." Dan sat in the chair, then hurled himself and the chair against the wall.

"Well, are all of them like that?" Levy asked.

"All the ones I tested."

"How many did you test?"

"Over two hundred."

In the summer of 1974, the Toronto and Chicago companies of Second City briefly traded places, sending Dan's troupe to Chicago, while up to Canada went the Chicago cast, led by a mustachioed Bill Murray. In Chicago, the Canadians' opening sketch portrayed a CIA operative plotting to invade Canada, disguised in a lumberjack shirt and Mountie boots laced to the knees.

President Nixon resigned during Dan's Chicago residency. That very night, Dan worked up an impression of the former president starting a new job: "Now that I've got some time, I'd like to invite you to San Clemente Dodge Chrysler."

When a *Chicago Tribune* reporter visited backstage, he found Catherine O'Hara sitting on the lap of sweet John Candy and Gilda Radner bouncing up and down across the legs of a somnambulant Dan—she and Dan had been dating. The scene cut a sharp contrast to the aggressive alpha-male vibe at *National Lampoon*, where the sheer physicality of Belushi and Chase had driven some cast members away.

Dan worshipped at Chicago's urban temple of blues. He spent evenings at great clubs, Wise Fools and Kingston Mines in Lincoln Park, and the Checkerboard Lounge on the South Side. He made a pilgrimage to Maxwell Street, the legendary South Side flea market. Scanning the daily papers for material, he found an item about legislators plotting to tax the city's Catholic schools. Chicago's powerful church hierarchy objected, and the tax plot died. Dan filed the idea away for later.

Dan and the other Torontonians returned to Canada at the end of August. Not long after, they received a visit from an oddly proportioned, white-scarfed Albanian.

Chapter 8

You're the Pits

A FTER JOINING THE SECOND CITY cast for a nightly improvisation in Toronto, John Belushi followed the group to the 505 Club,
the after-hours speakeasy. Dan Aykroyd didn't usually open up around
new people, but he felt immediately at ease with John, especially after
the improv session. Improv had a way of baring a performer's soul.
"Your mind is going so fast," Dave Thomas said, "you don't have time
to put up facades." In their brief mind-meld, John and Dan had felt an
instant bond.

"I knew that this was someone who understood me, and someone
whom I understood," Dan said.

Dan and John talked for hours, John downing whiskey, Dan cracking
beers. John loved Dan's threadbare tavern. He loved the music Dan was
playing on a phonograph atop a refrigerator.

"What is this?" he asked. "This is a great record."

"Oh," Dan replied, "it's just a local blues band."

John explained that he was from Chicago—naturally, he had heard
the blues. "But I'm into heavy metal."

"Well, John, you show me heavy metal, and I'll show you the blues."

Dan played John more blues. He spun records by Fenton Robinson
and Magic Slim, the Chicago blues guitarists, schooling John on the
music of his own hometown. John listened with growing interest. "This
stuff is amazing," he said.

"Yeah, well, do you play?" Dan asked. "Do you sing?"

Dan didn't know of John's work in *Lemmings*, let alone his drumming and dirty "Louie Louie" stylings in his high school band the Ravins. John filled him in, and Dan recounted his harmonica exploits in the Ottawa clubs.

"Maybe we should put a band together sometime," John mused.

Dan said he already had one in mind: an R & B duo, modeled on Sam and Dave but whiter and seedier, a pair of "classic recidivist American characters." The kind of guys who had done time in Joliet Prison.

Howard Shore, a local musician of some renown, overheard their conversation. He offered, "You could call it 'The Blues Brothers.'"

John told Dan he wanted to hire him for the *National Lampoon Radio Hour*. He could get Dan an American work permit, and Dan could eventually take a spot in a *National Lampoon* touring company that John would direct.

Dan knew *Lampoon*. He loved the idea of working for John and of working in the States. But he had just signed on to do another Second City show in Toronto. He had a lucrative gig on Canadian television and a profitable, if illicit, tavern to run. At age twenty-two, Dan was, he claimed, "making more money than the prime minister of Canada." He politely demurred.

The two new friends traveled to El Mocambo, the Toronto nightclub, for a performance by Wayne Cochran, a white James Brown disciple with a giant blond pompadour, who sang blue-eyed soul with an R & B big band. Dan had followed this kind of music since childhood. To John, it was fascinating and new.

John returned to New York, and the two new friends vowed to meet again.

Back in New York, John made a round of telephone calls to Harold Ramis, Joe Flaherty, and Gilda Radner, all Second City standouts. He offered them dream jobs, working on the most popular college radio show in America and assembling a *National Lampoon* road show. One by one, he ensnared them all.

Ramis was the first to arrive, in September 1974. "I walked right into the studio and went straight to work," he said, on a *Radio Hour* send-up of *Moby Dick* titled "Moby!" and credited to the Little Worth Community Theater of Sabbathday Lake, Maine.

A musical-comedy farce, "Moby!" imagined that Ahab's birthday was coming, and no one had bought him a gift. "We did a parody of every popular Broadway songwriter, from Sondheim to Gilbert and Sullivan," said Brian McConnachie, the lead writer. Bob Tischler outfitted the Radio Ranch with floorboards to mimic the sound of a ship's deck.

John's Captain Ahab opens the show with a mournful lament about losing his leg and his solvency to the great white whale: "When he bit my leg off, I'm certain Moby knew / That in my pants I kept my money. Now the mortgage payment on my ship is due."

The crew catch Moby Dick and present the whale to Ahab as a present. The captain closes with a celebratory chorus: "Moby, you weren't an easy catch, natch / Though you may look like a monster to a landlubber, Moby, you ain't heavy, you're my blubber."

Reunited in New York, the Second City troupe reprised its Chicago routine, gathering daily at a restaurant to scan the papers and sketch out ideas. And so commenced a cross-pollination of two great forces in American postcollegiate comedy. The Second City performers brought to the Radio Ranch a legacy of improvisational genius, combining elements of Hyde Park intellectualism, Chicago machine politics, and Toronto lunacy. John's *National Lampoon* colleagues contributed Harvard erudition, Madison Avenue cynicism, Bleecker Street cool, and lingering obsessions with Watergate and war. John again emerged as an unlikely leader, commanding by sheer force of presence. It didn't hurt that he and Judy had the nicest apartment.

John asked Janis Hirsch to come over with her film projector one evening so he and Judy could screen an old home movie someone had shot on prom night. Together, they watched a younger, thinner, clean-cut, sober John arrive at the Jacklin home in his white jacket, black bow tie, and two-dollar haircut to pick up Judy in her ruffled dress and white shoes. "Somebody's father was holding the camera, and they waved," Hirsch recalled. The couple posed against rococo wood paneling inside Judy's suburban home, looking like a cake topper.

* * *

That autumn, Dan Aykroyd climbed on his Harley-Davidson police motorcycle and rode nine hours from Toronto to New York. He found Greenwich Village and parked outside a biker bar. "And there's all these beautiful Harleys lined up," he said. "And I go in, and there's guys dressed exactly like me, black jeans, leather jackets with neckerchiefs hanging out of their pockets. I have a beer, and we're talking bikes." Dan found a pay phone, telephoned John, and announced he was down the street at a biker bar.

"Yeah," John said. "That's the heavy-metal gay bar."

Perhaps that episode inspired John's next move. Dan wanted to score some pot. John got weed from a man named Dale, who roomed with Janis Hirsch and was "very gay," she said. "He had this big, fluffy, curly hair and always wore pink-tinted Erica Jong glasses."

John told Dan he would take him to his dealer. "But I've gotta tell you, this guy is a motherfucker. Keep your head down. Don't make eye contact. Have exact—do you have exact change? Are they crisp, clean bills? Do not give this guy old, crumpled—do not fuck with this guy, Danny. Do you hear me? Just give him the money, and he'll give you the pot, and then we'll leave. Got it?"

By the time John and Dan arrived at Hirsch's door and rang the bell, Dan was shaking. Dale appeared at the portal, wearing a Marilyn Monroe T-shirt and short-shorts.

Dan helped out on an episode of the *Radio Hour*, playing drums on a parody of a Helen Reddy song. Then, he returned to Canada, savoring his deepening friendship with John.

John and his Second City friends traveled to Philadelphia in November to mount the new *National Lampoon* stage show. The material played, predictably, as a mash-up of Second City and *Lampoon*. The troupe members marched onstage with underwear on their heads, singing the old Cole Porter tune "You're the Top," repurposed as "You're the Pits." Gilda Radner played a blind "Rhoda Tyler Moore" in a cruel parody of an iconic television show. To the tune of *The Mary Tyler Moore Show*'s familiar theme song, Radner tossed her hat into the air and missed it coming down. John, cast as an abusive boyfriend, fought off imaginary robbers and rapists, alternately hitting his blind girlfriend and stepping in to save her. Then, he humped her leg.

"Ooh, what's that?"

"That's just the dog, honey."

"Well, he sure is friendly."

The new show had none of the genius of *Lemmings*. And yet, the cast featured four of the most talented performers John had ever met: Radner, Harold Ramis, Joe Flaherty, and Bill Murray, who joined up a week into the tour to replace his brother Brian, who was recovering from a brief, heartrending fling with Radner.

The troupe journeyed to Canada, where the production ran into trouble. The performers had only enough material for one set. On opening night in Ontario, the drunken patrons didn't leave after that first set. Backstage, the cast fretted about what to do in the second show. Someone suggested they perform the same show again and improvise new punch lines, unleashing the Second City magic.

Ivan Reitman, the young Canadian filmmaker, caught a show in Toronto. He remembered the improvised second set as "one of the most spectacular examples of thinking on your feet and cleverness you could possibly imagine. I've never seen anything like it before or since. Basically, I was watching them do a completely new improvisation based on another improvisation that they'd just done, not an hour before. About five percent of the audience was really drunk, and they started yelling, 'What the fuck are you doing? We heard that before?' And then, slowly, they all came to the realization of what they were witnessing."

After the Toronto shows, the cast repaired to the 505 Club, Dan Aykroyd's after-hours bar, to smoke weed. An underground rock station gave the performers little hash pipes emblazoned with its call letters. When the group headed to the airport for the flight home, Michael Simmons, the tour manager, begged them, "Do not carry the hash pipes."

"And, of course, who carried his hash pipe anyway? John Belushi," Simmons said. After some fuss, customs cleared them for departure.

*   *   *

On December 28, the *Radio Hour* aired its last episode. Dozens of stations had dropped the show after the death penalty episode. John and
his remaining castmates commenced rehearsals for a new *National Lampoon* show, with Ivan Reitman at the helm. The young Canadian had
talked his way into the job, though his chief credit was a schlock horror
comedy called *Cannibal Girls.*

The National Lampoon Show opened in March at the New Palladium
on West Fifty-First Street, in New York, with John joined by both Murray brothers, Radner, and Ramis. They recycled material from the prior
revue, and John reprised his *Lemmings* emcee role. At the end of the
show, John grabbed a megaphone and shouted that the entire house
was under arrest.

"Actually," a *New York Times* critic sniffed, "it is the cast that is
'arrested'—handcuffed by its own material."

But no one could miss the aura of raw talent amassed on the New
Palladium stage. Doug Kenney, *Lampoon*'s spiritual leader, caught one
of the final performances with Jim Belushi. As they watched, Kenney
pointed to the players in turn and appraised them: "Brian, he's got a
great face for the screen. Billy, he'll always work. Gilda, everyone will
love Gilda. But your brother, your brother's gonna be a big star."

In July 1975, *The National Lampoon Show* closed, making way for a
nine-month tour with a new cast. The old cast demurred. Belushi, in
particular, had been traveling "for the greater part of a year, and he
missed Judy," Matty Simmons said. John's parts went to a better singer,
who went by the stage name Meat Loaf. Simmons let the old performers
go, rejecting pleas to keep them on retainers. After four years of breathless work and ceaseless accolades, John Belushi found himself jobless.

Chapter 9

Saturday Night

O N INDEPENDENCE DAY WEEKEND in 1974, NBC president Herb Schlosser summoned Duncan "Dick" Ebersol to his summer residence on Fire Island. Just twenty-six, Dick Ebersol wore the veritable face of youth at rival ABC, where he worked in the sports division. Schlosser had tried and failed to poach the wunderkind executive for NBC's own sports department. Now, he told Ebersol cryptically, he wanted them to talk "about something that isn't sports."

The two men took a long walk on the beach. Schlosser explained his dilemma: "We've got a problem to solve on the weekends. Saturday nights, to be specific."

Johnny Carson, king of late night, had decreed that NBC would stop showing weekend reruns of his *Tonight Show*, which aired Monday through Friday. Schlosser wanted to keep Johnny happy. He had ordered up some specials. Now, he wanted to find a regular show for Saturday night.

Schlosser asked Ebersol to develop a program and move to NBC as its new head of weekend late-night programming. Ebersol left ABC the next month. He envisioned the new late-night show as a comedy vehicle, like *Tonight*, but for younger viewers. "Johnny was the most brilliant person in the world," he said, "but his show wasn't for teenagers." Ebersol imagined a weekly "variety wheel," with rotating hosts. He spent the autumn of 1974 bouncing from Los Angeles to Chicago to Toronto to New York, meeting with comics and comedy producers. His first choice for host was Richard Pryor, arguably the greatest stand-up comedian of the era. A delicate round of negotiations with Pryor yielded a tentative deal. Lily Tomlin signed on, then George Carlin. Someone pitched a duo of Steve Martin and Linda Ronstadt. Dozens of agents approached Ebersol with ideas. In December, a young Canadian producer suggested a show with the same sensibilities as the Kentucky Fried Theater, a comedy troupe that parodied the television medium. Sensing a kindred spirit, Ebersol filed away his name: Lorne Michaels.

Over the 1974–75 winter holiday, the mercurial Pryor pulled out, and Ebersol's project seemed to collapse. He reported the bad news to Herb Schlosser. Then, he telephoned the Canadian.

The partnership between Lorne Michaels and Hart Pomerantz had frayed by the time the Canadian Broadcasting Corporation aired the last *Hart and Lorne Terrific Hour* in late 1971. Tired of playing the straight man, Michaels branched out into producing other CBC broadcasts. In 1972, he pitched the network a show aimed at younger viewers, people weaned on television and weed, boasting that his show could be a breakthrough. One of the executives shot back, "If you're that funny, why are you here?" Within Toronto's entertainment community, it was widely held that anyone with real talent would eventually flee to the United States.

Michaels traveled to Hollywood. He pitched his show to NBC executives. To help them understand his novel concept, he played clips from his *Hart and Lorne* show and mixed in scenes from *Monty Python's Flying Circus*, the brilliant, absurdist sketch-comedy show from Britain. Michaels had been watching *Monty Python* on Canadian television since 1970. The show hadn't aired in the States. The NBC executives laughed through the tapes, but when the screening ended, Schlosser's programming chief stood up and barked, "What are you, crazy? We can't do this stuff."

In 1973, a mutual friend introduced Michaels to Lily Tomlin, a breakout star of *Laugh-In*. Michaels landed a writing job on *Lily*, an hour-long special scheduled to air that fall on CBS. Michaels shared her obsessions. "Lily used to use the phrase 'cultural feedback': playing the culture back to itself," he said.

Michaels worked with Tomlin on two more specials, rising to the rank of producer and collaborating with a growing circle of talented,

gently subversive writers and performers. The second special introduced viewers to Valri Bromfield; like Michaels, Bromfield was trying
to break through in Hollywood. The third broadcast added Christopher Guest and twenty-three-year-old Laraine Newman, from the
Groundlings improv group in Los Angeles. The specials would win
three Emmys, but Tomlin and Michaels and their collaborators battled
ceaselessly with the networks over boundary-pushing content and were
forced to decamp from CBS to ABC between specials two and three.
Neither network picked up *Lily* as a regular series, which was the ultimate goal. Thus, by the time he met Dick Ebersol, Michaels was more
or less out of work.

Michaels again pitched his idea of a television show for the television
generation. "I felt that American kids knew TV as well as French kids
knew wine," Michaels remembered, "and that there was such a thing as
good TV. The problem was that no one in TV was accurately expressing
what was going on. *Carol Burnett* sketches were dealing with the problems of another generation: divorce, Valium, crabgrass, adultery."

In January 1975, Michaels invited Ebersol to join him in an outing to
see the Kentucky Fried Theater, a troupe of former University of Wisconsin students who were staging a revue in West Los Angeles. The group
was exploring the same cultural feedback loop Lily Tomlin had tapped
in her specials. Ebersol didn't much like the Kentucky Fried Theater,
but he liked Michaels and took to inserting his name into conversations
with Herb Schlosser. On February 11, 1975, Schlosser issued a memo to
his staff. "I would like a thoroughgoing analysis done on a new program
concept called 'Saturday Night,'" he wrote. The show "should originate
from the RCA Building in New York City, if possible live." Schlosser said
the show "should be young and bright. It should have a distinctive look,
a distinctive set and a distinctive sound. We should attempt to use the
show to develop new television personalities." Schlosser was describing
the program Michaels had pitched to Ebersol.

Later that month, the two producers met with senior NBC executives
at the Polo Lounge in Beverly Hills. Michaels said the show had to be
live, reprising the anything-might-happen excitement of *Your Show of
Shows*, the live, ninety-minute Saturday-night program NBC had aired

from 1950 till 1954, featuring comedians Sid Caesar and Imogene Coca. Michaels said he would need a commitment to twenty shows, nearly a full season, to get the format right.

The network suits had suggestions. Perhaps the producers could tap Rich Little, the Canadian American impressionist, as a *Saturday Night* host. The USC Trojans marching band could play musical guest. The executives paled when Michaels said he would prefer Pryor and the Rolling Stones. Michaels wanted *Saturday Night* to give viewers the impression the adults had gone home and the kids had taken over the studio.

After the meeting, the two producers retreated to Michaels's suite at the Chateau Marmont, the fairy-castle hotel on Sunset Boulevard, to plan *Saturday Night*. Michaels visualized a permanent repertory company of six or eight performers, mostly young unknowns drawn from Second City and *National Lampoon*. He envisioned live music, rock and soul and political folk, sounds you didn't often hear on TV in 1975. He would film commercial parodies so expertly produced that they looked real, and a satirical news program patterned on *That Was the Week That Was*, and short experimental films. Hosts would rotate weekly, like faces on the cover of *Rolling Stone*.

Lorne Michaels had not yet signed a contract with NBC. On April 1, 1975, he and the network agreed to terms: $115,000 for seventeen shows, although they offered no assurance *Saturday Night* would last that long.

To mentally prepare, Michaels drove his Volkswagen convertible out to Joshua Tree National Monument. He traveled with Tom Schiller, a young writer and filmmaker who would join the *Saturday Night* staff. They took seven-dollar rooms at the Joshua Tree Inn, a brick and terra-cotta motel ringed by cactus and boulders. After they settled in, Michaels "brought out these mushrooms to take," Schiller recalled. "And as he got high, he didn't seem to change." Michaels sat by the pool, tripping as he took calls from network executives and conjured hallucinatory visions of his show.

Michaels returned to New York and hired Dave Wilson, a forty-something director who would be one of the few "adults" on a staff of mostly twenty-something performers and writers. Michaels reached out to Michael O'Donoghue and Anne Beatts, comedy royalty from *National*

Lampoon who were nearly broke a year after storming out of the *Radio Hour*. Over dinner at the couple's brownstone apartment, Beatts and O'Donoghue played hard to get, dismissing television as a lava lamp with sound. Beatts asked Michaels why he was calling the show *Saturday Night*.

"So the network can remember when it's on," he replied dryly.

At that, Beatts and O'Donoghue were in, and they gave Michaels cachet with the overlapping tribes of Second City and *National Lampoon*. Beatts would join Rosie Shuster, Michaels's talented wife, in a crucial female writing bloc on the *Saturday Night* staff.

Michaels arranged for Dick Ebersol to meet Gilda Radner. Now a seasoned performer of twenty-eight, Radner had won Michaels over in her *Godspell* days and was his first choice for the *Saturday Night* cast. She arrived at Ebersol's office with a tall, scruffy male friend, "very, very young, brash, but funny, likable," Ebersol recalled. After they left, he asked Michaels, "Who was that guy?"

Radner's boyfriend, Michaels replied. "He's a young comic from Canada."

By the spring of 1975, Dan Aykroyd must have felt like the last comic left in Toronto. Valri Bromfield had decamped to Hollywood. Belushi had lured Radner to New York. Two more Second City Canadians, Eugene Levy and John Candy, had fled to Pasadena to open a new Second City operation. At twenty-two, Dan was now the senior member of Second City Toronto, anchoring a cast that included relative newcomers Catherine O'Hara, Andrea Martin, and Dave Thomas.

Dan and Dave Thomas formed a potent improvisational team. Onstage, they would claim to have degrees in sound effects from the Massachusetts Institute of Technology and challenge the audience to stump them with suggestions, tapping Dan's bottomless trove of technical knowledge.

Dan knew Thomas had worked in advertising. Dan asked him one day, "Do you think we could get money writing spots for local advertisers?"

The Second City players were making $145 a week. "A thousand bucks for a thirty-second script was a lot of money back then," Thomas said. "So, we started writing these spots together," scripting lucrative radio ads that they could also narrate. They cowrote a script for a Canadian children's show, *Dr. Zonk and the Zunkins*, whose premise required Gilda Radner and John Candy to dress up as giant vegetables. They tripled their income.

On a hiatus from Second City in early 1975, Dan had climbed into his Chevy Biscayne with a friend and traveled from Toronto to New Orleans, Tijuana, and Los Angeles, where Michaels hosted the visitors at the Chateau Marmont. "Dan," Michaels had told him, "I'm going to reinvent the live television of the '50s." When the time comes, Michaels had said, "I'll call you."

In June 1975, Michaels and Ebersol held a procession of interviews on the West Coast. The big hire was Laraine Newman, who was about to make her national television debut playing a proto–Valley girl on a Lily Tomlin special. Back in New York, they recruited Garrett Morris, a playwright and actor and the lone Black artist at *Saturday Night*. Michaels hired Chevy Chase as a writer, though his telegenic looks would ultimately land him in the cast. Chase took a spot atop the *Saturday Night* hierarchy alongside Michael O'Donoghue and Michaels, thirty-something journeymen leading a mostly younger cast and crew.

On July 7, Michaels held the first staff meeting. *Saturday Night* would do sketches, he said, not skits. Carol Burnett did skits. *The Carol Burnett Show*, in fact, embodied everything that *Saturday Night* would avoid. The show was too broad, an industry term for anything slapstick, pie-in-the-face, or otherwise unsubtle. *Carol Burnett* players cracked up at their own jokes. That wouldn't happen at *Saturday Night*.

Michaels's top lieutenants, Chase and Michael O'Donoghue, urged him to hire Belushi. Michaels went to see *The National Lampoon Show*, the one that featured John, Harold Ramis, Radner, and the Murray brothers. John "sort of dominated the show," Michaels recalled. "I thought he was funny, but I think maybe because I was there, he was working really hard, playing to the back of the house. That tends to work better onstage than in front of a camera." John overplayed his informal audition, just as he had overplayed his informal audition with Tony Hendra at Second City a few years earlier. Worse, Michaels thought John might seed trouble in the *Saturday Night* camp.

Still, Michaels agreed to meet him. John arrived in a T-shirt, jeans, and sneakers, his face concealed behind a full beard. Once the introductions were past, John announced, "Television is crap." He bounced around Michaels's office on an animated, anti-television tirade: the medium was shallow and degenerate, the networks run by insufferable suits, all creativity snuffed out by the censors. John said his own television was covered in spit. "TV sucks," he yelled, several more times, his invective echoing through the halls of 30 Rockefeller Center.

Michaels patiently explained that not all television was bad. *Mary Tyler Moore* was good. *Dick Van Dyke* was good. Jackie Gleason was good.

That was old stuff, John said. The new stuff was shit.

Michaels asked, Why, then, are you here?

John explained that he knew Michaels had hired O'Donoghue and Radner. Television sucked, but maybe this show would be different.

Michaels sensed that John wanted the gig, that perhaps his television-sucks bluster was a defense mechanism born of fear that he wouldn't be hired. Michaels ended the meeting by inviting John to attend a cattle-call audition in August. "You'll have to shave off your beard," he closed.

"I blew it," John sighed to Judy when he returned home, tossing things around their apartment. He knew Gilda Radner had been hired without an audition.

Once again, John was staring into the abyss of unemployment, "just another out-of-work actor waiting by his telephone," the *Village Voice* reported in a July feature. "In two years in New York, he has never had to audition, and the prospect unnerves him."

Michaels scheduled auditions for two days in August at the old Steinway & Sons piano studio on West Fifty-Seventh Street. Ads in the trade papers drew hundreds of applicants, most of them wildly inappropriate for the show. Michaels and Dick Ebersol positioned themselves on folding chairs in the large, windowless room, outfitted with mirrors, a piano, and a modest stage, joined by writers and performers who had already made the cast. "A sad odor of showbiz heartbreak hung in the air," by one account. Every so often, one of the writers would lighten the mood, Chevy Chase taking a pratfall over folding chairs or Michael O'Donoghue invoking his impression of talk-show host Mike Douglas having needles jabbed into his eyes.

Jane Curtin, a prim Bostonian with improv credentials and movie-star looks, impressed the judges with a scene of Midwestern housewives chatting about the annual tornado. Many in the room already knew Bill Murray, who came in as a sleazy Vegas lounge singer.

The audition schedule fell hours behind. Tempers flared. On day two, a man burst into the room carrying an umbrella and attaché case and wearing a derby. "I've been waiting out there for three hours and I'm not going to wait any more and I'm going to miss my plane," he ranted. "That's it, gentlemen, you've had your chance." He turned and stormed out. Dave Wilson, the director, turned to Michaels and asked, "What the hell was that?"

"Oh, that was just Danny Aykroyd," Michaels replied. "He's probably going to do the show."

Belushi arrived for his *Saturday Night* audition wearing a bathrobe and carrying a wooden clothing rod from a closet, hair tied in a knot. He had prepared a new bit.

"There was a station in New York showing a samurai movie," John said later, explaining the genesis of his scene. "It was Toshiro Mifune. Oh, my God, I couldn't believe it. The sword fighting was fabulous. And I was fascinated, so I just got doing it around the house. Like, I would take a broomstick that we had in the house, and I would stick it in my belt, and I'd go, *woo-tee-bayaaahs*. I'd go up to my cats, you know, with the sword, and I'd go, *heedayyyy*."

John stood for hours in the audition hall, swinging his wooden rod as he waited his turn. "Someone better hire him before he kills somebody," Tom Schiller quipped. But when John's moment arrived, he entered the room in silence, grunting, rubbing his chin and arching his eyebrows as he stalked around the room, playing imaginary billiards with his imaginary sword. By the end of John's ten minutes, the observers packing the room were mesmerized, much the same effect sparked by John's audition at Second City, a half decade earlier.

After the auditions, the *Saturday Night* staff repaired to Michaels's apartment. Several very good performers vied for three available jobs. Dick Ebersol wanted Jane Curtin, for both her talent and her WASPy good looks. Two slots remained for male performers. Several writers lobbied for Bill Murray. Michaels instead chose Aykroyd, whose career he had followed since the teenage Ottawan first set foot in his production office at the CBC.

Everyone involved in *Saturday Night* seemed to want Belushi except Michaels. "John will be trouble," he said.

About a week later, the brain trust gathered to decide John's fate. "The thing that finally turned his mind was, I said I would take responsibility for him," Ebersol remembered. "I made a vow to Lorne that if he's the nightmare some people think he'll be, I'll take care of him. I'll be the minder of Belushi."

All summer, Michaels and Ebersol competed for talent with Roone Arledge, Ebersol's old boss at ABC. The ABC Sports chief was developing his own variety show, *Saturday Night Live with Howard Cosell*. Michaels had planned to call his own show *Saturday Night Live* until he learned of the rival program's name and quietly dropped the "Live." The two productions courted many of the same performers and writers, but the ABC show looked decidedly more conventional. Howard Cosell, the celebrity sportscaster, would host. Frank Sinatra and Paul Anka signed on as guests. The ABC program would debut in the eight p.m. time slot. Arledge offered cast jobs to three of John's former colleagues from *National Lampoon*, Bill and Brian Murray and Christopher Guest, and christened them the Prime Time Players.

By the autumn of 1975, Dan Aykroyd had been in and out of Lorne Michaels's orbit several times. But nobody had told Dan he had a job on *Saturday Night*. After the indignity of auditions, Dan accepted an offer from Bernie Sahlins to join his friends John Candy and Joe Flaherty in the fledgling Second City production in Pasadena. Dan and John Candy packed up a Mercury Cougar in Toronto and drove forty hours straight to Los Angeles. "And it was like the beginning of our dreams," Dan said. "We played old music, and we sang and talked and wrote routines and focused in on what we were going to do when we got older, and where we wanted to go."

They arrived in Pasadena and started rehearsals. Two days later, Joe Flaherty recalled, "we're talking about scenes and stuff, and the gal from the office comes in: 'Dan, there's a phone call for you.' So, he goes out in the lobby. He comes back: 'Well, I've just been offered a job. NBC's doing a show called *Saturday Night*. They want to know if I want to do it. What do you guys think?' We thought, NBC? Television? 'Go ahead, Dan, do it.'"

Dan flew to New York and moved in with John and Judy on Bleecker Street, sleeping on a foam mattress in the living room. "They were sort of like my aunt and uncle," Dan said. Soon, John and Dan were inseparable.

"Who's to say what makes people friends?" Judy said. "It seemed that John and Danny were attracted by some similar energy, almost like magnets. They were on the same wavelength and understood each other, although they didn't always think alike." Dan was "controlled and studied, John chaotic and spontaneous. Danny held things in. John wore his feelings on his face. Actually, there was a similar attraction to that between John and me, except that John and I were partners in life." John and Dan would be partners in everything else.

Michaels had summoned Dan to New York, compelling him to quit his Second City job and purchase an airplane ticket with his own funds. Even then, Michaels expected him to endure another audition. In September, Dan and John sat for screen tests. John appeared in a brown blazer and button-down shirt, his beard finally shaved. He loosened up with a spectacular display of raised eyebrows, then proceeded into his mesmerizing Brando, first *On the Waterfront*, then *Godfather*. He closed with a menacing Rod Steiger. Whatever his private fears of losing the *Saturday Night* gig, John looked the picture of assured calm, and the camera warmed to his moon-pie features.

Dan appeared in a blue blazer and vest, hair parted, a mustache concealing his youth. He opened as a newscaster soliloquizing on a new Soviet rocket. He morphed into a television pitchman touting "a very personal male product." He continued as a Louisiana crab fisherman reporting an alien abduction, a scientist pontificating on shale, and a French Canadian sawing a desk in half. "You want more characters, more accents? A cleaner look?" he asked sarcastically at the end. Off-camera, someone taunted, "Thanks for coming to New York."

The premiere of *Saturday Night Live with Howard Cosell*, ABC's competing broadcast, arrived on September 20, three weeks before the debut of NBC's *Saturday Night*. The latter show's newly hired writing team of Al Franken and Tom Davis hosted a viewing party, with a large bowl of weed as a centerpiece. Michaels brought his twenty-year-old cousin, who smoked too much weed and locked himself in the bathroom as a line formed outside. Someone summoned Dan, the most grounded party guest, to intervene. "This is Dan," he said, invoking his television voice. "You probably smoked some of that weed, you're probably paranoid, and you probably think you're the only one. Let me tell you, my friend, you're not the only one. We're all paranoid, we're all stoned." Dan talked him down.

Once the ABC broadcast began, no one in the apartment could hear it over the laughter. The Roone Arledge production was a disaster. Howard Cosell held court in a tuxedo on an orange-curtained stage, cueing a procession of variety acts: the Broadway cast of *The Wiz*; an overripe Sinatra telling bad jokes; magicians Siegfried and Roy, via satellite from Las Vegas; and tennis star Jimmy Connors, sweating profusely as he sang Paul Anka's "Girl, You Turn Me On." The Prime Time Players barely registered on-screen. When the *Saturday Night* staff returned to work on Monday, they decided to answer *Saturday Night Live* with open mockery. If Arledge wanted to call his cast the Prime Time Players, Michaels would call his the Not Ready for Prime Time Players.

In truth, Michaels wasn't entirely confident in his players. For the October 11 premiere, he hedged, lining up two musical acts, two stand-ups, an Albert Brooks film and a Muppets segment, this on top of several long monologues allotted to George Carlin, the nominal host. "Everyone in the cast was pretty disappointed by how little airtime they had," Judy said. "John, as usual, was probably the most vocal."

Days before the debut, John pushed Michaels a bit too hard, and Michaels fired him. John "stormed off in a huff, went across the street and disappeared into the Pig n' Whistle, this dive bar on Forty-Eighth Street," Anne Beatts said. She found him, drank with him, and persuaded him to return and apologize.

By mounting a live show, Michaels courted danger, and the premiere did not disappoint. An hour before broadcast, George Carlin announced that he would not perform in the program's marquee sketch, something about Alexander the Great at a high school reunion. Michaels cut it. The show was still too long. In a panic, he told the two stand-ups they would have to trim their acts from five minutes to two. Valri Bromfield agreed, but the other, a rising talent named Billy Crystal, refused. A half hour before air, workers were still setting the stage lighting. Dick Ebersol kept one eye on the lights and the other on Belushi. Fifteen minutes before he was due onstage for the opening sketch of *Saturday Night*, John was backstage, refusing to sign his contract with NBC.

Chapter 10

I'm a King Bee

A LL THROUGH THE SUMMER, John Belushi had balked at signing a contract to perform on *Saturday Night*. The network had sig-
natures from the other performers. John had read the document from
cover to cover. It was not, in fact, a particularly good contract. It guaranteed him a not-ready-for-midtown-rents salary of $750 a week for the
first year of *Saturday Night*, rising to $1,600 by year five, if the show lasted
that long. The network would allow John up to six guest appearances
per year on other networks. Otherwise, NBC effectively owned Belushi,
reserving the right to place him on any other program if *Saturday Night*
were canceled, an event that seemed inevitable.

A junior executive chased John around backstage, waving the con-
tract and warning that he could not go on the air unless he signed.
Dick Ebersol joined the fray, which soon drew the attention of Bernie
Brillstein, Michaels's manager.

John turned to Brillstein. "Would you sign this contract?" he fumed.

"I designed the fucking contract," Brillstein replied. The agent
explained that the document guaranteed every *Saturday Night* performer the same treatment. If any player reaped a new benefit, so would
everyone else.

"You telling me the truth?" John said, arching his eyebrow.

"Yes, goddammit," Brillstein said.

John considered. "If you manage me, I'll sign," he said. Brillstein
agreed. John signed. Two years earlier, John had held Matty Simmons
and *National Lampoon* hostage to leverage a job for Judy. Now, he had

held Lorne Michaels and *Saturday Night* at gunpoint to poach Michaels's manager, putting him on equal footing with his new boss, rendering him untouchable.

The October 11 premiere opened on a set that looked like Archie Bunker's living room. Michael O'Donoghue sat in an easy chair, wearing a brown suit, a trimmed beard, and a comb-over. John walked on looking very much like an Albanian immigrant, wearing a fur-lined hat and carrying a bag of groceries. The sketch unfolded as a variation on the language-class scene that Dan and Valri Bromfield had worked up at Second City. O'Donoghue said, "Good evening." John replied, "Guuuuhd eeeevuh-ning." The dialogue strayed into absurdist *Monty Python* territory. O'Donoghue recited, "I would like . . . to feed your fingertips . . . to the wolverines," lines John dutifully repeated. After a few more exchanges, O'Donoghue seized his chest, as if stricken by a heart attack, and collapsed to the floor. John arched an eyebrow in contemplation, then clutched his own heart and fell to the floor. After a brief silence, Chase walked onstage, wearing a headset and carrying a clipboard, as if he were one of the crew. He paused to survey the scene, turned to the camera, broke the fourth wall, and cried, "Live, from New York, it's *Saturday Night!*"

The bedraggled set, painstakingly assembled inside NBC's Studio 8H, cut a sharp contrast to the Vegas-lounge stylings of the typical 1970s variety show. The music that exploded after Chase's introductory line sounded less like network television and more like a pot-scented Bruce Springsteen record, all wailing saxes and funky bass. Don Pardo's voice rang out over a montage of late-night city scenes, showcasing all the things viewers could be doing if they weren't sitting at home, getting high and watching *Saturday Night.*

After the credits, George Carlin came on wearing a T-shirt beneath a three-piece suit, the result of a bizarre wardrobe compromise with network management, and delivered a few minutes of his stand-up act as an opening monologue. Dan appeared next in *Saturday Night*'s first filmed commercial parody, "New Dad Insurance," a play on late-night ads. Dan faded out of a smiling family portrait, and Chase walked on as the replacement "new dad."

The program's most daring sketch featured a special guest, stand-up comedian Andy Kaufman, who unfurled an odd piece of performance art. He stood, visibly uncomfortable, and cued a phonograph to play the theme song from a Mighty Mouse cartoon. He remained motionless until the lyric reached the third line and Mighty Mouse roared, "Here I come to save the day." Andy broke from his trance and mimed that line, smiling, wobbling his knees and slicing his hand through the air. Then he fell silent, shuffling, casting his eyes bashfully around and shakily pouring a glass of water as the song played on. The two-minute segment would set *Saturday Night* forever apart from the rest of the television pantheon.

Belushi returned to the stage as a man who claimed to have been attacked by a shark as a stunt to get on TV, called out by an intolerant Jane Curtin. Chase debuted as anchor of "Weekend Update." The newscaster role secured him a future on *Saturday Night*, as the one performer who introduced himself by name every week. John squeezed into a ridiculous bee costume for an inane sketch titled "Bee Hospital." John would come to loathe the bees. An interminable Muppets segment ate up precious minutes. Dan's only live showcase came near the end, in a scene opposite John and Gilda Radner. As he awaited his entrance, Dan told himself, *If this sketch doesn't work, I will return to Canada, buy a plow, and start a new career as a snow-clearance contractor.* The sketch worked, Dan invoking his pitchman's voice as a home invader who pauses in mid-crime to tout a home security system.

The episode ended with a relaxed swing jam scored by Howard Shore, *Saturday Night*'s Canadian music director, and sounding like an outtake from a Rolling Stones album.

In smoky living rooms around the nation, Steve Martin and Tom Hanks and other young performers watched the closing minutes of the new show and marveled. Someone had finally captured "our generation's loose, weirdo, hairy, nontraditional bent—Belushi's manic energy, Aykroyd's subversiveness, Chase's smartass leading man thing, Radner's woman-child daffiness—into something that could be presented on network television," Martin Short reflected.

Saturday Night had survived its first broadcast. On Monday, Dick Ebersol dispatched an exultant memo to Michaels. "The reaction from the network has been extremely encouraging this morning," he wrote. "*Everybody* is in love with Chevy."

New York and Los Angeles did not, however, erupt in spontaneous celebration. A few papers published brief reviews. A *Chicago Tribune* critic termed the program "superb." The *New York Daily News* opined that Carlin had "bombed badly." The commercial parodies left most reviewers baffled. The *New York Times* wrote nothing at all.

Michaels continued to hedge. For the second *Saturday Night* episode, he abandoned the formula established in the first, staging an extended musical special that exploited a reunion of folk-pop duo Simon and Garfunkel. Paul Simon and Michaels had become friends. Michaels reasoned that a set of Simon and Garfunkel tunes on live television would deliver solid ratings while freeing the staff to work on sketches for week three. Apart from Chevy Chase, the Not Ready for Prime Time Players appeared only once, in their bee costumes. That was an inside joke: no one liked the bees, not the network, not the cast, and Belushi least of all. Instead of cutting the bees, Michaels doubled down, trotting them out to gather awkwardly behind Simon, who awkwardly dismissed them. The scene played on the general ennui at *Saturday Night* and the stirrings of insurrection among the cast.

Two days later, *New York Times* reviewer John J. O'Connor weighed in on *Saturday Night*. "Even an offbeat showcase needs quality, an ingredient conspicuously absent from the dreadfully uneven comedy efforts of the new series," he wrote. O'Connor had struggled to discern the real commercials from the fake ones. His confusion suggested a generational divide. Older viewers couldn't quite comprehend the humor of *Saturday Night*, let alone appreciate it. O'Connor was forty-two. Kay Gardella, the *Daily News* scribe who had declared Carlin a bomb, was fifty-two. By contrast, Gary Deeb, the *Chicago Tribune* columnist, had found the fake commercials "devastating." He was twenty-nine.

The third episode of *Saturday Night* restored order, positing a rough format from which Michaels would seldom stray again. For host,

Michaels tapped Rob Reiner, who played Michael "Meathead" Stivic on television's number-one show, *All in the Family*. Reiner had feuded with Michaels and the writers all week. His opening monologue as a sleazy lounge singer missed badly. That failure left Reiner rattled for the rest of the night, tapping on microphones, sweating profusely, looking both ill and ill prepared, a syndrome that would afflict many future hosts. The indignant writers didn't cast Reiner in many sketches. His absence opened a door, finally, for the *Saturday Night* performers. Jane Curtin cemented her standing as a parodic talk-show host, glamorous, poised, and caustic. Laraine Newman emerged as a delightfully deadpan reporter opposite Chase's smart-aleck "Weekend Update" anchor. Dan shone as a uniformed everyman, equally comfortable playing doctor, huckster, and plumber. Even Garrett Morris, whose talents would be criminally underused on *Saturday Night*, found a recurring role, delivering news, loudly, to the hard of hearing.

But Belushi stole the show. John knew when to play to his strengths. Midway through the Rob Reiner episode, he took the stage as Joe Cocker, writhing, grimacing, wincing, spouting beer from his mouth, and flopping to the floor in a spastic fit. It was easily the funniest thing yet aired on *Saturday Night*, with the possible exception of Andy Kaufman. John brought Studio 8H to life.

Michaels continued to chip away at the fourth wall, allowing the backstage tension and tumult to bleed out onstage. In the middle of a scene at a restaurant staffed with bees—again—Rob Reiner exploded, halting the sketch and venting some of the wrath he had directed at Michaels and the writers all week. "All right, all right, that's it, that's it. Stop it," he whined. "Hold the music. No, no, no. It's ridiculous. Really. I mean, I'm not going to go on with this thing. This is absolutely ridiculous. I was told when I came on this show that I would not have to work with the bees. And here they are."

John walked up, interrupting Reiner's rant. "I'm sorry if you think we're ruining your show, Mr. Reiner," he said, blinking, looking on the edge of tears. "See, you don't understand. We didn't ask to be bees. You see, you've got Norman Lear and a first-rate writing staff. But this is all they came up with for us. Do you think we LIKE THIS?" John's voice was rising, antennae flapping wildly. "No. No, Mr. Reiner. But we don't have any choice." The other bees applauded as John retreated, his speech seemingly over. Then John pushed back into Reiner's space, jabbing a finger at the Meathead actor as the strains of "Battle Hymn of the Republic" rose up behind him. "We're just like you were, five years ago, Mr. Hollywood, California, number-one-show big shot. That's right. We're just a bunch of actors looking for a break, that's all. What do you want from us, Mr. Rob Reiner, Mr. Star? What did you expect? *The Sting?*" John retreated. The host looked ashen, speechless, spent.

For episode four, Lorne Michaels recruited Candice Bergen, the first woman to host *Saturday Night*, the first movie star most of the cast had ever seen up close. She was also the first host to arrive at 30 Rock as an avowed fan of the show, honored at the opportunity. And she was gorgeous. John, Dan, and the other boys on the seventeenth floor ran around "like puppy dogs" all week, competing for her favor.

Michaels and Bergen were sitting with Michael O'Donoghue in Michaels's office, mapping out ideas, when Dan and John crashed in, Dan in a black biker jacket, John in clothes he might have slept in. Michaels introduced them. The boys gushed praise of Bergen's films. They babbled about a sketch they wanted to do, a tribute to Sam Peckinpah, the director with a penchant for violent westerns. They acted it out, John's voice rising as he talked Bergen through the scene. Suddenly, John leapt at the actress, grabbed her arms, pulled her up from the couch, and tossed her onto the floor, as Michaels looked on in horror. John straddled Bergen, grabbed her head in his hands, and theatrically bashed it against the floor, over and over. Michaels sat frozen. O'Donoghue smiled and played along, hoping to seed the impression that this sort of thing happened every week at *Saturday Night*. Bergen just laughed.

The Candice Bergen episode opened with Chevy Chase portraying a bumbling President Gerald Ford, saying he was "truly honored to be asked by you to open the *Saturday Night* show with Harvey Cosell," a dig at the rival series. John crept onstage during Bergen's opening monologue dressed as a bee. Chase came out and tried to shoo him away.

John sneaked back and planted his chin on Bergen's shoulder, bobbing his eyebrows like Groucho Marx as she smiled indulgently.

The full cast collaborated on a "Jaws II" sketch, sending up Steven Spielberg's blockbuster film. Chase played a shark who talked his way into young women's apartments. John showed his range as an excitable Richard Dreyfuss. On "Weekend Update," Chase introduced his signature line, "I'm Chevy Chase, and you're not." Bergen gamely performed a commercial parody as Catherine Deneuve with a bottle of Chanel stuck to the side of her head. Dan and John played a pair of New Zealand kiwi trappers in camouflage hats and dark glasses, a sketch that ended with them chasing Bergen around the set and trapping her in a sack, reenacting the scene in Michaels's office. At the close, each cast member presented the delighted host with a red rose.

On the day of the Candice Bergen episode, the *Washington Post* published the first significant feature on *Saturday Night*. The author was the celebrated critic Tom Shales, who had just turned thirty-one. He seemed to understand the show on a cellular level.

"NBC's *Saturday Night* can boast the freshest satire on commercial TV, but the show is more than that," Shales wrote. "It is probably the first network series produced by and for the television generation—those late-war and post-war babies who were the first to have TV as a sitter. They loved it in the '50s, hated it in the '60s and now they are trying to take it over in the '70s." Shales said the new show had come within one rating point of meeting "the high standard set by Johnny Carson on weeknights." NBC had sold every available commercial slot through year's end.

Saturday Night was a success on every level. A network exec wrote a breathless memo to Michaels suggesting he hire Candice Bergen as permanent host. Michaels ignored it—he didn't want the same cover on his magazine every week. Dick Ebersol gushed that the show was "getting the most attractive audience on television today." Two early episodes had drawn the largest share of viewers in the coveted eighteen-to-forty-nine age group of any show on the air.

Two episodes later, John O'Connor of the *New York Times* publicly reversed his opinion of *Saturday Night*. Perhaps Shales's write-up had changed his mind. "For however long it lasts," he wrote, "'Saturday Night' is the most creative and encouraging thing to happen in American TV comedy since 'Your Show of Shows,'" the legendary 1950s variety program that had inspired Michaels.

Plaudits piled up. In December, *Newsweek* declared *Saturday Night* a hit, which was even better than declaring it good. A *Los Angeles Times* critic termed it "the only new comedy program to originate on American television in the last five years which enriches and expands the form."

The coverage pleased everyone but John. Most critics singled out Chevy Chase above the other *Saturday Night* players. Chase's rising currency didn't bother Dan, who didn't even want his own name broadcast on the air, but it bothered John. Back at *National Lampoon,* John was the star, and Chase had dwelt in his shadow. The very structure of *Saturday Night* seemed to turn the tables. John raged to Judy: Chase was getting roles that should have gone to him, carving out time that could have been his. John figured that, taken together, Chase's Gerald Ford stunts, his "Weekend Update" gig, the weekly host's segments, the musical guests, the Albert Brooks films, and the accursed Muppets ate up four-fifths of the camera time on *Saturday Night.* One Saturday, as John and Judy walked to a noon breakfast, someone on the street yelled, "Hey, it's the bee!" John seethed.

Michaels and Ebersol trained the spotlight squarely on Chase, rolling him out at the start of most episodes to perform his trademark pratfalls and again in mid-broadcast to anchor *Update.* Other performers competed for Michaels's attention and approval, but Chase sat in the inner circle, Michael O'Donoghue his only equal. If O'Donoghue was the lead writer, Chase was the lead actor.

John had never been upstaged. Now Chase overshadowed him without really trying. A mid-December issue of *New York* magazine put Chase on its cover, beneath the headline, AND HEEEERE'S TV'S HOTTEST NEW COMEDY STAR! The piece proclaimed Chase "a hot property at NBC," potential heir to Carson.

In the second week of December, Michaels took his biggest gamble yet, inviting Richard Pryor to host episode seven. Pryor agreed, on the condition that he import an entourage of Black talent, including Paul Mooney, the brilliant writer, and Gil Scott-Heron, the singer-poet who had recorded "The Revolution Will Not Be Televised."

Pryor feared the all-white writing staff would pen racially insensitive material, which seemed a safe bet. The staff treated Pryor with polite deference all week. Network executives feared he would curse on the air, though Carlin had not, so they conspired to broadcast the show with a five-second delay. This they arranged in utter secrecy, for fear Pryor might discover the ruse and walk out.

The episode's most daring sketch cast Pryor opposite Chase in a job interview, a *Monty Python* setup emboldened by racial wordplay. Chase gave Pryor a word-association test, which ventured into tense rhetorical terrain:

CHASE. "White."

PRYOR. "Black."

CHASE. "Negro."

PRYOR. "Whitey. . . ."

CHASE. "Colored."

PRYOR. "Redneck. . . ."

CHASE. "Jungle bunny."

PRYOR. "Honky."

CHASE. "Spade."

PRYOR. "Honky honky."

CHASE. "N-----."

PRYOR. "DEAD honky."

Amid the taut laughter that followed, Pryor's face quivered in comic rage as Chase backpedaled frantically. No one but Pryor could have delivered the scene.

The program also marked the *Saturday Night* debut of John's samurai. The scene, written by Tom Schiller, played on the notion of John's wordless swordsman running a hotel. Michaels had brought John over to

Pryor's hotel room to preview the sketch. Seeing it, Pryor had beamed, "I gotta do that." The scene opened at the hotel's front desk, John grunting as he thrust letters violently into mail slots. He babbled menacingly at Chase, cast as a hapless guest. The hotelier summoned Pryor, his samurai bellhop. The two staged a noisy sword fight over who would carry Chase's bags. It ended with John declaring, "Yo' mama-san." At that, Pryor swung his sword and cleaved the reception desk in two. John broke character then and ad-libbed, "Well, I can dig where you're coming from."

With the samurai sketch, the group dynamic on the seventeenth floor shifted yet again.

John "had been the top banana," Michaels recalled. "And [then] it was all about Chevy, all the time. And that was driving John crazy. Then, with the samurai on Richard Pryor's show, that was sort of the breakthrough." Belushi's star was rising.

Around this time, Steven Spielberg traveled to New York to meet the Not Ready for Prime Time Players. He attended an after-show party at One Fifth, an art deco–style restaurant. Spielberg was twenty-eight, just the right age for *Saturday Night*. He told John he was working on a new film set after Pearl Harbor in a Los Angeles seized by fears of imminent Japanese attack. John's samurai character would be perfect for the Japanese submarine captain. John grabbed a coat rack and lifted it into the air, maneuvering it like a periscope. "You want see my Japanese sub, skipper?" he asked Spielberg in a burst of Mifune-inflected grunts. John spent the rest of the evening in character.

John and his castmates weren't exactly famous, but *Saturday Night* was reaching the right people. One was Mitch Glazer, a young reporter for *Crawdaddy*, a rock zine that dwelt in *Rolling Stone*'s shadow.

"Everybody was focusing on Chevy," Glazer recalled. "But John, I don't know, his energy and the danger of him, the kind of excitement whenever he came on screen was jarring, and a comedy I hadn't seen before." Glazer resolved to write a story on *Saturday Night*'s feral samurai.

As the 1975–76 Christmas break approached, Dan felt creeping ennui. He asked John to join him in a cross-country road trip. They found an

Oldsmobile Ninety-Eight that awaited delivery to the West Coast and tricked it out with a music system and CB radio. They set out with a six-pack, aviator sunglasses, and a copy of Jack Kerouac's *On the Road*, which John read aloud as Dan drove. John played with the CB, affecting an effeminate voice and cooing to truckers, "I'd like to meet some of you boys," until threats of violence chased him from the air. The two friends talked about women, about John's love for Judy, about cars, the road, and UFOs. They slept in the scariest Norman Bates–type motels they could find, sharing a king-size bed. They stopped at the University of Arkansas campus in Little Rock and walked around to see if anyone would recognize them. No one did.

"The show's a real flop," John said. "Nobody has seen any of the work. What's it all worth?"

Dan timed their drive to hit Las Vegas before dawn. He motored through the city, running red lights while John slept. He knew that if John awakened, he'd trap them in Vegas for days. When John eventually stirred, the casinos lay fifty miles behind them. He was furious. But Dan got them to California in time for a few days' rest before their return to New York for the next show.

John caught up with Joe Flaherty, ensconced in Los Angeles with Second City, and asked him for advice.

"John, you know," Flaherty said, "they're not using you the right way." He urged John to do "the big stuff, when you work yourself up into a lather and just fall over. Try to play the more aggressive characters. Do something physical." Flaherty was right: John's big splashes on *Saturday Night* had come with his broadest characters, Joe Cocker and the samurai.

"Yeah, yeah, yeah," John replied. "I want to do more of that. I just got to get them to fucking write it."

A Christmas episode with Candice Bergen had sputtered, sending Michaels into a crisis of confidence. He and Michael O'Donoghue worked through the holidays to write good material for the first outing of 1976.

The January 10 episode opened with the Dead String Quartet, a macabre sight gag that played off the absurdist tradition of *Monty Python* and the gallows humor of O'Donoghue and *National Lampoon*. Elliott

Gould, star of the 1970 antiwar movie *M*A*S*H*, came on with a winsome song and dance. The best sketch of the night exploited John's Brando, casting him in a group therapy session.

"Vito was telling us about his feelings toward the Tattaglia family," said Gould, the pipe-smoking therapist. "Vito?"

"The Tattaglia family is causing me great personal grief," John fumed, summoning his Brando-as-Corleone voice. "Also, things are not going so well at my olive oil company."

"Oh God, Vito," Laraine Newman replied, in character as a blond stewardess from the Valley. "I think you're blocking."

"Blocking what?" John growled.

"Your true feelings about the Tattaglia family. Ga-yeee."

John then parodied the famous Vito Corleone death scene, a wedge of orange peel in his mouth.

For the January 17 episode, Michaels tapped Buck Henry, the Hollywood comedy writer. Henry arrived in New York full of ideas about *Saturday Night*, perhaps the first host to glimpse its full promise. Shortly before the hosting gig, Henry had attended a glamorous Hollywood party, "and everything stopped so they could watch this show," he recalled. "I thought, 'Oh, my God. They stopped drinking and doing drugs to watch a television show.'"

Henry asked the *Saturday Night* writers to show him sketches other hosts had turned down. The writers loved him. Michaels loved him. Early in the week, Henry asked him, "Do you want to do the samurai again?" Michaels had mostly avoided repeating sketches, but he agreed to broadcast "Samurai Delicatessen," and John sliced a tomato in half in midair on live television.

In the sleepy closing minutes of the broadcast, with little fanfare, Henry introduced "Howard Shore and His All-Bee Band." The camera panned to Shore, pianist Paul Shaffer, and the *Saturday Night* band, the musicians dressed as bees, Shore as beekeeper. John stood at a microphone, Dan behind him with his harmonica, in bee costumes and amber-tinted sunglasses. "All right now, are you ready for the blues?" John cried, antennae bobbing. "Lemme hear you say yeah! Yeah," he replied, answering his own appeal, sensing a listless audience beyond the stage lights. He launched into the old Slim Harpo tune "I'm a King Bee," summoning a convincing blues growl. At the instrumental break, John executed a manic, painful-looking sequence of cartwheels, somersaults, and pratfalls. In the closing bars, he halted the band for a series of single, staccato snare-drum blasts, cycling through his Joe Cocker impression and several others, finally stirring the somnambulant audience. The song ended to rousing cheers.

Before every *Saturday Night* episode, the house band would warm up the studio audience with music, mixing in monologues from cast members. "And I was playing a lot of blues," Howard Shore said. "The band was created from my love of Junior Walker, Stax-Volt, that era. King Curtis. And Danny played a little harp, and he asked me if he could sit in. And I said, 'Sure.' And John, of course, wanted to get in the act." Some musicians winced at allowing amateurs to join them, but Shore could hardly object— he had given the duo its name. He introduced them as "those brothers in blues, the Blues Brothers." And thus, the Blues Brothers had debuted off-camera in November 1975, "and it was an instant success and sensation," Paul Shaffer recalled, "because it was so high-energy and up-tempo."

John and Dan worked up a blues act, learning a few standards that John could sing while Dan goaded him on with the harmonica. They pushed Lorne Michaels to let them perform on the air. John's Joe Cocker had blown the roof off, and his pop-star fantasies conspired with his resentment toward the *Saturday Night* musical guests for hogging precious camera time. "Why can't one of the group sing?" he asked.

Michaels resisted putting the untried act on live television. An epiphany came to Dan one night while John was complaining about the damnable bee sketches. "Fuck Lorne," John said. "This is my last one."

"Wait a minute," Dan said. "I've got an idea. What if we get the band to put on bee costumes, and we all play Slim Harpo's 'I'm a King Bee'? I'll play harp and you'll sing the shit out of it."

"How's it go?" John asked. Dan walked him through the lyrics.

"Let's do it," John said.

Ever since adolescence, Dan and John had dreamed of fronting bands in smoky clubs. Now, their moment had arrived.

Chapter 11

Bass-o-Matic

THE WORK WEEK at *Saturday Night* commenced in Lorne Michaels's office around five p.m. Monday, closing time for most of the city. Michaels introduced the episode's host. The writers delivered pitches for that week's show, ranging from a few words to a literal walk-through of a six-minute scene. Dan emerged as a consummate writer, though NBC neither paid nor credited him for the work. In the Monday meetings, Dan would unleash his unbridled muse, leaping atop chairs and scaling Michaels's desk as he acted out a sketch, voicing every part, before storming dramatically out of the room, repeating a pattern established in his audition. At meeting's end, writers filed out in twos and threes for dinner, to flesh out ideas on napkins and menus, returning by midnight and working until dawn. The nocturnal schedule resumed on Tuesday, as writers polished scenes. On Wednesday afternoon, Michaels gathered the performers and host to read through scripts for the Saturday broadcast. Around five p.m. Wednesday, Michaels and a few aides returned to his office to assemble the show, calling in writing teams one by one to announce the fates of their scenes. Work began in earnest on sets, costumes, sound effects, and props for any scene that might earn actual airtime. Set designers and writers worked through the night. On Thursday afternoon, set pieces trickled in from a Brooklyn studio, supplemented by artifacts procured from antiques stores and boutiques and garments from the Brooks–Van Horn costume house on Seventeenth Street: Michaels strove for realism in every detail. Performers attended "blocking" sessions Thursday and Friday, a tedious procedure to synchronize cameras to scenes. After dinner Friday, wardrobe workers fitted performers into costumes. Dan, for whom dress-up remained serious business, traveled with reference books of uniforms and weaponry.

Cast and crew assembled Saturday afternoon for a run-through of the full show. After an hour-long dinner break, the players perused the last of many revisions to the weekly script. Dan, with his near-photographic memory, would flip through the pages and note any changes with a curt "Got it." Belushi and most of the others relied on cue cards. Dress rehearsal began around eight thirty. Someone timed the sketches with a stopwatch. Dress often ran twenty or thirty minutes long. Michaels then announced a final round of cuts, abandoning a week's work on entire truckloads of sets, costumes, and scripts. Dress rehearsal sometimes ran until 10:50, forty minutes before showtime.

John sleepwalked through rehearsals and came alive on the air, a routine familiar to anyone who had watched him on the Wheaton Central football team. Dan, by contrast, sometimes delivered his finest performance in the Monday writers' meeting and ran out of gas by week's end. In time, he learned to pace himself.

Michaels held final meetings in his office just before air, cutting a minute here, a sketch there, sometimes restructuring the entire broadcast.

Through the ninety-minute program, Michaels stood at a monitor with a glass of wine and read along with each sketch, sotto voce. Performers took the stage wearing two or three costumes in layers, each one slit down the back and closed with Velcro strips for easy removal. Wardrobe changes played out in a crowded hallway. "A clothesline and a bedsheet separated changing and fitting areas for the boys and girls," Laraine Newman recalled, "and the guys were not modest at all." Some of them didn't wear underwear. A sign eventually appeared, reminding the boys to bring a pair on Saturdays.

Dan and John spent endless hours together in a windowless office known as the Cave. "There were dirty clothes in piles several feet high in the corners, cartons and boxes stacked on the floor, loose pages of scripts littered everywhere, cassettes with the tape streaming out of them in long swirls, scattered collections of armament magazines, industrial manuals, liquor bottles, and motorcycle parts," by one account. "Beneath it all, somewhere, was a cot. Soiled panties sent in by fans, Polaroid shots of gas station attendants, and other oddities were pinned to the walls, which were scarred with holes, fist-sized and larger, and messages scrawled in Magic Marker." John often slept on the cot.

"It was like being in a college dorm, ya know?" Dan said. "We had beers and smoked the herb."

The partners wrote at desks pushed together in an L shape. "When they were working, it was very quiet," Tom Schiller said. "It was like a library."

John loved Judy and seemed unable to survive without her. Yet, he went to great lengths to avoid going home to their Bleecker Street apartment. Michael O'Donoghue joined him in midday outings to pinball parlors and horror movies. They were the odd couple, O'Donoghue fastidious, John slovenly. John messed with O'Donoghue's obsessive-compulsive mind by walking into his manicured office and subtly shifting objects around. John would not have noticed if O'Donoghue had emptied a wastebasket onto the floor of the Cave.

John and O'Donoghue bonded in resentment toward their respective romantic partners, who had become immersed in assembling a book of female humor titled *Titters*. Judy left her job at *National Lampoon* not long after the *Saturday Night* debut, the better to arrange her time around John's increasingly busy schedule. Then the women's book project heated up, keeping Judy and Anne Beatts away from John and O'Donoghue for days on end. Judy had grown accustomed to coping without John; John seemed unable or unwilling to cope without her. "I think an unconscious part of John was that ethnic man who likes the idea of his wife at home in the kitchen," Judy said. "On a conscious level, however, he wanted an equal."

John blamed Beatts for taking Judy away from him. Jealousy poisoned him toward Beatts's contributions to *Saturday Night*. He refused to perform scenes she wrote with Rosie Shuster, whom he sarcastically termed "the boss's wife," although their marriage was effectively over. All through the first season, relations soured between John and roughly half of the women on the *Saturday Night* set, though he grew close to Laraine Newman and adored Gilda Radner. He waged a particularly bitter feud with Jane Curtin, who had once counted him as a friend.

He and Curtin had auditioned together for the Howard Cosell show. "And he was just another actor who was looking for work and had a lot of promise, and he was very sweet and very considerate, and we would sit on my stoop and talk about what we wanted out of the business," she said. "And I liked him, I liked him very much.

"And then when the show started, I saw that something had gotten to John, and I don't know whether it was ego or ambition—a lot of it had to do with the drugs—and he was no longer this guy I could relate to. So, working with him was hard, because he didn't respect me, or at least he appeared not to respect me, and he didn't seem to respect the other women on the show, or the women writers."

Back at Second City and *National Lampoon*, John had embraced his female castmates like a protective older brother. Now, John regularly begged Lorne Michaels to fire "the girls." The next day, he would walk in with flowers and apologies.

It wasn't just John. All of the men at Second City, *National Lampoon*, and *Saturday Night* straddled two eras, and perhaps all struggled to perceive their female colleagues as artistic equals. Once, Curtin recalled, she performed a scene with Chevy Chase that required them to frolic in bed while Supreme Court judges looked on. After the performance, Chase asked Curtin, "Does your husband ever get upset at you doing things like this?"

"No," Curtin answered.

"Really," Chase said.

"He's an actor," Curtin said. "No, he doesn't. Would you get upset?"

"Yeah," Chase replied, "I would."

John's twenty-seventh birthday arrived on January 24, 1976. Friends presented him with a cake in the shape of a giant Quaalude.

Pot smoke pervaded the *Saturday Night* offices. If the staff had any qualms about lighting up in a skyscraper filled with network executives,

Michaels put them to rest. "When we had our early meetings in Lorne's office, and everybody was crammed in, one of the first things he did was light a joint and pass it around," Tom Schiller said. Schiller remembered riding up in an elevator with a white-gloved operator, "and when the doors opened on the seventeenth floor, this pot smell would billow out." Belushi showed Schiller how to roll a joint.

As the season wore on and fatigue mounted, pot gave way to cocaine. Michaels managed his own stress by ordering cases of top-drawer Chablis on the network's dime. He sipped through the week, cutting an image of refined calm that cloaked internal turmoil.

Dick Ebersol recalled the time Al Franken and Tom Davis pooled their meager salaries to buy their first blow. "So, they have the cocaine on the desk, they're, like, literally staring at it," he said. "Suddenly, this figure comes roaring through the room. Unbeknownst to us at the time, he had a straw in his hand. He gets to the table, and he has half of that stuff up his nose by the time they knew who it was: Belushi. They didn't know whether to be thrilled that Belushi had just done this to their coke, or to be absolutely decimated, because that represented about half the money they had in the world at that time."

On the March 13 edition of "Weekend Update," Chevy Chase introduced John as the program's new meteorologist. John had written the weatherman sketch with Michael O'Donoghue, a bid to build his brand in the ongoing contest with Chase, whose star continued to rise. John came on wearing a wig that looked like a parody of Chase's mid-'70s coif and launched into a goofy commentary that played on the notion of March coming in like a lion and going out like a lamb. "Do you know that March behaves differently in other countries?" he asked. "In Norway, for example, March comes in like a polar bear and goes out like a walrus. Or take the case of Honduras, where March comes in like a lamb and goes out like a salt-marsh harvest mouse."

Chase shuffled in his anchor chair and subtly aped John's movements, a Chase signature that drew attention from his guests. But John gathered steam, twitching with nervous energy and waving off Chase's interruptions. Chase put a hand on John's shoulder. John shook it off violently, looking like he might attack. Chase reached in with both hands. John nearly knocked him from his chair. John erupted: "THE WEIRD PART . . . THE WEIRD PART . . ." He collapsed to the floor.

But Chase remained the star. The next week, John and Dan traveled to Washington, DC, for the Radio and Television Correspondents' Association dinner, playing Secret Service agents to Chase's Gerald Ford. John arrived at the White House without an ID. During their visit, the group "spent an afternoon buzzing from landmark to landmark in an NBC limousine, at each point launching into a ragged improvisation on the spot," Tom Shales reported. "At the reflecting pool near the Lincoln Memorial, Belushi grabbed a stick and became a growling, limping old legislator, with Aykroyd, playing a reporter, chasing after him down the length of the pool and yelling, 'But Senator! Senator, please! Senator!'"

Saturday Night had sufficient currency that Ford himself taped some material for an upcoming show, echoing Chase's catchphrase with "I'm Gerald Ford, and you're not." After recording the segment, the president became entangled in his lapel mic, setting off one of the very blunders Chase so ably lampooned. Ford's press secretary, Ron Nessen, hosted the April 17 broadcast. News coverage focused on the president and Chase, overshadowing a bizarre faux commercial from Dan that would seed *Saturday Night* legend.

The Aykroyd family included an aunt, Hélène Gougeon, who hosted a cooking show; Dan termed her the Julia Child of Canada. On a childhood visit, Dan watched her lower a whole trout into a blender. "Aunt Helen," he asked, "what about the eyes, the head, the bones?" Aunt Helen chirped, "Oh, it's a bouillabaisse, it doesn't matter." Ten years later, Dan wrote it up as a sketch.

"Here's how it works," Dan cried in his breathless pitchman's voice, wearing a jacket that looked like a cross-stitch nightmare. "Catch a bass, remove the hook and drop the bass, that's the whole bass, into the Super Bass-o-Matic '76." Dan lowered an actual bass into an actual blender and hit the button. The explosion of fish guts and water triggered an explosion of laughter from the studio audience, startled by the sheer, manic strangeness. The camera cut to Newman, who drank from a murky glass and beamed, "Wow, that's terrific bass."

The next week, Michaels arranged a stunt that underscored how quickly and completely *Saturday Night* had captured the zeitgeist, even as he and his writers mocked their own hubris. Michaels sat at a desk, flanked by a photograph of the *Saturday Night* gang posing with President Ford. He boasted that twenty-two million Americans were watching his show. "But please allow me, if I may, to address myself to four very special people, John, Paul, George, and Ringo—the Beatles."

Michaels said he had heard talk of a Beatle reunion. He understood that various conflicts of personality or law might frustrate a regrouping, or perhaps no one had offered them enough money. "Well, if it's money you want," he said, "there's no problem here. The National Broadcasting Company has authorized me to offer you a certified check for three thousand dollars," Michaels said, holding it up to the camera. Laughter erupted at the absurd sum. "All you have to do is sing three Beatle tunes. 'She loves you, yeah, yeah, yeah.' That's a thousand dollars right there. You know the words. It'll be easy."

Michaels offered the world's most famous band these parting words: "You divide it any way you want. You want to give Ringo less, that's up to you."

If anything, Michaels underestimated his program's currency. Two Beatles, John and Paul, were watching *Saturday Night* that very night in John's apartment at the Dakota. They briefly considered crashing the live broadcast, a surprise visit that would have ranked among the greatest moments in television history, had it only come to pass.

In the spring of 1976, any new episode of *Saturday Night* brought weekend activities to a halt, at least for denizens of the television generation. Bob Woodward, thirty-three, tuned in to the May 8 episode and watched Aykroyd and Belushi perform a scene adapted from *The Final Days*, Woodward and Carl Bernstein's new book about the turbulent terminus of the Nixon presidency.

"Henry, get down on your knees and pray. Pray with me," Aykroyd's Nixon pleaded to Belushi's Kissinger.

"Mr. President," Kissinger replied, "you've got a big day tomorrow. So why don't vee just get in our jammies und go sleepy-time?"

"Don't you want to pray, Jew boy?" Nixon snapped.

Watching his scene unfold on television's hottest show, Woodward thought, *Now, it's real.*

On May 17, *Saturday Night* won three Emmy Awards: the Television Academy agreed with Tom Shales that Michaels had created the best comedy variety show on television.

For the May 29 episode, Michael O'Donoghue wrote an ingenious parody of *Star Trek*, the sci-fi series that NBC had unceremoniously canceled in 1969. With their none-too-subtle jab at the network, O'Donoghue and the gang bit the hand that fed them. "The Last Voyage of the Starship Enterprise" imagined network suits boarding Captain Kirk's ship and turning out the lights. Dan seemed the obvious choice for Kirk. He had already done a perfect Shatner at Second City. But John wanted the role. He had been watching *Star Trek* reruns. He told O'Donoghue he could do Bill Shatner.

"And then, all through the rehearsals, he couldn't do Bill Shatner," O'Donoghue recalled. "At all. It was just awful." Just before air, O'Donoghue hissed, "You better pull this off, you son of a bitch."

And then the sketch went live, and John executed a flawless Shatner, a template for all future Shatners, from the Thinker pose to the halting, oddly syncopated speech: "I have a hunch, Mr. Spock, that we are about to face something deadlier than the Romulans, the Klingons and the Gorns . . . all . . . rolled . . . into . . . one," he deadpanned, to a round of reverential applause.

Denied Kirk, Dan showed his range by voicing both Scotty and Dr. McCoy. Elliott Gould came on as an evil network executive, announcing that *Star Trek* would be canceled for low ratings. Chase, as Spock, fruitlessly attempted his Vulcan death pinch. Gould said, "Nimoy, I'm sorry, we'll have to take your ears back, too," and plucked them from his head.

John rang out the sketch with an entry in his captain's log. "We have tried to explore strange new worlds, to seek out new civilizations, to boldly go where no man has gone before. And except for one television network, we have found intelligence everywhere in the galaxy."

Chapter 12

Albanian Oak

A S *SATURDAY NIGHT* neared the end of its inaugural season, Bernie Brillstein took a call from a representative for Paul McCartney. The former Beatle was having "a little birthday party," the caller said, and wanted to pay Belushi $6,000 to do his Joe Cocker impression for the guests.

A paying gig? McCartney? John was overjoyed. The party was slated for June in Los Angeles. Dan and John organized another road trip. On top of the McCartney party, the boys were due in California to work with Michaels on a Beach Boys special for NBC.

Michaels took the gang to the Joshua Tree Inn, the desert retreat where he had mapped out the show in a mushroom haze a year earlier. They celebrated their success with a barbecue and a binge of 'shrooms, cocaine, tequila, and weed, with John claiming the lion's share. He topped it off with Quaaludes.

"We drank a lot and stayed up really late," Michaels said. "Then at about five o'clock in the morning, the sun was way too bright and woke me up. There was some sort of noise outside, so I staggered to the door. When I opened it, I saw Danny standing in the archway just a few feet away, and he's in the same shape I'm in, and we look out and there's John, on the diving board, doing these cannonballs. He goes straight up, hits the board, comes down, and then flips over into the pool. This was just for our benefit, Danny's and mine, because there was nobody else awake or watching it." Dan looked at Michaels and said, "Albanian oak."

On June 20, the boys dressed up as California Highway Patrolmen, to Dan's delight, for a scene in the Beach Boys special, marching into Brian Wilson's bedroom and hauling him off for failure to surf. Producers titled the sequence "Brian's Nightmare"—the lead Beach Boy feared both water and surfing. They filmed it on Wilson's birthday.

"Good afternoon, Mr. Wilson," John deadpans through dark shades in the filmed scene. "We're from the Highway Patrol, Surf Squad."

"Brian," Dan continues, "we have a citation here for you, sir, under section 936-a of the California Catch-a-Wave Statute. Brian, you're in violation of paragraph twelve. Failing to surf, neglecting to use a state beach for surfing purposes, and otherwise avoiding surfboards, surfing, and surf." Dan and John drag Wilson out of bed in his bathrobe, load him into a patrol car, and drive him to the beach, where they compel him to catch a wave.

A few days later, John and Dan performed for McCartney and one thousand guests beneath a giant tent on the old Harold Lloyd estate in Beverly Hills.

Later that summer, Dan invited John to visit him at the Aykroyd farm, an Ontario property that had been in the family for more than a century. John managed to cross the border without so much as a driver's license. He stepped out of his car and greeted Dan's parents with a running somersault.

Dan needed a new motor to navigate the lake on the family boat. He decided to borrow one from the local marina. Dan still got a high from flirting with crime, but he dared not involve John, who was not Canadian and might get in real trouble. Dan found some bolt cutters and a friend named Speedo and prepared for the heist. As they pulled away from the house in an old Buick, John ran out and cried, "Where are you going?"

"To get a motor," Dan replied.

"How?"

"We're going to steal it."

"I want to go."

"No."

"I want to help."

Dan relented. John climbed in. They found a fifty-horsepower John-son outboard motor at the marina. John and Speedo carried it to the car. The boys sped off. They drank beer, water-skied, swam, drove around in an old Chrysler pickup, and slept in a farmhouse where Dan's grandfather had held séances. At the end of the weekend, they quietly returned the motor.

At intervals through the first season of *Saturday Night*, Michaels had cracked the fourth wall to reveal the drama playing out behind the scenes. On July 15, *Rolling Stone* published a magazine-length account that pulled the wall down. A raft of features on *Saturday Night* would appear that spring and summer, but *Rolling Stone* seemed driven to estab-lish itself as the publication of record on *Saturday Night*, an endeavor edi-tor Jann Wenner had immediately recognized as a product of the same generation that had produced *Rolling Stone*.

"Nobody can stomach the Muppets, really, or the dull guest sing-ers," *Rolling Stone* reported, after interviewing most of the cast. "The consensus is that the players, when they're working together as comic actors, not celebrity-guest pawns, could hold the whole show by themselves."

Naturally, the most caustic quotes came from John.

"Look, I think that now, we, the players, have become, well, bigger than some of the stars who're booked as hosts," John said. He railed against the bees: "I hate the fucking bees." And against Chase: "Once we bend to a fucking star system here, everything changes." And against the hosts: "If there has to be this host, I'd like to see each one of *us* doing it." And against costars who had reaped recurring roles: "Get rid of *all* the old standard characters, the stale stuff, catchphrases." Soon enough, John would have catchphrases of his own.

A few weeks before the season-two premiere of *Saturday Night*, Tom Shales of the *Washington Post* announced that the program's "most visible comic performer," Chevy Chase, might leave. His contract up, Chase had negotiated a new deal with NBC that paid him $1.6 million to produce up to three specials. In effect, the network had raided its own show.

The remaining *Saturday Night* staff reaped huge raises, a reward for the Emmys and rising ratings. John and the other performers saw their annual pay approach $100,000.

The second season began on September 18, 1976, with Lily Tomlin and a surreal entourage of magicians and dwarves parading into Rockefeller Center as if in a scene from *Magical Mystery Tour*. Chase joked about his uncertain future. Then he injured his testicles in a pratfall, taking him out of commission for the next two episodes, a mishap some colleagues read as psychosomatic. "Chevy was ready to injure himself," Rosie Shuster said. "He didn't know where he was going."

Joe Cocker, withered and worn after years of debauchery and drink, gamely appeared as musical guest on the October 2 episode. John had met Joe some months earlier at a New York jazz club. John asked if Joe hated him for the palsied impression. "No, I don't," Joe replied enigmatically, "but some of my friends do."

In the *SNL* broadcast, when Joe was midway through "Feelin' Alright," John joined him onstage, matching his outfit and aping his moves. Cocker was in on the joke, but he looked more uncomfortable than amused, and he refused to take John's hand at the end. Afterward, John told *Rolling Stone* he would retire his Joe Cocker.

John invited Harold Ramis, his old Second City crony, to meet with Michaels in New York about a writing job. Ramis turned it down. "It just didn't feel good to me," Ramis reflected. "I could tell that the work habits at *SNL* were not healthy, just not good at all. John was already starting to look exhausted, and not just physically."

Chase performed his final episode of *Saturday Night* on October 30, with Buck Henry hosting. In the obligatory samurai sketch, John swung his sword with a bit too much abandon and slashed Henry across the forehead. Henry looked stunned. At the end of the scene, Henry botched a jump through a stunt wall, ripping open his leg. More than an hour of live broadcast remained. Henry gamely remained in the show, stitched up, ironically enough, by John's personal physician, who happened to be on scene. Henry resurfaced with a bandage on his forehead and no ready gag to explain it—until Chase took the stage for "Weekend Update," wearing a bandage on his own forehead as he announced, "Our top story tonight: Buck Henry cuts himself in the fore-head in a sketch on the *Saturday Night* show, as a far-gone and downed and drugged-out John Belushi hits him with a sword." By the show's end, the entire cast sported Band-Aids and crutches, a warm gesture that captured the dangerous magic of *Saturday Night*.

Chase's quip cut close to the truth. His impending departure should have seeded John's ascent. Instead, it triggered his collapse. John had trash-talked Chase for months. Now, John's moment had arrived. Instead of rising to meet it, he imploded, bingeing day and night on cocaine. It didn't help that he had free use of a limousine, hired by NBC to shuttle the cast to a remote Brooklyn studio it was using during elec-tion season, while the NBC news team needed Studio 8H. When John figured out that the driver would keep driving until he said otherwise, he steered the limo all over town, partying harder than ever. Sometimes he stopped by the midnight recording sessions for the next *National Lampoon* album. Just two years earlier, John had worked at *Lampoon* for $300 a week. Now, he spent more than that on coke. Judy hired more limousines to drive him around at night, partly to keep tabs on him and partly to spend money John might otherwise piss away on coke.

Dan and John had a week off after the October 30 episode. The presi-dential election loomed. They set off on a bleary weeklong road trip financed by Jann Wenner, the *Rolling Stone* editor. In exchange, the boys would pen a Hunter Thompson–style travelogue. They rented a Chevy Caprice. John outfitted it with a $3,000 sound system at *Roll-ing Stone*'s expense. They took a room in the Bellevue-Stratford, the grande dame of Philadelphia hotels, where twenty-nine conventioneers had just died of a mystery illness. They traveled to Atlanta and crashed Jimmy Carter's headquarters on election night. They stayed with one of Dan's old Ottawa friends in New Orleans. Before dawn one morning, they crank-called Wenner, Dan assuming a Cajun accent and saying his writers had hit a man with their car, which was filled with Class A nar-cotics, terrifying the sleepy editor for a few priceless minutes. The boys motored on to San Francisco.

"John used to love the gas stops," Dan said, "going in to chat with guys behind the counter there. There were lots of cigarettes, continuous tapes being shoved in, listened to and discarded, John getting really mad at me for driving too fast," though Dan never dared give John the wheel. "He had so much to say, so much to object to, and it was my job as the driver to take it."

Around the time the boys returned to New York, Michaels assigned Dick Ebersol to babysit Belushi. Ebersol flew John back to California with him on Sunday mornings, "directly from the party to the plane," to live at Ebersol's house until Wednesday, when the two would fly back. Ebersol once left a "While You Were Out" note on Michaels's desk that read, "I have the Albanian. Everything is under control."

Ensconced at the Ebersol home, John "would sleep all day, stay up all night and just generally be John," Ebersol recalled. "Things seemed to be going well until I was walking down the hall one morning and noticed smoke coming out from under his bedroom door. I ran in and saw that he'd fallen asleep with a lit cigarette, and his mattress was on fire. I woke him up and threw water on the bed to put it out. He just shrugged, moved over to the other bed and went back to sleep."

Back in New York, Judy confronted John. She challenged him on his coke habit, and asked whether they were ever going to wed and whether John might be bothered to help with the laundry once in a while.

"You don't know what it's like to be me," he pleaded, without further explanation. He sighed, "Things will be better when I'm dead."

Judy kicked him out. John found his way to the Sherry-Netherland Hotel, where his friend Penny Marshall had a suite. Penny telephoned Judy.

"I got him."

"Keep him," Judy replied.

Ensconced with Penny, John reprised his nocturnal schedule. When Penny politely suggested he ease off the drugs, John screamed, "Don't be my mother!" He decamped to Lorne Michaels's loft. One night during that stay, he fell asleep while smoking, starting another fire. He spent time at Essex House, the luxury hotel on Central Park. When a publicist arrived there for promotional work, he found John with another lit cigarette, passed out on another bed, averting yet another fire.

Tom Shales of the *Washington Post* visited the *Saturday Night* studio shortly after Chase's departure. He found the mood grim, the cast defensive, the after-party funereal. Reflecting on Chase's exit, John said, "All of us get restless and think about leaving." Dan concurred: "By next winter, I'll be gone."

After Thanksgiving, John went to see a New York addiction specialist. The doctor asked for his medical history and insisted he answer honestly. He made a list: Three packs of cigarettes a day. Cocaine habit. Quaalude addiction. Amphetamines. Regular doses of mescaline.

The doctor told John he had to stop.

"I give so much pleasure to so many people," John said. "Why can I not get some pleasure for myself?"

"Because you'll kill yourself."

"My whole life is being conducted for me," John said. "Schedules are set and I have to be there." Cocaine brought energy. Quaaludes brought sleep.

The doctor urged John to see a psychiatrist. John said he was too busy.

John's romantic misfortunes unfolded just as Dan's love life was heating up. Dan had dated Gilda Radner during their Second City run. He was seeing Catherine O'Hara when he arrived at *Saturday Night*. In the autumn of 1976, he started dating Laraine Newman, his sultry costar. The displaced Angeleno was just twenty-three when the show debuted, four months older than Dan, the youngest performer. Dating Dan helped her feel less alone. One morning, Newman was feeding fruit into a noisy juicer when Dan's voice boomed out of the bedroom, screaming, "Oh God, I'll tell. Oh, God." The grinding noise had inspired him to invoke the dentist scene from *Marathon Man*.

Candice Bergen returned in December to host the *Saturday Night* Christmas episode. No one had enjoyed hosting more than Bergen. Yet, she arrived to find that most of the fun had departed. "Everyone had been affected by this incredible notoriety," she recalled. "Certain people had become household names and others hadn't, yet they were all on equal footing on the same show. John was obviously one of the ones who'd caught on. They were under incredible pressure. People suddenly had money, and so anything they were inclined to pursue in terms of recreational drugs was no longer off-limits."

The Christmas episode had Bergen pouting in her dressing room, hung up over unrequited love for Belushi, an idea that triggered howls of laughter.

"When he held me in his arms, we had something special," Bergen said through the locked door, as Jane Curtin consoled her.

"Candy," Jane Curtin replied, "that was cellulite you felt."

Curtin huddled with Michaels, who went off to find Belushi.

"Candy," Curtin pleaded, "look what you're doing to yourself."

"I don't care, Jane. Why won't John at least talk to me?"

"Because he's an animal," Curtin replied. She meant it.

Belushi came to the door, dressed in bow tie and tails, and unfurled his best Bogart.

"Candy, baby, I know how you feel, but it's over."

John sweet-talked her as they walked into a *Casablanca* fog, Paul Shaffer playing "As Time Goes By" on piano in the background.

Bergen pleaded, "What about us, John?"

"Well, we'll still have Paris. And the Muppets."

Jimmy Carter's victory in the fall election paid off handsomely for Michaels, who had lost his Gerald Ford. Dan developed a potent Carter impression. In the Christmas episode, he addressed the *Saturday Night* audience with a fairly prescient forecast of the four long years to come.

"During my campaign for president," he drawled, "I promised to keep every promise I made. Tonight, I'm here to tell you that, well, unfortunately, that will be impossible."

In a consumer-protection spoof, Dan morphed into sleazy television pitchman Irwin Mainway.

"Mr. Mainway," Bergen deadpanned, "your company manufactures the following so-called harmless playthings: Pretty Peggy Ear-Piercing Set, Mr. Skin-Grafter, General Tron's Secret Police Confession Kit, and Doggie Dentist. And what about this innocent rubber doll, which you market under the name Johnny Switchblade?"

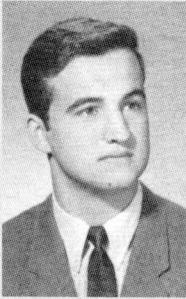

JOHN BELUSHI
Class Council 2,3; Forensics 4; Key Club 3,4; Plays 3,4; Varsity Show 2,3,4; Thespians 3,4, Secretary 4; Choir 4; Football 1,2,3,4, Co-Captain 4; Wrestling 1; Track 2,3; Baseball 1; Homecoming King 4.

John Belushi, decorated senior, Wheaton Central High School, 1967.
(*Courtesy of Community Unit School District 200, Wheaton, Illinois*)

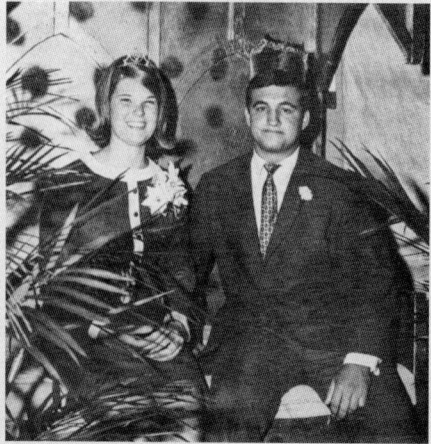

Belushi, reluctant homecoming
king, Wheaton Central
High School, 1966.
(*Courtesy of Community
Unit School District 200,
Wheaton, Illinois*)

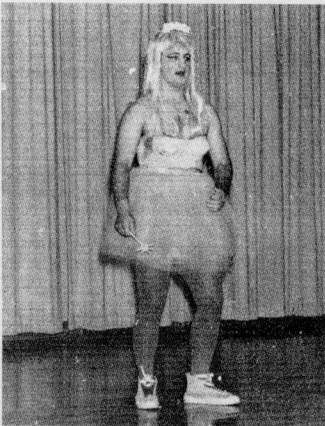

Belushi plays against type as the Blue
Fairy at the Senior Men's Fashion Show,
Wheaton Central High School, 1967.
(*Courtesy of Community Unit School
District 200, Wheaton, Illinois*)

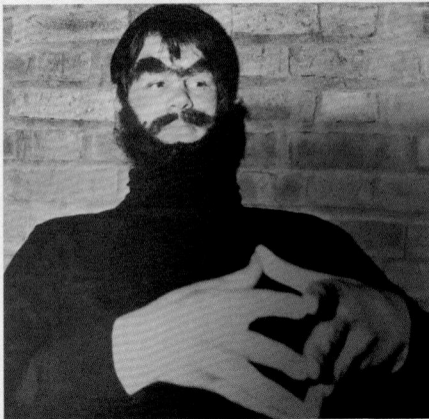

Dan Aykroyd dons a disguise at St. Patrick's High School in Ottawa, 1968–69. (*Courtesy of St. Patrick's High School*)

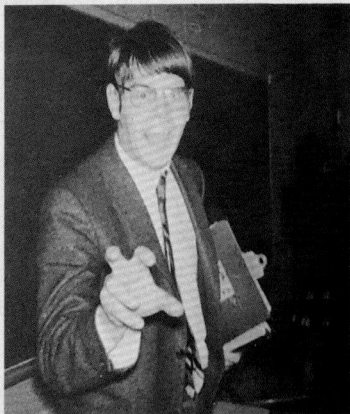

Dan Aykroyd in Catholic schoolboy attire at St. Patrick's High School in Ottawa, 1968–69. (*Courtesy of St. Patrick's High School*)

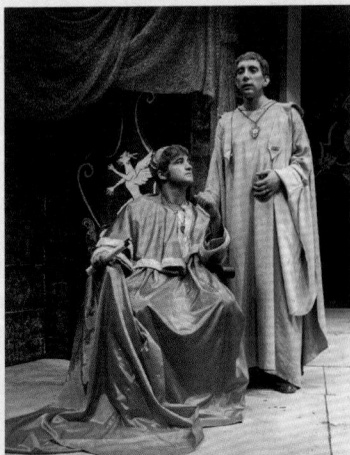

Belushi as Cardinal Wolsey in *Anne of the Thousand Days*, with Victor Caroli as Thomas Boleyn, summer stock theater, Indiana, 1967. (*Courtesy of Victor Caroli*)

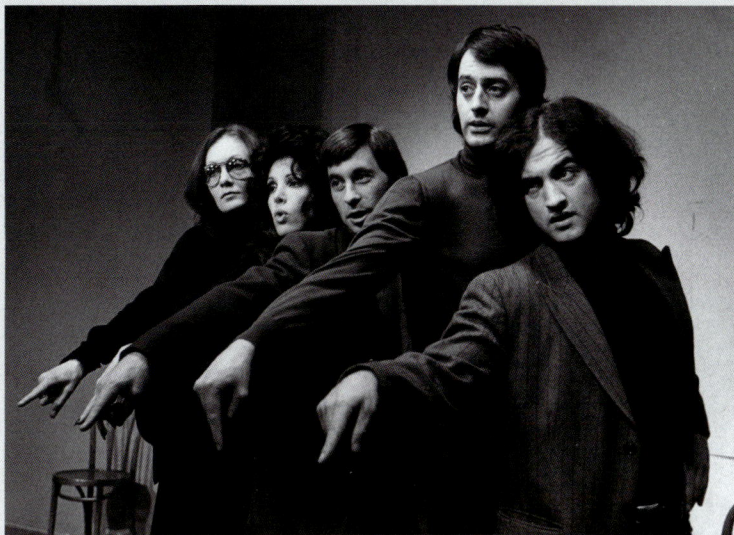

Second City's Next Generation, around 1971. From left: Judy Morgan, Eugenie Ross-Leming, Jim Fisher, Joe Flaherty, John Belushi. (*Courtesy of The Second City, Inc.*)

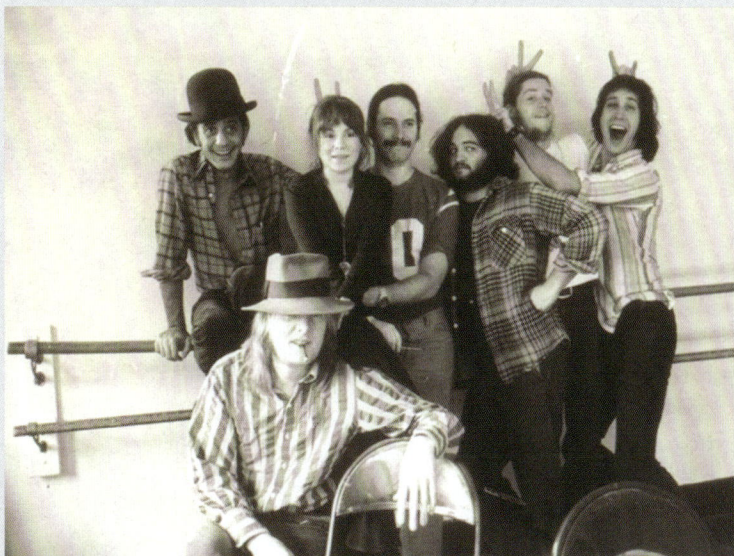

The *Lemmings* cast, 1973. From left: Gary Goodrow, Alice Playten, Christopher Guest, John Belushi, Paul Jacobs, Chevy Chase. Seated: director Tony Hendra. (*Courtesy of Magnolia Pictures. Photo by Michael Gold.*)

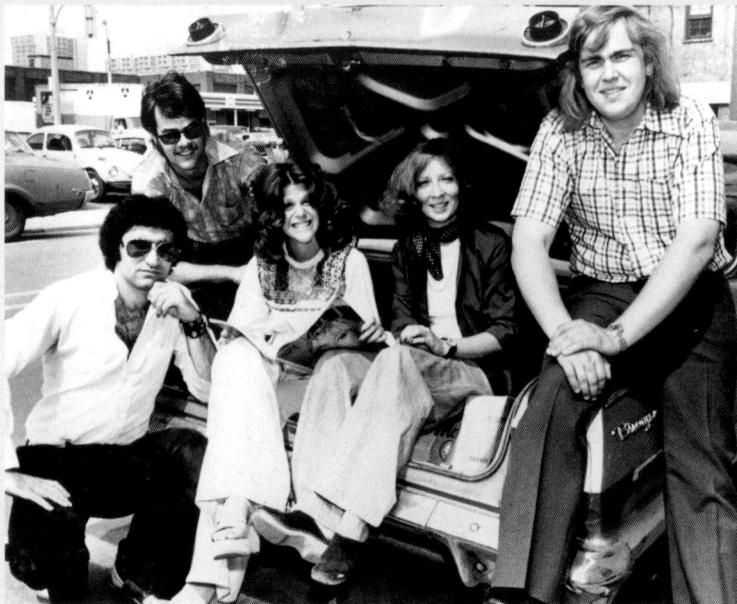

Second City's Toronto cast gathers around one of Dan Aykroyd's cop cars, 1974. From left: Eugene Levy, Aykroyd, Gilda Radner, Rosemary Radcliffe, John Candy. (*Courtesy of The Second City, Inc.*)

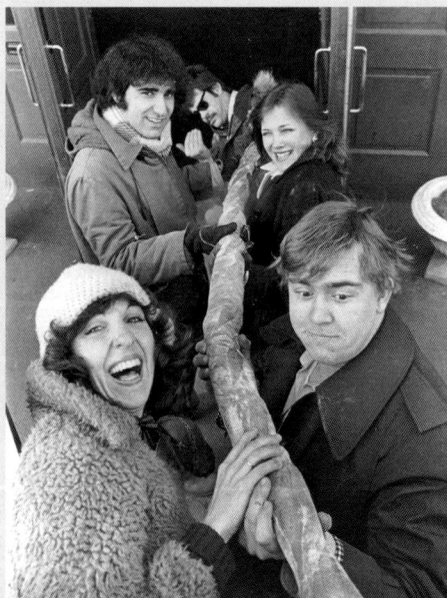

Second City's Toronto cast, future stars all, at the Old Fire Hall, 1975. Clockwise from bottom left: Andrea Martin, Eugene Levy, Dan Aykroyd, Catherine O'Hara, John Candy. (*Courtesy of The Second City, Inc.*)

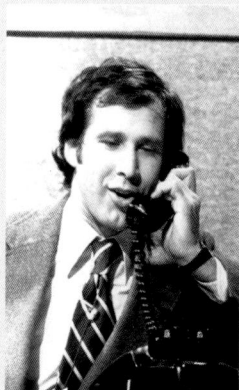

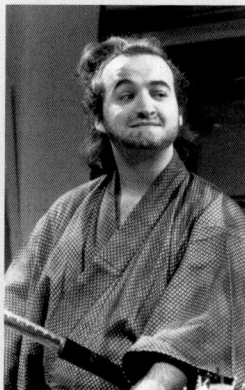

Chevy Chase rode "Weekend Update" to fame in season one of *Saturday Night*, which debuted in the fall of 1975. John Belushi's star ascended with the debut of his samurai that winter. (*Author's collection*)

Dan Aykroyd pitches the Bass-o-Matic on *Saturday Night*, inspired by his French-Canadian aunt and her cooking show, 1976. (*Author's collection*)

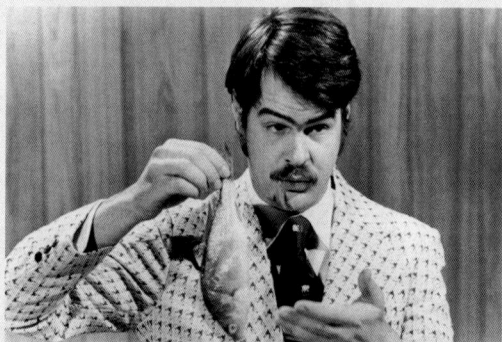

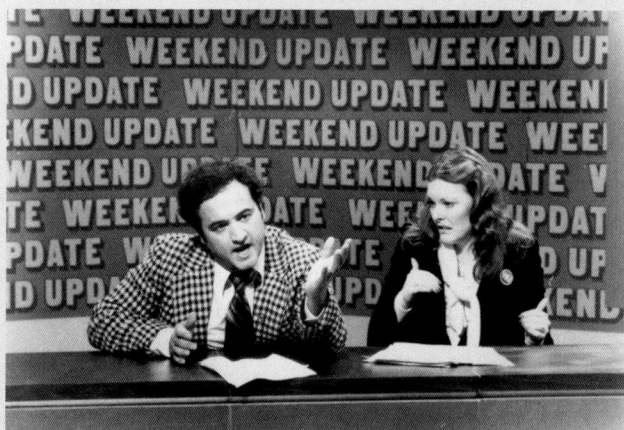

Belushi and Jane Curtin, dispositional opposites on *Saturday Night*, a slovenly Chicagoan and prim Bostonian. (*Author's collection*)

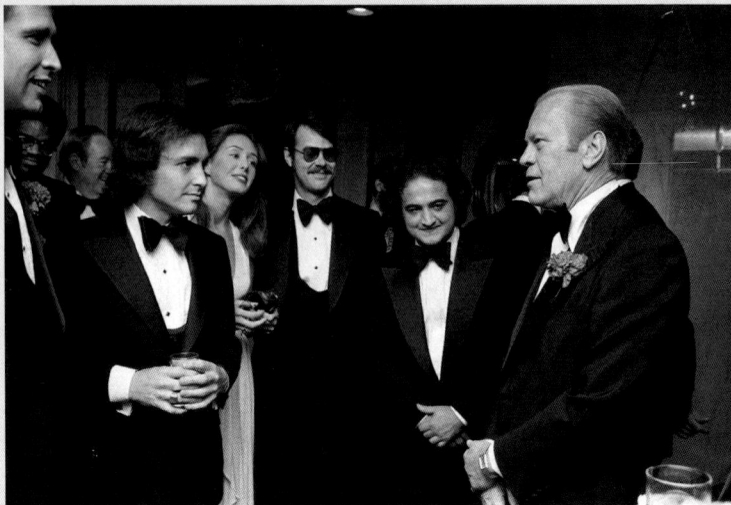

Belushi and Aykroyd with Lorne Michaels, Chevy Chase, and Gerald Ford at the Radio and Television Correspondents' Association dinner, 1976. (*Courtesy of the National Archives and Records Administration*)

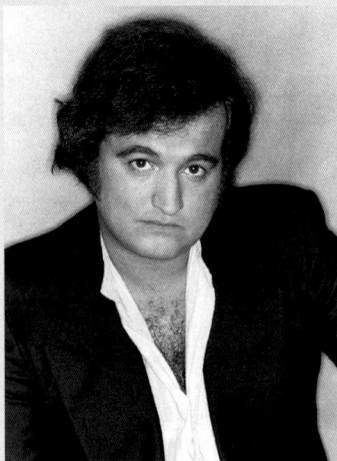

Belushi cast photo, *Saturday Night Live*. (*Author's collection*)

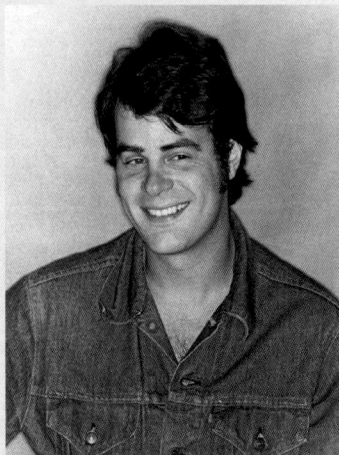

Aykroyd cast photo, *Saturday Night Live*. (*Author's collection*)

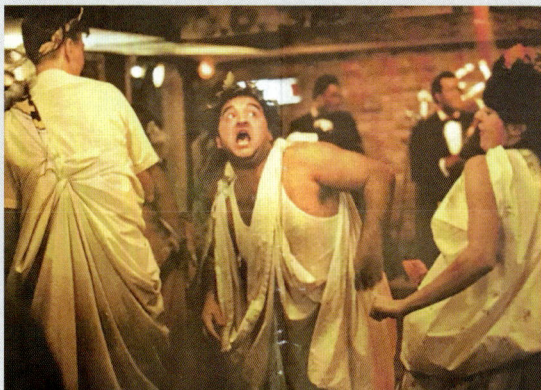

John and Judy Belushi dance at the infamous toga party in *Animal House*. Two years later, Judy would have another cameo as a cocktail waitress in *The Blues Brothers*. (*Author's collection*)

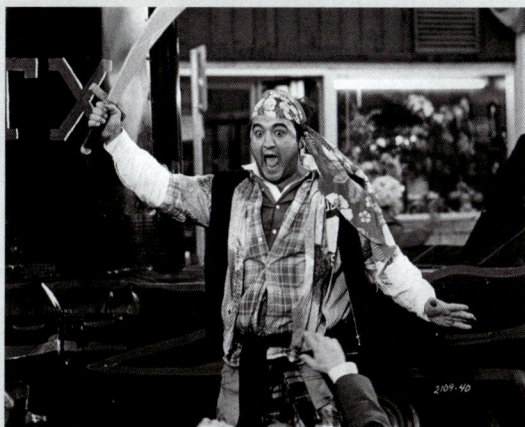

Belushi the pirate, *Animal House*. (*Author's collection*)

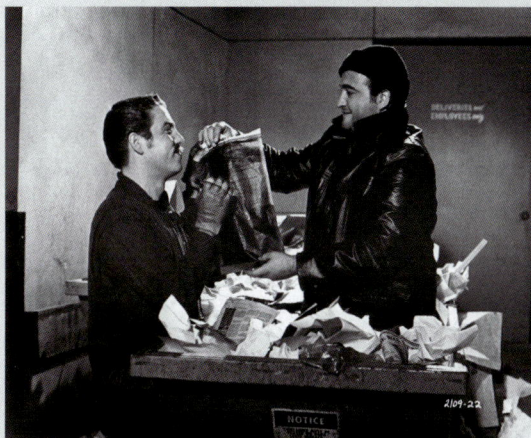

Bluto with D-Day, the biker part in *Animal House* written for Dan Aykroyd, who was too busy at *Saturday Night Live* to take it. (*Author's collection*)

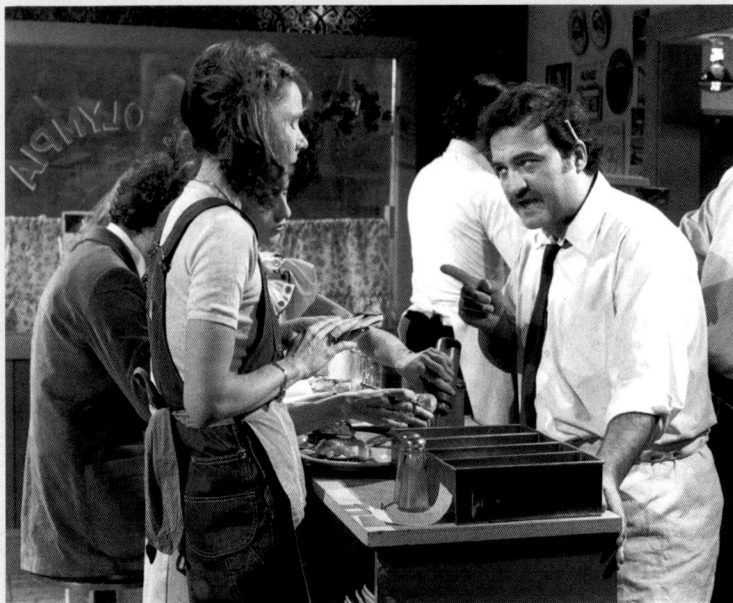

Belushi with Jill Clayburgh in the Olympia restaurant, 1978. Don Novello wrote the *Saturday Night Live* sketch from his memories of Greek diners in Chicago. Serendipitously, Belushi's father had owned one. (*Author's collection*)

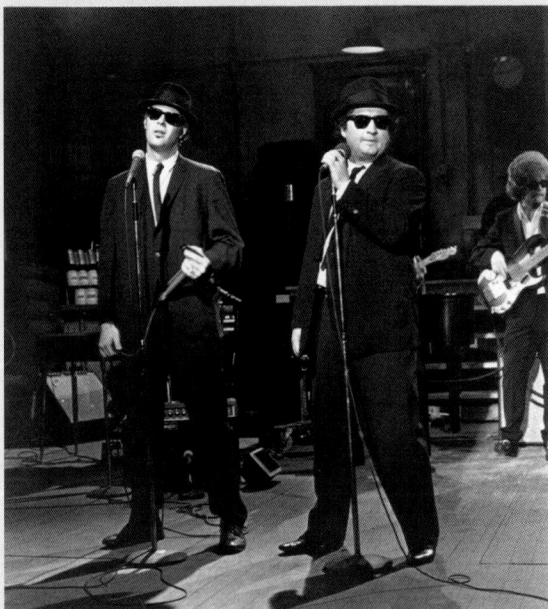

The Blues Brothers, with bassist Donald "Duck" Dunn to the right, perform on *Saturday Night Live*, November 1978. Viewers didn't know if the act was serious or satiric, and in the end, they didn't care. (*Author's collection*)

Dan corrected the name of "Johnny Switchblade Adventure Punk," and then backpedaled shadily. "I mean, so Barbie takes a knife once in a while, or Ken gets cut."

Bergen pressed on. "Well, we'd like to show you another one of Mr. Mainway's products. It retails for $1.98, and it's called Bag of Glass. Mr. Mainway, this is simply a bag of jagged, dangerous glass bits. . . ."

"We're just packaging what the kids want." Dan adjusted his tie. "I mean, it's a creative toy, you know? If you hold this up, you know, you see colors, all the colors of the rainbow. I mean, it teaches them about light refraction, you know? Prisms and that stuff."

In a tragicomic holiday scene, Bergen announced the "Adopt Belushi for Christmas Contest." Rosie Shuster wrote the sketch from real life: John was indeed alone for Christmas.

"Judy had given John the heave-ho, because he was howling at the moon," Shuster explained. "I wanted a slow, rotating stage for John to sit on, like a car in a showroom," but there wasn't time to build one.

"Now, we all want to help John," Bergen said in the live appeal. "But then we've all helped him so much already, putting him up, talking over his problems with him, lending him money. So now, it's your turn to help."

John addressed the camera: "Hi. I'm John Belushi. Ah, but you can call me Bah-loosh, just like my close, personal friend Chevy Chase does. You know, it's corny, but I love Christmas. Hey, I'd love to sit around the yule log and play with your daughter. . . . I'm not fussy. I'd like some candied yams, plum puddings, roast goose stuffed with drugs."

The cast gathered for a *National Lampoon*–style serenade to a mass murderer, "Let's Kill Gary Gilmore for Christmas."

Bergen had led one of the finest *Saturday Night* episodes to date. Yet, for her, the production had lost its soul.

Chapter 13

Night of the Seven Fires

J UDY ADOPTED BELUSHI for Christmas, allowing him back into the Bleecker Street apartment before the holidays. "He showed up in great shape, made a beautiful apology and plea for another chance," she said. They decided to greet the new year with Judy's brother in Colorado.

On the third day of their Colorado visit, Judy overheard John and Rob Jacklin discussing a wedding. She realized they were talking about hers. She and John had discussed marriage, but with all their recent problems, she had put the thought aside.

Judy confronted John: "I heard you tell my brother that we were going to get married."

"Well, yeah, aren't we?"

"Well, sure, but you don't just get married. You need blood tests and a license. You have to plan, John."

"Oh."

The Belushi and Jacklin clans flew in for a ceremony. Around five in the afternoon on December 31, 1976, John and Judy exchanged vows. They toasted with champagne and Halloween masks and honeymooned in a renovated farmhouse.

By season two, *Saturday Night* had enough young fans to support occasional forays to the local college circuit. With Chevy Chase gone, John was the big draw. He would drive out by limousine with Dan or Michael O'Donoghue in tow. The college shows played meaner than Michaels's broadcasts, closer to the misanthropic spirit of *National Lampoon*. A performance might commence with O'Donoghue at the lectern. John would take the stage and beg for drugs.

"No, John," O'Donoghue would reply. "You've had enough."

After some pleading, O'Donoghue would produce a giant syringe and give John a mock injection, enough juice to power a seventy-five-minute show. O'Donoghue might read some "Weekend Update" jokes that had been pulled by network censors. John would do his samurai act. They would set fire to a sack filled with real fan mail. As a grand finale, John would cleave the podium with a chain saw.

In early January, Dan and John traveled together to a Rhode Island campus for a college gig. "He was really fucked up that day," Dan recalled. In mid-show, in character as Catherine the Great and wearing a towering wig, John attempted a breathtaking leap. "Unfortunately, there wasn't any stage where he landed," Dan said. "About three quarters of that leap was incredible. The last quarter was a little rough." John landed in the hospital with torn cartilage in his left knee, missing the first *Saturday Night* of the new year. As with Chase's injury of the previous year, the timing of John's accident suggested a psychological component.

"On morphine and Demerol, he was pretty out of it," Judy said. "Still, he very much wanted to do the show and was angry the doctors were taking so long to decide whether they should operate or not." John kept asking for more painkillers. Judy realized a friend was bringing him cocaine, which he hid inside his cast. She escorted the visitor into the hall and barked, "Can't you see that it works against his medication? It might even be dangerous," she added, her understatement born of 1970s naivete.

John's absence, following Chase's, left the program two men down. Michaels chose the January 15 program to introduce Bill Murray, the odd man out in the auditions of two years prior. Murray had joined brother Brian and Christopher Guest on Howard Cosell's *Saturday Night Live*. That show had lasted eighteen episodes, a historic flop. Michaels held off Murray's debut for as long as he could, to minimize unflattering comparisons to Chase. With John laid up, Michaels could wait no longer.

But Dan carried the January 15 show, trotting out a dazzling display of road-tested characters and introducing a new one, Beldar Conehead. Dan had toyed with the idea of pinhead lawyers from France. Michaels didn't like the thought of poking fun at human deformity. Dan repurposed his pinheads as aliens, a topic that, like ghosts, had transfixed the Aykroyds for generations. Dan wrote up the Coneheads as a bizarre sitcom family.

The Coneheads delivered an instant hit. The studio audience shrieked with laughter when Dan walked on set and removed his knit cap to reveal the phallic cone, a liquid-latex marvel that took twenty minutes to apply and several painful minutes to remove.

"Daddy, where do we come from?" pleaded Laraine Newman, just returned from a difficult day in public school.

"France," Dan monotoned, after a meditative pause. "Just keep telling them you come from France."

John returned to *Saturday Night* the next week. Once again, Michaels wrote backstage drama into the script. For the opening, Gilda Radner wheeled John out in a chair, his head lolling, stubble darkening his face. In front of the cameras, Michaels argued with a physician about John's fitness to perform: "I can't put this man on television. He's barely awake." That wasn't far from true. Michaels asked the doctor why he insisted that John perform. The doctor explained: if John didn't perform, he wouldn't get paid, and the doctor would cut off his drugs. At this, John's head snapped up, his eyes popped open, and he yelled the opener: "Live, from New York, it's *Saturday Night*!"

To Judy, John's wheelchair scene rang a bit too real. She had never seen him so addled. She feared he was mixing cocaine and Quaaludes. He later confessed he was snorting heroin, a habit formed when the hospital meds ran out. She persuaded him to see a psychiatrist. He left her a note one day as he went off to see the shrink, promising, "I'm going to lick this thing." After a few months, he stopped the sessions. He told Judy drugs were no longer a problem.

Mitch Glazer, the reporter from *Crawdaddy*, shadowed John that spring for a cover story. After chasing John from club to club for weeks,

Glazer earned his friendship. He wondered how long his new friend could sustain his pace.

"About three months ago," John told Glazer for the story, "or close to that, I thought real seriously about killing myself. I finally had almost everything I thought I could want, and all these people started to involve themselves in my life. Pushing me in different directions. . . . I remember looking out a window from up here one night. You know, looking out and thinking, 'What the fuck. I could just walk out there.'" The writer watched John drain a bottle of tequila, spilling the last of it down his leg.

"What can I say? The man's a genius," Dan told Glazer. "Only sometimes, he departs. Leaves the land of the living, becomes somebody else. That's the comedian's disease."

John showed up late to cast meetings and rehearsals. He feuded constantly with Michaels, who repeatedly fired and unfired him. "Quite often, he just wants to be told that he's needed," Michaels said to a visiting reporter, sounding like a beleaguered parent. "Sometimes he responds best to that. And sometimes he responds best to being yelled at."

John wrote less and less with Dan. He looked pale and sickly, onstage and off. Yet, the *Saturday Night* audience embraced him more than ever. Belushi was a violent teddy bear, a cuddly monster, lovable and vulnerable and real.

In a March episode, Dan played Jimmy Carter opposite Bill Murray's Walter Cronkite in an imaginary call-in show, Murray's stentorianwindbag impression pushing the unflappable Dan to the brink of real laughter. The scene played on Dan's encyclopedic mind. His President Carter instructed a postal employee on the proper use of an automated letter sorter. He talked down a teen who had taken some bad acid, an exchange that replayed Dan's encounter with the young partygoer who had locked himself in a bathroom.

"I'm afraid to leave my apartment, and I can't wear any clothes," the youth pleaded. "And the ceiling is dripping."

The president asked, "Peter, what did the acid look like?"

"They were these little orange pills."

"Were they barrel-shaped?"

"Uh, yes."

"OK, right. You did some orange sunshine, Peter."

Explosive laughter.

"How long ago did you take it, Peter?"

"Uh, I don't know. I can't read my watch."

"All right, Peter, now just listen. Everything is going to be fine. You're very high right now. You will probably be that way for about five more hours. Try taking some vitamin B complex, vitamin C complex. If you have a beer, go ahead and drink it."

"OK."

"Just remember you're a living organism on this planet, and you're very safe. You've just taken a heavy drug. Relax, stay inside, and listen to some music, OK? Do you have any Allman Brothers?"

The episode won an Emmy.

A few weeks later, John paired with Dan in an opener about Soviet premier Leonid Brezhnev negotiating to appear on *The Tonight Show*. Dan unfurled a superb Russian accent as Brezhnev's interpreter. "He says he wants to be on with Johnny," Dan instructed, as John murmured in his ear. "No guest hosts. No David Brenner. No McLean Stevenson." When John's Brezhnev heard a response he didn't like, he mimed a nuclear explosion with his mouth and hands.

That spring, Dan started a relationship with Rosie Shuster, the *SNL* writer and proverbial boss's wife, although she and Lorne Michaels had drifted apart. A year earlier, John had blamed Anne Beatts for taking Judy away from him. Now, he blamed Shuster for making off with Dan.

"He was mad because I was with Danny," Shuster said, "and he had big plans with Danny, and he didn't want Danny distracted with me."

Dan and John performed less together because they wrote less together. Dan begged John to slow down, back off the drugs, and focus on his craft, echoing Judy's increasingly desperate pleas at home.

If anything, Dan faced more pressure than John. The friends now split a writing credit and an extra $275 a week, but Dan did nearly all of the writing. Dan worked against constant deadlines and relentless stress, and he was not a calm man. Fist-size holes pocked the walls of the office he and John still shared. Dan once came offstage and punched through a glass-framed poster, bloodying his hand. On another bad day, he put his fist through the glass frame of a 30 Rock directory, leaving a trail of blood from the seventeenth floor to the infirmary, ten stories down. When his prized bong disappeared from his office, Dan went berserk, crushing ceiling tiles to dust, pulling doors from cabinets, bending metal support beams, and splintering a Barcalounger. This time, network maintenance staff left the damage untouched, punishing Dan like an errant child.

At moments in *Saturday Night*'s second season, colleagues could hear Dan arguing with John behind closed doors. In a particularly bitter row at season's end, Dan exploded: "If you're not going to be a writer, then don't take the money, don't waste my time."

"I don't want to be a writer," John screamed back. "I want to perform. I don't want to write. Keep the money."

"I don't care about the money," Dan said. "You can have the money, but don't pretend you're a writer. Don't even show up."

Dan and John had yelled plenty, but not at each other. As Dan raged, John's face sank into raw vulnerability, visible "around the eyes and cheeks, but mostly on his mouth." Dan would never forget it.

When *SNL* broke for the summer, John binged. One evening in late May 1977, he ran into Bill Boggs, host of a popular New York television talk show, at the hot new dance club, Studio 54.

"Who's on the show tomorrow?" John yelled, straining to be heard above the beat.

"Well, we got Michael O'Donoghue," Bill Boggs replied. John nodded. "We got David Brenner." John grimaced. "We got Steve Allen."

"Steve Allen? I love Steve Allen." Allen had helped to create *The Tonight Show*.

"Why don't you come and be on the show tomorrow?" Boggs offered. John reached into a pocket and produced a piece of paper and a little pencil. He wrote down his telephone number and handed it to Boggs. Boggs told him to be there at eleven o'clock.

"Call me in the morning," John countered, "and keep calling until I pick up."

The next morning, eleven o'clock came and went. Boggs called John again and again. At length, someone picked up. "John, it's Bill Boggs," the host said. "Fuck you," John replied, hanging up. Boggs called back. "John: Steve Allen. Steve Allen." There was a pause. "Uh, all right, I'll be there."

"So, a half hour into the show, Belushi comes in the back door, crawls across the floor like a lizard, crawls up onto the set into a chair," Boggs remembered. "We put a mic on him." John wore a blue trucker's cap and dark sunglasses over a tan blazer and a striped shirt, unbuttoned past his sternum.

John rambled, interrupted the host, and dropped an f-bomb. "You don't perform your best on drugs, and you don't necessarily write your best on drugs," he slurred, clearly on drugs.

The show spiraled into chaos. O'Donoghue extinguished his cigarette in his water glass. At that, John grabbed his own water glass and emptied it into a potted fern. Boggs goaded John to do an Elvis impression. John grimaced, but the host whipped up the audience until he had little choice. John sang a few lines of "Jailhouse Rock." Then he picked up another water glass, threw it at Boggs, and kicked over the host's table, upending more water glasses and several plants.

"He put me on the spot," John shrugged to the stunned studio audience. "Whaddaya want me to do?" Boggs removed his wet shirt. Steve Allen looked stricken.

A *Rolling Stone* reporter reached Lorne Michaels for comment on the spectacle. Michaels said he had never seen anyone in his cast so much as smoke marijuana.

Not long after, John journeyed up to Canada, alone, to visit Dan at the Aykroyd family farm. Dan nursed him off heroin.

That summer, John and Judy rented a cottage in an East Hampton enclave that housed Lorne Michaels, Jann Wenner, and other famous friends. John appeared at Wenner's daily staff briefings, where the editor plotted *Rolling Stone*'s move from San Francisco to New York. John "would make an entrance crawling on his hands and knees," Wenner said, and work the room with his Jann Wenner impression. On Sunday mornings, John would arrive at Michaels's house on a moped, carrying a Sunday *Times*. "It was a nice gesture," Michaels said. "Then, of course, he'd open the refrigerator, empty it and sit down and call Cairo. The initial gesture allowed him carte blanche for the rest of his visit."

During the summer hiatus, a script arrived in John's mail. The film was called *National Lampoon's Animal House*. Producers wanted John for a part that sounded like lead animal.

By the summer of 1975, most of the best performers from *National Lampoon* had landed jobs on national television, half on *Saturday Night*, the rest on Howard Cosell's doomed *Saturday Night Live*. Harold Ramis remained free. Ivan Reitman offered him $2,500 to write a film treatment. Ramis sketched out a story, called "Freshman Year," based on his time at Washington University in St. Louis. "It was too personal, too sentimental," Ramis recalled. No one liked it.

In early 1976, Doug Kenney attended a *Saturday Night* cast party. The *National Lampoon* cofounder was a comedy genius, a millionaire at twenty-nine. But *Lampoon*'s star was falling, and *Saturday Night*'s was rising. *Lampoon* staffers both mocked and envied the *Saturday Night* defectors, who were fast becoming household names. That night, Michaels mockingly offered Kenney a job: "Let me help you pick up the pieces of a shattered career."

That did it. When he recovered from the slight, Kenney told Matty Simmons he wanted to leave *National Lampoon*. Simmons asked for time to think. Then he called Kenney into his office: "You can't leave. We're going to do a movie."

Simmons wanted Kenney to write a film loosely based on the magazine's celebrated yearbook parody. Two years earlier, *Lampoon* had released a full-length send-up of a 1964 high school annual, an instant classic, much of it penned by Kenney.

Simmons paired Kenney with Ramis. They retooled Ramis's treatment as "Laser Orgy Girls," adorned with copious sex and drugs and a Manson-esque cult. They called in one more partner, Chris Miller, the *National Lampoon* writer who had penned the magazine's funniest frat-house stories, invoking his own boozy college memories from Dartmouth.

The three writers met for brunch at a Greenwich Village restaurant. Over Bloody Marys, they tossed out outrageous college stories. Ramis took notes on a legal pad. Miller mentioned that his Dartmouth fraternity had been known as the Animal House. He observed, "At the center of any great Animal House is a great animal." The collaborators looked at each other and said, "Belushi."

The writers set their story in the brief, innocent era between the deaths of Joseph McCarthy and John Kennedy, a time of crew cuts, jackets and ties, keg parties, and hair spray. Just fifteen years had passed, but it might as well have been fifty. When Belushi stopped by Kenney's apartment, the writers taunted him: "Hey, John, we're writing a movie for you."

"What? What is it? What's it about?" John begged them to let him read it. They refused.

The typical film treatment filled ten or twenty pages. The *National Lampoon* writers handed in 114 pages. "It was funny as hell," Matty Simmons said, "but it was like *War and Peace*." The working title was "Night of the Seven Fires," drawn from one of Chris's *Lampoon* pieces. Many scenes involved regurgitation.

Aging film executives of the 1970s didn't understand the emerging television generation any better than their counterparts in the television industry. Auteur classics *Bonnie and Clyde* and *Easy Rider* and *M*A*S*H* had seeded a cinematic revolution, but the industry still favored comedy stylings of the martini era, films written by Mel Brooks and Neil Simon and Blake Edwards, men born in the 1920s.

Simmons shopped "Night of the Seven Fires" around the studios. No one wanted it. He talked his way into a meeting with Ned Tanen, the mercurial production chief at Universal Pictures. Simmons and Ivan Reitman flew to Los Angeles. Tanen took the treatment and said he would read it.

Accounts diverge on what happened next, but Tanen evidently shelved the tome. Thom Mount, a young Universal executive, unshelved it.

"I was a huge fan of the *High School Yearbook*," Mount said, referring to the *National Lampoon* parody. And here was a treatment for a *High School Yearbook* movie. "Night of the Seven Fires" was a funny, scattershot mess, whose plot involved fraternity brothers becoming sufficiently drunk to extinguish fires with vomit. Mount persuaded Tanen to take another look.

Tanen shared the treatment with Sean Daniel, another junior executive. "Everyone around here hates it," Tanen growled. "Lemme know what you think."

Daniel loved it. He told Tanen the "Seven Fires" treatment could yield a movie funnier than anything else circulating inside Universal's Black Tower.

Tanen summoned Simmons and Reitman back to LA. In Simmons's account, Tanen growled, "I hate this treatment. Everybody is drunk, or high, or getting laid." And then, without batting an eye, he asked, "Can you make this movie for two million?" Simmons had no idea what a movie cost. He looked at Reitman. Reitman shrugged. He turned to Tanen. "Absolutely!"

The "Seven Fires" writing team spent several months working up a script. None of them had written one, but their styles gelled, and Kenney's rapier wit set a high bar. They renamed the project *Animal House* and set it in 1962 at fictional Faber College. The finished script included a scene of Belushi's character hurling a beer keg at a parade float shaped like John Kennedy's head. The keg punctured the float like an assassin's bullet.

Sean Daniel delivered the script to Ned Tanen. "It's hilarious," Tanen told him, after reading it. "And you've gotta be out of your fucking mind if you think that this studio is gonna make this movie. Who the hell is gonna direct this?"

Ivan Reitman had hoped to direct. But Universal did not want to entrust a movie to the man responsible for *Cannibal Girls*. The executives approached several established directors. No one wanted it.

Sean Daniel had a girlfriend working on a film called *The Kentucky Fried Movie*. The project shared comedic DNA with Second City, *National Lampoon*, and *Saturday Night*. It unspooled as a parody of cinema and television, a barrage of mock ads, previews, and newscast snippets, climaxing with a thirty-minute martial arts parody titled "A Fistful of Yen." In one sketch, a gorilla from the zoo rampaged through an insipid television morning show. In a high-gloss commercial parody featuring real-life television star Bill Bixby, scientists demonstrated a pain reliever by repeatedly hitting people on the head. Big-name actors Donald Sutherland and George Lazenby made cameos in a preview for a disaster film titled "That's Armageddon." Between sketches, a newsbreak anchor announced, "I'm not wearing any pants. Film at eleven."

The Kentucky Fried Movie marked the film debut of Kentucky Fried Theater, the LA comedy troupe Lorne Michaels had channeled as inspiration for *Saturday Night.* The ensemble had hired a young director named John Landis.

Chapter 14

Schlock

JOHN DAVID LANDIS was born in Chicago but moved to Los Angeles with his family in infancy. His father, Marshall Landis, was an interior designer who popularized the minimalist Danish-modern style of decor in American homes. Marshall Landis died in the autumn of 1956, shortly after John's sixth birthday. John's mother, Shirley, then married a man in the construction business. John grew up in Westwood, near UCLA, with two older sisters, a stepsister, and a half brother. "We lived in a middle-class neighborhood, but we never had money," he said. "We'd always shop at Sears or Penney's."

The Landis home shared a fence with a veterans' cemetery. John and his friends would ride homemade skateboards into the cemetery to watch military funerals. "We'd be in T-shirts and cutoffs and our tennis shoes. And we'd go to hear the gunfire, and they would eject these shells into a bucket." He and his friends collected the spent shells. The boys built a tree house among the eucalyptuses in an unused portion of the cemetery. A few years later, Landis lost his virginity among the trees. Then the Vietnam War heated up, and the military replaced trees with graves.

Hollywood studios lay a bicycle ride away. Landis sneaked in to marvel at the soundstages and sets. At age eight, he saw the fantasy epic *The 7th Voyage of Sinbad*, featuring Ray Harryhausen's renowned stop-motion effects. "It was my first real movie," he said. "I went bananas." After that, when adults asked what he wanted to do when he grew up, Landis said he wanted to make movies.

Landis attended Ralph Waldo Emerson Junior High School in Westwood, a public campus dotted with future stars; his friends included David Cassidy. Landis had a spotty academic record. "I was never diagnosed as ADHD, but I'm sure I was," he said. "I would get A's in English and A's in history, and I would always fail math. I'm sure I was a behavior problem. I wasn't a bad kid, but I would often be in trouble." He gravitated toward the school's audiovisual geeks: "We were the guys who were into the movies."

In October 1964, at age fourteen, Landis joined a class trip to the Santa Monica Civic Auditorium to see the T.A.M.I. Show, a multi-act concert, the film of which would help introduce James Brown to white America. Landis cheered when the Godfather of Soul took the stage with his Famous Flames.

For high school, Landis transferred to Oakwood School, a private campus with a looser structure and an artsy curriculum. He attended on a scholarship and studied alongside the children of Hollywood composers and writers. He grew his hair and fell in with the budding hippie movement.

"In the sixties, when you had long hair, it really did identify you: 'He's antiwar. He probably respects Black people. He likes rock 'n' roll,'" Landis said. "We would hitchhike to San Francisco or San Diego or Tijuana all the time, because it was easy. Someone else with long hair would pick you up."

In tenth grade, Landis lost his scholarship over disciplinary lapses. He wound up in an experimental program at UCLA, teaching younger students. The program eventually lost funding. Thus, when he departed the experimental school at sixteen, John Landis was a high school dropout who had taught at UCLA.

Landis went to work in the mailroom at 20th Century-Fox. "Being the mail boy was boring," he said, "but the access I got was incredible." He made regular trips to the makeup department to watch John Chambers, the artist who had created Spock's ears on *Star Trek*. He chatted up a drunk Richard Burton and lunched with George Stevens, director of *Giant*. He forged Raquel Welch's signature on publicity photos bound for GIs in Vietnam.

In 1969, Landis traveled to Europe. He worked in Yugoslavia on the set of *Kelly's Heroes*, the World War II action comedy, and befriended Donald Sutherland, the quirky Canadian star. He vagabonded around Europe, working as a stuntman, extra, and production assistant in spaghetti westerns, learning to fall off horses. He returned to the States in 1970 for more stunt work. In *The Towering Inferno*, he was set aflame and filmed crashing through a window. He sought more fulfilling work as an assistant director, but lack of a diploma and funds hindered his progress. So, he wrote and directed a film of his own, *Schlock*, a parody of drive-in monster movies. He shot it for $60,000, much of it raised from friends and relatives.

Filmed in 1971 and released in 1973, *Schlock* drew a cult following and made money. Landis landed a spot on *The Tonight Show*, a film director at twenty-two. Someone from the Kentucky Fried Theater troupe saw him on *Tonight* and arranged a meeting. The theater boys asked Landis how to write a script. He ran out to his car and returned with a script he had written, titled *An American Werewolf in London*. The boys borrowed it, went off, and wrote their own script for a movie that parodied the *Airport* disaster film. Landis loved it, but no studio wanted it. They settled on an alternative: The Kentucky Fried Theater should make a movie from the sketches on its show. Landis would direct.

Sean Daniel's girlfriend, Katherine "Boots" Wooten, worked as script supervisor on *Kentucky Fried Movie*. Daniel gave her the *Animal House* script to read.

Wooten asked, "Who are you looking at to direct this?" Daniel said the studio heads wanted a big name. "And I said, 'No, no.' A heavy-handed comedy director would encase it in formula, and I felt like this movie needed to breathe, and John was the one to put breath into it." She urged Daniel to consider Landis for *Animal House*. Daniel met with the director at the tiny bungalow Landis shared with his girlfriend, costume designer Deborah Nadoolman, in Laurel Canyon. Landis showed Daniel a rough cut of *Kentucky Fried Movie*. Daniel loved it. He feared Ned Tanen would hate it.

Landis traveled to the Black Tower with a short reel tailored for older studio executives: "Sight gags and tits," Thom Mount recalled. Mount and Daniel corralled Tanen into a screening room. "Ned lasted eight minutes," Mount said. On the way out, Tanen instructed the junior executives, "OK, hire the guy. But don't expect a budget on this thing."

Daniel gave Landis a copy of the *Animal House* script. "It was the funniest thing I'd ever read," Landis said. "But it was also a mess." Still, Landis rejoiced at working for a major studio. He went to the Universal canteen for a tense meeting with Daniel, Mount, and Tanen, who sat with his arms crossed. Visibly nervous, Landis sat down and promptly spilled a glass of water. He recovered and launched into a shrewd critique of *Animal House*. The script was hilarious, but parts of it crossed a line: the misogyny, the vomiting, the beer keg flying through President Kennedy's head. "We can't film that," Landis said.

"You're fucking right, we can't film that," Tanen growled. He was warming to the guy.

Lose the Kennedy gag and the vomit, Landis said, and filmgoers would fall for *Animal House*. "This is a really heartwarming movie about people that you love," he said. "The audience knows these people. They were these people, or their brothers were these people, or their fathers were these people."

Landis flew to New York to meet with Matty Simmons and the scriptwriters in the offices of *National Lampoon*. The writers eyed him warily.

"He was an outsider, and an obnoxious one," Harold Ramis said. In their first meeting, Landis referred to *Animal House* as his movie. "We'd been living with it for two years, and we hated that. But he did seem to understand the material."

Landis envisioned *Animal House* arcing on a simple us-versus-them, good-versus-evil conflict between rival fraternities. Ramis and his cowriters had scripted Delta House as protagonists, a house of beer-chugging losers fighting for their Greek lives. Their foil was Omega House, a band of well-heeled assholes set on destroying the Deltas. The writers had done a fine job with the villains, but the Deltas emerged as equally repellent. Landis insisted on rewrites that sweetened the Deltas into heroes.

The studio provided an office in its New York headquarters on Park Avenue, a space outfitted with antiques and hunting-lodge artwork, for the writers to polish the script. "I remember Doug drawing little rats on the paintings with a ballpoint pen that you wouldn't notice at first look," Ramis said. "And I remember stuffing towels under the door to keep the smoke in the room."

Ramis and his collaborators wrote parts for their friends from *National Lampoon* and *Saturday Night*. They imagined Chevy Chase as Otter, the frat-house lothario. They wanted Dan Aykroyd for D-Day, a leather-clad biker. Ramis saw himself as Boon, the nominal romantic lead. Belushi, of course, would play Bluto, Delta's most slovenly slob.

But Landis didn't want Ramis, who looked too old for the part. Nor did he want Chase, whose star power might transform *Animal House* into a Chevy Chase film.

Belushi wasn't a household name, but he was a star. The Universal bosses told Landis to get him for Bluto if he wanted to make *Animal House*. In August 1977, Landis traveled to New York for a screening of *Kentucky Fried Movie*. At the theater, someone introduced him to Belushi.

"Jesus," John said as he shook the director's hand. "You're young. Where are you staying?"

"The Drake," Landis replied.

"I'll see you there later," John said. He turned and walked off.

After the screening, Landis returned to his hotel to wait for John, who hadn't given a time. At last, a knock on the door announced his arrival. Landis admitted him.

John burst in and "started making all these insane demands about the script, the character," Landis recalled. Much like the *National Lampoon* writers, John regarded Hollywood types as the enemy. "It was outrageous, and at the end of it, I said, 'No! No! Are you crazy?'" Once again, John was sabotaging a job interview, daring Landis to reject him for a part he dearly wanted and feared he wouldn't get.

They settled into calmer conversation. John liked the script, but his scenes added up to only about a quarter of the film, with scant dialogue. John wanted to be the lead. Landis patiently explained that Bluto could not be in every scene. Landis saw Bluto as an explosive blend of Harpo

Marx and Cookie Monster, a man of voracious appetites and few words. Bluto's volcanic energy could not burn on-screen for long.

Talk turned to *Kentucky Fried Movie*. John had loved the film, especially the martial arts parody. "And then he got animated," Landis remembered. As they spoke, John picked up the phone and dialed room service, over and over again. "He ordered some shrimp cocktails," Landis said. "He ordered hamburgers. He ordered prime rib." Landis realized the actor was auditioning, then and there. He was Bluto.

"Listen," John said, at last. "I have to go." He left Landis alone in the suite. Landis telephoned Sean Daniel. "I think we got him," he said. As they spoke, Landis heard another knock on the door, which he opened to "an army of waiters with trays and tables of food," like a Marx Brothers scene. The bill was $150. Landis paid.

In the days to follow, John waffled on committing to *Animal House*, compelling Doug Kenney to lobby him on Landis's behalf. John had done the same thing with Lorne Michaels and *Saturday Night*. In truth, John wanted *Animal House* just as badly as he had wanted *Saturday Night*. "They can't do it without me," he told Bernie Brillstein, his manager. Brillstein negotiated a $35,000 contract for John to play Bluto, a significant paycheck for a performer with no film experience.

While Landis had balked at Ramis and Chase, he thought Dan Aykroyd would make a great D-Day, the biker brother in Delta House. No one wanted Dan in *Animal House* more than John. But Dan wasn't interested. *Saturday Night* was his job. Lorne Michaels was his boss. Michaels had just lost Chase, and now he was losing John, whose attention was already divided between work and his ongoing bacchanal. Dan declined the role. John was crushed. Dan consoled him: "You do it. It's your movie."

Around this time, Brillstein took a call from another film producer. Jack Nicholson wanted Belushi for a small role in a western he was shooting in Mexico. John would play a Mexican lawman, a casting inspired by John's Eli Wallach impression in a *Saturday Night* sketch. It was a measly part, but John accepted: He wanted some film experience before *Animal House*. He loved Jack Nicholson. John's father would love seeing him on a horse. Adam Belushi cherished his *Bonanza* reruns.

John signed on to *Goin' South* at $5,000 a week for five weeks, with an understanding that his work would end in time for the September 24 season premiere of *Saturday Night*. Jack Nicholson was surprised to get him. "What the hell does John Belushi want to do this for?" he asked his producers.

John arrived in Mexico asking the same question. The long journey to Durango left him agitated. Someone summoned a producer to Jack's rented home, where John was pacing the floor in slept-in clothes.

"I got to get out of here," John said, avoiding the producer's eyes. "I got to go. I've got to get back. I can't live here." He seemed to be cracking up. He opened a kitchen drawer and removed a knife. He muttered about the tiring journey and the shitty hotel where they expected him to stay.

The producer reasoned with the knife-wielding actor. He didn't want John stabbing someone, nor did he want to fire him—Nicholson wanted him in the film. A second producer arrived. He tried to talk John down: "Maybe you ought to take a nap. You're really acting like an asshole." John sat down and fell asleep.

The next day, John apologized to the producers and to Nicholson. The star had no standing to lecture John about drugs—much of the cast and crew of *Goin' South* were snorting coke. Instead, he offered professional advice.

"If these producers weren't my friends," he told John, "they would write you out"—eliminate John's part and send him back to New York. "And this would hang around your neck for ten years."

Judy flew down to offer support. She and John rented a house near the shoot. John fell ill from the intense summer heat. A botched explosion injured his hand. Judy examined the shooting schedule and realized he would never finish in time for the *Saturday Night* premiere. If John bailed on his tiny part, he might not work in Hollywood again. The Belushis were marooned in Mexico.

Chapter 15

Little Chocolate Donuts

SATURDAY NIGHT RETURNED to live broadcast on September 24, 1977, as *Saturday Night Live*, a name Michaels politely reclaimed from Roone Arledge and ABC. John flew in from Mexico, where relations with the producers of *Goin' South* were going south. John and Dan reported to work in separate offices; the Cave was no more. Dan wanted to write alone. He installed bunk beds in his new space so John knew he remained welcome.

"You're my best friend. I'm gonna miss you," Dan told John in the opening shot of the season premiere, in character as President Carter bidding farewell to a corrupt aide. John, sweating profusely, drew warm applause.

Backstage that night, John reprised a passive-aggressive game he had played with his employers since the Second City days, hinting to a visiting columnist that this season of *SNL* might be his last. "It's sort of like the fifth year of college, you know? The fourth year: great. But the fifth year, you feel like you're hanging around and you don't really belong."

Steve Martin, a rising star of American comedy, made his third appearance as host. Though prematurely gray, Martin was only thirty-two. He was touring behind a hit album, *Let's Get Small*, and propagating a national catchphrase, "Ex-cuuuuuse me."

The premiere trotted out Dan to narrate a commercial parody about a rabbi performing a bris in a moving sedan. Dan and Martin performed a sketch about a pair of Czech immigrants called the Festrunk brothers, clad in striped polyester pants and clashing disco shirts, unbuttoned to the navel, visibly "swinging" as they unfurled awkward translations of misbegotten pickup lines such as "So, how much do you weigh?" to a horrified Curtin and Radner, asking to hold their "big American breasts."

The writers incorporated John's Mexico ordeal into "Weekend Update": a slideshow depicted John presenting a dubious "scholarship" to a Durango boy in exchange for a bulging sack of weed.

Dan now shared "Weekend Update" duties with Jane Curtin, playing himself. Dan preferred anonymity, an ironic and ultimately futile quest for an actor on national television. Out on the streets, Dan sometimes literally hid behind John, trailing him on sidewalks. Fans mobbed John and ignored Dan, who seemed to will himself invisible. He could still ride the subway without drawing a crowd.

On the seventeenth floor, a cumulative fatigue set in. Production lagged. Few scenes came together in time for Wednesday script readings. "For the first time," by one account, "there were read-throughs where no one laughed."

John flew back and forth to Durango to fulfill his duties on *Goin' South*, which mostly meant sitting around. "By the end of the shoot," Judy said, "John desperately wanted to be gone, and the producers wanted him gone, too." When they summoned him to Los Angeles for additional voice work, John demanded $100 per diem. Filmmakers delivered it as a bag of change.

Dan had no film project, but he bore stresses of his own. He felt underpaid and exploited, and he blamed Michaels. That autumn, a network accountant sent a form letter to Dan and several colleagues, seeking repayment of $400 in expenses accrued on a trip to the Emmys to collect an award. In reply, Dan defaced the walls of the seventeenth floor with demented graffiti, scrawling "I am Beelzebub," threatening the accountant's life, and scripting a four-foot-high "Fuck you." Perhaps Dan hoped Michaels would fire him. Workers quietly repainted the walls.

The approaching October shoot of *Animal House* put *Saturday Night Live* and *National Lampoon* on a comedic collision course. John Landis filled out his cast with young, mostly unknown actors, whose presence on-screen would not distract viewers from their Delta House personas. Landis had Belushi, but studio bosses wanted a movie star.

"Who the fuck is John Belushi?" Ned Tanen growled to Sean Daniel. "Get me some faces that moviegoers know."

Landis knew Donald Sutherland, star of *M*A*S*H* and *Klute*, from the *Kelly's Heroes* shoot. Landis had babysat his son Kiefer. He sent the *Animal House* script to Sutherland, who liked it. Thom Mount reached out to negotiate his fee for a part that would require two days' work. Sutherland agreed to a princely sum of $50,000, the same amount Universal was paying Landis to direct, more than the studio was paying Belushi.

As the shoot drew near, Tanen terrorized Daniel, telephoning at random hours, hissing, "Two million dollars, Daniel," and hanging up. None of the older executives inside the Black Tower liked the script. And for all Ned Tanen's bullying, the assigned budget ($2.4 million, in the end) was barely enough to make the film.

"It was way too expensive to shoot on the studio lot," Daniel said, "so we had to find an actual college." One hundred colleges turned them down, including all three of the screenwriters' alma maters, Harvard, Dartmouth, and Washington University. The project looked doomed. At last, Daniel found a receptive audience in William Beaty Boyd, president of the University of Oregon. "As long as you don't say it's the University of Oregon, you can shoot here," he instructed.

The cast arrived in Eugene, Oregon, in October with long hair and beards, looking nothing like a Kennedy-era fraternity. Landis put everyone up at a Rodeway Inn and arranged haircuts. John and Judy hosted a World Series party; it was Yankees versus Dodgers, perfect for an assemblage of actors from New York and Los Angeles. Someone rolled a piano into a motel guest room, which became a party hub.

Landis had sharpened the *Animal House* script into a contest between the lovable boozers of Delta House and the privileged assholes in Omega, who would spend most of the movie trying to bring Delta down. If Dartmouth and Harvard emblemized American elitism, *Animal House* emerged as the quintessential cinematic expression of anti-elitism, a film directed by a high school dropout and starring a world-class slob.

Nothing captured its spirit better than a sweatshirt designed for Bluto by Deborah Nadoolman, Landis's girlfriend, with COLLEGE emblazoned across its front.

Landis urged his actors to embrace their roles. He encouraged them to spray-paint graffiti on the walls of the dwelling he had rented as Delta House. When actor Mark Metcalf arrived at the Rodeway Inn restaurant to start work as Douglas C. Neidermeyer, one of the hated Omegas, Landis sat with the Deltas at a corner table. "That's him!" Landis cried. "That's Neidermeyer!" Belushi leapt up, screaming and hurling food at the stranger. The others followed suit.

Peter Riegert, a Broadway actor with movie-star looks, flew in to play Donald "Boon" Schoenstein, the part Harold Ramis had written for himself. Riegert recalled his introduction to Oregon as "a week of rehearsals in which we did no rehearsals, except partying. The movie's about an hour and forty minutes and change. That's what we did seven days a week for seven weeks. It was a party."

Almost no one in the cast had belonged to a fraternity. One evening, the Delta actors attended a party at a real fraternity, to polish their method. They soon found themselves encircled by real fraternity brothers. One of them said, "You Hollywood fags think you're gonna come up here and steal our women."

In the tense moments that followed, Jamie Widdoes, the sandy-haired actor cast as the Delta president, thought, *Wow, I may get the shit beat out of me, but that is such a great line.*

As the actors turned to leave, the lead bully offered, "Have a nice night, asshole." Widdoes reached out and popped the student's beer into his face. The fraternity brothers jumped the actors. As they limped home to the Rodeway Inn, Widdoes apologized profusely to the others for starting the fight.

"No, wait a minute," said Bruce McGill, the Texan cast as D-Day. "This is perfect. We're bonded now. We are the Deltas."

John was heartbroken at missing the fight. He had flown home to do *SNL*, an exhausting weekly routine he would continue through the shoot. John worked on *Animal House* from Monday to Wednesday, then flew to New York, leaving Judy in Oregon—they could not afford to buy her a ticket. On Saturday nights, the *Animal House* cast gathered to watch John on TV. John returned in time to watch Chicago Bears games on Sunday afternoons in Oregon. Sometimes he brought bagels from the city.

Back in New York, John could no longer enter a nightclub without drawing a crowd. In Oregon, he remained sufficiently anonymous that he could sneak into a university classroom to hear a lecture. Once, when John raised his hand to ask a question, the professor glared and asked, "Why are you always coming in late?" John replied that he had a job in a steel mill.

Thom Mount, just a year older than Belushi, immediately spotted his drug habit. "I had worked with Richard Pryor," Mount said, "so I knew how to work around a drug problem." Producers leased the Belushis a house off campus to honor John's star billing, a development that conveniently kept him clear of the Rodeway Inn parties. By most accounts, John remained reasonably clean through the shoot. Landis busted him once smoking pot in a dormitory bathroom; shouting, "Come here, you fuck!" he physically dragged him out. John felt oddly moved.

Weed and wine circulated freely among the *Animal House* cast and crew. Landis himself "never did a drug," one colleague recalled. "He never drank coffee. Landis is Landis. He was just high on life."

The director tailored the movie to John, trimming his lines, compelling him to act with his face and body, building scenes around his comings and goings. Landis never kept John on-camera for long: Bluto played best in brief, explosive segments. John had begged the director to include him in the lengthy road-trip scene, but Landis refused: Bluto could not simply sit in a car.

"John was a fun, really talented sketch player," Peter Riegert said. By contrast, Riegert and most of the other *Animal House* players were theatrically trained actors, accustomed to inhabiting a part across the full run of a ninety-minute script. "There's a big difference in my mind between sustaining a character for five minutes and an hour and thirty minutes."

Still, Bluto set a high bar. In his opening scene, he turned to greet two Delta pledges while holding a beer and urinating prodigiously, showering their pants and shoes. Then he led them into Delta House and caught a flying beer bottle (hurled by Landis from off-screen), an unscripted moment that showcased his gridiron reflexes.

Shooting proceeded amid relentless drizzle. Landis kept the energy high.

"He would yell at us," Widdoes said. "'BE FUNNIER. DO IT AGAIN. BE FUNNIER.' And you're like, OK. We'd do it again. 'THAT'S NOT FUNNY.'" Landis kept the performers on their toes by hurling props and pens. "He needed results, and he needed them fast. Thirty-two shooting days. No money."

Most *Animal House* actors followed the script; John improvised. One scene re-created a Kennedy-era toga party, a bacchanal inspired by the Greco-Roman pretensions of an era when the typical Ivy Leaguer studied Latin. John had attended a toga party at Wheaton Central High School. In the movie sequence, Bluto walked up to a beatnik character who was serenading some women (one played by Judy) with an acoustic guitar, singing the folk standard "I Gave My Love a Cherry." Bluto stopped in his tracks. His face morphed through a series of expressions: puzzlement, revulsion, resolve. He grabbed the guitar and smashed it against the wall. He was supposed to hit the wall once, but the guitar refused to splinter. Bluto erupted in fury, swinging the instrument back and forth against two walls until only the neck remained. He handed the stump back to the beatnik with a gentle "Sorry."

Another scene called for Bluto to lead his frat-mates into the dean's office with a horse, by cover of darkness, as a prank. With the cameras rolling, John slipped on wet grass and fell. Landis bellowed, "Keep going!" John popped back up and improvised a series of goofy, SWAT-team hops that elevated a trivial connecting shot into a ballet of Buster Keaton–esque slapstick.

Landis coached John through a riotous sequence in the college cafeteria. Bluto walked down the serving line, wearing a greasy cutoff sweatshirt, filling his tray and his mouth as Landis barked instructions: "What is that? It's Jell-O! Swallow all of it!" John executed it to perfection, filling his pockets, piling food high on his tray, arching an eyebrow as he slurped down a plate of green Jell-O in one gulp. Then he danced over to a table filled with appalled Omega villains.

"See if you can guess what I am now?" he asked. He stuffed a ball of mashed potatoes into his mouth, then slapped his cheeks, food exploding all over the Omegas. "I'm a zit. Get it?" Bobbing his eyebrows, Bluto led the Omegas in a chase around the cafeteria, seeding chaos and yelling, "Food fight!" He did the scene in one take.

John elevated one of the film's gratuitous nude scenes, obligatory in a *National Lampoon* movie. Bluto climbed a ladder to watch sorority girls in a pillow fight. Unsated, Bluto hopped the ladder, pogo-stick style, to reach another window and watch a coed dreamily undress. John broke the fourth wall, turned to the camera, and bobbed an eyebrow at the audience, a gesture that satirized the scene's essential sleaze. Then Bluto's excitement overcame him, and he and the ladder toppled to earth.

Landis and his star made the most of Bluto's limited dialogue. In a pivotal plot point, the dean expelled the Deltas for cheating on an exam, the battle seemingly lost. As the brothers sulked in the ruins of Delta House, Bluto unfurled the immortal line "Seven years of college down the drain." Matty Simmons claimed to have written it.

"It's perfect for the character," Peter Riegert said, "because John looked thirty."

Bluto leapt up to rally the dejected troops. "Over? D'you say over?" John cried. "Nothing is over until we decide it is. Was it over when the . . . Germans bombed Pearl Harbor?"

A puzzled Delta brother murmured, "Germans?" His seatmate instructed, "Forget it. He's rolling."

On a rare weekend off from *SNL*, John and Judy headed downtown and caught a show in the ballroom at the Eugene Hotel. The night's entertainment came from the Crayhawks, a mash-up of two house bands, one led by a superb young blues guitarist, Robert Cray. John sat transfixed by the singer, a harmonica virtuoso named Curtis Salgado—who looked and dressed and sounded like a real-life Blues Brother. In mid-song, Salgado felt a tug at his pants. "Hey!" the man said. "Belushi wants to meet you." Salgado knew nothing of Belushi or *Saturday Night Live*. "I'm singing," he replied. "Fuck off."

At the break, Salgado jumped off the stage and headed toward a group of female friends. The same man grabbed his arm and spun him around. A stranger extended a hand. "I'm John Belushi," he said. Salgado craned his neck toward the women.

"Hey, I like your music, and I like what you're doing," John said. "You remind me of this friend of mine. His name is Dan Aykroyd. He plays the harmonica, too." John said he played in "this variety show" back in New York. The singer tried to break free.

John continued: "I'm really excited about this, because I get to do a show with Ray Charles."

That got Salgado's attention. "What?"

"Yeah, Ray Charles." John turned to walk away. Now, Salgado grabbed his arm.

"Whoa, wait a minute, come here. You've gotta ask him about Guitar Slim."

"Who's Guitar Slim?"

Salgado explained: Guitar Slim was a New Orleans R & B guitarist from the '50s who influenced Jimi Hendrix and, thus, the course of rock 'n' roll.

"Why don't we go upstairs and smoke a joint?" John offered. In the empty hotel mezzanine, John asked Salgado about the songs he had just sung: What were they? Who wrote them? Dan would have known, but Dan wasn't there. Salgado told John about "Hey Bartender," the Floyd Dixon standard, and "I Don't Know," by Chicago singer Willie Mabon, and "Soul Man," by Sam and Dave.

"Do you know Ray plays alto sax?" Salgado offered. "He did on *Live at Newport*, on a song called 'Hot Rod.'" John listened attentively.

The next weekend, on November 12, Ray Charles played a rare sax solo on *Saturday Night Live*. Someone mentioned it to Salgado. *I did this*, he thought.

Some days later, John telephoned Salgado: "Hey, bring your records over." Salgado arrived at John's rented house with a stack of R & B vinyl. "Blue Öyster Cult was on the turntable," he remembered. "I took that off and put on some Magic Sam."

John returned to the Eugene Hotel. At the end of a set, Salgado let him sing "Hey Bartender" with the Crayhawks. John did his Joe Cocker voice, which was his comfort zone. "And the audience just went apeshit," Salgado remembered.

After the show, John asked, "What did you think?"

"John," Salgado replied, "it's Joe Cocker." He reached over and tapped John on the heart. "You gotta be yourself," he said, "and you gotta come from here. That's what music is about."

"Yeah, you're right," John replied.

Curtis Salgado launched John on a Belushi-size blues bender, rekindling his passion for the Blues Brothers. John chatted up Landis about his ambitions for the characters. He took new interest in the *Animal House* soundtrack, much of it drawn from the set lists of bands like the Ravins. Landis allowed him to sing a version of "Money (That's What I Want)," the Barrett Strong hit, which played in an opening scene.

The final battle in *Animal House* unfolded at the homecoming parade. D-Day, the part written for Dan Aykroyd, driving a sleek, souped-up black sedan the Deltas had christened the Deathmobile, crashed into the officials' viewing platform. Bluto, dressed as a pirate, leapt from a roof, grabbed a hanging banner, and sailed down to the street like Tarzan.

Rain had drenched cast and crew throughout the shoot. On the day of the parade sequence, rain turned to snow. Landis caught pneumonia. Production photos show him swaddled in blankets.

On the last day of filming, actor Stephen Furst, who played a particularly hapless Delta pledge, approached John for an autograph. John took the still and wrote, "To Frank." He crossed it out and wrote, "To Bob." He crossed that out and wrote, "To Jimmy." He crossed that out and wrote, "To Steve, I hate you. Leave me alone, you scumbag fuck face. Belushi."

Back at *Saturday Night Live*, Dan Aykroyd slipped into John's customary role as agent provocateur. One night in November, he happened upon a document on Lorne Michaels's desk that showed the program's weekly budget. Doing the math, Dan calculated NBC was budgeting more money for the *SNL* writing staff than he and the other writers actually received. Dan rushed around the seventeenth floor like a union rep, asking all the writers about their weekly pay. When he tallied the numbers, he found a shortfall of roughly $10,000 per show. The writers gathered in Michaels's office on the night of November 17, Michaels's thirty-third birthday. Dan wanted Michaels to explain where the extra money was going. Michaels was out celebrating.

The next day, Dan assembled the writers outside Michaels's office and launched into a "magnificent tirade," by one account, pace quickening, volume rising, and face reddening as he gathered steam. At the end, he turned and smashed a boot-clad foot into the wall. Michaels emerged.

"What's up?" he asked coolly.

Dan thrust a finger in Michaels's face. "You're fucking spending all your time in that office and going out to dinner with Candice Bergen," he said. "And the fucking show is going to hell, and we have five writers who are writing the show, and eighteen people on the credits."

Michaels listened in silence, periodically nodding his head. When Dan was through, the boss turned, walked back into his office, and slammed the door.

Michaels quietly hired two new writers. One, Don Novello, became a productive contributor offstage and on, creating a gossipy priest character named Father Guido Sarducci. The other, Brian Murray, dwelt in the shadow of his ascendant brother.

The November 19 episode offered perhaps the greatest commercial parody John Belushi would perform on *SNL*. Scripted by Franken and Davis, the film opened with John dressed for an Olympic decathlon, in the style of 1976 gold medalist Bruce Jenner, and completing a spectacular high jump, then winning a long-distance sprint. The camera cut to John sitting at a breakfast table, wearing a sweater and holding a cigarette, deep furrows beneath his eyes.

"I logged a lot of miles training for that day," John said. "And I downed a lot of donuts. Little Chocolate Donuts. They taste good, and they've got the sugar I need to get me going in the morning. That's why Little Chocolate Donuts have been on my training table since I was a kid."

Announcer: *Little Chocolate Donuts. The donuts of champions.*

John had been a serious athlete. Ten years later, he looked like a parody of an athlete. He went along with the shoot until some kid off set cried, "I like the fat guy." At that, John retreated to his trailer and sulked.

The next show began with host Mary Kay Place calling out the tired cast, and John in particular, for lack of "pep." John walked onstage late, mirroring his habitual tardiness in rehearsal. Jane Curtin jumped in: "You've been a disciplinary problem since the show began." John revived then and led the cast in a high school cheer, climaxing with him bursting through a giant paper hoop.

Anyone who doubted John's pep need only have shadowed him into the next day. After the official *SNL* after-party, the cast repaired to the Lone Star Café, the famed Texas-themed club on lower Fifth Avenue. Willie Nelson, that week's musical guest, played a late set.

"This was their regular post-show stop," Jamie Widdoes said. "There was a stage, and there was a balcony up above that they would close off for the cast members and their guests. Willie performed. And sort of in the middle of it, Willie said, 'Now we have some special guests, Jake and Elwood Blues.'"

Inspired by Curtis Salgado, John had talked Dan into staging the first live performance of the Blues Brothers outside the *Saturday Night Live* cocoon, playing the Big Joe Turner song "Flip, Flop and Fly" and a few others. Though they had performed for millions on live TV, the boys were frightened to join Willie Nelson onstage. Their host was not amused.

"I remember looking at Willie, and Willie had this look of *What the fuck is going on?*" Widdoes said.

John's musical education continued. On New Year's Eve, 1977, he went with Mitch Glazer to the Palladium to see Levon Helm and the RCO All-Stars. Helm, drummer for The Band, was a rock 'n' roll heavyweight. His All-Stars featured Stax Records legends Steve Cropper and Donald "Duck" Dunn on guitar and bass, Dr. John on keyboard, Paul Butterfield on harmonica, and the *SNL* horn section. As they played, John turned to Glazer and said, "If I ever put a band together, I want that band."

* * *

A sketch in the January 28, 1978, episode opened in a Greek diner, a place much like the eateries John's father had run in Chicago. In the vérité spirit of *SNL*, Dan Aykroyd flipped real burgers on a working grill. Jane Curtin, an impatient customer, ordered a tuna sandwich and fries.

"No," said John, the cashier. "No tuna."

"You're out of tuna?"

"No tuna. Cheesebooger? Cheesebooger? Come on, come on, come on. We ain't got all day. We gotta have turnover, turnover." He turned to Garrett Morris, the next customer. "What are you gonna have?"

"I think I'll have grilled cheese and a Coke."

John turned to Dan at the grill. "Grilled cheese?"

"No grilled cheese," Dan barked.

"No grilled cheese," John barked.

"Uh, cheeseburger and a Coke."

"No Coke. Pepsi."

"OK, Pepsi, and french fries."

"No fries. Chip."

Cheesebooger. Pepsi. Chip. John shouted the orders to Dan and Bill Murray in the kitchen, who parroted the words back. This was a uniquely American take on the old *Monty Python* sketch about a cheese shop that had no cheese. At the Olympia restaurant, patrons could order whatever they wanted, as long as they wanted a cheeseburger.

Don Novello, the new writer, penned the diner sketch from memories of the Billy Goat Tavern in Chicago. Mike Royko, the columnist and Belushi family friend, all but lived at the Billy Goat. The staff didn't ask you what you wanted to eat—they told you. Novello called his fictional diner the Pyreaus Café. "John asked me to change it to the Olympia," he said, "because it was his father's restaurant." John's character, Pete, honored Uncle Pete, who had corralled customers at the real Olympia.

Chevy Chase returned to *Saturday Night Live* to host the February 18 show. It was sweeps month, and a reunion would fire up the ratings. The mood at 30 Rock was predictably strained. Michaels and John had trash-talked Chase since his defection from *Saturday Night*. Others in the cast and crew resented Chase's return. John did his best to stir things up, especially with Bill Murray, who had replaced Chase only to emerge as the better sketch performer. "And I'm sure Billy wanted to take me down," Chase said.

The week unfolded in tension. John walked out of a promotional photo session with Chase, huffing, "I don't want to do no more fucking publicity." Dan followed. The photographer filed a letter of protest.

Minutes before the show began, Chase appeared at the dressing room where Bill and John were sitting on a couch. Voices rose. Bill instructed Chase, "Go fuck your wife," an unsubtle allusion to Chase's marital woes. Chase countered, "I'm gonna land Neil Armstrong on your face if you don't shut up," pointing up Bill's complexion problems. Words came to blows. The fists mostly rained on John, who had stepped in. No one landed a good punch, but Bill got off the best line, pointing at Chase and bellowing, "Medium talent." At the show's end, John, Dan, and Bill gathered conspiratorially at the rear of the stage, visibly distancing themselves from Chase.

For the March 11 episode, Tom Schiller recruited John to visit a Brooklyn cemetery and film a short piece that imagined Belushi as an old man, the last survivor of *SNL*.

The film's title, "Don't Look Back in Anger," played on the Dylan documentary *Dont Look Back* and John Osborne's British class-conflict drama *Look Back in Anger*. Schiller shot it in black and white. The scene opened in a railcar, then cut to John pacing through the cemetery on a cold winter's day, with a soundtrack of stark, Teutonic strings that evoked an Ingmar Bergman film.

John turned to the camera. "Yeah, they all thought I'd be the first to go," he said, his voice falling halfway between a geriatric Gene Hackman and Jimmy Stewart. "I was one of those 'Live fast, die young, leave a good-looking corpse' types, you know? But I guess they were wrong." He gestured to a tombstone with his cane. "There they are. All my friends. This is the Not Ready for Prime Time Cemetery." Nervous laughter from the audience. "Come on up."

John gently mocked his costars by imagining their fates, the script turning alternately whimsical, sad, and cruel. Of Dan, he said, "I guess he loved his Harley too much. They clocked him at 175 miles an hour before the crash. It was a blur. I had to be called in to identify his body. I recognized him by his webbed toes.

"The *Saturday Night* show was the best experience of my life," John continued. "And now they're all gone. And I miss every one of 'em. Why me? Why did I live so long? . . . I'll tell you why. Because I'm a dancer!"

John dropped his cane. Gypsy music swelled, and he launched into a spirited dance, the audience clapping along.

Later that month, on broadcast day, John lumbered down a hallway at 30 Rock in faded jeans and a sweatshirt, giant green claws flopping on his hands and feet. He stomped into his dressing room, grabbed a banana, and inserted it into his mouth whole, disgorging an empty skin. Dan walked in and greeted him with "Hello there, Thing." The claws were for a mock film preview lifted from real life. John was famous for showing up unannounced at the homes of friends and costars and sundry celebrities in the middle of the night, rampaging through their kitchens, playing their records, and setting fire to their furniture. In this episode, John would play "The Thing That Wouldn't Leave."

John didn't like the claws. They made no sense. From that topic he turned to *Animal House*, a production in which he now felt cheated. "Bullshit money, no points, but I'm gonna be the fucking star anyhow, those cheap bastards," he fumed, spitting banana peel at an *Animal House* poster taped to a mirror.

He griped to a visiting *Rolling Stone* reporter who was preparing a profile of Dan. In a calmer moment, John examined their friendship.

"Here's the difference between us: see, I never carry any ID, no driver's license, no passport when I travel, nothing. I couldn't care less. He," Dan, "always carried this big ID wallet, big as a purse, that he kept chained to his belt at all times. When he lost it, I was laughing my ass off.

"He's Mr. Careful, and I'm Mr. Fuck It. I can't always figure him out, but whenever I'm around him, I feel safe."

Chapter 16

Joliet Jake

B ACK IN NEW YORK, Belushi remained obsessed with the trappings of rhythm and blues. He bought a dark brown fedora, black Ray-Bans, and a dark suit coat. His pockets bulged with R & B cassette tapes. He would storm into the home of Bob Tischler, the *National Lampoon Radio Hour* producer, pull blues albums from his shelves, and play one song from each, leaving them in a teetering stack on the floor. At home, he would serenade guests with a frenetic barrage of 45s. He would spin one for a few bars, then say "Nah," rip it from the turntable, and snap it in two.

"What he was doing," Judy said, "was finding out which songs people responded to," building a Blues Brothers set list in his head.

John and Dan had drifted apart. John was newly married. Film commitments distracted him from his job at *SNL*, though he remained the program's unrivaled star.

John started visiting Manhattan clubs, dressed in his Blues Brothers getup, leveraging his celebrity to jump onstage with various bands to sing "Hey Bartender" or "Sweet Home Chicago" or some other blues standard, the same routine teenage Dan had followed back in Ottawa with his harmonica.

Lorne Michaels witnessed one of John's sets. John had taken Curtis Salgado's advice, moving past his Joe Cocker impression to find his own voice, a crude but effective growl. After John sang, Michaels offered, "Why don't you warm up the show with the band on Saturday night?"

John alerted Dan, and together, they metamorphosed into the Blues Brothers. They purchased black suits and ties to complement the hats and Ray-Bans. They acquired a 1967 Dodge Monaco and painted it black. Someone dubbed it the Bluesmobile.

Though Howard Shore had christened the Blues Brothers, the concept came mostly from Dan, the blues hound, who honored the great blues duos of the 1960s: Sam and Dave, who had scored monster hits with "Soul Man" and "Hold On, I'm Comin'"; and James and Bobby Purify, known for "I'm Your Puppet" and "Shake a Tail Feather." The funereal black suits were "straight from Lenny Bruce, who said, 'You've always got to wear a suit and tie, man, to fool the straights,'" Dan said. The hat and shades recalled urban bluesmen like John Lee Hooker, who had electrified the Delta blues with a driving boogie beat. More broadly, formal dress linked the white bluesmen with the grand tradition of Black rhythm and blues. R & B icons of the pre- and post-war eras were always impeccably dressed, from Lonnie Johnson and Cab Calloway to B.B. King. By the 1970s, most white rock stars had ditched jackets and ties for torn jeans and tie-dye, but many Black artists had not. Even the King of the Blues knew better than to travel in slovenly dress, lest he be endlessly harassed by racist whites. Dress like you're going to the bank to borrow money, B.B. said.

The sunglasses were less about race and more about dope. Musical artists Black and white wore sunglasses, even at night, to conceal dilated pupils and that bloodshot look. Dark sunglasses allowed John to hide the evidence of debauchery. They freed Dan from the awkward business of eye contact.

Back in 1975, jamming with the *Saturday Night* band, John and Dan had harbored no real ambitions beyond living out childhood rock-star dreams. Now John shared Dan's messianic zeal for spreading the gospel of rhythm and blues. As usual, John charged forward with boundless energy and impeccable instincts but no real plan. Dan, the obsessive method actor, would write one.

On a Monday in April 1978, they met with Tom Malone, multi-instrumentalist and arranger for the *SNL* band. They described the Blues

Brothers, "two ne'er-do-well blues musicians who wore sunglasses day and night," Malone recalled. "They were orphans with very little emotional response to anything. They lived in a cheap, tiny apartment next to the elevated train tracks in downtown Chicago. They drove an old Illinois state police car." On Wednesday, the band rehearsed "Rocket 88," Ike Turner's prototypical rock 'n' roll stomper, with John and Dan fronting.

"We thought it would be fun," Dan explained, "to put together an act that venerated the African-American songwriters and the songbook and the artists in a way that had humor, which was always there, if you recall. The classic band leaders—Wynonie Harris, Cab Calloway, Jimmie Lunceford, Johnny Otis—they were great musicians, but they were funny too. And they were great frontmen. They featured artists and stars that were much more talented, in terms of virtuosos on horns and piano and guitar. But the frontmen were very important."

Already, Dan was dreaming bigger than blues. Wynonie Harris and Cab Calloway wore crisp suits and led big bands, musicians who read music and populated the "race" charts of the 1930s and '40s, which gave way to the rhythm-and-blues charts of the 1950s. They sang mostly about sex and women who liked it too much or too little, smiling as they unfurled bawdy verse in thinly veiled metaphor. In one 1949 side, Wynonie Harris sang, "All she wants to do is rock, rock 'n' roll all night long." Not for another half decade would the white arbiters of propriety and taste puzzle out what he meant.

When the Blues Brothers strode out onstage to lead the *Saturday Night Live* band in musical warm-ups before the April 8 show, they were auditioning for a gig as Michaels's musical guests. They played "Rocket 88." The next week, they worked up a version of "Hey Bartender." John and Dan pushed to perform on the show. Michaels said he didn't see anything funny.

After that, John and Dan said they were done: "We're wasting our time if Lorne won't let us on." The fate of the Blues Brothers hung in the balance.

And then, Lorne Michaels relented, although memories diverge on exactly how. By one account, a musical act dropped out. By another, Michaels determined the next show was running short. Or maybe

Michaels just gave in, awarding his stars a coveted slot as musical guests opposite a red-hot host, Steve Martin. Better still, the Blues Brothers would perform the cold open, the first sketch of the night.

That Saturday night, April 22, 1978, marked the real debut of the Blues Brothers on *Saturday Night Live*, not in bee costumes but clad in jazz-junkie chic, and again backed by the powerhouse *SNL* band.

Paul Shaffer introduced them: "In 1969, Marshall Checkers of the legendary Checkers Records called me on a new blues act that had been playing in small, funky clubs on Chicago's South Side." That was a winking reference to Marshall Chess and Chess Records, the legendary Chicago blues label. "Today, with the help of Ahmet Wexler, Jerry Ertegun, and the staff of Pacific Records"—a send-up of Jerry Wexler and Ahmet Ertegun at Atlantic Records—"their manager, Morey Daniels, and with the support of fellow artists Curtis Salgado and the Cray Band, they are no longer an authentic blues act, but have managed to become a viable commercial product." Here, the audience laughed politely, although few would have recognized the name of Curtis Salgado, the Oregonian who had helped teach Belushi the blues.

Jake and Elwood Blues stormed through "Hey Bartender" as if their very careers depended on it. The performance ushered in the strongest ninety-minute episode in the brief history of *Saturday Night Live*, maybe the finest ninety minutes Lorne Michaels and his performers would ever deliver on the stage of Studio 8H.

The opening credits billed the Blues Brothers as special guests, a distinction that ensured the Blues Brothers brand belonged to Dan and John, rather than NBC. Dan and Steve Martin, the host, returned as the Festrunk brothers, characters who had somehow grown wildly popular in the months since their quiet debut. When Martin announced, "We are two wild and crazy guys," the studio audience exploded.

Martin held court in an instant-classic sketch titled "Theodoric of York, Medieval Barber." John came onstage as a hunchback. "Say, don't I know you?" Theodoric asked. "Yeah," John replied. "You worked on my back."

On a "Weekend Update" segment called "Point/Counterpoint," a send-up of the dueling-commentary format, Dan and Jane Curtin traded ad hominem attacks. One of Dan's lines launched a catchphrase: "Jane, you ignorant slut."

Not to be outdone by the Blues Brothers, Martin trotted out a high-gloss musical number called "King Tut," poking fun at the traveling *Treasures of Tutankhamun* exhibit that had captured the zeitgeist. "He gave his life for tourism," Martin deadpanned during the disco break. Released as a single, the song sold more than a million copies.

Not to be outdone by Steve Martin, John and Dan reclaimed the stage to perform "I Don't Know," by Willie Mabon. John sang like a drunk guy at a blues bar, dancing maniacally, turning clunky cartwheels, and firing up the Studio 8H audience with a spoken-shouted interval that Salgado had taught him: "I said, 'Woman, you going to walk a mile for a Camel, or are you going to make like Mr. Chesterfield and satisfy?'" John savored every word, and the crowd clapped and whooped along like parishioners at an evangelical sermon. "And she said, 'That all depends on what you're packing, regular or king size.'" At that final double entendre, the crowd exploded in rapture.

Writer Tom Davis would later term the episode "the only time I remember the show being good from beginning to end. Everyone was happy after that show. But that's how rare that was. It's the only one I can remember."

By this date, no one had to wander far in the *SNL* offices to find cocaine. One reliable spot was the band dressing room, known to insiders as the departure lounge. John appeared at the door one night and beckoned to one of the musicians: "You got any blow?"

The musician "pulls out a little vial that has a little dust in one corner," Tom Malone remembered. "This is all I have, John," he announced, handing John the vial. John returned it: "That won't even get me started." He hustled out.

A few minutes later, Malone recalled, the musician turned to his bandmates and asked, "Anybody want blow?" He produced a full vial. "Hey," Lou Marini protested. "I thought you were out."

"That was my Belushi bottle," the musician replied. Soon, every musician at *SNL* carried a Belushi bottle.

When *Saturday Night Live* broke for the summer, John and Judy rented a house on Martha's Vineyard, playground of the rich and powerful. They visited the home of James Taylor and Carly Simon. Simon was struggling with her husband's heroin addiction. She could tell John was on coke. Even so, John harangued her with a delusional speech. He was worried about James. James was out of control. He, John, was in control. Drugs were bad, sure, but they released an artist's muse. The trick was control.

Simon walked off and found Judy on the sunporch. They commiserated. Judy had found it hard to shake her own coke habit. Everyone used it, and the lift helped her match John's energy through the long nights, the better to steer him clear of real trouble.

"I've tried doing drugs with him," Judy said, shaking her head. "I've tried not doing drugs with him. I've tried going to a shrink and not going to a shrink. We've tried going to a shrink together, and we've tried going to a shrink separately."

Simon burst into tears. If Judy couldn't get her husband off drugs, then what chance did she have?

John was still riding high on the Blues Brothers. He and Dan got Bernie Brillstein to find a contact in the record business. Brillstein found Michael Klenfner, an executive from Atlantic Records, the longtime label of Aretha Franklin and Sam and Dave and Ray Charles. Klenfner visited John and Judy on the Vineyard. They talked for hours, Klenfner recalled, "about how great the *SNL* performance had been and how we should do a record."

Klenfner took the idea to Jerry Greenberg, president of Atlantic. "Jerry," he urged, "this is gonna be fucking huge." The label president was unmoved. Klenfner arranged to have the Brothers meet Ahmet Ertegun, the label co-founder.

The meeting quickly soured. The label president turned to John and Dan and said, "You guys oughta cut a disco cover of 'Stairway to Heaven.'" Disco had colonized the charts that summer, with Andy Gibb's "Shadow Dancing" leading the assault.

Dan pulled Michael Klenfner out of the meeting. "What the fuck are you doing to us?" Dan hissed. They walked back in. Klenfner said,

"That's not gonna fly." The boys wanted to cut an authentic blues album. "And they want to do it live."

Bernie Brillstein negotiated a $125,000 contract with Atlantic. He set the Brothers up to open for Steve Martin in a nine-night stand at Universal Amphitheatre in Los Angeles in the fall. Martin's own fame was exploding, thanks largely to his appearances on *SNL*. John and Dan would earn $17,000 for the shows: "birdseed," in Bernie Brillstein's parlance. But the extended engagement offered several chances to capture a live show for a Blues Brothers LP.

John and Dan needed to polish their act. John contacted the owner of Lone Star Café, the hip western club that hosted the *SNL* after-after-parties, looser and noisier than the official after-parties where Lorne Michaels held court. The Lone Star's owner put John in touch with Doc Pomus, the legendary R & B songwriter. Doc introduced John to Roomful of Blues, a rhythm-and-swing revival band. They agreed to back the Blues Brothers one Monday night at the Lone Star. The crowd loved them. But Duke Robillard, the band's founder, lead guitarist, and alpha male, walked off in mid-set.

"You can't have John and Duke onstage," Dan explained. "One or the other."

John approached Robillard after the show, pleading, "You can't do this to me. You need me. I have a recording contract."

"I don't need you," Robillard fired back, drunkenness emboldening him. "And I wouldn't play behind you again for a million dollars. You couldn't sing your way out of a paper bag, Belushi. You should stick to TV."

"But they liked me," John protested. He couldn't grasp how deeply the band resented the Blues Brothers for upstaging them, celebrity dilettantes peddling an inferior act. Dan, still harboring doubts about the Blues Brothers mission, quietly concurred with the Duke: "He's right, man," he told John. "He's really right."

The producers chose Denver, the heart of Middle America, for the first public screening of *Animal House*, around Memorial Day, 1978. "There was a big fraternity gathering in Denver at the time," Peter Riegert said.

Real fraternity brothers squeezed in around Lew Wasserman, the Universal boss, who wanted to see how his money had been spent. The lights dimmed, and the courtly Elmer Bernstein score kicked in.

If there was a moment when *Animal House* announced itself as a *National Lampoon* film and as an artifact of the irreverent television generation, it was the arrival of two pledges at Delta House. The freshmen gazed up and beheld a mannequin crashing through an upstairs window, cueing perhaps the most famous song in comedy-soundtrack history, the Kingsmen's slurry "Louie Louie," one the Ravins had let Belushi sing. The preview audience exploded. "You couldn't hear through the laughter," said Sean Daniel, the young Universal executive.

After the screening, John Landis telephoned Belushi to deliver a report. "How did it go?" John asked.

"It was great," Landis replied. "I'm sorry you weren't here." The director said he wanted John to hear something. He lifted a tape recorder to the receiver and hit play. John heard tinny laughter and screaming. What is that? he asked.

The audience, Landis replied.

Animal House premiered on July 27, 1978, at the Astor Theatre in New York. Landis penned a note to John that read, "John, I love you. You bless my movie and my life."

This time, the film played to modest laughs from a crowd peppered with envious *National Lampoon* staffers, jaded executives, and aloof critics. Midway through, John padded out to the lobby and found Sean Daniel huddling with Bernie Brillstein.

"Wait till we get to Chicago with this," John said, speaking to himself as much as to them. "Best comedy city. New York, they're all pussies."

When the champagne flowed at the Village Gate after-party, no one looked happier than Matty Simmons, who knew a hit when he saw one, and Doug Kenney, who had realized his dream of making a film.

Off in a corner, Ned Tanen shoved Thom Mount against a wall. "You take that fucking scene out of the movie," he hissed. Tanen thought the Black roadhouse sequence was going to spark walkouts.

Tempers cooled the next day. The *New York Times* ran a review by Janet Maslin, the first volley in a critical skirmish over the legacy of

Animal House that would reveal a fresh generational divide. Maslin was twenty-eight. "At its best," she wrote, "the movie isn't strictly satirical, because it doesn't need to be. The filmmakers have simply supplied the appropriate panty-girdles, crew-neck sweaters, frat-house initiation rites and rituals of the toga party, and let all that idiocy speak—very eloquently, and with a lot of comic fervor—for itself."

Rex Reed, of the *New York Daily News*, a decade older than Maslin, termed the film "stodgy, predictable and amateurish." Harry Themal of the Wilmington, Delaware, *News Journal*, several years older than Reed, told his readers that *Animal House* "offers little but sophomoric humor that even a high school freshman would scorn."

But most critics, and nearly all younger critics, loved the film. Gene Siskel, the *Chicago Tribune* reviewer, called it "terribly funny." Roger Ebert of the *Chicago Sun-Times* went further, as he often did: "The movie is vulgar, raunchy, ribald, and occasionally scatological. It is also the funniest comedy since Mel Brooks made *The Producers*."

All through the next week, John stopped by *Animal House* screenings around Manhattan, chatting up managers about box-office receipts, scanning lines of moviegoers, Bluto made flesh.

John was right about Chicago. He arrived as a conquering hero and led Sean Daniel on a triumphal nocturnal tour of favorite Old Town taverns. He repeated the pub crawl every subsequent night, even the one before his big day with the Chicago press. At first light, a procession of reporters and morning-show producers awaited him.

"Belushi is due to be awake and in the lobby of the hotel," a *Tribune* columnist wrote.

He sleeps through his first wakeup call. He sleeps through his second wakeup call. He sleeps through his third wakeup call. He sleeps through sustained pounding on his door. Finally, the man who is trying to wake Belushi summons a hotel security guard, and the guard unlocks the door to Belushi's room—only to find that the door is chained shut. So, the guard finds a metal tool, reaches inside the door's narrow opening, and removes the chain lock from the inside wall. Belushi still sleeps. The security guard and the man looking for Belushi walk over to the bed and shake him awake. Belushi says good morning.

John had clearly, and impressively, pissed off the columnist. But the resulting article praised the actor and the film. "Chicago loved the movie," Sean Daniel recalled, "and that meant the world to John."

Back in New York, John approached Paul Shaffer. "We want you," he said.

"To play piano on the record?" He knew the Blues Brothers were about to make one.

"No, to be our band's musical director."

Shaffer politely reminded John that he had no band.

"We'll put one together. You and me."

John, Shaffer, and Dan assembled a band. Or tried to. "John was becoming a movie star that very week," Shaffer said. "I'd go to his apartment every day, and he'd have to keep taking calls and giving interviews. Not much got accomplished."

The first hire was Steve Jordan, the *SNL* drummer. The Brothers tapped *SNL* saxophonist Lou Marini and trombonist Tom Malone. Malone recruited trumpeter Alan Rubin. They auditioned guitarists, but no one sounded sufficiently bluesy. They returned to Doc Pomus for counsel.

"I know just the guy," Pomus said: Matt "Guitar" Murphy, a blues master who had played with Howlin' Wolf. John and Dan found Murphy at a New York blues club, trading licks with Johnny Winter and James Cotton. When the dust cleared, the Brothers approached him: "Hi, I'm John and this is Danny. We're making an album. Would you like to help us make it?"

Murphy said he would be delighted. They talked about pay. John suggested $650.

"Oh, well, I think maybe it should be a little more than that," Murphy replied.

"Oh, no, no, I'm sorry," John countered. "Did I say $650? I meant $6,500."

The New York players convened at John's apartment for a band meeting. John laid out his vision in a forty-minute spiel. "OK," he said at the end. "The business meeting is over. Let's hang out."

At this, Tom Malone recalled, "John pours six Quaaludes into his hand, puts them in his mouth, takes out a bottle of Courvoisier, *glug, glug, glug, glug.* He hands me the bottle, and it's half empty."

John raised one last item of business: "Everybody has to have a middle name," like Matt "Guitar" Murphy. "If anybody can't come up with a middle name, we'll come up with one for you."

Tom Malone suggested "Bones," a name he'd picked up in high school. Marini said, "How about 'Blue' Lou Marini?"

Matt "Guitar" Murphy played lead. Paul "Shiv" Shaffer thought the band should hire a rhythm guitarist, someone to play licks in the grand Stax Records tradition of Sam and Dave.

Tom "Bones" Malone offered, "I've been playing in this band with Levon Helm. Steve Cropper and Duck Dunn play with us, and they're both available."

Steve "The Colonel" Cropper and Donald "Duck" Dunn were the guitarist and bassist, respectively, for the legendary Stax house band. John didn't know them, but the pair had helped create the sound he and Dan sought to emulate in the Blues Brothers. John made some phone calls and, after convincing Cropper and Dunn he was the real Belushi, snagged the two Memphis legends.

John himself wasn't quite a legend, but he no longer greeted the press with reverent acquiescence. When reporter Charles M. Young of *Rolling Stone* showed up to do a cover-story profile, John enlisted the writer to help him move. Young lugged boxes from the Bleecker Street apartment into the Bluesmobile, bound for a new home on Morton Street, two floors of a nineteenth-century brownstone with sixteen-foot ceilings, elegant chandeliers, and marble fireplaces. It cost $1,650 a month. Dan called it the Reich Palace.

The *Rolling Stone* writer trailed John to a sushi restaurant in Los Angeles for a celebratory dinner with John Landis. Steven Spielberg, the celebrated director, walked up wearing an *Animal House* T-shirt.

"I've seen it three times," he told Landis.

In the weeks following the Blues Brothers' debut on *SNL*, Dan and John talked about creating short films to air on the show, featuring the Brothers in character acting out various scenes. Up in Canada during summer break, Dan fleshed out a backstory for Jake and Elwood Blues. For Dan, fully occupying a character, disappearing into a role, meant scripting a creation story, even if it remained inside his head.

One late-summer day, John and Dan telephoned Sean Daniel at Universal. *SNL* made short films. Universal made long ones.

Elwood, not Dan, took the receiver. He told Daniel the legend of the Blues Brothers: two orphans on a quest to reunite their band and raise $5,000 to save their orphanage. Elwood called it a "mission from God."

"Sounds like a movie to me," Daniel said.

Animal House remained box-office gold. Word had spread through Hollywood of a possible Blues Brothers film. Every studio wanted it. "It was on me to make sure it was made at Universal Studios," Daniel recalled.

"We're doing this," Daniel told Elwood. "Don't go anywhere." Bernie Brillstein took the phone and closed the deal.

Daniel telephoned Ned Tanen, now the film-division president. "Belushi, Aykroyd, Blues Brothers. How about it?"

"Great," Tanen replied. "Wait'll Wasserman hears this." The last line he said with a mischievous cackle, because both he and Daniel knew any film that starred the Blues Brothers was going to be trouble.

If anything came of the breathless negotiations, this would be the first *Saturday Night Live* film. Lorne Michaels would have seemed the natural choice for executive producer, responsible for shepherding the project to the screen. But John and Dan told Bernie Brillstein they wanted him.

The Brothers' decision "was nothing against Lorne," recalled Brillstein, who managed all three men. "Lorne had always been the boss, but this was their way of symbolically leaving home. John and Danny wanted to be in control, and this was their shot."

Not long after, Dan telephoned Thom Mount and Sean Daniel at Universal.

"OK, here's the problem," Dan said. "We've got to save the orphanage."

"OK," Mount replied. "A tried-and-true trope."

"First, the Blues Brothers have to get out of jail. And then, the Blues Brothers have to get the band back together. But no one wants them to do that: the wives, the girlfriends, the cops."

Someone had to write the Blues Brothers story. Dan was already mapping it out in his head. The time had come for field research.

"I need some cash," he instructed.

"We can get you an advance," Daniel replied. They settled on $20,000, an advance on a screen-writing fee, not for a short film, but for a full-length motion picture.

"I need a remaindered California Highway Patrol car."

"OK," Mount replied. "We can get one of those."

"I might need two or three months on the road, but I'll bring back a script."

John and Dan booked studio space for a week of Blues Brothers rehearsals for the Universal Amphitheatre shows. Word came down that Atlantic Records had balked at covering the spread between their advance and the cost of rehearsing and performing the album. "We were looking at spending between $150,000 and $200,000 in the space of a month, which was more than John had made from two years of *SNL*, *Goin' South* and *Animal House* combined," Judy said. The couple invested $50,000 of their own funds.

For the first full band meeting, John and Mitch Glazer decorated the courtyard of John's Morton Street apartment. "It was like date night," Glazer said. "John was gonna pitch the idea of doing the movie."

If Steve Cropper and the others harbored any doubts of Belushi's sincerity, they melted away when the band reached the Vault, John's soundproof studio. "He had the best collection of blues I had ever seen in my life," Cropper recalled. Glazer put on a compilation of Stax Records songs, serenading the rhythm section that had played on most of them.

Rehearsals commenced at the start of September. This was Jake and Elwood's first time playing with Matt "Guitar" Murphy, Cropper, and Dunn, all rhythm-and-blues royalty. When the Colonel arrived at the studio, Dunn pulled him aside. "You're gonna have to help these guys," he said. "They're doing a bunch of blues songs that'll never sell."

Dan and John had populated a set list with old and old-sounding rhythm-and-blues songs, including "Hey Bartender," "Flip, Flop and Fly," and "I Don't Know," all from the 1950s.

At the session's end, the Colonel turned to John and said, "How 'bout doing something people can dance to? How about Sam and Dave?"

"Give me a song," John said.

"How about 'Soul Man'?"

They played it. "Man, that was great," John said at the end. "But it's too high for me." The musicians dropped the key from G to E, lowering the vocals into John's narrow range.

The professionals coached the amateurs, telling John how to time the lyrics so they fit within the beat of the song, teaching him dynamics, soft and loud, and how to draw out a note.

"At the beginning," Dan said, "it was mainly John's burden and John's bag to carry, because he had the bulk of the vocals." As the week progressed, Dan found spaces in the songs for harp solos, dance moves, and his own brand of swooping, glissando background vocals, sliding down the scale, masking his own insecurity as a singer.

On the third night of rehearsals, the horns arrived. Most of the musicians already knew each other through the RCO All-Stars. Still, the gathering seemed ripe for a clash of cultures and egos, pitting a mostly self-taught southern rhythm section against a New York horn section that read charts. Alan "Mr. Fabulous" Rubin, the trumpeter, had studied at Juilliard.

And then they started playing. "There was something about this combination of such disparate elements, Duck and Steve's Memphis shit, the horn section," Marini said. "There'd never been a horn section like that in a band like this. It was just razor-sharp." Curious celebrities and top-drawer musicians came and went from the sessions.

"They were flipping out," Marini said. "After a couple of nights with the horn section there, we realized that this was more than just a casual, fun gig."

Between songs, John and Dan taught the musicians the story of the Blues Brothers. Judy worked as a roadie, booking studio time, renting gear, purchasing plane tickets, and reserving hotel suites. By night, the gang "threw ideas around, listened to blues records until our ears bled, and then scoured the city for even more inspiration," Judy said. "I designed a logo for the band and ordered T-shirts, buttons and everything a band should have. A day or so before the first show," scheduled for September 9, "somebody called and told me it had all been delivered. I drove over to the amphitheater. By the time I got there, every last bit of it had already been stolen: 'liberated' would actually be the better term." Judy ordered more.

John prepared for the Los Angeles shows with a stay at La Costa, the luxury resort and spa near San Diego. Landis joined him. They spent lavishly on herbal wraps, massages, and facials. John also brought $1,000 worth of cocaine, which Landis discovered and discarded. John howled.

One night at the spa, they ran into William Holden, the aging star of *Sunset Boulevard*. Holden treated his young colleagues to a Norma Desmond–size rant about the Hollywood press.

"They'll hate you if you die in your sleep," he growled. "You know why? Because it's bad copy."

The day before the first Universal Amphitheatre performance, Dan was still sweating the details, playing Mr. Careful to John's Mr. Fuck It. "The glasses are crucial, man," he lectured John, who was soaking in a hot tub in the house the Brothers had rented in a canyon. "The band has got to have the right look or the whole thing won't work." Dan waved a pair of Wayfarers in the air as John sank deeper into the tub.

"There's nothing to do anymore," John replied. "The band's as tight as it can get, and all this other bullshit is gonna have to come together without me."

Inside, Judy and a friend sorted through a stack of black suits and white shirts. Dan asked, "Where's the handcuffs and the briefcase?"

On the morning of September 9, John Landis wed Deborah Nadoolman, his longtime girlfriend, in a small ceremony at their home. After exchanging vows, the couple hosted a reception for John and Dan, other friends and loved ones, and most of the band. "I learned one thing," Landis said. "Never be the host of your own wedding." That night, the happy but exhausted couple took their parents to see the Blues Brothers.

An hour before the show, John and Dan sat in their trailer at the venue. "I want a chili dog," John pleaded. An aide suggested he graze the trays of fresh fruit and vegetables in Steve Martin's dressing room. "You don't understand. I need a chili dog," John replied. "Carrots won't put me in the right mood."

Dan sat quietly at a fake-walnut Formica table, testing his handcuffs, resetting his digital watch, arranging his harps inside the black briefcase, pulling out a battered microphone. "Jagger used this on 'Honky Tonk Women,'" he told his guests.

The lights dimmed. The capacity crowd exhaled a collective roar. The musicians took the stage. Paul Shaffer counted in "I Can't Turn You Loose," the Otis Redding hit. Dan summoned his radio-pitchman baritone and spoke from the wings:

"Well, here it is, the late 1970s going on 1985. You know so much of the music we hear today is preprogrammed electronic disco. You never get a chance to hear master bluesmen practicing their craft anymore. By the year 2006, the music known today as the blues will exist only in the classical records department in your local public library. So tonight, ladies and gentlemen, while we still can, let us welcome, from Rock Island, Illinois, the blues band of 'Joliet' Jake and Elwood Blues, the Blues Brothers!"

Dan strolled out. John bounded from the wings in a triple cartwheel. Five thousand fans leapt to their feet, and suddenly, everyone knew Steve Martin's opening act was no joke.

Chapter 17

Briefcase Full of Blues

M ANY IN THE SOLD-OUT Universal Amphitheatre audience had arrived with gag arrows through their heads in totemic tribute to the headliner, the hottest comedy act in America. Yet, for forty minutes on that September night, the crowd forgot all about Steve Martin. The Blues Brothers played their parts to perfection, transfixing patrons with reverent dance moves John choreographed over the churning rhythms of the world's finest Memphis soul band.

"Blue" Lou Marini stood near the edge of the stage. "And I'm out there looking at Jack Nicholson," he said. "And we're playing '"B" Movie Box Car Blues.' And he looked up at me, and he lifted up his sunglasses, and he went, 'Wow.'"

After the set, the first in a nine-day residency, the scene backstage unfolded like a rock 'n' roll dream. Dan and John pulled drummer Steve Jordan into their trailer and popped a bottle of Dom Perignon. A knock sounded at the door, and Mick Jagger and Linda Ronstadt walked in. Jackson Browne, Joe Cocker, and Henry Winkler milled around outside. Walter Matthau pocketed a Blues Brothers button for his kid.

John and Dan talked with Mitch Glazer about the Blues Brothers movie script. John wanted Dan to write it with Glazer, who was working on a second *Crawdaddy* article that told the Brothers' backstory. "But I didn't have the confidence, really," Glazer said. He demurred.

Two days later, in the *Los Angeles Times*, rock-music critic Robert Hilburn paid John and Dan the respect of covering them as a serious act, "a lively, surprisingly authentic tribute to the spirited blues style of people like Muddy Waters and the R & B flash of Sam and Dave." He even praised John's singing, "a gruff, intense vocal style that is able to convey both the plaintive and mocking undercurrents of the blues."

Overnight, Dan and John had risen a step on the ladder of fame. Hugh Hefner invited them to the Playboy Mansion. When the boys realized the offer did not include the band, they turned it down. A procession of Hollywood directors filed into the amphitheater to pitch film roles. John's parents turned up from Chicago. He assigned Bernie Brillstein to babysit them. Agnes Belushi beamed with stage-mom pride, acting, by one account, "as if John were an eight-year-old boy who had just tap-danced in an amateur show." She pressed Brillstein for complimentary tickets and limousine service to hot Hollywood shows. John told Brillstein he would cover the costs, happy to distract her. Adam Belushi mostly sat quiet, asking only whether John was "a good boy." Yes, of course, Brillstein replied.

Every night onstage, John would scale the scaffolding that held the stage lights and "make it down, twenty-four bars later, in time to sing," Paul Shaffer said. John almost seemed to be acting out the climbing-the-towers episode at Woodstock that he had mocked in *Lemmings*. "It didn't look safe."

But the amphitheater run went off without a real hitch. The biggest scare came on the night someone in the sound booth took a telephone call and heard a familiar voice: *This is Bob. Could you turn it down a little?* Bob Hope owned a sprawling estate near the Universal lot. The band turned it down.

During the Universal residency, John, Sean Daniel, and Landis attended a screening of *Throne of Blood*, the Akira Kurosawa classic. They sat in the back row. John contributed the occasional samurai grunt, but his heart wasn't in it. He had contracted laryngitis from overtaxing his vocal cords. He seemed preoccupied. Every so often, a silent red light blinked to summon him away for a telephone call.

At the film's end, John headed to a food stand outside the Universal lot for a chili dog, accompanied by Mitch Glazer, who was preparing his Blues Brothers article.

"It is a smog-brown late afternoon," Glazer wrote. "John has a strange, contained smile on his face, as if he's eaten a laugh track. Finally, he stops at an overpass that bridges a rusty trickle of water."

"I got the Spielberg movie," John said. He had scored a small but lucrative part in the *Jaws* director's next film. "I think this means I'm set. I mean, I don't ever have to worry about money again."

John leaned over the concrete wall and gazed down at the Los Angeles River.

"It's an old tradition to throw a penny in there for luck," Glazer said. "Belushi reaches into his pocket and pulls out a crumpled $20 bill. His eyebrow arches, and a close-mouthed smile curves across his face. Cars shoot by on the freeway, exhaust whipping our jackets."

"Thank you, LA," John said softly, ripping the bill into confetti and tossing it over the wall. "Thank you, Hollywood."

Jaws, released a few months before the 1975 debut of *Saturday Night*, had performed well enough to coin a new Hollywood term, "summer blockbuster." The film eventually reaped nearly $500 million at the box office and reigned as the highest-grossing film until *Star Wars*, the 1977 summer blockbuster. Spielberg's next project, *Close Encounters of the Third Kind*, ranked second in ticket sales that year.

Now, Spielberg wanted Belushi for his World War II film. He decided against casting a white actor as a Japanese submarine commander, despite his fondness for John's samurai stylings. He told Bernie Brillstein he wanted John instead to play Wild Bill Kelso, a crazy, cigar-chomping bomber pilot. With the success of *Animal House,* John's asking price had risen tenfold, to $350,000. Spielberg was ready to pay.

After reading the script for *1941*, Brillstein urged John to pass. It wasn't funny.

"I can't turn down Spielberg," John replied.

A few weeks later, Spielberg visited John and Dan in Los Angeles.

"I want you to meet Sergeant Tree, tank commander," John announced, pushing Dan forward. He wanted Spielberg to cast Dan for the part of a patriotic army sergeant. On cue, Dan rattled off obscure data on military hardware. Spielberg loved it.

* * *

By its fourth season, *Saturday Night Live* routinely drew a thirty-nine share in the ratings, meaning that two-fifths of the available television audience tuned in. Factor in public viewings in dorms and bars, and perhaps twenty-five million Americans watched *SNL*. Much of the bump came from *Animal House*, which would close out 1978 as the highest-grossing comedy film to date, earning $120 million on a $3 million final budget.

If the King Tut episode in season three had marked the artistic apex of *SNL*, the season-four premiere probably brought the show closest to the center of American popular culture.

A few years earlier, Lorne Michaels had made tongue-in-cheek overtures to the Beatles. In the autumn of 1978, Michaels landed the second-greatest act in the rock pantheon, the Rolling Stones, as hosts and musical guests. The Stones were riding a wave of artistic resurgence powered by a splendid comeback album, *Some Girls*.

The Stones spent the week of October 7 partying and practicing. They rehearsed at a studio on West Fifty-Second Street, with besotted *SNL* staffers at their feet. After hours, some of them assembled at the Reich Palace to jam with John and Judy in the Vault. The musicians turned up late at Studio 8H on Friday night, arriving with an arsenal of vodka, scotch, and cocaine. They were late again on Saturday. Only Mick Jagger seemed to grasp how the program worked. The writers risked casting him in a few sketches. They cut Keith Richards when he missed an entrance in one sketch and failed to remember the one line he had been assigned in another.

The band tried to tweak the studio audience to its specifications, instructing in a memo, "No sophisticated 'Elaine's,' Upper East-Siders, no moms and pops, no show-biz folks." Sophisticates and showbiz folks turned up anyway. A network censor apprised an *SNL* costume designer that Mick's tight trousers revealed too much of the append-age they strained to conceal. The wardrobe woman replied, "If you want to go up to Mick Jagger and tell him he has to wear underwear, be my guest."

The opening monologue fell to Ed Koch, mayor of New York. Koch presented a certificate of merit to Belushi, "a great New Yorker." This was the writing staff needling John over his dizzying rise. John took the stage in jeans beneath a black Blues Brothers jacket and tie.

"This is a very nice certificate of merit," John said haltingly. "I could put it on my wall. It'll . . . Mr. Mayor, is this it? This piece of paper here? I mean, isn't there a key to the city or something? I mean, Dolly Parton got a key to the city, you remember?"

"John," Koch replied, "the key to the city is a different kind of honor."

"Yeah, it's a bigger honor. You know? I mean, I lived here for six years, you know? A blonde with a rack rolls in from Nashville and you give her the key to the city. She lives in LA, in a trailer. Was she in a movie? I mean, *Animal House* has made sixty million dollars, you know?" Applause. "Sixty million dollars? Does New York have sixty million dollars?" John's voice rose. "Sixty million dollars for . . . Universal Studios. That's right. And you know what I got out of it? Nine hundred bucks."

John ranted on. "I could have stayed in Hollywood, taken all those big offers, had a house on Mulholland Drive. But nooooooo." Cheers. "I gotta stay here, come back to New York City and work for these late-night TV wages. Four hundred and fifty bucks a show. That's how much we get. You know how much they get on *Laverne and Shirley*?"

Once again, Michaels and his writers drew inspiration from real life. John was heading off to make another movie and taking Dan with him. Bill Murray was making his first big film, *Meatballs*, a summer-camp comedy. Laraine Newman was starring in *American Hot Wax*. Garrett Morris was mulling a Broadway show. Gilda Radner had many courters. Michaels stood to lose his cast.

"I've encouraged them all to do other things," Michaels told a *Newsweek* reporter, "but it's the scale of them that concerns me now."

All week, the network had feared the Stones might say or do something untoward. In the end, the lone breach of taste came from Dan. A sketch cast him as a refrigerator repairman summoned to the home of the Nerds, a family of chess-club types. Dan's repairman arrived wearing a comically tight T-shirt. When he turned around, low-slung pants revealed half of his bare buttocks.

"The moon came out surprisingly early," Bill Murray observed.

"No wisecracks," Gilda Radner chided.

Rosie Shuster had written the sketch with Anne Beatts. She and Dan were still dating, and the relationship would inspire several memorable *SNL* scenes.

"Danny used to do that at home sometimes," she said of the plumber scene. "He would be down fixing something at ground level, and he had this extraordinary, footlong moon."

The censors ordered Dan not to tuck his pencil into his butt crack for comic effect. Naturally, he did.

Three years earlier, *New York* magazine had sent John's ego into a tailspin with a cover story on Chevy Chase. In October 1978, *Newsweek* put John on its cover. The photo pictured Bluto in a toga, a laurel wreathing his head.

"Eleven years ago, in 'The Graduate,' Dustin Hoffman proved that a movie leading man need not be tall, chiseled and dashing," *Newsweek* opined. "Now John Belushi has demonstrated that he can even be a slob."

John offered, "My characters say it's okay to screw up," explaining both his own fame and the broader allure of *Animal House.* "People don't have to be perfect. They don't have to be real smart. They don't have to follow the rules. They can have fun."

John Landis chimed in with prophetic candor: "If he doesn't burn himself out, his potential is unlimited."

The cover of *Newsweek*, with a circulation of nearly three million, ranked not far behind the cover of *Time* in gravitas. In Studio 8H, the spotlight shone ever brighter on John, who still could not tolerate its glare.

With ratings soaring, *SNL* would finally turn a profit in season four. Michaels's salary jumped to more than $750,000. Performers earned roughly $200,000. Agents and studio executives dropped by the seventeenth floor to pitch film deals. Wine, flowers, and gourmet food adorned the weekly read-throughs. Network contractors expanded offices and outfitted them with new furniture, carpeting, air-conditioning, and track lighting.

Egos swelled apace. Lowly production assistants found they were no longer permitted to speak to performers. Cast members who had once curried favor with the press now rebuffed interviews.

Bernie Brillstein went to see Thom Mount at Universal. He asked the studio to give John a retroactive percentage of the *Animal House* profits, reminding him that Universal had paid him only $35,000. Mount said no. In that case, Brillstein countered, how about a bonus? All right, Mount replied, but he wanted a three-film commitment from John. Universal would pay $350,000 for the first project, *1941*, $500,000 for the second, and $750,000 for the third. Fine, Brillstein replied, but what about the bonus? Mount balked.

"I'll go out for ten minutes," Brillstein said. "Give me your best shot."

Brillstein telephoned John for his thoughts. Whatever the amount, John said, get the check today. Brillstein returned to the meeting room. Mount offered $250,000. The full deal, announced in a November press release, would deliver $1.85 million to John and Judy.

Everyone at Universal assumed the second film in John's new Universal deal, with the attendant $500,000 paycheck, would star the Blues Brothers. Mitch Glazer's demurral left Dan to tell that story alone. Dan had read the occasional film script, but he had never written one.

More than ever, Dan and John needed somewhere to blow off steam, an address far from 30 Rock and the nightclub throngs. They scouted locations for a new 505 Club, the Toronto speakeasy Dan had set up as an after-hours crash pad for Second City friends. By lucky chance, Dan had just found space to store his growing motorcycle collection, in the basement of a four-story tenement at Hudson and Dominick Streets, near the Holland Tunnel. "Then it took us only about a week to realize, 'Hey, this would be a great place for a party,'" he said.

When John and Dan showed up to inspect the property, no one had the key. John crushed the doorknob with a cinder block. Behind the steel door, they found a fetid, black-windowed space framed by peeling wallpaper, with wet floors and a truly frightening toilet. "It was such a shithole that it took my breath away, literally," Glazer recalled.

Dan converted the Lovecraftian dwelling into another illicit club, a place for cast, crew, host, musical guests, and celebrity friends to gather after Lorne Michaels's after-parties. He stocked the jukebox with singles from Bleecker Bob's Records. He planted a red plastic rose inside the foul women's room.

John hated playing in drag. Perhaps as an act of spite, Lorne Michaels persuaded him to appear on Weekend Update in cruel mockery of Elizabeth Taylor after the actress had drawn mirthful headlines for choking on a chicken bone. The November 11 episode, poking at Taylor for struggles with her weight, tickled the more mean-spirited *SNL* writers.

Bill Murray introduced the bit by touting Liz as the actress "whose face has set the standard for screen beauty for so many years." John appeared, wearing a beehive wig, chandelier earrings, and a black lace dress and gnawing on an enormous chicken leg. Murray cooed, "I don't care how much you weigh, just so your cheeks don't puff up over those beautiful violet eyes that I've been in love with since *National Velvet*."

Just as Murray asked, "Will there be a *Cleopatra II*?" John gagged, eyes bulging, hands on his throat, teetering in his chair, beehive bouncing atop his head. He gave himself the Heimlich maneuver. Chicken flew from his mouth.

The Blues Bar opened that night. Keith Richards and Francis Ford Coppola tended bar. The Grateful Dead raised glasses with the cast. Drinks were free, and a small stage beckoned. Here, John and Dan could play out their Blues Brothers fantasies, performing blues standards with a pickup band that might include David Bowie, James Taylor, or members of ZZ Top for an intimate audience of elite friends. Every weekend, the Blues Bar filled up with A-list celebrities while fending off the army of music-industry executives, agents and publicists, paparazzi and press who buzzed around *SNL*. Dan often doubled as bartender and bouncer. One Monday, he showed up at 30 Rock with a black eye.

Reporters pressed in on John like never before, revealing little embarrassments that only seemed to enhance his fame. A *Daily News* reporter shadowed John and Dan on the week of the November 18 episode, featuring *Star Wars* princess Carrie Fisher and the return of the

Blues Brothers. The reporter captured an ugly run-in between John and a photographer. "Get that fucking thing outta my face before I break it over your head," John screamed, before Dan seized him in a bear hug and pulled him back. Sometime later, the reporter watched John sneak up behind a young woman on the set and nip at the back of her jeans. She shrieked. "Sorry," he said.

"He's basically a sweet person who is very sorry for much of what he does," John Landis offered.

"John is his own worst salesman," Lorne Michaels observed.

"John scares the hell out of me all the time," Dan said. "But even at his worst, he's lovable."

Ten minutes before air, Michaels ducked into the dressing room where Dan and John straightened their Blues Brothers ties. "John, it's cut," he said.

"What?"

"The Blues Brothers. It's cut."

"Why, you . . ." John lunged. Michaels laughed and slammed the door.

Quite the contrary: the November 18 episode unfolded like a promotional video for the Blues Brothers LP, titled *Briefcase Full of Blues* and slotted for release ten days later. Soon, John and Dan would be competing with other *SNL* musical guests in the record racks.

The show opened with the tight rhythms of the Blues Brothers band, everyone wearing sunglasses. Garrett Morris introduced Jake and Elwood, "direct from a statewide automobile tour of Illinois and Indiana." John and Dan strode coolly onstage, looking measurably more confident than in their *SNL* debut a few months earlier. John produced a key on a chain and ceremonially unlocked Dan's handcuffed hand from his black leather valise. Dan opened the case and produced his harmonica, as John snapped his fingers and chewed gum. The band halted. John turned a nimble cartwheel. The musicians launched into "Soul Man," and the Brothers exploded in dance.

This was the act that had brought the Universal Amphitheatre throngs to their feet, John's good-enough singing and the Brothers' electric moves backed by a pitch-perfect Memphis soul revue. In mid-song, the band added four extra bars for Dan to take a brief harp solo. It wasn't half bad.

After "Weekend Update," the Brothers returned for two more tunes. The first, "(I Got Everything I Need) Almost," paid tribute to the Downchild Blues Band, the white Toronto blues outfit whose songs had caught John's attention the first time he walked into Dan's 505 Club. Dan stood a pace or two behind John, at his right, his comfort zone, blowing harmonica fills, joining his partner in a little dance at the musical break. The second number, "'B' Movie Box Car Blues," showcased the dueling guitars of Steve Cropper and Matt "Guitar" Murphy in a song penned by Delbert McClinton, the white Texas bluesman. The brisk vocals taxed John's limited powers of intonation, but this was a showcase for the band. Midway through, the Brothers actually lay down onstage to allow a clear view of the musicians, who charged into a double-time boogie workout. Then the Brothers rose and jitterbugged in jubilation. The set closed with John locking the cuffs back on Dan's hands as the band played an outro in the anachronistic style of an R & B showcase.

Shared love for partying probably fueled the backstage friendship that blossomed between John and Carrie Fisher.

"Everyone was completely loaded in those days, but at that point it was really fun and no one was really scared about it yet," Fisher recalled. "John wanted me to date Danny so that we could hang out more. I was about twenty-one and dating Paul Simon at the time, and Danny was living with Rosie Shuster. But John thought that we would be a good couple and we could all have fun together. So, he invited me down to his house in the Village, and then he invited Danny over to join us, and then he passed out. That was his version of a blind date."

Dan and Fisher commenced "this clandestine affair where we would meet in parking lots and make out," Fisher said. "That was John's favorite thing ever. In getting Danny and me to have the affair, he got to be part of it."

John's matchmaking also complicated the romantic lives of Rosie Shuster and Paul Simon, two of Lorne Michaels's closest friends, at a time when John's own rapport with the *SNL* boss was wearing thin.

With money pouring in, the Blues Brothers opened a business office on Fifth Avenue in the Flatiron district, with a secretary, a lounge, and a reception area designed like a travel agency to throw off groupies and autograph seekers.

"Every day John was in town, he'd storm into the office barking, 'Get me the Jenkins file. Please!' Then he'd burst out laughing," said Karen Krenitsky, the secretary. "Besides being John and Danny's official business headquarters, it was also kind of a clubhouse where their friends could drop by and a museum where they could display all their memorabilia. The work part was a little crazy. You were never sure where to locate John. You were never sure John was going to make a plane when you booked it. You were never sure he'd make it to his hotel room when the plane landed."

Briefcase Full of Blues dropped around Thanksgiving. John and Dan had rejected record-company pleas to put their names on the cover. They remained in character, offering "very special thanks to Dan Aykroyd and John Belushi" in small print on the back. The first pressing of fifty thousand copies sold out in a week. By early 1979, the album was climbing toward the top of the *Billboard 200* album chart. Neither of the two postwar blues giants, B.B. King or Muddy Waters, had cracked the top twenty.

"Disco was on its way out. That's what you have to remember," Dan said. "Disco was dying and New Wave hadn't started yet. There was nothing on the radio."

The top ranks of the *Billboard 200* in February 1979 revealed a bewildering jumble of consumer tastes. Billy Joel, a politely rocking singer-songwriter, vied for supremacy with crooners Neil Diamond, Barry Manilow, and Barbra Streisand; funk masters Chic and Earth, Wind and Fire; and Rod Stewart in his own regrettable disco phase.

Music critics had indulged Dan and John through their Universal stand and occasional *SNL* appearances. Most of them greeted the new Blues Brothers album with surprising goodwill, a testament to the currency *SNL* still enjoyed in the counterculture.

John's powerful onstage presence didn't translate well to disc. But Bob Tischler had captured superb performances from the backing band. Cropper and company "were so good," Tischler said, that he could splice together song snippets from any of the nine nights. They fit perfectly, because the musicians played every song to metronomic precision, every night. The producer recalled only one significant mixing-board edit. In the Sam and Dave classic "Soul Man," John had impishly changed "give you hope" to "give you dope." Tischler made him change it back.

"Their genius lies not in an ability to surpass or even rival the classic material they choose to cover, but rather in the unpretentious sense of fun with which they imbue each song," Timothy White wrote in *Rolling Stone*.

"The studio-superstar backup band isn't exactly long on personality, but it rocks, and almost every song ranks as an under-recorded classic," wrote Robert Christgau of the *Village Voice*, unofficial dean of rock critics.

Not all were so kind. In Chicago, hometown to Belushi and the blues, a reviewer sniffed, "Can white comedians sing colorless renditions of the blues and earn a gold record for their efforts? Apparently so."

The biggest problem with the Blues Brothers wasn't Belushi's voice or Aykroyd's chops. They were two white guys fronting a mostly white band that played historically Black music. In *Rolling Stone*, Dave Marsh theorized that the presence of Cropper and Dunn, the white Stax masters, was "the only thing keeping the Blues Brothers from slopping over into racist parody."

Across the overlapping film and music industries, the Blues Brothers, their film deal, and the million-selling album sparked backlash. A *Washington Post* writer noted that the all-star backing band, however well paid, would reap none of the royalties going to Dan and John for *Briefcase Full of Blues*, which would soon top $1 million. An executive from Alligator Records, the blues label, told the *Chicago Tribune* he had asked *Saturday Night Live* to book his artists. Someone in the music department said no—"After all, we've got the Blues Brothers." That was not what the Brothers had intended.

In New York, Duke Robillard of Roomful of Blues was still badmouthing Elwood and Jake. "Musically, it was obvious that Belushi and Aykroyd had no talent whatsoever," Duke told the *Berkeley Barb*. "We had to show Aykroyd what harp to use before each song: he didn't know the keys. That was totally unbelievable. Then we heard Belushi sing, and that was unbelievable, too."

Dan didn't like playing in drag any more than John did. For the December 9 episode of *SNL*, Franken and Davis persuaded him to play Julia Child in a sketch inspired by an actual mishap during a visit by the celebrity chef to Tom Snyder's show.

Slicing into a chicken, Dan pretended to cut into his hand. "Now I've done it," he crooned, in a falsetto that impressively echoed Child's dowdy upper-crust warble. "I've cut the dickens out of my finger."

Fake blood spurted from a concealed hose. The audience howled.

"First, we must stop the bleeding," he said, swaddling his gushing hand with his apron. "The best way is with direct pressure on the apron, like so. Now, you want to raise your hand over your head so the blood has to be pumped all the way up. Well, the apron doesn't seem to be working . . ." The segment concluded with Dan's delirious chef collapsing on the counter. Never, perhaps, had an *SNL* studio audience laughed so hard for so long.

Belushi's exploding celebrity, first with *Animal House* and now with the Blues Brothers album, set off a chain reaction of envy and emulation at *SNL*. Over the winter break, Lorne Michaels and Paul Shaffer helped Gilda Radner plan a comedy-variety record of her own, tentatively titled *Gilda Radner, Live from New York*. Friends and VIPs filed into a studio at Seventh Avenue and Fifty-Second Street for a live taping of songs and sketches, much of the material pulled from *SNL*.

Radner "was demanding parity of attention with John and Danny," one *SNL* writer observed. "It was dueling egos."

John and Dan flew to California to join Steven Spielberg on the set of *1941*. After *Jaws* and *Close Encounters*, Spielberg chose a promising script based on a brief panic in Los Angeles shortly after the Pearl Harbor attack. The director wanted to make his own *Animal House*. Under Spielberg's lead, *1941* evolved from a dark comedy into a star-studded, scenery-shredding farce. The budget swelled to $35 million, nearly twice the cost of *Close Encounters*.

John had found a role for Dan. He encouraged Spielberg to award small parts to Joe Flaherty and John Candy, standouts from the old Second City. The two performers now starred on *Second City Television*, a Canadian sketch-comedy series launched in direct response to *Saturday Night*—Bernie Sahlins was tired of losing stars to Lorne Michaels.

On the *1941* set, the Second City gang quickly surmised that Spielberg could not do comedy.

"One day he called me into his trailer, showed me a take of the scene we'd just shot and asked, 'Was that funny?'" Flaherty said. "I just stared at the screen and thought, Oh jeez, we're in trouble."

Following a familiar pattern, John found a local artist with drug connections and more or less transformed him into "Captain Preemo," drug dealer to the stars, with John as his main customer. He hung out for hours on end at the man's West Hollywood home, joined by growing ranks of *1941* cast and crew, sometimes pouring out a long line of coke on an overturned mirror and challenging someone to race him to the middle.

One December day, John pulled up to the set ninety minutes late in a car driven by Lauren Hutton, the supermodel. He could barely walk.

"You can do this to anyone else," Spielberg huffed, "but you can't do it to me." No one had ever shown up so late or so stoned to a Spielberg set.

Spielberg assigned an associate producer to babysit John. John asked her to drive him to the home of Ron Wood, the Rolling Stone, where events unfolded as one might expect. The babysitter found she could barely keep pace with her charge. One night at three a.m., she slipped out of a studio where John and Dan were jamming with the Stones. John grabbed her and asked why she was leaving so early.

Curtis Salgado, who had inspired John's blues crusade, flew down for a visit. He and John dined at a sushi restaurant. John produced a pile of Blues Brothers buttons and passed them out to fellow diners. Over dinner, John challenged Salgado to a wasabi-eating contest. John liked to pin four pieces of sushi between his thumb and forefinger and wad them into his mouth, mocking a delicate culinary ritual.

John and Judy had rented a mansion high above Sunset Boulevard in the Hollywood Hills. Salgado glimpsed a strategically placed copy of *Newsweek* on a table, the one with Belushi on the cover. John took him on a tour, showing him the hot tub adorned with three cherub statues, steaming water flowing from their penises. They paused in the kitchen, and John opened up about working with Spielberg.

"This movie has no script," John said. "I mean, they're just making it up as they go along."

Dave Thomas and Eugene Levy were writing their own script for Columbia during the *1941* shoot. At lunchtime one day, they walked over to the set to see how the boys were doing.

"And there's a thousand extras just sitting there, sitting around," Thomas said. "Spielberg's sitting on a crane camera." Thomas walked up to the director and asked what everyone was doing.

"We've been here since seven a.m.," Spielberg replied gloomily. "We're waiting for Belushi."

"Where's Danny?"

"He's looking for him."

While shooting a scene at Indian Dunes in Valencia, John slipped on morning dew and fell headfirst from the wing of a P-40 Tomahawk. "Luckily, his fall was broken," Spielberg recalled. "But unfortunately, it was broken by a human being who happened to be standing there." Both parties recovered.

Between Blues Brothers gigs, film shoots, and *SNL* episodes, Dan somehow found the time to crisscross the Upper Midwest, seeking visual inspiration for his script. Piloting a former cop car, his dream ride, Dan "basically took the trip that he wanted the Blues Brothers to take in the movie, and he took lots of photos," said Bob Weiss, a big, bearded producer who had worked with John Landis on *Kentucky Fried Movie*. Already, Universal executives were planning for Landis to direct, and Weiss to produce.

Dan returned and assembled a crude slideshow from color Xeroxes of photographs he'd snapped on the road.

"There's Joliet Prison, there's the Bluesmobile, there's the Curl Up & Dye salon, there's the bridge over the Chicago River," Weiss recalled. "Danny had a pitch that went with the slideshow. This was a very hard movie to explain. You saw that it was kind of a postmodern, soulful Midwestern odyssey."

Dan had photographed men in broad-brimmed hats and wide-lapeled suits on Maxwell Street. He had visited the Old Joliet Prison, where the fictional Jake Blues earned his nickname. Other shots showed shadowy streets beneath the Chicago "L" tracks; a late-1970s Chicago Police car; various drawbridges and swing bridges, set pieces for an epic car chase; and a giant air-raid siren that sat outside Dan's old elementary school, its cinematic value yet unknown. One shot pictured Dan himself, exiting a fleabag hotel.

"Jake" was close to John. "Elwood" came from Elwood Glover, a talk-show host whom Dan considered the most boring man on Canadian television. Jake and Elwood had grown up in the Rock City orphanage, a name that vaguely suggested Rock Island or Rockford, a pair of Illinois cities oddly named, as most of the state was pancake flat. The nuns tormented the Brothers by day. At night, they sought solace with Curtis, the Black janitor, who taught them the blues. (The boys named Curtis after Salgado.) They formed a band and crisscrossed the prairies in their jet-black Bluesmobile. Then the cops busted them, sending Jake to Joliet Prison. The band scattered to day jobs. Jake sat in his cell, dreaming of busting out and getting the band back together.

On New Year's Eve, 1978, the Blues Brothers band traveled to San Francisco for an epic show, opening for the Grateful Dead at a farewell party for Bill Graham's legendary Winterland Ballroom. John and Dan arrived in character. At this stage of their careers, neither man would answer a reporter's question unless the inquisitor directed it to Jake or Elwood. Timothy White of *Rolling Stone* tagged along and played along, eventually submitting an entire article that treated Blues Brothers fiction as fact.

Backstage, they spoke of their movie script, which Dan had half finished, under the working title "Joliet Jake." He was working off a simple treatment that John Landis had crafted from Dan's Blues Brothers backstory.

"We play ourselves," John explained. "Here's a simple synopsis: It starts with me getting out of jail after three years, and I expect the band to still be together."

"He got three years on a five-year rap," Dan broke in. "Armed robbery at a gas station."

John continued, "But anyhow, the film is about finding the band members and trying to get it all back together again."

"We hunt them down like cops, like detectives," Dan said.

Word of Dan's progress would have set off celebrations inside the Black Tower at Universal.

"Without a script, of course, we didn't know if we were gonna make a movie," Thom Mount said. "All we had was a writing deal with Danny. That was the only thing on paper. We had a development meeting every week. I would say, 'Where are we on *Blues Brothers*,' and we would all look at each other, like *Have any of us heard from Danny?*"

The Blues Brothers played a raucous hour-long set at Winterland. At the end, John took a glass of champagne from an outstretched hand. He drained it in one long gulp. John had warned the band not to eat or drink anything offered by outstretched hands. At length, John apprised Judy that he was tripping.

The group repaired to a Victorian painted lady in Haight-Ashbury, where Jefferson Starship was throwing a party in the Brothers' honor.

"God," John marveled when he arrived, looking clear-eyed and calm. "Isn't everybody dressed nice?"

Back in New York, on January 24, 1979, the couple celebrated John's thirtieth birthday, dining alone in the Reich Palace. A few days later, *Briefcase Full of Blues* reached number one on the *Billboard* album chart. John had starred in the biggest comedy film of the past year, and he anchored the most popular late-night television show in America.

Chapter 18

The Phone Book

A S A SORT OF THIRTIETH-BIRTHDAY resolution, John told Judy he would do coke "differently—not every day," she recorded in her diary. A few weeks later, Keith Richards rolled into New York. He and John embarked on a coke-fueled binge.

John arrived at Studio 8H the next day, February 24, 1979, "totally out of it, almost unable to perform," Al Franken recalled. He staggered into his dressing room, collapsed on a couch, closed his eyes, and moaned that he was too sick to go on. Someone summoned a doctor, who examined John and summoned Lorne Michaels.

The doctor said John could not perform: "His lungs are filling with fluid."

"I understand," Michaels said. "But it's only another hour and a half, and then he can rest."

"No," the doctor said. "He can't do it."

"Well, what happens if he does it?"

"He might die."

"What are the odds of that?"

"Fifty-fifty."

"I can live with those odds."

At that, John's eyebrow popped up. "He looked at me with as close to a smile as he could muster," Michaels recalled. Even near death, Belushi liked a good line.

John donned a suit and tie. Aides plied him with coffee. Just before air, NBC staffers guided him into a chair behind a desk for the cold open with Dan, Jane Curtin, Gilda Radner, and Kate Jackson, the host, a send-up of Kate's hit show, *Charlie's Angels*. The program opened to the largest television audience of the season, twenty-eight million homes.

John limped through the scene as a hoarse, pale, sweating Fred Silverman, the new NBC president. The episode would go down in *SNL* lore as John's worst. One writer recalled it as "the one and only time I ever remember John being messed up at airtime." Outside the inner circle, hardly anyone noticed.

The next day, Judy Belushi updated her diary: "John trouble."

Dan surfaced in March with another classic character, Fred Garvin, male prostitute. This one had arisen in the bedroom with Rosie Shuster, Dan role-playing as a working-class gigolo with a Chicago accent: "C'mere, little lady." He and Shuster turned the tables on an old-boys cliché in the resulting skit. Margot Kidder played a bank officer who arrived in rural Moline, Illinois, as a guest of the Great Lakes Feed and Grain Company, whose principals routinely dispatched a call girl to a visiting executive's hotel room. With the genders reversed, the befuddled men sent Fred Garvin. He arrived in a plaid sport coat and brown trilby and announced in square syllables, "I have a work order here which specifies that I am to roger you roundly till six fifteen tomorrow morning."

Two years earlier, John and Dan had more or less severed their writing partnership. Now, even Dan scarcely had time to write for *Saturday Night Live*. He was spending every free moment finishing his Blues Brothers script. "I wrote a lot of it at the Blues Bar," he remembered. "I wrote a lot of it at the farm in Canada. I wrote a lot of it at *SNL*," toiling inside his 30 Rock office. He emerged from one writing session and asked Paul Shaffer, "What's the most dramatic Catholic imagery imaginable?"

"The stigmata," Shaffer replied. Dan retreated to his desk and wrote down a character name, Sister Mary Stigmata.

Dan hired an assistant to screen calls and repel visitors. Once, the assistant screened John, and John fumed. During idle moments on the *1941* set, Dan pecked away at the script in a bungalow. John helped him with the Chicago scenes.

"I really didn't know how to write movies," Dan said. "I was told that most screenplays were 120 to 150 pages long, but when I sat down to write *Blues Brothers*, there were so many descriptive passages in there, just paragraphs and paragraphs of shots and concepts and ideas. Eventually, it kind of ballooned up."

With the script nearly finished, Dan returned to 30 Rock one day and could not find his only copy. After a frenzied search, he spotted the pages in a stack of old *SNL* scripts, headed to the shredder.

Bob Weiss had signed on to produce the *Blues Brothers* film. All involved had assumed directing duties would fall to John Landis, on the strength of *Animal House* and his rapport with Belushi.

Back in the summer of 1978, the *Blues Brothers* film "was really kind of a vanity deal," Landis said. "Universal was trying to keep John happy." No one had assigned the project a firm date. Landis started work on a Lily Tomlin film called *The Incredible Shrinking Woman*. Over the winter holiday, Universal had released *Moment by Moment*, a romantic drama starring Tomlin opposite red-hot John Travolta. *Moment by Moment* died at the box office, poisoning both actors' prospects.

Inside the Black Tower, Sean Daniel had lobbied Ned Tanen for weeks to forget *The Incredible Shrinking Woman* and redeploy Landis on *The Blues Brothers*. When the receipts came in for Tomlin's flop, he saw the opportunity.

Tanen telephoned Landis in early February with an update on *The Incredible Shrinking Woman*. "Your budget was $12 million," he growled. "It's now $3 million." Landis had already spent nearly $1 million on costumes and sets. He said he could not make the film for that sum. "All right, then, we're shutting it down," Tanen replied.

"I think Ned wanted me to say, 'It can't be done,'" Landis reflected. The director obliged. In the press, Tanen blamed Landis and his waxing ambitions: "We didn't want it to turn into 'Close Encounters of the Fifth Kind.'"

Landis was free. Two days later, Tanen telephoned again. "Can you get *The Blues Brothers* done by August?" August lay a half year away—impossible.

"Sure," Landis replied. On March 14, 1979, *Variety* announced that Landis would direct *The Blues Brothers*. His salary would be $625,000.

* * *

In late March, Bob Weiss took an anonymous phone call. "Be on your property tonight," the caller said, then hung up.

"It had the tone of a ransom call," Weiss said. He recognized the voice.

Some hours later, Weiss heard something land in his yard with a concussive thud, a sound "equivalent to, I'd say, five copies of the Sunday *Times*," he said. Weiss walked outside and found a thick parcel wrapped in the cover of a Los Angeles telephone book. Inside, he found Dan's script, dated March 22 and titled *The Return of the Blues Brothers*. The credit line read, "Scriptatran GL-9000." He telephoned Sean Daniel.

"The good news is, the first draft finally got here," Weiss said. "The bad news is, it's 324 pages. We have a lot of work to do."

Dan also dropped off copies at the homes of Landis and Daniel, each one wrapped inside the cover of a different telephone book. "It was classic Aykroyd," Daniel said.

Inside the Black Tower, Thom Mount tore through the massive tome. As a rule of thumb, one script page translates to a minute on film. At 324 pages, Dan had written more than five hours' worth of movie. He had, in fact, written enough for two movies. He had scripted long narratives for every musician in the Blues Brothers band.

"The characters were wonderful, the scenes were great, the ideas were fabulous," Mount said. And yet, "with all the insane flying-through-the-air cars and destruction of property, the movie was not going to be cheap."

The screenplay opened with a Blues Brothers concert at a hotel in fictional Falls End, Wisconsin, in the summer of 1982. From there, it leapt forward to Jake's release from prison, a few years later.

Many familiar scenes are already here, albeit in elongated form, and with names and plot points that would change in later drafts. Jake walks out of Stateville Prison, not Joliet. Elwood jumps a bridge, and then another, and another, to impress his brother with the new Bluesmobile. The Brothers visit the Penguin and learn that her orphanage owes delinquent taxes. Jake tells her she's up shit creek. She swats them with her ruler. They stop at the Triple Rock Church, but no epiphany comes to Jake inside. Two cops pull the Brothers over, triggering the first of many car chases. The pursuit careens onto a country-club golf course, setting up a gag involving the Bluesmobile and a groundhog, a sight that would have prompted quizzical comparisons to a competing film from the *National Lampoon* gang, had it wound up in *The Blues Brothers*. The boys escape to Elwood's fleabag apartment. They track down "Guitar" Matt on Maxwell Street, but not in a diner. They find their keyboard man at a cheesy Ramada Inn, fronting a band named Paul and the Plushtones. They buttonhole Mister Fabulous at a swanky downtown restaurant. They stop at the propellant plant where Elwood works. Jake's jilted lover stalks them with an anti-tank gun. Those scenes, and a few others, eat up 120 pages of script, enough for an entire film. And Dan had written two hundred pages more.

Mount asked Landis what he thought of Dan's script. "It's daunting," Landis replied.

"Do you think we can get it made?"

"Yes," the director replied. He set about sculpting Dan's phone book into something filmable.

One week in LA, still working on *1941,* John developed an ear infection. A doctor advised him not to fly. John feared Lorne Michaels might fire him. The telegram he sent on April 4 to announce his absence did not help his case. He addressed it to "cast and crew of Saturday Night Live and some of the writers," implying ill will toward the others. He closed, "I miss almost all of you."

John asked Spielberg and Landis to film something he could send to Michaels in consolation for his absence. "He wrote this little sketch," Landis said. "We shot it up at Steven Spielberg's pool. It was John lounging with all these playmates in bikinis, eating sushi out in the gorgeous sunshine, holding up a doctor's note, saying, 'I'd really like to be there for the show, but . . .' Meanwhile, it was freezing in New York. I think it pissed them off even more."

Ironic or not, John's film had given Michaels the finger. He responded in kind: the segment never aired on *SNL*.

The rift refused to heal. By the season four finale of *Saturday Night Live*, on May 26, John's departure seemed scripted. "I think probably John won't be back," Michaels told Tom Shales of the *Washington Post*.

Summer arrived, and John's future remained unsettled. "Whatever Belushi decides, I'll abide by his wishes," Michaels told the *Daily News*. He added a passive-aggressive note: "The success of 'Animal House' and the Blues Brothers has caused enormous confusion in John's life." The columnist reached John on Martha's Vineyard. "When I have something to announce, I'll call you," John said.

On June 15, John and Judy returned to New York for a momentous meeting with the Blues Brothers band. John gathered the musicians and announced he was stepping down as bandleader. The Blues Brothers belonged to Universal now. John and Judy circled back to Martha's Vineyard and stayed until month's end, attending parties and digging oysters as they awaited a July 1 flight to Chicago to start work on the film.

On June 28, Gilda Radner's birthday, Paul Shaffer and Howard Shore flew to the Hamptons in a chartered plane. They arrived at a small gathering at Michaels's house with a surprise birthday present: the master tape of Radner's album. The rising currency of the Blues Brothers had infected Radner's project. Someone suggested adapting the album into a Broadway show and then a movie.

The rivalry cut both ways. John had begged Paul Shaffer not to work with Radner. One night at *SNL*, he had grabbed Bob Tischler, his record producer, and thrown him against a wall, hissing, "You're not doing the Gilda album. It's going to be a piece of shit." Tischler was committed to producing both acts.

Michaels's listening party soon soured. The record sounded half-baked. Radner locked herself in a bedroom, disconsolate. The group talked of recording her show again in a Broadway theater.

That afternoon, Bernie Brillstein telephoned Paul Shaffer. "Lorne will do anything not to have you in Chicago next week," he said. Shaffer had planned to fly to Chicago to start work on *The Blues Brothers*. Brillstein represented both John and Radner. Shaffer, too, had loyalties to both performers. He would have to choose. He loved leading the Blues Brothers band, but the role put him in conflict with Belushi, the band's brightest star. Some nights on the Universal Amphitheatre stage, John had introduced Shaffer as the musical director, and some nights he had not. "John," Shaffer would say, "let me conduct, and you be the star." But John didn't really want to share the baton.

Shaffer chose Radner. He couldn't bear the thought of letting her down.

Brillstein called John to tell him Shaffer's decision. John exploded: "The fucking movie's off! Shaffer's out! He'll never be a Blues Brother!"

Brillstein absorbed the rant. Then he challenged John: "Does your life depend on a piano player?"

John paused. "Wait," he said. "I've got the guy." A few phone calls later, John had enlisted Murphy Dunne, a Chicago singer and keyboard man who had performed in Second City. Problem solved.

Dan would earn $250,000 to costar in *The Blues Brothers*, half of Belushi's pay. Dan was half as famous as his partner. He liked it that way.

John Landis assembled the crew that would make the film. Among them: Bob Weiss, the producer, charged with overseeing the schedule and budget; Stephen Katz, the cinematographer, responsible for cameras and lights and the film's overall look; George Folsey Jr., the editor, who would splice the film together; and David Sosna, the assistant director, responsible for executing the director's directions. All but Sosna had worked with Landis before, on *Kentucky Fried Movie* or *Animal House*. Most were in their twenties or early thirties.

"And we started storyboarding: 'What do we want this film to look like?'" Stephen Katz said. "I looked at Dick Tracy comic books, and that became my kind of palette. I saw it as kind of a comic book."

Cinematographers work with a range of film speeds assigned arbitrary numerals. A rating of 100 ASA (for American Standards Association) bespeaks a "slower," less sensitive film that absorbs light less quickly, ideal for bright outdoor scenes. Film rated 200 absorbs light twice as quickly, and so on. For *The Blues Brothers*, Stephen Katz chose film with the highest ASA ratings available. More sensitive film would push the contrast between the brightest whites and the deepest blacks. "It gave the film a look. I was pushing it to its limits."

Katz ran camera tests on stand-ins for the Blues Brothers, dressing them in the G-man suits and Wayfarer sunglasses. He learned to light them from the side, the only angle that eliminated glare on the lenses. Side lighting would complement the pronounced bone structure of Belushi's face.

Katz drew inspiration from the French masters Jean-Luc Godard and François Truffaut, from Orson Welles, and from *A Night to Remember*, an old British film about the *Titanic*. He wanted to shoot *The Blues Brothers* with "hard light," a technique that yields sharper focus and harsher shadows, common in noir cinema. For the musical numbers, his blueprint was *Singin' in the Rain*; Katz had worked for Stanley Donen, the film's codirector and co-choreographer. "Great dance," Donen had said, "is on the stage. You sit back and let it happen."

To complete the film's distinctive look, Katz would shoot with ultra-wide lenses, "like the fourteen-millimeter, which the studio hated." Wide lenses captured a broad field of vision, delivering an almost hallucinatory sense of depth. "I wanted depth," Katz said. "I wanted a lot of depth. And I wanted everything in the world," meaning in the shot, "to be in focus. It's a style. It's the way comic books are." Terry Gilliam, director of the Monty Python films, favored the fourteen-millimeter lens for its acid-dream effect, enlarging faces (and especially noses) in close-up and warping the edges of the screen.

George Folsey, the editor, shared Katz's vision of a wide-angle epic. Folsey pushed Landis to film in CinemaScope, a process that employed complementary lenses to shoot and project a film more than twice as wide as tall. Common in westerns and epics, CinemaScope had little use in madcap comedy. And wide-angle films translated poorly to rebroadcasting on 1970s televisions, which were nearly square. Landis settled on the more standard ratio of 1.85 to 1. He feared anything wider would "hurt the comedy." To preserve some of that epic feel, Landis and Katz would shoot much of the film with a fourteen-millimeter lens.

David Sosna, the assistant director, went to see the production manager at Universal. To shoot Dan's script would require dozens of stuntmen, drivers, and extras, and police to block off city streets. "When we first laid out the script," Landis remembered, "there were eleven stunts that we knew would be impossible." A preliminary breakdown included such directives as "Flamethrower blows up phone booth" and "Nazi wagon falls into hole in street."

The production manager "told us in no uncertain terms we could have no more than twelve walkie-talkies," Sosna recalled. "The sound union said if you had more than twelve, you needed a walkie-talkie guy." The studio didn't want to pay for a walkie-talkie guy.

"The studio honestly didn't understand the size of the picture John [Landis] wanted to make," Sosna said. An item that spring in *Variety*, the film-industry bible, put the film's budget "in the neighborhood of $5,000,000." *Animal House* had cost less. Sosna knew *The Blues Brothers* would cost more.

As the Chicago shoot approached, "everybody was nervous," Bob Weiss said. "And when I say everybody, I mean the studio. We knew what we wanted to make."

In the weeks to come, Landis would trim Dan's 324-page telephone book into something filmable. The streamlined story began with Elwood Blues arriving at Joliet Prison to greet brother Jake upon his release from three years' incarceration. They travel in the Bluesmobile to the Catholic orphanage that reared them. They meet with Sister Mary Stigmata, who tells them the county will close the orphanage unless someone can raise $5,000 in delinquent property taxes. The brothers proceed to church, where an epiphany seizes Jake: they'll put the band back together!

The inciting incident, the narrative spark that launches the Blues Brothers on their quest, came from Dan. He remembered, from his time in Chicago with Second City in 1974, reading about Chicago politicians scheming to tax parochial schools. Landis didn't like it, "because you can't really tax church property," he said. He told Dan the plot point strained credulity. "Really?" Dan replied, unfamiliar with American tax codes. Landis left it in; quite a lot in the *Blues Brothers* script strained credulity.

Dan's script supplied no central villain—no Omega House, no Dean Wormer. But the boys encounter plenty of adversaries and obstacles, most of them arising from their own past sins, which are many. At every turn, Jake and Elwood face skeptical bandmates, disapproving wives, angry girlfriends, and a growing armada of angry police. From the moment of the traffic stop that opens the second act, *The Blues Brothers* read like one long car chase.

Landis wanted to make a movie in the slapstick tradition of the Keystone Cops. Dan drew inspiration from *Smokey and the Bandit*, the Burt Reynolds–Sally Field car-chase film from 1977; and from *Bullitt*, the Steve McQueen car-chase film of the previous decade. Stunt drivers had crashed more than eighty vehicles in *Bullitt*.

The car chase begins with a routine traffic stop, initiated by a pair of Chicago patrolmen when the Bluesmobile runs a red light. The filmmakers named the officers Daniel and Mount, honoring and ribbing the young Universal executives who had championed their cause. The officers discover that Elwood is driving with a suspended license after amassing 116 parking tickets and 56 moving violations. They order Elwood out of the car. Instead, Elwood speeds off. "They're not gonna catch us," he tells Jake. "We're on a mission from God."

That line came from Landis, a winking nod to Dan, whose passion for rhythm and blues had shaped *The Blues Brothers* into a musical.

Chapter 19

The Mission from God

A T THE CLOSE OF THE 1970s, the nation's concert patrons and record buyers had all but forgotten the titans of rhythm and blues. *It's hard times befallen the soul survivors*, Donald Fagen of Steely Dan lamented in "Hey Nineteen," a song that name-checked Aretha Franklin, Queen of Soul.

Aretha Louise Franklin, born in 1942, was the daughter of the Reverend C. L. Franklin, the celebrity preacher, and she first drew notice singing potent gospel in his Detroit church. She rose to modest fame on Columbia Records in the early 1960s, but the label's timid producers restrained her gospel fire. She moved to Atlantic Records in 1966 and reclaimed her roots, recording a string of stunning singles. Songs like "Chain of Fools" and "Respect" were hard soul in the Memphis and Muscle Shoals traditions, performed by racially integrated bands, unconcerned with prudish white sensibilities, in sharp contrast to the sugarcoated soul of Motown. Diana Ross was Franklin's competition, but Otis Redding and Wilson Pickett were her artistic peers. Her signature song, "Respect," reinvented Redding's romantic plea as a powerful feminist anthem. Franklin and her music became symbols of Black Power, as well, and she sang at the 1968 funeral of Dr. Martin Luther King Jr. By the mid-1970s, though, Franklin's fire had dimmed. She released an album in 1979 titled *La Diva*. It stalled at 146 on the *Billboard 200* album chart.

In the spring of 1979, John Landis approached Franklin and other legends of rhythm and blues and invited them to perform in *The Blues*

Brothers, to reintroduce them to white America and to immortalize their music on film. That was Dan's mission from God.

Dan had written most of the parts not knowing who might play them. He wanted the film to "recognize these veteran, venerable artists," heroes of the 1950s and '60s, forgotten giants. Landis understood Dan's mission on a cellular level. He had seen James Brown at the T.A.M.I. Show.

Landis enlisted Franklin to play the long-suffering wife of Matt "Guitar" Murphy. He met with Ray Charles, the Genius, at his Los Angeles home. Between Brother Ray's dirty jokes, the director persuaded him to play the pawnshop dealer who sells the Blues Brothers their gear.

Ray Charles Robinson, born in 1930 and blind from age seven, had played piano for lesser artists before striking out on his own, leveraging classical training to blend gospel, jazz, and blues into the new genre of soul. His piano-jazz stylings, modeled on those of the great Nat "King" Cole, landed Charles a spot in 1952 on the roster of Atlantic Records, the young, white-owned rhythm-and-jazz label. In 1954, he scored a breakout hit, "I've Got a Woman." That song and his other defining 1950s hits, "Hallelujah I Love Her So," "Drown in My Own Tears," and "What'd I Say," reveal a breathtaking range, transporting the listener from piano bar to church pew to dance hall and back again.

Charles moved to the ABC-Paramount record label in 1959, signing a contract that delivered money, artistic control, and eventual ownership of his master tapes, rare commodities for a Black artist in that era. He immediately rewarded the label with a cover of Hoagy Carmichael's "Georgia on My Mind," a chart-topping smash that Georgia would claim as its state song. With the landmark 1962 album *Modern Sounds in Country and Western Music*, Charles almost single-handedly reconciled the working-class music of white and Black America. He was an artist who, on top of his instrumental virtuosity and compositional brilliance, possessed a singing voice that white artists could invoke only in pale imitation.

By the late 1970s, the Genius remained on the road. But changing tastes confined him to such venues as the Lane County Fairgrounds in

Eugene, Oregon, the city that had hosted *Animal House*. Brother Ray's albums barely charted anymore.

Landis wanted Little Richard, whose "Tutti Frutti" had led the rock 'n' roll revolution, to play the singing preacher whose sermon inspires Jake's epiphany. The director flew to Tennessee and met with Richard Penniman at his church. "And he was lovely," Landis said. The director watched Penniman lead a mesmerizing service and joined him in a raucous meal. In the end, though, the mighty singer announced that fealty to Jesus precluded his participation.

Filmmakers approached James Brown, the Godfather of Soul. He agreed to play the preacher, "which surprised us," Landis said, coming from the singer of "Hot Pants" and "Get Up (I Feel Like Being a) Sex Machine." The Godfather replaced Little Richard. No one else could match Penniman for raw power.

James Brown entered the world in 1933, grew up mostly in Augusta, Georgia, and formed a gospel quartet with some cellmates in juvenile detention. He evolved from gospel into R & B with a vocal group called the Famous Flames. In 1956, they released a single called "Please, Please, Please," a traditional ballad with a most unusual vocal, more rhythm and lust than melody. After that, Brown reeled off a string of chart-topping hits, developing a style of raw, rhythmic vocals that picked up where Little Richard left off when he retreated from "Tutti Frutti" fame into the ministry. With a landmark 1963 album, *Live at the Apollo*, Brown crossed over to success in the white pop market. In a sequence of iconic singles, including "I Got You (I Feel Good)" and "Cold Sweat," Brown and his band squeezed out the chord changes and repurposed every instrument as percussion. Some listeners consider his 1965 hit "Papa's Got a Brand New Bag" the recorded debut of a new musical genre called funk.

On April 5, 1968, the day after the King assassination, Brown performed a live concert in Boston. Through sheer force of charisma and will, Brown persuaded Bostonians to mourn the fallen leader in peace. Boston remained calm that night while many American cities burned. A few months later, he recorded a seminal anthem of Black Power, "Say It Loud—I'm Black and I'm Proud."

Brown led the funk genre into the 1970s, stripping the music down to its rhythmic bones. Yet, by the late 1970s, the Godfather had lost a step. His 1979 release, *The Original Disco Man*, reached 152 on the *Billboard 200*. That summer, the Godfather performed at a lonely dinner theater in Bloomington, Minnesota.

Landis needed someone to play Curtis, elegant mentor to Elwood and Jake. He flew to Dallas to watch a performance by the great Cab Calloway.

Cabell Calloway III, born in 1907, had risen to prominence in the 1920s in Chicago as a scat singer, leveraging the human voice to mimic an instrumental jazz solo, a technique he learned from Louis Armstrong. Calloway moved to New York in 1929 and led a big band at the famed Cotton Club. In 1931, he recorded "Minnie the Moocher," one of the first songs by any Black artist to sell a million copies. Calloway became a massive star, charting hits with "The Jumpin' Jive" and "The Honeydripper" and performing opposite Lena Horne in the 1943 film *Stormy Weather*, one of the only golden-era Hollywood musicals to feature a Black cast. Onstage, Calloway perfected a gliding back step, a stage trick that passed through the decades from Calloway to James Brown to Michael Jackson, whose followers rechristened it the "moonwalk." Calloway hosted a nationally syndicated radio show, one of the first Black entertainers to do so. He toured Europe with his big band, attracting top-drawer sidemen with lofty salaries that only Duke Ellington could beat. When the band toured the American South, Calloway hired private train cars to insulate the musicians from the enduring horrors of segregation.

Calloway charted singles in five decades. Yet, when he signed on to play Curtis in *The Blues Brothers*, he hadn't cracked the top forty on any chart in thirty years.

For an outdoor sequence on Chicago's famed Maxwell Street, Landis wanted someone who had actually performed on Maxwell Street, a master of hard blues. He hired John Lee Hooker.

Hooker, born in either 1912 or 1917, made his name as a swamp-boogie singer and guitarist in Detroit. But he was, in fact, one of the great Delta bluesmen. A sharecropper's son, Hooker learned Delta blues standards on acoustic guitar before moving north for better-paying work. In 1940s Detroit, Hooker developed an electrified "urban" variant of the acoustic country blues he had left behind. Muddy Waters and Howlin' Wolf, Hooker's Delta-blues contemporaries, charted a similar course in Chicago. Hooker's recording career set off with a bang: "Boogie Chillen'," recorded by Modern Records, the Bihari brothers' "race" label, in 1948, soared to number one on the R & B charts on the strength of Hooker's voice, guitar, and stomping foot. Hooker was the first Delta blues guitarist to top the *Billboard* R & B chart: Genre giants Robert Johnson, Son House, and Skip James remained all but unknown outside Mississippi, and the guitar itself was a backbench instrument. John Lee Hooker would change all that, alongside his Delta brethren Muddy Waters and Howlin' Wolf and B.B. King, the titans of postwar blues.

Hooker crossed over to reach white audiences in the folk-blues revival of the late 1950s and early 1960s with a series of long-playing albums that exploited his old boogie-blues singles. Dan Aykroyd would later cite Hooker as source material for the Blues Brothers look, although few, if any, images of the bluesman from that era picture him in a black suit and shades.

By the late 1970s, Hooker had achieved broad fame. But never had he scored a smash hit, let alone a string of them, and his career had cooled by the time he met John Belushi at the Lone Star Café during John's *SNL* heyday.

"Hi," Hooker had said, blankly.

"You know: John Belushi. I'm on TV."

Hooker had peered through his shades.

"Oh, yeah. You one of them Muppets, ain't ya?"

Landis approached B.B. King, the biggest name in blues. But unlike most of his peers, B.B. was busy, playing three hundred gigs a year. Sid Seidenberg, B.B.'s canny manager, apprised Landis that B.B. was booked. Only years later did the blues monarch learn he had been up for a part in *The Blues Brothers*. He was crushed.

Universal executives balked at some of the artistic choices Landis presented them. Cab Calloway and James Brown were ice-cold. In place of Aretha Franklin, someone suggested Rose Royce, a funk-disco group assembled to record the theme song to the hit film *Car Wash*. Landis declined.

Some of the artists seemed to share the studio's skepticism, and a few balked at singing their own classic material. Calloway pressed Landis to let him perform a disco version of "Minnie the Moocher," released to marginal success in the prior year. Landis preferred the bluesy original. Franklin wanted to play "Respect," her signature hit. Landis explained that he and Dan had written another Aretha Franklin hit, "Think," into the script. She would sing it to Matt "Guitar" Murphy as he threatened to leave her and rejoin the band. The Queen grudgingly agreed.

By May 4, John Landis had completed a 139-page rewrite of Dan's *Blues Brothers* script: long, but still filmable. Over the next month, the script passed back and forth between the two writers, each contributing edits.

"Danny's ideas are so unique and interesting, and he has such an insane point of view on so many things," Landis said. "He had this very specific way of speaking for Elwood," the character Dan had written for himself. "He wrote a scene where they jump in the car, and Elwood says, 'It's 106 miles to Chicago. We have a full tank of gas and half a pack of cigarettes.'" Landis ran those lines through his head. Then he added one of his own: "It's dark, and we're wearing sunglasses."

On June 4, Landis and Aykroyd completed a 144-page *Blues Brothers* screenplay. Over the next two days, the director trimmed it to a 125-page shooting script, the one he would take to Chicago.

Landis fretted about how Aretha Franklin and Cab Calloway would receive the screenplay. On June 8, he sent a copy to Calloway with a cover letter that said, "As you will read, this is a crazy movie filled with music and action. Please read the entire script to get the feel of just what kind of an insane picture we are making. I am anxiously waiting your reaction to the project."

On June 25, 1979, Warner Brothers announced the second feature film from *National Lampoon*. *Caddyshack*, a comedy farce about class conflict set at an upper-crust country club, would star *Lampoon* alumni Chevy Chase and Bill Murray alongside Rodney Dangerfield, a comedic actor of Johnny Carson's generation. The timing seemed calculated to distract attention from *The Blues Brothers*. The *Animal House* alumni now sat in competing camps, Landis and Belushi with *The Blues Brothers* at Universal, Harold Ramis and Doug Kenney piloting *Caddyshack* at Orion Pictures. In the months to come, the parallel projects would inspire (mostly) good-humored rivalry about which cast was snorting more cocaine and whose film would fare better at the box office. For the hypercompetitive Belushi, though, the contest would turn ugly, John bitterly accusing Kenney of trying to sabotage his film.

John stayed clean on Martha's Vineyard as he and Judy rested for the looming shoot. "He's much more alive without cocaine," Judy wrote in her diary. "I'm getting nervous about going to Chicago."

On July 1, John and Judy flew to Chicago. As the unrivaled star of *The Blues Brothers* and a hometown hero, John faced a crucial first task: to convince the new mayor to let a film crew tear up her city.

Jane Byrne had taken office that spring, at forty-five, as Chicago's first female mayor. Before her ascent, Dan and John would have stood little chance of filming their Chicago car-chase musical in Chicago. Precious few films had shot in the city, a prohibition that dated to the early years of Mayor Richard J. Daley. A powerful Irish American politician from the city's Southwest Side, Daley assumed office in 1955 and indulged film and television crews until 1959, when an episode of a now-forgotten series called *M Squad* portrayed a Chicago cop taking bribes. Chicago hosted almost no movies for the next two decades, while its urban peers reaped millions in tax dollars and priceless celebrity as cinematic settings: New York with *Saturday Night Fever* and *Manhattan*, San Francisco with *Dirty Harry*, Philadelphia with *Rocky*, Los Angeles with *Chinatown*.

"There wasn't an official policy or anything," the *Tribune* recounted later. "Movies did shoot here. Brian DePalma shot *The Fury* here," in 1977. "A lot of commercials were shot here. There was even a cottage porn industry in River North. But the cooperation needed for a large-scale Hollywood production—the kind Belushi, Aykroyd and director John Landis had in mind, only bigger—was out of the question."

Now, Daley was gone, and the new mayor had other plans. Jane Byrne had agreed to host *The Blues Brothers* months before the summer shoot. But her power extended only so far. She could allow the crew to drive a convoy across Daley Plaza. She could not permit them to shoot inside the Daley Center itself—that building fell under the county's purview. Nor could she corral the city's powerful unions.

Landis visited Sidney Korshak, an attorney and fixer whose friends included Frank Sinatra, Ronald Reagan, and Lew Wasserman, the Universal studio chief. Korshak had grown up in Chicago and made his name defending Al Capone before pivoting into a prosperous labor practice. His meeting with Landis opened doors that Chicago's mayor could not.

"I was given his phone number," Bob Weiss said. "And I was told, 'If you ever have a real problem in Chicago, call this number. But if you call it, make sure you've got a problem.' He was a heavy, heavy hitter. And not somebody you spoke idly about or to."

By the time Mayor Byrne summoned Aykroyd, Belushi, Landis, Daniel, and Weiss to her downtown office, the meeting was pro forma, more photo op than negotiating session. Before signing off on the project, though, Byrne wanted to make the filmmakers sweat.

When the group arrived at city hall, John was already sweating. "I thought he looked sick, to be honest," Byrne said. "To the point that his hair was getting wet. I was a fan of his. But, of course, I wasn't going to say this right away." She greeted the party as Boss Daley would, "nodding like Buddha."

"I know how Chicago feels about movies," John offered. The mayor nodded. John said the studio wanted to donate money to Chicago orphanages. "How much money?" the mayor asked. "Two hundred thousand," he replied. She nodded.

"So, what's this movie about?" she asked.

"Well, it's about these two characters, Jake and Elwood, and they've got about ten thousand traffic tickets."

Byrne offered to take care of them. The mayor was funny. The filmmakers laughed.

"All right," she said. "If we can't help you with those tickets, what else can we do for you?"

John kept talking, and talking, and talking. "Finally, I just said, 'Fine,'" Byrne recalled. "But he kept going. So, again I said, 'Look, I said fine. Is there anything else I can help you with?'"

"Wait," John said. "We also want to drive a car through the lobby of Daley Plaza. Right through the window."

Daley Plaza's namesake had died in 1976. Three years later, most of his former cronies had lined up against the new mayor. They called her "crazy broad" and "skinny b---h" and worse. They had owned the city for years and thought they owned it still.

"I wouldn't have a problem with that," the mayor replied.

Dan entertained the mayor with his Jimmy Carter impression. She asked the boys to appear with her onstage to open ChicagoFest, a celebration of music and food on Navy Pier. John and Dan agreed. They vowed the mayor to secrecy, lest the festival be overrun with Belushi fans.

When the meeting was over, the new mayor had given the *Blues Brothers* crew permission "to land a helicopter next to the Picasso in Daley Plaza," Thom Mount remembered. Nothing seemed off-limits.

John took Dan on a tour of Chicago memories. Both friends had lived in the city, performed at Second City, and partied in Old Town, but not at the same time. They drove to the University of Illinois at Chicago Circle, the university named for a freeway interchange. John showed Dan the storefront that had housed the West Compass Players. They happened upon John's old landlady.

"Mr. Belushi!" she cried.

"I still owe you for a month's rent," John said. He produced $100 and handed it over.

At Second City, the cast greeted the boys like visiting deities. One night, John appeared backstage and approached Tim Kazurinsky, a short, bespectacled impressionist who stood out among the main-stage players. John told Kazurinsky he would go far. Kazurinsky invited John to pop onstage for a few minutes, a rite of passage for famous Second

City alumni. John demurred. Kazurinsky begged. John refused. After more begging, he agreed.

"All he did is walk out on the stage and stand there," Kazurinsky said. "And the place went nuts. It just blew up. I had never seen anything like it in my life. People jumped out of their seats, knocked over tables, sent drinks flying. It was like somebody put jumper cables on their chairs. It was big, and it was frightening."

John retreated, overcome with emotion. "And he had trouble talking," Kazurinsky said. "He didn't perform that night. He couldn't."

Over Fourth of July weekend, John and Judy watched a Cubs game, caught the downtown fireworks from a rooftop perch, and toured the old bars. John played pinball and snorted coke. When Judy confronted him, John said he'd gotten the blow from Bob Weiss. Judy raged at Weiss. "Don't give him fucking coke," she shouted. John couldn't backslide now. The movie hung in the drug scales. "It's your career," Judy said, "but it's my life."

Weiss hadn't given John coke, but he didn't want to tell Judy her husband was lying.

In the week of July 12, 1979, disco songs filled the top three slots on the *Billboard Hot 100*: "Bad Girls" and "Hot Stuff" by Donna Summer, and "Ring My Bell" by Anita Ward. All three celebrated sexual freedom from a Black and female perspective. They marked high points in the disco movement, born in urban nightclubs, like Studio 54, where people of all races and sexual orientations reveled in dance and drink, androgyny and drugs, and rebelled against the strictures of "rock."

Over the decades, rock 'n' roll had evolved from its Black origins into a high-stakes party, hosted mostly by straight, white males in vast caverns like Universal Amphitheatre. Along the way, the genre had lost much of its rhythm and its "roll." You couldn't dance to it, and that suited many young, white rock fans just fine. By the close of the 1970s, white rock acts such as AC/DC, Led Zeppelin, and Van Halen vied with sequined, multiracial disco acts at the top of the charts. The arrival of disco had revived dance. Legions of rock fans resented that, along with disco's "urban" roots, playful gender-bending, and frank sexuality. A pop-cultural showdown loomed.

Steve Dahl, a young white deejay, lost his job on Christmas Eve of 1978, when his Chicago station, WDAI, transitioned from rock to disco. He joined a rival rock station, WLUP, and spent the spring and summer campaigning against disco.

On the night of July 12, Dahl hosted a bizarre promotion at Comiskey Park, the soulless South Side ballpark that housed baseball's White Sox, less-loved brethren of the Cubs. Bill Veeck, the White Sox owner, would try anything to boost sagging ticket sales. Between games of a twi-night doubleheader, Veeck staged "Disco Demolition Night," an idea cooked up by his son Mike and the impish deejay. Anyone who surrendered a disco record at the gates would get in for 98 cents. Dahl would blow the records up in center field between games. His minions would cheer from the stands.

The doubleheader sold out. Thousands congregated outside the park. More than fifty thousand people crowded into the stadium, some scaling the walls on makeshift siege ladders brought from their homes. Most were young, white males, primed on beer and weed. All night, vinyl discs sliced through the air like sharpened frisbees. Players took the field in batting helmets.

Between games, Dahl detonated his explosives, pulverizing a mountain of disco records and non-disco records by random Black artists. Fans rushed the field, ripping up the grass, setting fires, and uprooting bases. Throngs of men danced in circles around the smoldering shards, an ironic image in a protest against dance music. Outside Comiskey, vinyl bonfires lit the streets. Riot gear–clad police moved in to clear the scene.

Dan and John shared Steve Dahl's disdain for disco, but for a different reason. They saw its toll on the careers of Aretha Franklin and James Brown and the Chicago blues community. They hated seeing Cab Calloway dishonor his own legacy by disco-fying "Minnie the Moocher." "One of our intentions with this picture was to kill off disco," Landis said. When filming commenced, the "Disco Sucks" slogan appeared on the *Blues Brothers* set, emblazoned on camera mounts and crew T-shirts.

On the final weekend before production began, John and Dan drove up to Wisconsin with Judy and Rosie Shuster to vacation at a lakeside resort where the Jacklin family had summered in Judy's childhood.

"The trip was supposed to be a chance to relax, with the four of us sharing this tiny cabin," Shuster said. "But a bunch of fans somehow found out about it and descended on the place." The couples spotted the crowd as they prepared to head out. "Luckily, Danny had parked a getaway car in the back, because that's how Danny is. We had to jump out the back window into these thorn bushes and beat a hasty retreat to a drive-in movie." John watched the film with his head down.

Chapter 20

Sweet Home Chicago

U NIVERSAL INSTALLED most of the *Blues Brothers* cast and crew at a Holiday Inn. The crew set up a war room inside a downtown production office. They punched through walls to run dozens of cables for extra telephone lines to support daily communication with cast and crew, police, and extras. The production would work Tuesdays through Sundays, with most Mondays off, a schedule both punishing and costly: union workers earned double time on weekends.

Much of the Chicago shoot would play out on Chicago's streets and suburban expressways. The script comprised 389 scenes: starting around scene 72, when Jake and Elwood sped away from a routine traffic stop, the narrative unfolded as one long car chase. Dan had scripted the Bluesmobile as a retired cop car, purchased by Elwood at auction, a detail that honored his fascination with law enforcement and established an ironic camaraderie between the Brothers and their police pursuers. Landis reveled in the comic absurdity of fifty new cop cars chasing an old one.

Crew papered the office with maps of Lower Wacker Drive, the base of a double-decker roadway that ran along the Chicago River to separate commuters and shoppers from service trucks and deliveries in the upstairs-downstairs tradition of English manors. Crucial chase scenes would be shot along Lower Wacker, beneath the Lake Street "L" tracks and on windy stretches of expressway. Several Sundays would be set aside for "lockups," crew and cops blocking more than one hundred intersections and exits so a stray Sears truck wouldn't careen into a staged car crash. Locking up for a single shot required many people and walkie-talkies. Workers designed a light board on one wall map, with little blinking bulbs showing the progress of the Bluesmobile fleeing its police pursuers through downtown Chicago. "It was the first digital electric prop I recall anyone building," said David Sosna, the assistant director.

In late June, Sosna drove around the city and its suburbs with John Lloyd, the production designer, surveying possible sets. They planned to shoot most of the outdoor scenes in and around Chicago that summer. They beheld Richard J. Daley Plaza, the courtyard surrounding the county courts building, adorned with a Pablo Picasso statue that they dared not harm. They toured Maxwell Street, home to a famed Sunday flea market, where they planned to film John Lee Hooker's musical number. They spotted a flophouse on West Van Buren Street, a structure that shook when the L trains passed, a perfect lodging for Elwood Blues. They found a pawnshop on East Forty-Seventh Street, in the Bronzeville enclave, that would serve as backdrop for the Ray Charles number. For the James Brown sermon and song, they located an old Baptist church on East Ninety-First Street, its steeple adorned with a crooked cross.

Location scouts had reported an odd find with cinematic potential: an abandoned shopping mall. Dead malls weren't so common in the late 1970s, a moment near the peak of the mall era. But one Chicago mall had just closed: Dixie Square, a victim of crime, vacancies, and blight in the struggling Southwest suburb of Harvey. It had opened in 1966 and closed in 1978, after "stabbings on consecutive weekends in a bathroom," Sosna said.

"We got out of the van at the mall," Sosna recounted. "I remember peeking through a crack, a piece of plywood that was placed over the door." They beheld a dusty warren of empty stores. "And I'm standing there with John Lloyd, and John says to me, 'We can't show this to Landis.' We can't show him the mall because this is too big. They don't have lights. That means they don't have electricity. That means we have to put all that stuff in. We were afraid of the cost."

By the time the crew arrived in Chicago, executives at Universal conceded that *The Blues Brothers* would cost more than $5 million. The official budget, passed down from the studio to the local film commission to the press, now stood at $12 million. Sosna feared even that sum wouldn't cover the shoot.

Sosna and Lloyd didn't breathe a word of their mall find to Landis. Somehow, Landis found out. He asked his scouts why they were not preparing to film there. The scouts tried to explain their reservations. "Shut up and show it to me," Landis said. The dead mall was perfect. Landis would restore it to life.

A shooting schedule for *The Blues Brothers*, dated July 6, prescribed seventy-four days of production, starting August 6 in Chicago and ending November 5 in Los Angeles, with the occasional day off. But *The Blues Brothers* would announce itself to the city well before the official start date.

On the morning of July 22, a Sunday, fifty-four Chicago police cars chased the Bluesmobile, a 1974 Dodge Monaco 440, down Lake Shore Drive. The weekend shoot, with stuntmen posing as Jake and Elwood inside the Bluesmobile, ranked as the most ambitious among several pre-production shots scheduled in the days leading up to August 6. Pre-production work focused mostly on smaller sequences that could be filmed before the cast arrived. Thanks to their deal with the mayor of the nation's second-largest city, Landis and company wielded "control of the freeway that's impossible to even think about in Los Angeles," Sosna said. The studio enlisted seventy-six police officers to drive squad cars and direct traffic, paying the officers $16.50 an hour and the city $30 a day for each vehicle, plus a full tank of gas.

Weekend motorists found long stretches of the Lake Shore expressway and the landlocked Eisenhower Expressway closed to traffic, along with half of the bridges that traversed the Chicago River. "The resulting traffic jam must have proved a pain in the carburetor for thousands of motorists burning $1.03-a-gallon gas as they were summarily diverted from their self-appointed recreational tasks on a lovely summer weekend," a *Tribune* columnist huffed. Lakefront tenants telephoned the newsroom to report a high-speed chase.

While Landis and Sosna directed police out on the Chicago streets, giants of rhythm and blues flew in to record vocals for the big musical numbers that would power the beating heart of *The Blues Brothers*.

Ray Charles met the filmmakers at the Universal Recording studio at Walton and Rush Streets along the Magnificent Mile, an operation unrelated to the same-named Hollywood movie studio. He "brought braille music sheets with him," said Bob Tischler, who produced the session. Charles glided through a reading of "Shake a Tail Feather" on a Wurlitzer electric piano. Months later, on a Los Angeles soundstage, Brother Ray would lip-synch over the recording.

Aretha Franklin arrived the next day. She brought her own backup singers and her own arrangement of "Think," her decade-old hit. Lou Marini walked up to introduce himself. "She was sitting in a chair, smoking a cigarette," he recalled. "And I said, 'Ms. Franklin, I just want to say, it's an honor to meet you, and I'm a huge fan, and I'll be playing a solo on this tune.' Who knows what I said. And she sort of looked up to me, halfway, and I was wearing a yellow football jersey with black letters, '69.' And she looked at me and said, 'Sixty-nine, huh?'"

After hearing the prerecorded backing track, Franklin announced, "I'd like to change the piano."

"Of course," Landis replied. "Who would you like?"

"I'll do it," Franklin replied. She sat down at a Steinway and pounded out the song in an explosion of energy.

Franklin did two or three takes on the piano and two or three more at the microphone, recording her lead vocal, each performance strikingly different from the last. "She was in the moment," Marini said. When the session was over, Franklin shrank back into herself. "It was like letting air out of a balloon," Bob Tischler said.

"During playback," Marini said, "everybody was dancing around and freaking out over how great everything sounded." Franklin looked pleased.

By day, John and Dan hung out at the music studio, recording the rest of the *Blues Brothers* soundtrack with the band. The sessions began without Paul Shaffer, a huge loss, given his dual role as master key-boardist and musical director. "He had to be replaced by three or four people," Bob Weiss said. John sang lead vocals on some new songs: Taj Mahal's "She Caught the Katy," Steve Winwood's "Gimme Some Lovin'," and Solomon Burke's "Everybody Needs Somebody to Love," along with the local anthem "Sweet Home Chicago," the Elvis classic "Jailhouse Rock," and the *Rawhide* theme.

At night, the boys made the rounds of Chicago blues clubs, hanging and jamming with local talent, including harmonica virtuoso Big Walter Horton and Luther "Guitar Junior" Johnson. "They knew what we were up to, and they embraced it," Dan said. "Any of them that were available, we threw them in the movie."

When crowds grew too thick, the Brothers would hail a police car as if it were a cab and catch a ride back to their temporary home, the top floors of the Astor Tower, a modernist Gold Coast high-rise that had hosted the Beatles. Sidney Korshak, the powerful lawyer and fixer, had secured them the city's finest perch.

Soon, John and Dan drew thick crowds wherever they went. They faced a familiar dilemma: how to carry on a 24/7 bacchanal while retaining some semblance of anonymity.

"There were times when I had the de facto role of bodyguard," Bob Weiss recalled, "because [John would] get mobbed and I'd have to get him through and save him from autograph-seekers. There were times when fans would just materialize out of thin air. . . . This was why we had to have the Sneak Joint."

John Candy, Dan's old Second City pal, reminded the boys of the Sneak Joint. The Second City cast had haunted the bar, tucked within a yellow coach house across from the theater on Wells Street. They found the shuttered pub and took out a six-month lease at $500 a month. They bought a jukebox and stocked it with R & B sides. They imported a pinball machine and a pool table, polished the old bar fixtures, and reopened the space as the next Blues Bar, another pri-vate club, with oversize portraits of the late Mayor Daley adorning the walls. Steve Beshekas, John's comedy partner from their youth, came in to tend bar.

"It was glorious good fun," said Murphy Dunne, keyboard man in the Blues Brothers band. "The police would go in there and claim that they were closing it down, but then it would open up the next night. And Dan, during all of this, made a lot of friends who were cops. He would do ride-alongs. There were rumors the police would go out with Dan, and they would fire automatic weapons."

The Blues Brothers' speakeasy would not stay secret for long.

On August 3, a hot, sunny Friday, Mayor Byrne strode onstage at Navy Pier to welcome twenty thousand screaming fans to ChicagoFest and to bask in adulation for delivering Belushi back to Chicago. Word had leaked that the Blues Brothers would appear, and "an impassable mass of people" crowded the main stage for their ten p.m. set, by one account. The boys sang four songs, to rapturous cheers, between sets by local folk legend John Prine and blues titan Muddy Waters.

The Ray-Ban Wayfarers Dan and John wore that night came from a collection of more than one hundred pairs that *Blues Brothers* crew snatched up in the city's dingiest dime stores and hippest vintage boutiques, as the model had ceased production. Most of the extra pairs went to John, who kept giving them away to female fans.

Camera crews had spent the last week of July in shooting tests, setting up on Daley Plaza, inside the Cook County building, outside the Dixie Square mall, and beneath the Lake Street L tracks for dry runs of crucial scenes. Stephen Katz mounted a camera atop a mock Bluesmobile and ran it up and down Lower Wacker, shooting mock chase sequences. He filmed the familiar strobing blue lights of a late-1970s Chicago police car to see how they looked on-screen. Anyone who bought a ticket to *The Blues Brothers* would see a lot of them.

August 6, the scheduled start date for production, came and went. David Sosna, the director's top lieutenant, thought his crew wasn't ready. He asked Bob Weiss to delay the shoot by a week.

"There was a whole lot of stuff we weren't ready to do," Sosna recalled. The crew planned many ambitious scenes. One called for a speeding police car to crash into the side of a tractor trailer on an expressway. A split-second error in timing might send the cruiser through the cab of the truck. "We aren't ready to make that shot," Sosna pleaded to the producer.

And thus, *The Blues Brothers* already lagged a week behind schedule when production commenced. The film was now an eighty-one-day shoot, starting August 13 and ending November 21. The budget had swelled to $20.6 million, nearly twice the figure reported in the local press, more than Spielberg had spent on *Close Encounters*. The sum remained a closely held secret.

August 13, 1979, dawned as a cool, crisp Monday. The first day of production called for a series of sweeping aerial helicopter shots to establish the gritty gravitas of industrial Chicago. The crew filmed at South Works, a US Steel mill at the mouth of the Calumet River that had billowed smoke across the South Side since the turn of the century. The footage would open the finished film.

"We didn't have drones in those days," Stephen Katz said. The camera operator "was hanging out the door of the chopper with a rig."

Landis had not bothered to ask permission to film at the steel plant, "as we knew they would say no," he said. As the helicopter hovered, security men emerged from the factory with weapons and opened fire, briefly transforming *The Blues Brothers* into a war film. Landis ordered a retreat.

On the first morning of the shoot, Katz vomited. The cinematographer had worked with a tiny crew on *Kentucky Fried Movie*. Now, he supervised a small army of electricians and grips, and he was scared. "I was a young guy, twenty-nine, thirty," he said. "I got saddled with a Universal crew. There were a lot of old-timers, a lot of good old boys, a lot of them had drinking problems, and they weren't very friendly to me. They weren't nice." Katz was gay. His partner worked on the crew. An undercurrent of homophobia chilled relations with the union men.

Day two, August 14, brought the first scene to feature Jake and Elwood, mercifully simple. The Bluesmobile arrived at a red-brick house on a sleepy residential Chicago street, a narrow triplex of diagonal brick on a street of near-identical homes, a dwelling not unlike the brown-brick duplex on Walton Street that had once housed the Belushis.

The Brothers emerged from the sedan and knocked on the door. A matronly, olive-skinned woman answered. Rumor swept the set that she was Belushi's mother, though she wasn't.

"May we come in, ma'am?" Elwood asked, sounding like a cop.

"Please," she replied.

The Blues Brothers entered the home, and the scene was over.

"And the boys were in the living room," Katz said. "It was fun. I wasn't stressed anymore. It was my comic book."

Chapter 21

The Blues Bar

FOR THE FIRST big *Blues Brothers* musical number, on August 16, the crew set up along Maxwell Street, west and south of downtown. Founded by Jewish immigrants in the nineteenth century, the Maxwell Street market had evolved into a weekly celebration of Black music and culture. Landis hired hundreds of extras to fill the street, most of them locals. As he prepared to shoot, a police officer assigned to the set bellowed through a megaphone to the crowd, "All right, if anyone fucks up, I'm gonna put them in jail. Do you understand me? You're going to jail."

"Hey, wait. What are you talking about?" Landis cried. "They're going to work for us."

The officer turned to the director and replied through his megaphone, "You don't understand these people. We're not dealing with normal people."

Landis, his patience exhausted, shouted back sarcastically, "What are we dealing with? Negroes?" The officer backed down.

The filmed scene shows the Bluesmobile creeping through a dense crowd and arriving in front of the Soul Food Café, setting up the big Aretha Franklin number inside. Filmmakers didn't touch the gorgeous neon sign announcing the storefront's true identity, Nate's Delicatessen. With the café as a backdrop, John Lee Hooker leads a fiery rendition of "Boom Boom," fronting an all-star band, Big Walter Horton on harmonica, Pinetop Perkins on piano, Luther "Guitar Junior" Johnson on guitar, Calvin "Fuzz" Jones on bass, Willie "Big Eyes" Smith on drums. George Folsey, the film editor, cut back and forth between the band and street scenes: shots of the Cheat You Fair store, Italian sausages steaming on a grill, racks of R & B cassettes for sale, statues of zebras and sad clowns.

Hooker and his band marked an expansive divergence from the script, which called for "two old Black men" playing guitars into little Pignose amps on the sidewalk. One of those men was to be Muddy Waters. A day or two before the shoot, Muddy's people notified Landis that the great bluesman had the flu. Someone dispatched a doctor to examine him, and the physician pronounced that Muddy would need two weeks to recover. Alas, *The Blues Brothers* could not wait. Had Muddy been well, "Boom Boom" would have segued into one of Muddy's greats, "Mannish Boy" or "Hoochie Coochie Man" or "Rollin' Stone."

John Lee Hooker had partly inspired the Blues Brothers' look. In this performance, he wears a sleek mocha-leather jacket, a white hat with a woven band, a multihued earth-tone shirt, and alligator boots. Dan and John watch reverentially from the diner doorway. Dan smiles beatifically and says, "Yep," sounding too verklempt to say more as he takes in the glorious scene, his crazy blues dream made manifest.

Elwood's exclamation did not appear in the *Blues Brothers* script: Dan ad-libbed it. Many of the most memorable lines in the film, from Dan's "Yep" to Aretha Franklin's "*Shee-it*" to the SWAT team's "hut-hut-hut," would spring to life on the set or in postproduction, improvised by the actors or dreamed up by Landis or his lieutenants. "There are shoots where the script is the bible," said Katherine "Boots" Wooten, the script supervisor. "And there are shoots where the script is a clothes rack to hang things on, and that was the way with John."

The next day, August 17, the production traveled to the Calumet River, gateway to Chicago's unsung East Side, to film a spectacular jump across the Ninety-Fifth Street Bridge. In the filmed scene, Elwood vaults the open drawbridge to prove the worth of the new Bluesmobile to a skeptical Jake. A stunt driver executed the jump, driving a Bluesmobile that carried only a gallon of gas, to trim its weight and minimize fire risk. On the first try, the driver "hit with such an impact that the front bumper came off, and it went under the car and it blew out a couple of tires," crew member Morris Lyda recalled. "It wasn't a very graceful landing, and Landis just went ballistic." Lyda was on set with John and Dan to watch. "Dan wouldn't have missed that for anything." Landis filmed it again.

"Car's got a lot of pickup," Jake deadpans in the filmed scene.

Elwood replies with a classic Dan gearhead soliloquy: "It's got a cop motor, a four hundred and forty cubic-inch plant. It's got cop tires, cop suspension, cop shocks. It's a model made before catalytic converters, so it'll run good on regular gas. Whaddaya say, is it the new Bluesmobile or what?"

"Fix the cigarette lighter," Jake replies.

Much of the dialogue between Jake and Elwood in the *Blues Brothers* shoot would play out inside a moving Bluesmobile. To capture it, William B. Kaplan, the soundman, crouched down on the floor of the sedan's back seat for hours at a time with a tape recorder and microphone. Once or twice, filmmakers allowed Dan to drive the Bluesmobile at speed. Dan was a formidable driver with street-racer impulses. John remained a terrible driver, and stunt-driving terrified him. Kaplan recorded loud exchanges between driver and passenger, John screaming at Dan to slow down and to ease up on the next turn.

If any one episode betrayed the first flicker of danger that *The Blues Brothers* might bog down, might descend into a cinematic Vietnam, it arrived on August 19, the first Sunday on Lower Wacker Drive.

Lower Wacker lay nearly empty on Sundays, when most delivery vans and work trucks sat idle. Landis needed footage of police chasing Jake and Elwood through downtown toward Daley Plaza, the terminus of the epic pursuit. All told, the frames shot on Lower Wacker would fill only a minute or two of screen time. The crew employed an army of officers and production assistants to watch intersections. Stunt drivers drove the squad cars.

Filming the chase required all the ambient light the sun could shine on Lower Wacker, much of it seeping through at intersections and between bridge pilings.

"They had shot a whole bunch of tests, and it always looked good in the tests," recalled George Folsey, the film editor. But on the Sunday of the shoot, the sun refused to shine. "We ended up with pretty much the whole day's work unusable."

A surprise visit from Mayor Byrne, the production's most vital supporter, sparked further delay. "All of a sudden, this limo pulls up, and she's smiling and shaking hands," recalled Mark Hogan, an electrician on the set.

The crew would return to Lower Wacker on another Sunday and do it all again. In one memorable shot, the Bluesmobile vaulted over a police cruiser, shearing the flashing Mars lights off its roof. Landis had offered the driver fifty dollars as an incentive to pull it off.

Nearly every *Blues Brothers* scene would play out to an impromptu audience. Pedestrians and Belushi fans stood and gawked wherever the *Blues Brothers* crew assembled to shoot. Sometimes, it worked: a high-speed chase down a city street would naturally turn heads. But crowds also gathered to watch Jake and Elwood walk through a doorway. That did not work. Then, the crew would gently ask the throng to retreat behind the police barriers. Sometimes, they refused.

"You can't really tell people who are walking down the street while you get your shot, 'You can't watch our movie,'" David Sosna said. "'Hey, it's a public street, asshole.'"

Not long after the Navy Pier gig, Dan vented to a *Tribune* reporter. "Every time we try to film, thousands of people appear to watch and foul things up," he said.

"Playing ChicagoFest was a mistake," Donald "Duck" Dunn told the reporter furtively, giving his name as Dave. "All those people seeing Aykroyd and Belushi onstage got us too much attention. People mean well, but they don't leave us alone."

They spoke inside the Blues Bar, a hideout into which John and Dan could no longer sneak. Every night, "all these sycophants and groupies of both sexes hang around, trying to get in," a *Tribune* columnist lamented. "People you don't believe—officials from City Hall, and newspaper reporters, and television people. They all want to touch stardom or something." The writer ignored the irony of his own presence.

Groupies and fans flocked to the daily *Blues Brothers* shoot, a steady supply of lovely young women, who sometimes paired off with handsome young men from the mostly male crew. Someone tacked up poster board on the side of the grip truck and wrote answers to some obvious questions a visiting fan might ask: the name of the production, its budget, its stars. Drugs? Yes. Availability? Surely.

John's old insecurities remained: part of him craved the attention. One night, he donned a hat and sunglasses and headed to a bar with Bernie Brillstein. The camouflage worked: no one recognized him. After fifteen minutes, he tore off the hat and shades, leapt up, and cried, "Hey! Drinks for everybody!" Then he turned to his manager. "Hey, Bernie, you got a hundred bucks?"

Groupies and fans would pay more than that to get into the Blues Bar. Tabloid reporters offered thousands of dollars for backstage dirt. Early in the shoot, the *National Enquirer* approached Stephen Katz with $100,000 to "give them the scoop on Belushi." Katz asked a studio publicist to make them go away.

Oh, the stories Katz might have told.

At the start of production, John told Bob Weiss he needed a vitamin B_{12} shot for energy to sing his parts at the recording studio. Weiss reached out to a psychiatrist friend. The doctor insisted on first examining the patient. He met with John and took notes: Belushi was overweight, with pallid skin, clogged sinuses, glassy eyes, and raspy breath.

The doctor reported back to Weiss. "Is this guy a friend of yours?" he asked.

"Well, I hope we're becoming friends," Weiss replied. "It's mostly a working relationship. Why?"

"Well," the doctor replied, "if something isn't done, he doesn't have long to live."

But keeping John clean proved no easier on the *Blues Brothers* set than in 30 Rock or on the *1941* set. Coke was everywhere.

"Cocaine was a currency back then, and we were shooting nights," Dan said. Coffee would not suffice. "So, there was money set aside to get through the nights, and a little reward at the end of the nights for our hard-working crew."

"Bones" Malone recalled a soundman on the set "who was The Man. You could buy a gram from him for a hundred bucks."

There was no line item in the *Blues Brothers* budget for cocaine. But "almost everybody on the company, with the exception of Landis and me, were happily cocaine users. I don't mean they were junkies," David Sosna said. "They would party at Belushi and Aykroyd's bar, and Landis and I never went."

For John, the problem was not too little energy on the set; it was too much. Long hours of idleness between takes ill suited his metabolism. "He was like a kid who couldn't sit still," said Don Novello, the *SNL* writer. "He just had to be always moving. And that's why movies were so hard for him. You're sitting in trailers. And for someone like that, it was just hard."

John fell into his usual pattern, arriving late to the set; Wayfarers concealing bleary eyes, brimming with contrition. Layne "Shotgun" Britton, the septuagenarian makeup artist, did his best to paste over the damage, calling John "fat boy" right to his face as he worked. One rough morning, Shotgun took a look at John and said, "Jesus Christ, kid. You know, once I had to stand Robert Mitchum up against the wall and paint eyes on his eyelids, he was so fucked up." It was Shotgun's way of gently chiding Belushi to shape up.

Studio executives did what they could to track John's nocturnal travels. "We hired hot and cold running trainers to surround John, to try to keep him straight," Thom Mount said. "We had all kinds of men come and go who professed to have expertise in this area, and none of them succeeded. John eluded all of them."

For this shoot, John chose his own overseer, a Texan named Morris Lyda, on a recommendation from James Taylor. Lyda had worked with David Bowie and Linda Ronstadt. When Bob Weiss called Lyda, his wife picked up. She said he was out on his ranch, towing a tractor out of a bog. "He sounds like just the guy we need," Weiss replied.

Lyda flew to Chicago and served a dual role as driver to Belushi and road manager to the Blues Brothers band, which was not on the road. He helped John get up and out in the morning, ferried him to the set, and chaperoned him through the night as best he could. Lyda controlled cash flow to the musicians, each of whom earned $1,000 a week. He tried to control John's cash, so that at least Belushi couldn't buy blow with his own funds. But John got so much free coke that money hardly mattered.

In showbiz parlance, *The Blues Brothers* was a two-hander, a two-man performance, like a Laurel and Hardy film. The Brothers had no real costar, no one who would share the screen for more than a few minutes at a time. Among the dozens of character actors, comedians, film directors, and musical performers enlisted to play minor parts, the standout was Carrie Fisher, the diminutive *Star Wars* princess, daughter of screen legends Debbie Reynolds and Eddie Fisher. Dan had written a part for "Joliet" Jake's crazy ex-girlfriend. When the time came to cast it, Landis asked, "What about Carrie?"

John considered Fisher a kindred spirit, not least for their addictive personalities. "They're different," John once told Fisher, referring to Dan and Judy. "We're alike." John could talk Carrie into almost anything. She hated hard liquor; he got her drinking Wild Turkey. They did opium together.

Judy tried to forbid cocaine at the Blues Bar. She might as well have forbidden oxygen. Morris Lyda recalled a night when "some kid had got in there and got up to Belushi and said, 'You want a bump?' 'Yeah.' They went out back. The kid has a little brown bottle of blow. He dips his spoon in there and does a snort. He dips the spoon in and gives it to Belushi, and he blows it away." John emptied the bottle into the cap, tipped it back, and snorted it up. "That's how you do cocaine," he told the stricken boy.

Another night, Landis asked Fisher to mind John at the bar. As they sat, John pulled out a stash and offered her some.

"John, should you really be doing that?" she asked.

"Do you want some blow or not!" he screamed.

Fisher didn't even like coke, but John got her hooked. Dan grew concerned about her habit. He kept trying to get her to eat. One evening at dinner, Fisher choked on a brussels sprout. Dan performed the Heimlich maneuver, possibly saving her life. Then he proposed to her. She accepted.

"John's perfect double-date concept was me and Danny and him and Judy," Fisher said. "He was in love with Danny and I being in love, and his influence was such that he could make it happen. But the problem was that now Danny had two people to take care of, which was a lot for Danny to do." The engagement unraveled.

Carrie Fisher would appear in perhaps five minutes of the finished *Blues Brothers* film, captured in various states of alertness. When the crew shot her inside the Curl Up & Dye salon, painting her nails and flipping through a manual for an M-79 flamethrower, Fisher was "spaced out" and barely able to speak, Stephen Katz recalled. She and Penny Marshall had dropped acid before the shoot.

Yet, for all the drugs and delays and ambitious set pieces, *The Blues Brothers* progressed smoothly, at first.

Production entered its second week. The crew journeyed to Joliet on Tuesday, August 21, to film at the Joliet Correctional Center, a limestone fortress that had once housed Confederate prisoners. Already, delays had pushed the production more than a week behind schedule, but the prison shoot, painstakingly arranged with the warden, could not be moved.

Filmmakers had toured both Joliet and Stateville, another maximum-security prison a few miles to the north. Stateville, named in Dan's original phonebook script, featured a panopticon "roundhouse" design, with an armed tower at the center of a vast circle of tiered cells, "like Dante's *Inferno*," Landis said. Prison officials introduced Landis to Richard Speck, a Stateville resident who had slain eight student nurses in a Chicago town house. Some weeks after the crew's visit, inmates staged a violent standoff against the guards. Landis crossed Stateville from the location list.

Dan insisted on traveling the forty-five miles from Chicago to the Joliet Prison by motorcycle. David Sosna tried to stop him. "If you crash," he said, "we won't have a movie." Dan appealed to Landis. The director gave his blessing; Dan had ridden thousands of miles on his Harley.

The *Blues Brothers* production was awash in recreational drugs, so Sosna warned cast and crew not, for heaven's sake, to bring any to the prison. A couple of grips forgot his instruction. Prison officials found the contraband and sought to jail the offenders. Weiss and Landis talked them out of it.

Joliet Prison housed its own share of dangerous men. Between takes, John turned to a guard, gestured to a group of inmates, and asked, "What did those guys do?"

"You see that tall guy?" the guard replied. "He murdered his wife, his two children, his mother and father with a hatchet."

"Really?" John walked over to the tall convict.

"Hey, is it true you murdered your family with a hatchet?"

"Yes'um."

"What happened?"

The convict gazed at John. "I don't know, I just went crazy."

John walked over to his director. He and Landis gaped at each other and shared a spontaneous "Whoa," almost as if the cameras were already rolling.

In the filmed scene, a pair of guards frog-march Jake Blues through the antebellum prison, past real prisoners, and across the bleak grounds beneath a slate sky, the latter frames shot from a crane. Frank Oz, the puppeteer who had just voiced Yoda for George Lucas in *The Empire Strikes Back*, hands Jake his effects across a desk: "One Timex digital watch, broken. One unused prophylactic, one soiled."

Jake emerges from the prison through a steel gate that had not moved in thirty years. Landis "paid big money to get that thing opened up," said Dennis Wolff, the warden. Brilliant sunlight bathes Jake's body in an unearthly glow.

In keeping with the film's overarching spirituality, Landis wanted Jake Blues to make his entrance like "an otherworldly, Christlike creature," Stephen Katz recalled. Landis asked the cinematographer to invoke the blinding light that framed the aliens who emerged from the spaceship in Spielberg's *Close Encounters*. Sosna found a way to create the effect: The crew placed a giant white curtain behind Belushi and scattered white silica sand on the ground, all to reflect light back at the camera. When they shined ten-thousand-watt lights on the curtained scene, the white-hot glare rendered the background "bleached out and overexposed," Katz said. The effect "truly set the tone for the film. It wasn't based in any reality, more of a spiritual moment. Belushi the messiah had been set free." Landis shot the emerging Belushi mostly from behind: only when Jake and Elwood embrace, six full minutes into the film, would theater patrons see his face.

Not long after the prison visit, the filmmakers invited the warden and his wife to the Blues Bar. That night, revelers passed around a film can filled with weed. The can reached Jackson Browne, who unwittingly passed it to the warden. "The warden's holding it, and he's looking at his wife, and he realizes that he's holding a can of pot," said William Kaplan, the soundman. "And for a moment, he's like, 'Whadda I do now?' And he just passed it on."

Chapter 22

Get Off of That Picasso

L ORNE MICHAELS spent the summer of 1979 preparing for the Broadway opening of *Gilda Radner: Live from New York*, his answer to *The Blues Brothers*.

After four seasons, *Saturday Night Live* had spawned plenty of side projects and spin-offs. Michaels and much of the *SNL* brain trust had collaborated with some of the Monty Python gang on *All You Need Is Cash*, a brilliant 1978 mockumentary about a pop band called the Rutles, a send-up of the Beatles. The TV movie cast John Belushi as Ron Decline, a parody of Allen Klein, the fearsome manager; and Dan as Brian Thigh, a tubercular composite of several pinhead artists-and-repertoire men who had turned the Beatles away. Bill Murray had starred in *Meatballs*, a 1979 summer-camp comedy that launched, at last, the directing career of Ivan Reitman. Murray seemed destined for bigger things, including a collaboration with Chevy Chase and the *National Lampoon* gang on their big *Animal House* follow-up. That film, the directorial debut of Harold Ramis, would enter production in the autumn of 1979 on a golf course in Florida. But *Caddyshack* lay in the future, and the other projects paled beside the Belushi phenomenon. *Animal House* had put Bluto on the cover of *Newsweek*.

Radner's show opened August 2 at New York's Winter Garden Theatre to mixed reviews. Radner made *People* magazine, a story that included a quote from Michael O'Donoghue, now a former *SNL* writer, about Belushi driving around in a limousine with a shoebox full of cocaine. The indelicate remark offended both John and Dan, who telephoned

Bernie Brillstein from Joliet Prison after reading it. "I want nothing more to do with those people," Dan seethed, meaning those in Lorne Michaels's orbit.

Michaels approached the fifth season of *SNL* expecting to lose John but not Dan, who had pledged he would return. The rift with John over his ear infection and many other sins seemed unlikely to heal. Once again, it fell to Bernie Brillstein to deliver the bad news. He telephoned Michaels and told him Dan had decided to leave. The news hit the papers at the end of August. A spokesman for *SNL* said nothing was final, but a spokeswoman for Brillstein said John and Dan had "nothing planned beyond the movie," which sounded final enough.

John and Judy flew to Martha's Vineyard on weekends during the *Blues Brothers* shoot to house hunt. They settled on a $425,000, eight-acre oceanfront property that had belonged to Robert McNamara, the former defense secretary whose Vietnam policies John had protested in the fog of tear gas on the Chicago streets.

"Shit," John joked to Judy, "the press won't be able to pass this up, the opportunity to mention McNamara and Belushi in the same sentence."

Scores of news outlets picked up the story. The McNamara spread included a stretch of coastline that had been a nude beach before the defense secretary cordoned it off. That account, combined with Belushi's Bluto alter ego, inspired wild stories about a clothing-optional beachfront *Animal House*. John and Judy issued a statement promising that the beach would remain off-limits, which, oddly enough, was exactly what their new neighbors wanted to hear.

Dan purchased a nearby home. Now he and John would be neighbors on the Vineyard as well as in the Village, where Dan and Peter Aykroyd shared an apartment near John and Judy. The Brothers bought matching black Jeeps with sequential license plates.

On August 28, a crisp Tuesday, the *Blues Brothers* production entered its third week. The crew drove ninety miles to Milwaukee for a one-day shoot that called for a piece of unfinished roadway. Bob Weiss found one. "Not only did it go nowhere," he said, "it ended on a ramp high up in the air." It was the eastbound terminus of I-794, an abandoned bridge from one Milwaukee expressway to another at the shores of Lake Michigan.

Before the crew could shoot there, David Sosna had to persuade a skeptical Wisconsin road official to allow stunt drivers on the jagged stretch of unfinished bridge. Sosna and his crew met the official at the site. The road official, clean-cut and older, appraised the assembled long-hairs from Hollywood. He and Sosna chatted. "I don't think this will work," the official sighed, and the crew turned back toward their vans. Sosna made a desperate play.

"Your name: you're Jewish?"

"Yes."

"A landsman!" The term meant fellow Jew, countryman, friend. Sosna was Jewish in name only, but on this day, he embraced his faith.

The official smiled. Sosna smiled. The *Blues Brothers* troops returned from the vans. The two men schmoozed. Sosna played his ace. "I asked if he knew where I could get some decent pastrami in Milwaukee." The road man beamed. In that moment, Sosna could have married his daughter. "Instead, we got the bridge."

The bridge-to-nowhere sequence caps a cartoonish scene, some of it filmed a few days earlier in the city. A group of American Nazis who have joined the pursuit of the Brothers spot the Bluesmobile in downtown Chicago and give chase, tailing Jake and Elwood in an orange Ford Pinto station wagon. For the Nazi vehicle, Landis chose a "dinky little car" that had soared to infamy for bursting into flames if a collision ruptured its gas tank. Head Nazi Henry Gibson fires out of the passenger window to a soundtrack of Wagner's "Ride of the Valkyries." A bullet pings off the Bluesmobile's engine. "We've thrown a rod," Dan announces, diagnosing the problem on sound and gearhead instinct. Smoke billows from the hood, an effect achieved by a man tethered to the front bumper and holding a smoke machine while hurtling forward at forty-five miles per hour. Jake wipes grime from the windshield. Elwood, driving blind, flies past a construction sign, blasts through sawhorses, and screeches to a halt at the edge of a concrete precipice.

This was another dangerous shot. The crew held their breaths as Dan's stunt double hit the brakes, one for each wheel, in a custom-rigged Bluesmobile. The car was supposed to stop a few feet past the road's edge. Another foot or two, and car and stuntmen would plunge to earth. On the first try, the driver "stopped too short," Landis said. The director wanted another take, "and he wanted the driver to go much faster this time," said Gene Schuldt, an actor who played one of the Nazis. "Well, the driver overshot." The Bluesmobile toppled over the edge of the roadway and became ensnared in steel reinforcement rods that protruded from the ramp. Crewmen "ran over and held the rear end of the car down while the stunt guys crawled out of the windows," Schuldt said. A crane rescued the teetering Bluesmobile. The filmed scene blends both shots, cutting away from the too-fast Bluesmobile at the final second.

The Milwaukee shoot illustrated why *The Blues Brothers* was slipping ever further behind schedule. Cast, crew, and police stood ready to film by eight a.m. on August 28. But late arrivals and the scene's sheer complexity slowed production. Cameras didn't roll until 12:20 p.m. The orange Pinto hurtled up the freeway ramp, fitted with a dummy driver and tethered to another vehicle. "At the right moment, the dummy car was released and, in a screech of tires, hit a gravel ramp at an angle, flying off one side of the expressway stub," the *Milwaukee Journal Sentinel* reported.

Landis didn't like it. "He hit the ramp at an angle," the director sighed. "We've got to retake." The retake would have to wait until the following morning, expending another orange Pinto, one of several on hand for the *Blues Brothers* production. A one-day shoot became a two-day shoot, and then a three-day shoot, each day commencing with an orange Pinto flying off the ramp.

Bob Weiss struggled for days over a second piece of Looney Tunes lunacy that Dan and his director had envisioned. In the filmed scene, the Bluesmobile dangles off the concrete cliff. Elwood throws it into reverse and launches the sedan into a gravity-defying, end-over-end flip, sailing over the Nazis in their Pinto.

The easy choice would have been to film the scene with miniatures, scale models small enough to be thrown by an off-screen hand. But

Weiss wanted to do the stunt with a full-size Bluesmobile. "The thing about miniatures," he explained, "is you can only get so close before the illusion wears off."

Weiss requisitioned an industrial quantity of mercury, the dense, liquid metal. "We put a big tank of mercury in this Bluesmobile," one of thirteen models rolling around Chicagoland. When a stunt driver backed up the vehicle, he triggered "little pointy things" that descended from the undercarriage and dug into the asphalt, halting the car. The mercury rushed to the rear of the tank, shifting the vehicle's weight and rearing it up on its hind wheels like a bucking bronco. The producer resorted to miniatures for the next shot, filmed later on the Universal lot, showing the Bluesmobile flying backward through space. Then the camera cuts to a real Bluesmobile vaulting over the doomed Pinto.

September 1, a pleasant Saturday, kicked off Labor Day weekend. The *Blues Brothers* production crew set up at Daley Plaza for a three-day shoot that would make its previous efforts look like child's play.

Seventy-five police blocked off the plaza at seven a.m. Then the troops arrived: more than two hundred extras in street clothes, two hundred faux National Guardsmen, one hundred extras dressed like police, and seven mounted police on horseback, playing themselves.

The crew spent Saturday shooting the end of the car chase. In the filmed scene, the Bluesmobile arrives at the courthouse to pay the orphans' tax bill. "There it is," Jake yells. Elwood pumps the horn as he steers diagonally across the plaza, scattering pedestrians. The first man to leap away is John Landis, in a cameo à la Hitchcock, dressed in a beige camel-hair coat, reprising his stuntman days. The car skirts a subway entrance, narrowly misses the Picasso, scatters more bystanders, and swerves around a roadblock, plowing through a plate-glass window into the Daley Center. The Bluesmobile drives straight through the modernist civic skyscraper, scattering yet more pedestrians. Then it crashes through another plate-glass window at the far side, emerging onto Randolph Street outside the Greyhound bus terminal. Elwood steers around the corner onto Clark Street, jumps the sidewalk, hits a no-parking sign, and comes to rest outside the Cook County building, an old neoclassical fortress across from the plaza. Jake and Elwood leap from the sedan and dash toward the entrance.

"That was the last shot of the day," David Sosna said.

After John and Dan exited the battered Bluesmobile, Landis halted filming, and the crew rolled in another Bluesmobile, this one precut into dozens of pieces, stitched back together, and held in place with pins attached to a slender steel cable. A tug of the cable pulled the pins, and the car fell apart. A mechanical-effects operator had toiled for months on the vehicle. A forklift carried it to the set.

Guards watched the collapsible Bluesmobile till morning, when filming resumed. John and Dan found their marks on the sidewalk beside the new Bluesmobile, and the camera rolled. In the filmed scene, Jake and Elwood turn to see the Bluesmobile collapse into a hundred pieces behind them. Elwood, stricken by the loss of his mechanical friend, doffs his hat. The camera cuts to a pair of meditative statues, watching sadly from above. Jake yells, "Come on!" and the Brothers dash off again, disappearing through golden doors into the county building, police at their heels. Inside, they upend vending machines and drag heavy marble benches to block the doors.

Landis playfully cuts to business-as-usual calm inside the county building, where soot-faced Jake and Elwood approach a group of officers.

"Sir," Elwood beckons, tipping his hat, "where's the office of the assessor of Cook County?"

"Down the hall, turn right, take the elevator to 1102," an officer responds.

"Thank you, sir." Jake and Elwood race off.

Outside, an invading army of police and firefighters attack the barricaded golden doors with axes. The doors were props, replacing the real doors, which the crew had carefully removed. Inside, Jake and Elwood skid around a corner and reach the elevator. The cab arrives, and the door closes. Cut to a squad of SWAT officers leaping from a van, chanting "hut-hut-hut." A military jeep sweeps past the Picasso. Firefighters demolish the last shards of the golden doors. An entire military convoy rolls through Daley Plaza.

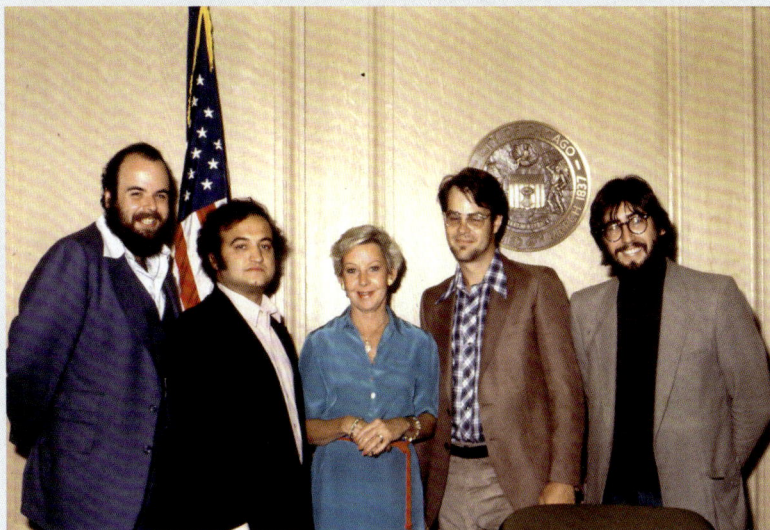

The gang meets Jane Byrne, Chicago's new mayor, who would give *The Blues Brothers* license to drive a convoy across Daley Plaza. From left: Bob Weiss, Belushi, Mayor Byrne, Aykroyd, John Landis. (*Courtesy of the Robert K. Weiss Collection*)

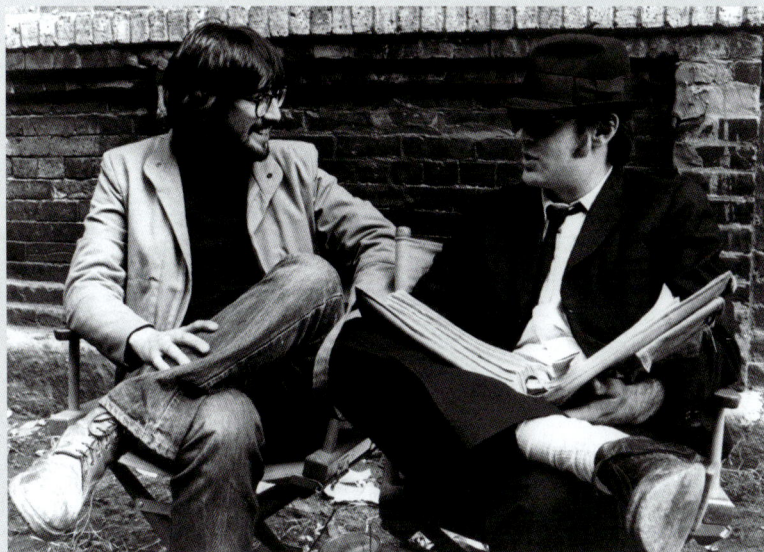

Landis and Aykroyd with *The Blues Brothers* script, 1979.
(*Author's collection*)

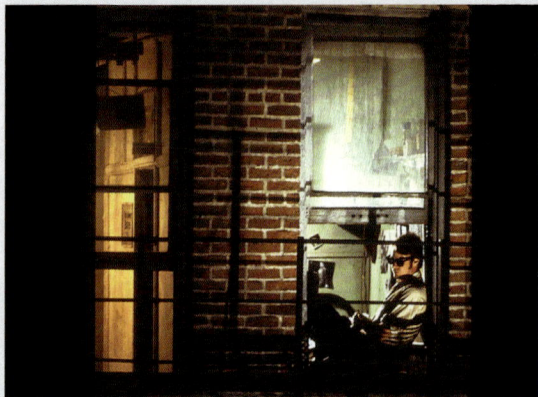

Elwood Blues at his apartment window, where the trains went by "so often, you won't even notice it." (*Courtesy of the Robert K. Weiss Collection*)

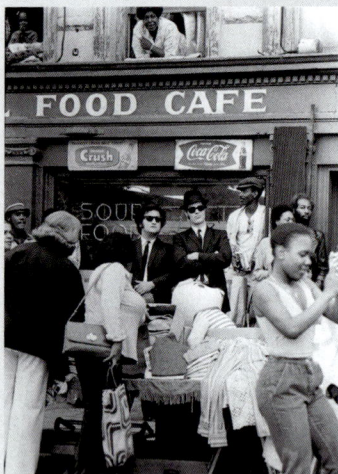

Jake and Elwood outside Aretha's Soul Food Café, where Jake would soon order four fried chickens and a Coke. (*Author's collection*)

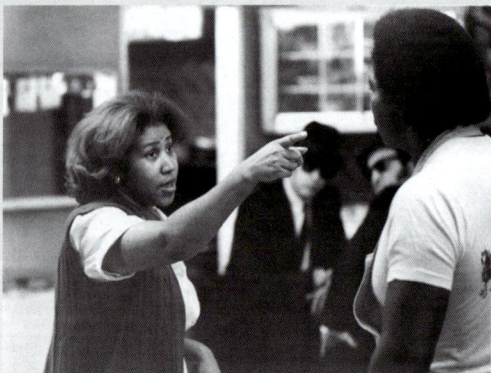

Aretha confronts her man, Matt "Guitar" Murphy, in perhaps the most celebrated musical scene from *The Blues Brothers*. (*Author's collection*)

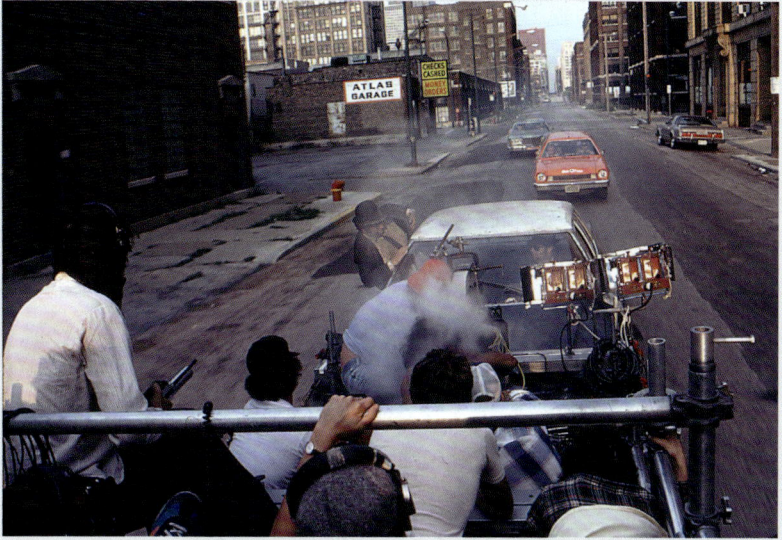

A camera crew films Jake and Elwood in the Bluesmobile, with the Nazis in pursuit. (*Courtesy of the Robert K. Weiss Collection*)

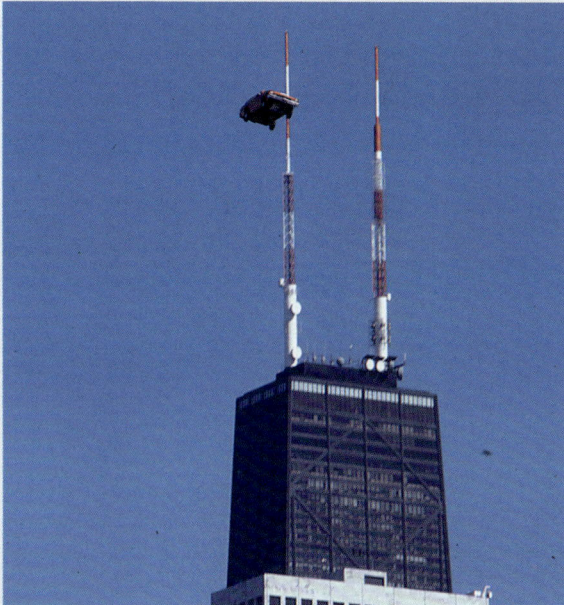

The Pinto drop, with the John Hancock building providing perspective. (*Courtesy of the Robert K. Weiss Collection*)

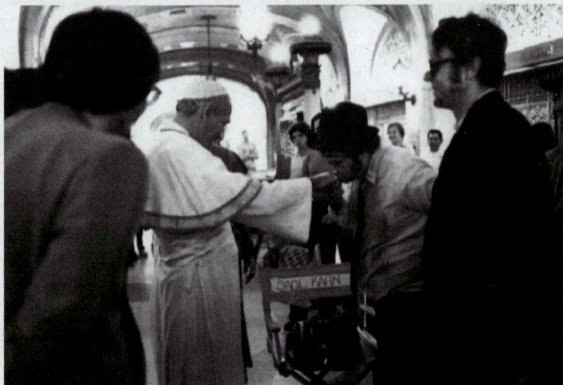

Jake and Elwood greet the fake pope. Cast and crew had thought they were meeting the real one. (*Courtesy of the Robert K. Weiss Collection*)

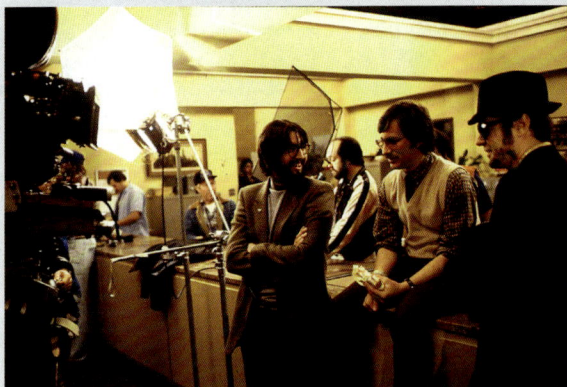

Landis with Steven Spielberg, cast as a humble tax clerk. (*Courtesy of the Robert K. Weiss Collection*)

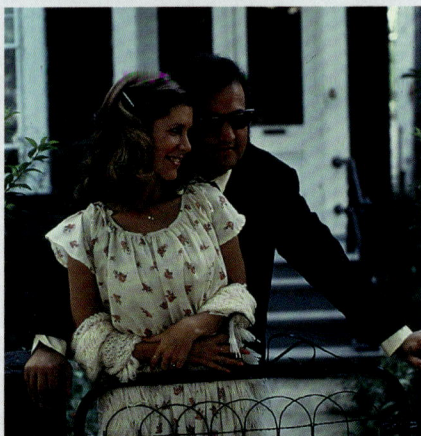

Belushi with Carrie Fisher, the Mystery Woman. During *The Blues Brothers* shoot, she and Dan Aykroyd were briefly engaged. (*Courtesy of the Robert K. Weiss Collection*)

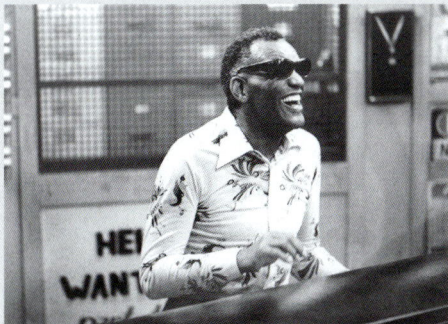

Ray Charles demonstrates the action on a beat-up Fender Rhodes keyboard. (*Author's collection*)

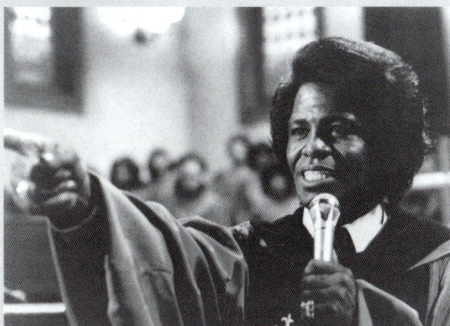

James Brown asks, "Have you seen the light?" (*Author's collection*)

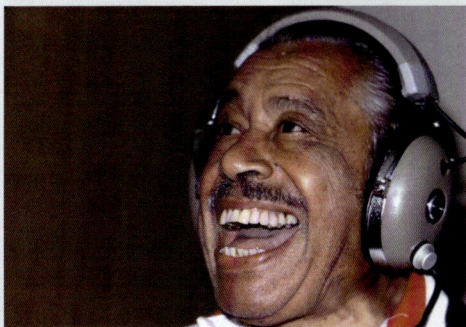

Cab Calloway recording the vocals for "Minnie the Moocher" in a Chicago studio. (*Courtesy of the Robert K. Weiss Collection*)

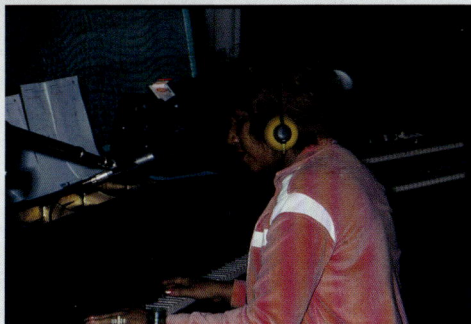

Aretha Franklin in the Chicago studio, recording the piano and vocals for "Think." (*Courtesy of the Robert K. Weiss Collection*)

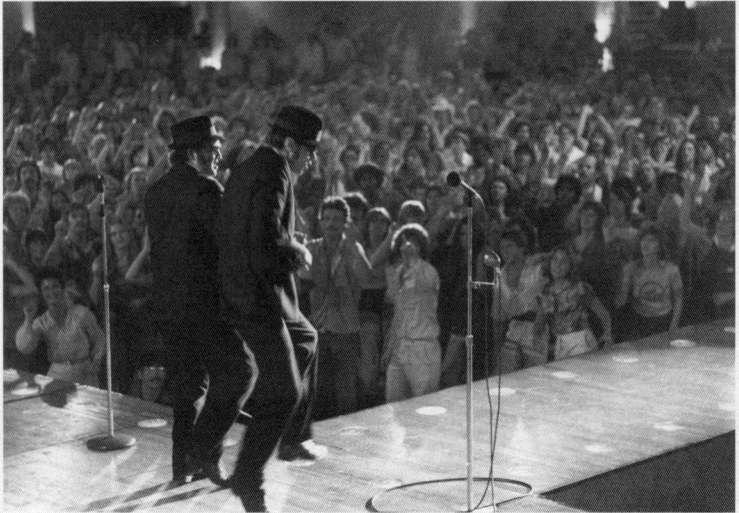

The Blues Brothers in concert at the Hollywood Palladium, the climactic scene in
The Blues Brothers. Local police tried to bust audience extras for smoking pot.
(*Courtesy of the John Landis collection*)

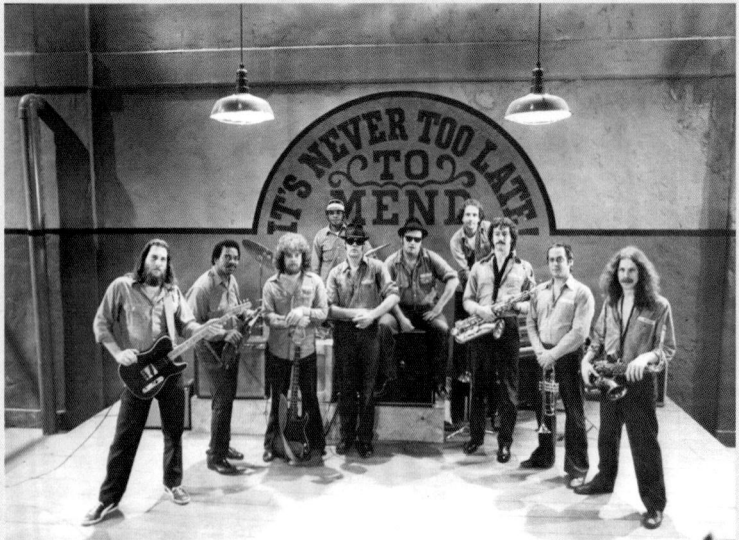

The Blues Brothers band. From left: Steve "The Colonel" Cropper,
Matt "Guitar" Murphy, Donald "Duck" Dunn, Willie "Too Big" Hall, Aykroyd,
Belushi, Murphy "Murph" Dunne, Tom "Bones" Malone,
Alan "Mr. Fabulous" Rubin, "Blue" Lou Marini.
(*Author's collection*)

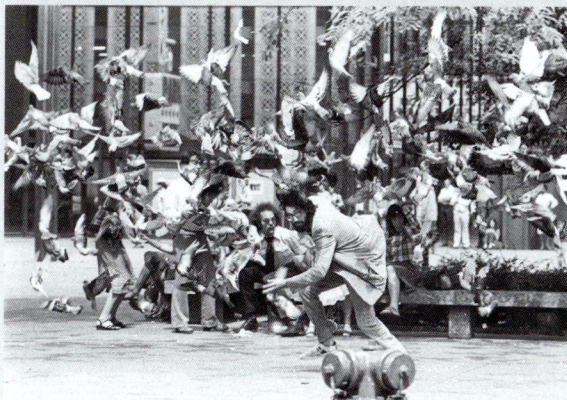

John Landis in cameo, leaping out of the way of the oncoming Bluesmobile. (*STM-002979452, Jim Frost/Chicago Sun-Times. Courtesy of the Chicago History Museum.*)

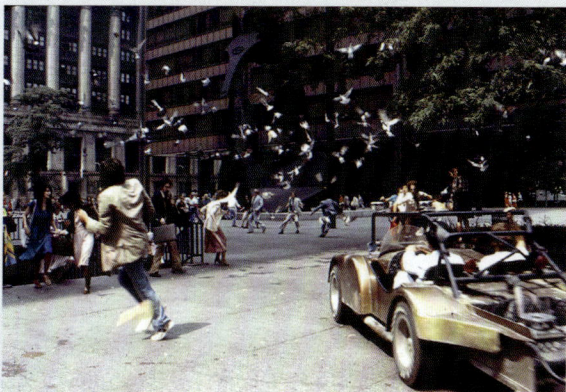

Having evaded the Bluesmobile, Landis turns to appraise the Daley Plaza scene as the camera car shoots past. He was, after all, the director. (*Courtesy of the Robert K. Weiss Collection*)

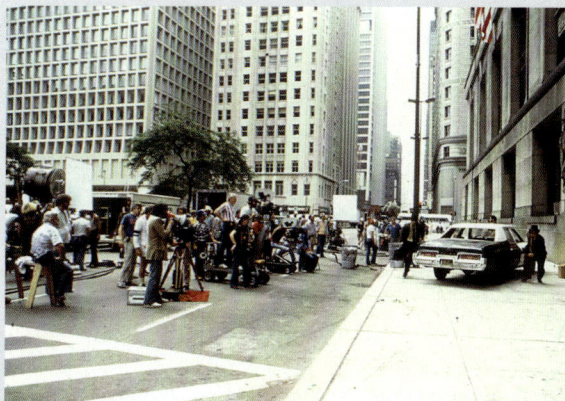

The Blues Brothers arrive at the Cook County building, Memorial Day weekend, 1979. John Landis stands behind the camera. (*Courtesy of the Robert K. Weiss Collection*)

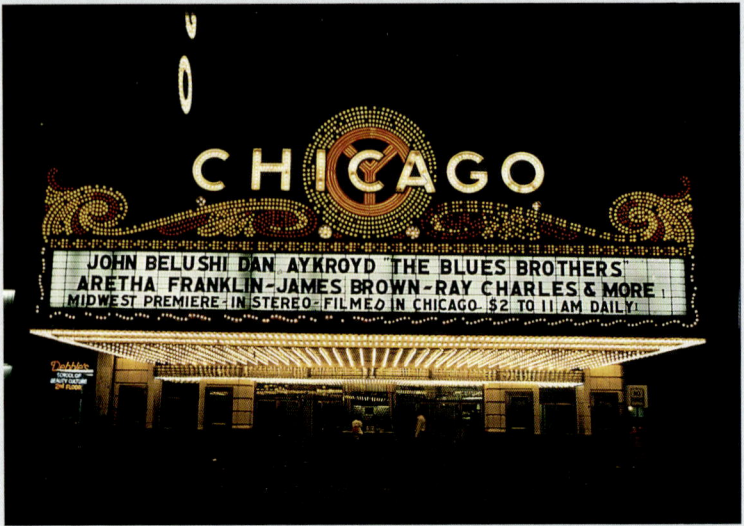

The Midwest premiere of *The Blues Brothers* at the Chicago Theatre.
(*Courtesy of the Robert K. Weiss Collection*)

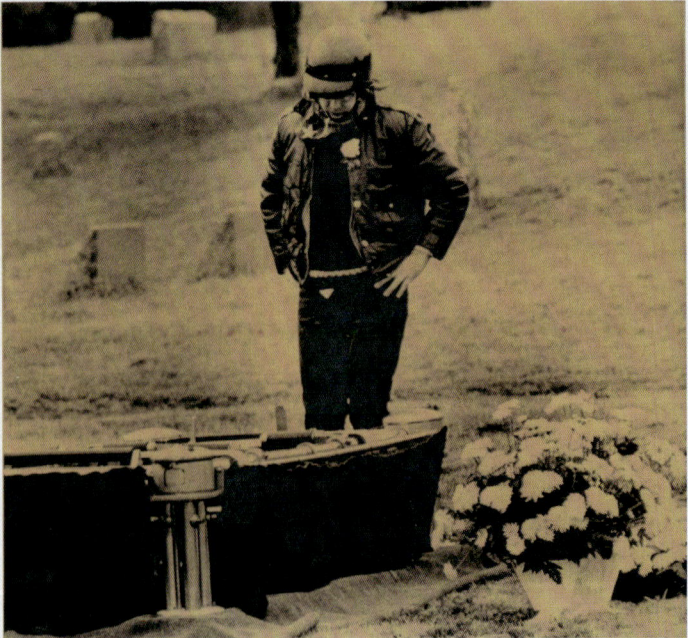

Dan Aykroyd at Belushi's grave, March 9, 1982.
(*Courtesy of the* Boston Herald *and MediaNews Group. Photo by Joanne Rathe Strohmeyer.*)

Cut to Jake and Elwood, jaws set, staring stolidly ahead as the elevator creeps up to the eleventh floor, the car silent save for a low pulse of Muzak: "The Girl from Ipanema," the bossa nova classic.

Back when he was filming *Animal House*, Landis had asked Antônio Carlos Jobim for permission to parody "The Girl from Ipanema" in a scene that showed Otter dressing for a tryst. Doug Kenney had written funny lyrics. Jobim "didn't find it funny and said no," Landis said. In revenge, the director repurposed the song as elevator music in his next film. Copyright law permitted him to use the song, sans parody lyrics, without Jobim's permission.

All day, the plaza and surrounding streets rattled beneath the combined weight of one Sherman tank, three hook-and-ladder trucks, four troop trucks, fifty squad cars, innumerable army jeeps, one SWAT truck, two hundred extras, one hundred state and city police officers, two hundred faux National Guardsmen, twenty firemen, and seven horses. Some in the crew feared the granite plaza might collapse. Helicopters sliced through the sky. SWAT men crawled across the roof and rappelled down columns. Some of the shaky aerial shots looked like war footage filmed with a handheld camera, which, in fact, they were.

Landis and Weiss had battled with a squeamish Federal Aviation Administration over the helicopters. A DC-10 had crashed on takeoff from Chicago's O'Hare International Airport just four months earlier, killing 273 people. Fearful aviation officials forbade Weiss to land a helicopter on Daley Plaza, restricting him to shooting footage from above. And then, on the morning of the plaza shoot, "I get the invariable six a.m. phone call," Weiss said. A fuel truck had backed into one of the helicopters, rendering it unusable, along with the fixed camera mount inside. Weiss told Stephen Katz, who would have to make do without his aerial shots.

"I said, 'Fuck it, take the handheld camera, go up,'" Katz recalled. "So, it's shot with a handheld camera. It's great, 'cause you feel like you're really in the helicopter. It reminded me of a Sam Fuller war movie." Weiss procured a perch atop the Gothic-style First United Methodist Church tower, once Chicago's tallest structure, to shoot some less-shaky aerial footage. In consolation for the lost helicopter, a repentant FAA allowed Weiss to land one of his remaining birds on the plaza.

In the filmed sequence, the army of troops stops at the checkpoint where Elwood asked directions.

"Excuse me," a squad leader asks, "did you see two guys come in here, black suits, black hats, one carrying a briefcase?"

"Yeah, I just sent 'em down there."

"Thank you," the squad leader replies, in muted understatement. Hundreds of troops swarm past and, finding the elevator in use, fly up the stairs.

Jake and Elwood reach the eleventh floor, find the assessor's office, and see a handwritten sign on the glass door: "Back in 5 minutes." (Landis had written it.) The Brothers fidget uneasily outside the locked office as hundreds of armed men storm across the plaza and up the stairs. At last, a clerk appears at the door: Steven Spielberg, in a cameo, chewing on a sandwich, a sequence filmed later on the Universal lot. "Can I help you?" Spielberg asks. Jack and Elwood hoist him by the armpits and carry him across his own office, planting him atop the counter. Spielberg calmly regards the boys and their paperwork as an army of men charges up the stairs and blasts through the glass doors behind them. Spielberg stamps the form and hands the boys their receipt for settling the orphanage's tax bill. Cut to a close-up of Jake's and Elwood's wrists as handcuffs snap around them.

The Daley Plaza shoot cost $3.5 million, more than Universal had spent on *Animal House*, more, reportedly, than any studio had spent on a single scene for any film in a big city. Miraculously, a weekend of pantomimed police actions yielded just two minor injuries. A stuntman tripped while bursting out of an elevator and fell on his foam fire ax. Belushi strained his back while helping Dan move furniture to block doors.

The studio spent $17,000 to replace the shattered nine-by-nine glass panels in the Daley Center, paying union glaziers double time to work on a national holiday so the panes would be in place when the city reopened the next day.

The studio's biggest fear had been that someone might land a helicopter on the Picasso, the odd, brooding aardvark whose demise many

Chicagoans would have cheered. At one point amid the mayhem, an extra had scaled the statue, prompting Landis to borrow David Sosna's bullhorn and bellow, "Get off of that Picasso," a line that surely no director had said before nor would utter again.

The *Chicago Sun-Times* ran a story on day two of the Daley Plaza shoot, marveling at the assembled forces and assuring readers that the broken plate-glass windows would be replaced. But the massive production did not draw the army of press Landis had feared. Even as they filmed in plain sight, the filmmakers nursed improbable hopes that no prying reporters would reveal their cinematic secrets to the world.

Just before the holiday weekend, however, word had leaked that *The Blues Brothers* was no longer a $6 million movie or even a $12 million movie. Syndicated columnist Marilyn Beck announced that the film "is now expected to cost at least $16 million," citing Bernie Brillstein, an executive producer. The production "is turning out to be larger than anyone realized," Brillstein said. *Variety* invoked the same $16 million figure in its August 29 edition, within a cover story published beneath the five-column headline U.S. PIC BUDGETS INTO MEGABUCK ERA.

Bob Weiss showed the piece to Landis and film editor George Folsey, noting that the production had spent $16 million already. "Well," Folsey mused, "no turning back now."

On September 5, as *The Blues Brothers* entered its fourth week of production, the studio took out four color pages in *Variety* for an ad that toyed with the film's many industry critics. On the first page, white letters against a black background spelled out "It's too late." Readers turned the page to behold a double truck featuring Jake and Elwood and the Bluesmobile against a bleak Chicago backdrop of power lines and girders: "Production has begun." The next page carried the traditional ad, names of cast and crew framing a group photo. Aykroyd was almost smiling.

"It was quite famous at the time," Sean Daniel recalled. "It was a message to the audience: 'This is coming at you.' And it turned out to be a fateful line for everyone who was working on the movie."

The crew headed to remote Wauconda, Illinois, that day to film a montage: the Bluesmobile driving along a suburban Main Street, down a country road, through an empty field, and past throngs of bathers, an enormous civil-defense speaker mounted on its roof. Dan modeled the mammoth speaker on the air-raid siren at his elementary school in Canada.

Cab Calloway appears in the tableau as Curtis, dressed to match Elwood and Jake and handing flyers to adorable orphans. In separate shots, filmed later in Hollywood, Aretha Franklin, James Brown, and Ray Charles hang posters for the Blues Brothers charity show. Brother Ray hangs his upside down.

The beachfront footage came not from Lake Michigan but from a private stretch on tiny Bangs Lake, a Wauconda recreation spot. One suburban homeowner refused to open his beach to the crew until John and Dan emerged from their trailer to pose for pictures with his family.

One hot late-summer day, the crew traveled to Jackson Park, a jewel in the necklace of sprawling urban parks that landscape architect Frederick Law Olmsted had planted around Chicago. Atop a historic Jackson Park bridge, they staged a demonstration by Illinois Nazis.

By introducing white supremacists into *The Blues Brothers*, Dan and Landis fed the film's narrative arc and honored Dan's "mission from God." The Nazis served as a symbol of entrenched American racism, which every great Black musical artist had battled. Until Jake and Elwood encountered the Nazis, the story delivered no real villain. Yes, the Brothers had adversaries, legions of police and troopers and cha-grined country-and-western musicians who would thwart their quest. But the officers were only doing their jobs, and the members of the Good Ole Boys band had a legitimate beef. The Nazis, alone among the Brothers' pursuers, counted as truly villainous.

"We had always intended to have some sort of white-supremacist thing," Landis said. "The Klan, we couldn't use them, because it was Chicago," not the South. Instead, Landis chose Nazis. And if the notion of a Catholic orphanage owing property taxes sounded far-fetched, the idea of neo-Nazis marching in Chicago did not. Illinois Nazis had planned a demonstration for the summer of 1978 in Skokie, a largely Jewish Chicago suburb. Amid howls of outrage, officials moved the rally downtown, where Chicagoans pelted the Nazis with eggs. The Skokie rally seemed a natural subject for *National Lampoon*–style parody: at one point, Harold Ramis and Doug Kenney had pitched it as the basis for a second *Lampoon* film.

Now, Landis re-created the standoff in verdant Jackson Park, a dozen faux fascists facing scores of screaming protesters. He recruited Henry Gibson, a former *Laugh-In* regular who had appeared in *The Kentucky Fried Movie*, as their leader. Landis wrote a speech for Gibson to deliver to the frothing crowd, larded with lines such as "the swastika is calling you." He transcribed the words verbatim from the answering-machine message of the real-life National Socialist Party of America, the group that had assembled in Chicago.

Before the cameras rolled, Gibson told Landis, "I want to speak to the crowd." He addressed the throng of extras: "I'm a nice guy. I don't mean any of the things I'm going to say."

The filmed scene starts with the Bluesmobile stalled in traffic at the stone bridge.

"Hey, what's going on?" Jake asks a passing cop.

"Ah, those bums won their court case, so they're marching today."

"What bums?"

"The fucking Nazi party."

The line in the script contained no expletive. The cop added it on his own. Landis kept it.

Elwood scoffs. "Illinois Nazis."

After a considered pause, Jake replies, "I hate Illinois Nazis."

Elwood screeches the Bluesmobile around the traffic jam and up the bridge, scattering Nazis into the lagoon, to ecstatic cheers from the protesters. Crew workers tossed dead fish into the water to float among the thrashing Nazis in their close-up.

At times, during those long weeks in Chicago, the *Blues Brothers* shoot came to resemble a montage of car crashes. In addition to renting active police cars for chase scenes, the *Blues Brothers* crew purchased more than sixty retired squad cars, at $400 each, for crash scenes. Every night, after a pileup, "the teamsters would be there with car carriers, and they would haul the cars that we had damaged back to a garage on the West Side of Chicago, a garage that was in a nasty neighborhood where people got shot," David Sosna said. Repairs to the fleet of sixty-odd cars would allow *The Blues Brothers* to set a record for cars destroyed in a film, 103.

The crew filmed many crash scenes on Sundays, when expressway traffic ran lighter. One Sunday, during filming in the western suburbs, an inconvenienced motorist "took his car, and he tried to run over a lady cop" at a freeway entrance, Sosna recalled. "So, the lady cop says on the radio, 'This guy's trying to kill me with his car.' And at that moment, I lose control of the set." The imperiled officer's comrades took off in their squad cars, "going the wrong way on the freeway," a scene as crazy as anything in *The Blues Brothers*. Officers swarmed the aggressive motorist and "beat the fuck out of this guy." Then they returned to their positions, and filming resumed.

For one particularly daring sequence, to be shot over three days, the shooting schedule dictated, "100 mph chase under El tracks." Mayor Byrne had granted filmmakers permission to shoot thirty cop cars chasing the Bluesmobile along Lake Street, a catacomb of trestles supporting elevated tracks, at racecar speeds. Only eight years had passed since the release of *The French Connection*, with Gene Hackman chasing a bad guy through Brooklyn in a speeding car beneath that Metropolitan Transportation Authority's elevated tracks.

David Sosna locked up every intersection and cleared the sidewalks beneath the tracks before shooting the breakneck pursuit. Stunt drivers replaced Dan and John, whose close-up images would be spliced in later.

In the filmed scene, Elwood steers the Bluesmobile through one calamitous intersection after another, running red lights, swerving around a panel truck, evading station wagons and even a pack of cyclists. The absurd procession of obstacles looked like something out of *The Kentucky Fried Movie*. Landis had pumped the crew for suggestions. He loved the idea of the Bluesmobile blowing past bicycles. David Sosna hated it. "Somebody's an eighth of a second late, he's gonna be dead," he fretted.

Landis himself rode in the "*Bullitt* car," a stripped-down Corvette with a camera mounted on top, designed for the Steve McQueen film, "going

110 mph with the stunt driver and talking into the walkie-talkie, cuing the trucks and the bicycles," the director said. "It was all done in one long take." He filmed John and Dan in a separate run at a much lower speed, shooting backward from a camera car that towed the Bluesmobile.

The L track chase ends in an epic pileup. The Bluesmobile hits a stopped cruiser. More cop cars hurtle into the scene, crashing into each other, flipping dramatically and launching off one another.

"We had to get permission from the city to drill holes in their streets so pipe ramps could be bolted into the street," David Sosna said. The pipe ramp, a piece of stunt-car technology, flipped a car on its axis if hit at the right angle. The ramp worked so well that the finished scene shows cars entering the frame already airborne and upside down. Film-goers had never seen the like.

The final smashup "took a hell of a lot of planning," Stephen Katz recalled. "I'm standing on the sidelines watching this. All the cameras are rolling, and I'm just hoping there's film in the cameras." As the scene unfolded, Katz turned to a visiting Universal executive and said, "I've always wanted to make an art film."

Most interior shots for *The Blues Brothers* would wait until the crew reached Los Angeles. But the location scouts wanted to film inside the flophouse at 22 West Van Buren Street. They repurposed it as the Plymouth Hotel, home to Elwood's one-room apartment on the L tracks in the West Loop. The script had the boys spending their first night together inside the narrow space.

"Well, it ain't much, but it's home," Elwood announces in the filmed scene as the pair enters the pistachio-walled room, a space almost too slender for a single bed.

"How often does the train go by?" Jake asks.

"So often you won't even notice it."

Elwood puts a record on the turntable. He toasts Wonder Bread on a bent clothes hanger over a hot plate. Jake falls asleep on the bed as the ceaseless trains roll past, visibly rattling the room.

"Those were my trains," David Sosna said. Landis wanted the apartment scene to play out against a constant rumble of passing trains.

Outside the window lay parallel tracks, enclosing the city center within a rectangular loop of elevated railway.

Sosna paid four motormen to sit at either end of each two-car L train and run them in opposite directions. "On the foreground track I had one train, and it would go right to left. And a second later, there'd be a car going left to right" on the other track, he explained. "And then both cars would stop, and they'd reverse." All this played out during a late-night lull in Chicago transit service. The scene defied reality: even at rush hour, L trains never pass quite that often.

Belushi had appeared healthy at the start of shooting. By the time of the nocturnal flophouse scene, he looked pale and sounded stuffy, the toll of relentless partying. The decision to conceal the boys' eyes behind dark sunglasses suddenly looked providential.

Chapter 23

The Pinto Drop

I F ANY SET IN *The Blues Brothers* rivaled Daley Plaza for sheer destruc-
tive ambition, it was Dixie Square mall. Within the abandoned retail
hangar, twenty miles south of downtown Chicago, set decorators had
spent weeks installing electricity, air-conditioning, and light, realistic
signage, and truckloads of real mall merchandise. Inside, they painstakingly recreated thirty-two storefronts, including such familiar Chicago
names as clothier Bigsby & Kruthers, Jewel supermarket, Lemmy's hot
dogs, and R.J. Grunts restaurant.

"They had to contact everybody and explain, on stationery, 'We're
making a movie, and we'd like to use your products,'" David Sosna said.
"The deal was, we would return what survived. We never knew from shot
to shot what was gonna make it to the end of the day."

Production commenced on September 10, at a reported cost of
$200,000 a day. The script called for a car chase through a parking lot
filled with seven hundred brand-new cars, rented from local dealerships
and driven to the set by teamsters and production assistants. The first
night, though, unfolded as a bewildering ballet of delays.

Stephen Katz, the painstaking cinematographer, toiled for hours
planting stage lights around the vast mall, "throwing a parabola of light
on each pilaster," David Sosna recalled. "Looked gorgeous. Took the
whole first half of the night to rig." In a more disciplined production,
crew would have set the lights beforehand.

"A quarter mile we lit," Katz said. "It was insanity."

That was the night the *Blues Brothers* cinematographer decided to fire his senior staff. "I was sick and tired of smelling alcohol on their breath," he said. The crusty Universal hands had battled Katz every day for a month. Now, at the start of a mammoth shoot, the cinematographer dismissed his top aides, the gaffer and key grip, and promoted younger assistants to take their place.

"The studio went berserk," Katz said. "They didn't want the wheels to stop. The wheels fucking stopped. Right there on the exterior of the mall. A million people. 'Goodbye.' John was right behind me," he said, meaning Landis. "John protected me, and I just kept going. And from that day on, the film took on a new life. All the young guys were like, 'Wow, let's do this.' And they were my guys. They became my army."

Later that night, Belushi vanished from the set.

"It was a cold night," Dan said. "It was about two in the morning, and lunch had been called," albeit at an unusual hour. "And it was over, and everybody was looking for Belushi." No one could find him. "Time and money were ticking away."

John had gone on one of his walkabouts, Morris Lyda's term for Belushi's disappearances. His wanderings usually ended hours later with a telephone call, a gravelly voice instructing Lyda, "Come pick me up."

On this night, the meter was running. Dan lit a cigarette and "stood under the stars, under the streetlamps," he recalled. Glancing around, he beheld "this path kind of leading out of the weed-strewn parking lot into a suburban neighborhood nearby." He followed it. "I walked into the neighborhood. I looked, and all the houses were dark," except one. On instinct, Dan walked up to the door and knocked. A man appeared in his bathrobe.

"Yeah?"

"We're shooting a movie over here," Dan said.

"Yeah, I know."

"And we're looking for one of our actors."

"Yeah, I know. Belushi. He came in here about half an hour ago. He raided my fridge. He's asleep on my couch."

Dan awakened his partner. "John," he said, "we've gotta go back to work."

In the filmed scene, the Bluesmobile pulls into the mall parking lot, trailed by two police cruisers. The stunt drivers tried not to hit the parked cars as the procession wove expertly around them on the slick pavement, which had been soaked with truckloads of water. Wet pavement reflected light back into the camera, defining the road surface.

"You got us into this parking lot, pal," Jake Blues quips. "Now you get us out."

"You want out of this parking lot?" Elwood asks menacingly. "OK."

Inside Toys "R" Us, a cheery cashier rings up a sale. "Will there be anything else?"

The customer holds up a Grover doll. "Yes. Do you have a Miss Piggy?"

The Bluesmobile crashed in, vaulting off a hidden ramp through the plate-glass window. The stunt car came sickeningly close to crushing a stuntwoman who stood in its path. (Look for the woman in light slacks and a red top.)

For the interior shoot, the crew had lit the rebuilt mall "like a mall was lit. I think we had every generator in Hollywood," Stephen Katz said. "We could go anywhere, three hundred and sixty [degrees], any time."

Stunt drivers spent the next several days reducing the mall's interior to "a screaming mess," per the script instruction, smashing through storefronts fitted with real glass, plowing through kiosks stocked with real merchandise, narrowly missing dozens of stunt actors cast as shoppers and standing in carefully prescribed spots, lest they be hit. Katherine Wooten, the script supervisor, swept in behind the stunt cars on roller skates, checking each camera for continuity, the sense of seamless visual consistency from shot to shot. The crew had sealed and blacked out every exterior door and window, to preserve the illusion of night. Screeching cars spewed exhaust fumes and burnt rubber into the enclosed space, befouling the air, already ripe from rotting produce in the supermarket. Cast and crew took periodic ten-minute breaks, filing outside to fill their lungs with fresh air. The scene ended with the Bluesmobile crashing out through a JCPenney window.

One stuntman strayed from his mark, edging toward the cameras to "increase his odds of being seen," Bob Weiss said. A shard of glass nicked his chin, requiring two stitches, the lone injury. The mall shoot became an $850,000 item in the *Blues Brothers* budget.

So far, so good, the producer thought. Then he received a summons to the mayor's office.

"I get to the meeting," he said, "and there's the head of the fire department, the head of the police department, politicos from Mayor Byrne's office. It's like, 'What the fuck did I do?'"

The city brass told Weiss they were concerned about an upcoming scene in the shoot: Landis wanted to blow up a building. His script had Carrie Fisher's vengeful Mystery Woman detonate the Plymouth Hotel as Jake slept inside. Producers had a deal with owners of the Wabash Hotel, a shuttered inn on Harrison Street in the South Loop. They would implode the building on film, a $30,000 stunt. Now, city officials told Weiss they feared the blast might rupture underground gas pipes, potentially triggering a chain reaction of unintended explosions around the city. The stunt could spark another Great Chicago Fire.

Weiss canceled the detonation. Months later, a special-effects crew in LA would fake the explosion with studio trickery, using flash powder and an enlarged still frame of the flophouse, a sequence interspersed with interior shots of balsa-wood bricks and beams falling on Jake and Elwood in a Hollywood studio.

Just one year earlier, filmmakers had been all but forbidden in Chicago. Now, the city hummed with cinematic activity. One Friday in late September, Landis and his crew watched from Lower Wacker Drive as a competing film crew sent a green Pontiac Grand Prix crashing through a cable fence on the fifteenth floor of the Marina City parking garage and sailing into the Chicago River.

Paramount Pictures had arrived to launch production on *The Hunter*, an action picture starring Steve McQueen, whose producers had sweet-talked Mayor Byrne into allowing them in behind *The Blues Brothers*.

McQueen occupied half of the presidential suite atop the Holiday Inn. John Landis and his wife, Deborah Nadoolman, shared the other half. "And he and I would come out at the same time in the morning and go to the elevator," Landis recalled, "like the coyote and the sheep" in the Looney Tunes cartoon. Landis and his crew menaced their Paramount rivals, stealing walkie-talkies and dispensing bad directions. One day at mealtime, the crews staged an *Animal House*–style food fight across the Chicago River.

Landis and his crew would not be upstaged by Steve McQueen and his crew. On the last day of September, a Sunday, a helicopter hired by Bob Weiss dropped an orange Pinto station wagon twelve hundred feet onto the north bank of the Chicago River.

"You couldn't ask Landis things like 'How high do you want to drop the car?' Because he had no idea what that meant," Weiss recalled. When the producer asked his director how far to drop the Pinto, Landis replied, "I don't know, five, six thousand feet?" Weiss realized "that he doesn't know what five thousand feet is. I said, 'John, let me ask you a question.' And I pointed to the Hancock," one of the city's tallest skyscrapers. "I said, 'How tall do you think that building is?' And he had this look on his face that said, 'I have no fucking idea.' I said, 'It's about twelve hundred feet.'" They settled on twelve hundred feet.

Dropping a car from a helicopter was "a big fucking deal," David Sosna said. The FAA had to certify the Pinto as an aircraft. Filmmakers ran twelve-hundred-foot drop tests in lonely fields to demonstrate that the wagon would land in a predictable spot. Storyboards showed one Nazi throttling the other as the wagon descended, a replay of the scene in *Animal House* in which the mafioso mayor comically strangled Dean Wormer. Landis scrapped that idea. Instead, he had the Nazi lieutenant turn to Henry Gibson in midair and declare, "I've always loved you." He filmed the exchange as the performers sat inside a Pinto held aloft by a forklift. The Pinto hung in front of a projection screen on a soundstage. The projector cast an image on the screen to create the illusion of the Pinto in descent.

On September 30, the crew filmed the Pinto's real descent, a stunt that ended off-camera, the vehicle reduced to "an eighteen-inch-high abstract sculpture," one observer reported. The landing spot, a vacant patch of scrub and dirt, sat near the hairpin S curve in Lake Shore Drive, subsequently straightened. A woman in a high-rise telephoned police to report a car outside her window. Weeks later, the crew would film a more whimsical landing, dropping yet another Pinto from a crane through a false section of pavement into a Pinto-shaped hole carved in a street on the Universal back lot.

Only one or two things could stop the movie's production in its tracks. One was a Chicago Bears game, which clogged city arteries for hours on some fall Sundays. Another was a papal visit.

Pope John Paul II arrived in Chicago on Thursday, October 4, for a two-day stay. Luciano Pavarotti serenaded him with "Ave Maria" at the city's Holy Name Cathedral. A million Chicagoans joined the pontiff in worship at Grant Park.

"It was like pope-a-mania," Bob Weiss said. "You could get 3-D masks of the pope. I had a Lincoln that I was driven around in, because I didn't know where anything was in Chicago. It looked like a limousine. The pope had a motorcade. My car accidentally became part of the procession. And people started cheering. And people thought, 'Here it is, this is the start of the pope parade.' But it was just this Jewish guy from the Bronx."

Amid the papal disruption, Landis masterminded a practical joke on the cast and crew, shooting downtown. "All of a sudden," Weiss said, "two limousines pull up, and out of the first limousine come two guys who look like cardinals, and they run to the other limousine and open the door, and out gets a guy who looks like the pope. The first thing that happens is, the Catholics on the crew hit the marble." Landis approached the pontiff. "And we're standing on the set, and people can't believe what's happening. This was the pope, visiting the set. The pope extends his hand, to shake Landis's hand. Landis extends his hand and grabs the pope by the balls. Literally gets a handful of testicles. You could feel the air getting sucked off the city streets."

By mid-October, *The Blues Brothers* sat two weeks behind schedule and several million dollars over budget.

"You didn't want to be the Universal Studios executive in charge of this production," Sean Daniel said. "And that executive was me."

Studio bosses occupied larger offices on upper floors. "We all parked in this underground garage, right next to the elevators," Daniel said. "Every day, I prayed that I would not be riding up in the elevator with either Lew Wasserman or Sid Sheinberg or Ned Tanen. It was really my unlucky day if it was two out of three.

"Lew Wasserman was famous for having a machinelike brain for numbers. My ride from the basement to the eleventh floor was a nonstop recitation of how far over budget the movie was: 'When is this going to end, Mr. Daniel? What do you intend to do about it?'" On other elevator rides, Tanen would vow, "I'm gonna pull the plug! I'm gonna go down there and pull the plug on this! It's outta control!"

Bob Weiss invited Daniel to bring Ned Tanen to Chicago. "I don't think you guys understand what we're doing," Weiss reasoned. "You don't understand the level of effort to bring this to the screen. This is not two cars having a fender bender at an intersection."

The executives flew in. Weiss led Tanen into the war room, with Lower Wacker Drive laid out in maps, and out to the yard where mechanics rebuilt demolished squad cars. He showed Tanen the logistics involved in locking down miles of downtown roadways. "As the day proceeded, and I took them to various parts of the operation, Ned's color, the pallor of his skin, got grayer and grayer," Weiss said. Tanen caught an early flight home.

The Hollywood press caught wind of the overruns, and reporters began folding *The Blues Brothers* into earnest trend stories about runaway budgets on film shoots. With a rumored $20 million tab, *The Blues Brothers* now cost more than Stanley Kubrick's *The Shining* ($19 million). A few more delays might push the production into the budgetary air space of Francis Ford Coppola's *Apocalypse Now* ($31 million) and Spielberg's *1941* ($35 million). Hollywood insiders began referring to the Aykroyd-Belushi film as *1942*.

On a chilly October morning, police secured four square blocks around Forty-Seventh Street and Prairie Avenue in Chicago's Bronzeville neighborhood to shoot crowd scenes for the Ray Charles number. The crew repurposed a pawnshop as Ray's Music Exchange, where the Brothers would negotiate the purchase of a used Fender Rhodes piano. Artists adorned the brick facade with an enormous mural honoring Black musical icons who did not perform in the film, including Muddy Waters, Mahalia Jackson, and Stevie Wonder. Landis put B.B. King front and center, hoping he would spot himself in the finished film.

Someone cranked up a recording of Brother Ray singing the version of "Shake a Tail Feather" he had recorded in the downtown studio. "Tail Feather" wasn't a Ray Charles song. Dan chose it because, he said, "we needed a dance number." The song paid homage to the Purify brothers, an obvious soul-duo touchstone for Jake and Elwood. More subtly, the selection honored the Five Du-Tones, the Chicago soul-vocal group that had originally recorded it in 1963. Charles was happy to sing it.

Dozens of dancers, mostly Black, a few white, filled the broad sidewalk and street like a modern-day flash mob. They cycled through the twist, the fly, the bird, the monkey, and the mashed potato. Dozens more bounced up and down on a distant L platform—not extras, but commuters who had spontaneously joined in. The filmed scene would cut jauntily from the chilly Bronzeville street to Brother Ray and the band on a Hollywood set, a sequence to be filmed weeks later. Hundreds of locals watched the spectacle from behind police barriers.

"What's curious about this," a visiting reporter noted, "is that all these Chicago Black people have gathered to gawk at all these white people from California who, inside their charmed sawhorse circle, are running around hollering at each other, talking urgently into two-way radios, messing with all this outer-space equipment, making themselves a movie about . . . Black Chicago music."

Between takes, dancers sipped hot chocolate, checked their watches, and shivered: autumn had arrived in Chicago.

By the fourth week of October 1979, *The Blues Brothers* lagged sixteen days behind schedule. Landis and company had once planned to shoot their last Chicago scene on October 11. Budget overruns were bad enough. Weather posed a bigger threat. The high temperature that Tuesday was forty-six degrees. Night shoots were frigid. After endless runs up and down water-soaked streets, numb crew members sometimes wiped ice from their faces.

"We have to go back to Los Angeles," David Sosna told Landis, "and we have to go now."

For the delays, some of the crew blamed Stephen Katz. "He was a very nice guy and a good cameraman," said George Folsey, the editor. "But the leap from *Kentucky Fried Movie* to *The Blues Brothers* was just too much."

Fussing over light levels with his contrast glass, Katz had pushed one-day shoots into two-day shoots. Volatile Chicago weather, random logistical setbacks, and the sheer complexity of the production all had cost the *Blues Brothers* crew precious time.

And then there was Belushi. Landis figured his star had cost them three or four days of cumulative delays with his chronic tardiness and propensity to wander off the set. And he was getting worse.

The week started with John and Dan in an all-night jam with the Eagles, in town for a gig at Chicago Stadium. Someone explicitly instructed John not to party with the Eagles, for fear he might go missing for days. But the band beckoned to him from the stage, broadcasting an invitation in an improvised song lyric: "Looking for Belushi / Let's go eat some sushi." John heard it, and after the show, the Brothers crowded into the Blues Bar with the band, Jackson Browne joining them on guitar. Libations flowed. "Thank God they had microphones to lean on," one attendee observed.

John recovered in time for the shoot on Tuesday, October 23, when the crew staged a spectacular pileup outside Wauconda, nearly fifty miles northwest of the city. In the filmed scene, Elwood rouses a sleeping Jake when he says, "I gotta pull over." And pull over he does, crashing through a guardrail, careening down a steep embankment, slicing through grass, and vaulting up to a surface street, with an armada of Illinois State Police in close pursuit.

The script called for the cruisers to tumble down the embankment, flipping side over side and flying over one another. The first time Landis filmed the embankment scene, however, the stunt cars stubbornly failed to flip. "They just drove down the hill, fully controlled, if slightly bumpy," David Sosna recalled.

"They're supposed to fucking flip," Landis observed. "Not drive. Flip."

The crew found shovels and dug a ditch parallel to the road, a few feet down the hill. When they ran the scene again, the stunt cars caught in the trench, flipping enough of them to seed the vehicular entropy Landis sought. In the pièce de résistance, a squad car sails into the side of a passing tractor trailer. This was the stunt whose complexities had prompted David Sosna to delay the start of production. Now, they were ready. Filmmakers sent a stunt driver off a 150-foot ramp into the trailer, which was moving slowly and equipped with breakaway sides.

"We were there two days," David Sosna said. "We had police on the first day. Someone in the production office fucked up and didn't get the cops on the second day." No cops meant Sosna had no one to post at freeway entrances to stop motorists from literally crashing the scene.

"So I'm out there, and I have no cops, and I'm the only one who knows this." Sosna rounded up seventy extras and dressed them as cops. He instructed them, "You are the law. Palm up and, by God, if they take another step, you're gonna kill them." Sosna planted fake police at the freeway entrances to stop real motorists from interfering with the fake police crashing real squad cars.

Late on the afternoon of October 25, a chilly Thursday, Landis and crew waited on John, who refused to emerge from his trailer. John had been downtown when the director summoned him to the suburbs for a dusk shot outside a lonely service station. "We left Chicago late," Morris Lyda said. "The rush-hour traffic made us later. Getting him in the car and moving was the problem. He was gassed when I picked him up."

"We get there late, and they've lost the light," Lyda said. "Landis goes fucking ballistic on Belushi. Belushi gets more pissed off than he was. He was pissed off coming to set, but then he got more pissed off." John felt scapegoated for the mounting delays.

John, already blasted, asked Lyda for a bottle of wine. "So, I took him a bottle of wine, but I watered it down," Lyda said. "Then he's pissed off with me because I've watered down his wine."

Landis, his patience exhausted, stomped up to the star's Winnebago and knocked on the door. Inside, John sat with hair disheveled, eyes vacant. Atop a desk sat a mound of cocaine.

"John, you're killing yourself," Landis cried. "Do not do this to my movie. Don't do this to me. Don't do this to Judy. Don't do it to yourself."

John's head bobbed woozily. Landis scooped up the white powder, "probably a hundred thousand dollars' worth," and flushed it down the toilet. That got a reaction. John stood, muttered, "Landis, you mother-fucker," and charged at his director, trying to get past Landis to the remnants of his stash. They grappled like drunken wrestlers. John burst into tears, and their grapple melted into an embrace. Landis burst into tears. "John, this is insane," he moaned. Judy burst in, drawn by the ruckus.

Dan finally coaxed John out to the set for a mercifully brief sequence at the gas station, Jake Blues glancing at his watch, smashing a bottle on the pavement, and prodding Elwood to get back on the road. John completed the take before passing out. Crewmen carried him back to his trailer. Judy summoned a nurse, who induced John to vomit. A driver took the Belushis back to their apartment at Astor Tower. Judy and Dan sat a bedside vigil. John vomited periodically through the night. Judy wrote in her diary, "What could be going on inside this person to make him so unhappy?"

The crew had built the faux country service station out on Route 59 in the far west suburbs. Over the final three days of Chicago shooting, October 25 through 27, they filmed a colorful scene that did little to advance the movie's narrative. Jake and Elwood arrive at Lloyd's Tire Clinic to gas up the Bluesmobile. A sporty convertible pulls up, driven, improbably, by Twiggy, the British model. She mistakes Elwood for an attendant. They flirt. She drives off. Elwood, mesmerized, forgets to turn off the pump. Jake and Elwood dash to their make-or-break gig. Jake tosses a lit cigarette butt out the passenger window. It triggers a massive explosion.

Filmmakers hauled a fifty-five-gallon drum of gasoline into the hut at the center of the station. A special-effects man planted sticks of dynamite around its rim. Just before the timed explosion, David Sosna turned to the police working the perimeter. "I said, 'Are we clear in the trees?'" It was nighttime, and trees ringed the gas station. "They said yes. I said, 'When was the last time you checked?' They said, 'Half an hour ago.'" Sosna asked them to check again. They did, and "sure enough, there were kids in the trees." Police dispersed them. The blast shattered windows and rattled homes.

John had little to do on-screen. Idle and restless, he slipped into a coke-addled fog. Twice that week, he failed to arrive on set. "Both times," Landis said, "we ended up taking the door off his room and calling the paramedics, because he had basically overdosed."

By the time the cast and crew of *The Blues Brothers* limped out of Chicago, the film's star and box-office draw had "almost died," not once but twice, Landis said. And the film was only half-finished.

Chapter 24

Have You Seen the Light?

T HE *BLUES BROTHERS* production crew shot its first scene on the Universal lot in Los Angeles on the day before Halloween in 1979, authentic Chicago streetscapes giving way to Hollywood artifice. Jake and Elwood enter the convent to meet with Sister Mary Stigmata, the nun who will set the Brothers on their quest.

Landis had already filmed exteriors in Chicago, fabricating an entrance to the fictional St. Helen of the Blessed Shroud in a South Side alleyway, part of the real-life Schoenhofen Brewery complex.

Stephen Katz, the perfectionist cinematographer, hadn't laid eyes on most of the Hollywood sets, which workers were building just in time to be filmed.

"That day," he said, "we were under pressure to shoot, and we hadn't seen the set, and it took me all morning, or all day, to light just the staircase. I got obsessed with the staircase and the Christ." He lit the set like a horror movie.

The Brothers climb creaky stairs, spooked by the giant Jesus statue that looms on the landing, eyes rolled back in his head, and by the door that closes itself.

Sister Mary Stigmata, whom Jake and Elwood call the Penguin, evokes Father Baxter, the short-fused, chalk-hurling priest of Dan's adolescence. Sister Mary, however menacing, reveals her humanity as she recounts her plight: her orphanage faces closure over a $5,000 tax bill from the county that it cannot pay. "No problem," Jake says. "We'll have it for you in the morning." The nun seizes the moral high ground when she refuses to accept the Brothers' "filthy stolen money." The boys squirm, seated in children's school desks. Jake tells the nun she's "up shit creek." She swats his hand with a ruler. She asks him to repeat himself. He tells her, again, that she is "up shit creek." She swats him harder. Soon, both Brothers are cursing, and Sister Mary is reaching for a wooden pointer. Belushi's stunt double clatters back down the stairs, desk and chair and all. Sister Mary banishes the boys and floats back into her office, carried by celestial winds. Landis conceived the floating-nun bit at the last minute, aided by a simple dolly.

Filmmakers took care to capture Jake's tumble down the stairs in a single take: a dangerous stunt, even for a stuntman.

A steeper challenge lay ahead. The crew faced a complicated shoot inside a Hollywood reconstruction of the Triple Rock Church, where preacher James Brown leads the congregation in song. Producers had attempted to record the number in the Chicago studio but found that no two takes of the Godfather's vocals sounded alike. Now they would tape him live, backed by James Cleveland's Southern California Community Choir, with a cameo from Chaka Khan, an ascendant diva of rhythm and blues. The production hired dancers and trampoline acrobats.

Again, Stephen Katz arrived to a set he had not seen. "They expected me to come in and light the thing in three hours," he recalled. "The extras, the dancers, I said, 'Send them home. This isn't gonna happen today.'"

Shooting commenced the next day. James Brown played the Reverend Cleophus James. The singer arrived on set looking "pretty spaced," Bob Tischler recalled. But Brown whipped the flock into a frenzy as John and Dan stood stone silent at the back of the church. The dancers and acrobats exploded in choreographed energy on "The Old Landmark," a blistering gospel stomper that Aretha Franklin had recorded on her *Amazing Grace* album. "I searched and found the fastest gospel song I could find," Dan recalled. Acrobats twirled through the air, vaulting off hidden trampolines and soaring past a blue neon cross, a prop whose construction Landis had ordered in a moment of inspiration. The Godfather delivered an impassioned vocal, a performance he would touch up later in a studio. Jake begins to tremble, seized by religious ecstasy. The sun bursts through the clouds and shines down through a stained-glass window, delivering Jake's epiphany: "The band!"

The glorious sunray "was hand-painted," David Sosna said, on a black card that filmmakers inserted at the precise line where church met sky.

"Do you see the light?" the preacher beckons. "Have you seen the light?"

"Yes! Yes!" Jake responds. "Jesus H. tap-dancing Christ, I have seen the light!" His stunt double backflips dramatically up the aisle. John himself dances a little jig at the pulpit. His fervor infects Elwood, who joins him. The aerobic scene taxed John, who had seemed near death a few days earlier. Between shots, he gulped oxygen from a tank.

The shooting script "makes a racial point more strongly" than the finished scene, writes R. J. Smith, Brown's biographer. The Reverend James asks Jake Blues, "My little lost, white lamb, have you come to join our flock?" Filmmakers cut the line. The scene spoke for itself, Smith said: "Brown, and all the performers in the movie, will lead white America to the promised land."

Amid this joyous chaos, David Sosna received word that Aretha Franklin was coming.

"We were told, without warning, to be ready in two days for her arrival," he said. "We had her for three days." Sosna would have to halt James Brown in mid-shoot to film Franklin.

"Well, that doesn't work," Sosna recalled. "We're in the church, trampolines, people jumping up in the air. We had dancers. Dancers aren't extras. Once you get them, you want to keep them. We can't move." Someone at the studio told Sosna he had no choice: "It's fucking Aretha."

Unlike James Brown, Aretha Franklin had waffled on *The Blues Brothers*. "She wasn't sure about playing a servant in her first movie role," said Cecil Franklin, her brother. She didn't want to wear a waitress dress. "But when it comes to confronting a no-good man, Aretha has no equal. She realized that this part gave her a chance to tap into that attitude.

The combination of her being real and then topping it off with a song was too great to resist."

Franklin, cast as the diner owner, had never made a film. Her prior contribution to *The Blues Brothers*, recording piano and vocals in Chicago, had been forgettable, another day in another recording studio. Now, arriving in Los Angeles, she beheld a perfect reconstruction of a Maxwell Street diner on the Universal set. The Queen was impressed.

In the filmed sequence, Jake and Elwood walk into the diner. Elwood orders plain white toast. Jake orders four whole fried chickens and a Coke: Landis had seen John order that much food. The setup reunites Jake and Elwood with Matt "Guitar" Murphy, Aretha's on-screen husband and fry cook, and "Blue" Lou Marini, their saxophonist/ dishwasher.

Landis instructed the musicians to be themselves. Franklin obliged, and she steals the scene, her voice dripping with withering, righteous scorn. "The Blues Brothers? *Shee-it.* They still owe you money, fool."

The script called for Jake and Elwood to jump into Franklin's musical number. When the time came, Dan recalled, "I didn't know whether I was gonna be able to stand, because when that track started and I saw her doing it, and the fluidity of the moves and the music, my stomach turned to jelly and I couldn't feel my legs."

Three backup singers, conveniently placed at the counter, rise and join Franklin in song. "Blue" Lou rips off his hairnet, liberating his shoulder-length hair, climbs atop the narrow counter, and raises his sax, playing along with his own prerecorded solo. "The lunch counter was, like, chest high," Marini said. "And the reality is that I'm gonna be doing that dance up there on this two-and-a-half-foot-wide thing with the stoves on one side. I'm an agile, athletic guy, but it was a little daunting."

Sadly, in much of the edited scene, Marini appears headless. The camera angle didn't capture his full body, and Landis thought a headless saxophonist was funny. When Marini saw it on film, he was deflated. An assistant cameraman deadpanned, "You signed up for a lot of money and a little head, and that's what you got."

Once the musical number began, it became painfully clear that Franklin could not remember the lyrics to her famous song. She seemed gloomy, distracted. William Kaplan, the soundman, wrote the lyrics on a pair of whiteboards and placed one at each end of the set, so Franklin could see them at any point in the routine. "But it didn't work," he said, "because she needed glasses, and she couldn't wear them."

Franklin struggled, as well, to lip-synch to her own impressionistic vocal track. Landis had to film several takes: a few too many, in Franklin's opinion. "But she pulled through," Landis said. "I knew she'd be a wonderful actress."

After the shoot, Franklin departed Los Angeles. The diner scene complete, David Sosna pivoted back to the Triple Rock Church. He had kept an entire troupe of dancers and trampoline jumpers on retainer, paying them not to take another job. Now, he summoned them back to the church set to resume filming with James Brown. As Sosna barked orders to dancers and extras and crew, Brown turned to him, smiled, and said, "I like you. You don't let them mess." The Godfather admired a man who ran a tight band.

John cleaned up admirably for the scenes with James Brown and Aretha Franklin. He and Judy had settled into a secluded cottage in Coldwater Canyon, rented from Candice Bergen. Dan worked and slept in an office on the Universal lot. John awoke early, swam, washed down vitamins with fresh orange juice, and even worked out a bit. His only lapse came during a visit to the home of Rolling Stones guitarist Ron Wood, an injudicious destination for a man avoiding drugs.

Belushi's sobriety wouldn't last. During the Franklin shoot, one of Landis's aides recalled, "a thousand-foot film can arrived in the camera department. A crew member opened it and showed me the contents, no film inside, filled to the brim with cocaine. I wasn't surprised or shocked. Obviously, it was for Belushi. Not a word was said."

Another day, a man showed up on the set to deliver drugs to John. Landis found out and had him arrested. "And John just went crazy," Landis said. John dragged him into a screaming argument that spilled out onto Lankershim Boulevard.

"You can't tell me who my friends are," John raged.

"I don't give a fuck who your friends are, and believe me, this guy's not your friend."

John told the director to go fuck himself. Then he stepped out into the street and stuck out his thumb. "Some perfect stranger, this long-haired dude in a convertible heading in the opposite direction, whipped his car around, did a complete one-eighty, and screeched to a halt next to John," Landis recalled.

"Hey, Belushi! Hop in, buddy."

John leapt into the passenger seat and instructed, "Take me to the Chateau Marmont," and they were gone.

Still, with the production safely ensconced in Los Angeles, Universal executives breathed easier. "The picture is only eleven days over schedule," Ned Tanen boasted to columnist Marilyn Beck. He predicted the production would wrap by year's end.

In truth, *The Blues Brothers* lagged nearly a month behind schedule. Rumor buzzed around Hollywood that its budget had passed $20 million, which it had, back in August. On the Universal back lot, some of the crew wore T-shirts that read, "I survived Chicago."

George Folsey saved Landis and the studio two days of shooting by persuading him to cut the brothel scene. Dan had scripted it as the Brothers' first stop after leaving Joliet Prison. The script described a set "furnished in bright orange shag carpeting, a couple of loud, plaid, convertible couches, chrome coffee table, a hot plate and toaster oven." There, just ten minutes out of prison, Jake Blues pairs off with a statu-esque brunette named Streak, retreats to a bedroom, and indulges his senses. It was the only thing in *The Blues Brothers* approaching a sex scene.

"John," Folsey pleaded, "I'm uncomfortable with this scene, the idea that they're going to see this nun, and they're gonna save this orphan-age, and the first thing out of the box, we take them to a whorehouse." Landis telephoned John Lloyd, the production designer, and told him not to build the brothel set. The resulting savings "probably paid my salary," Folsey said.

In another feat of narrative efficiency, Landis had combined sev-eral threads from Dan's phone-book-size script into a single scene that reunited Jake and Elwood with much of their band. In the streamlined script, Murph and the Magic Tones have settled into a cheesy residency in the Armada Room at a Holiday Inn near O'Hare. Landis shot the exteriors at an actual Holiday Inn near O'Hare, the interiors at a kin-dred hotel in LA. "We stayed there and shot there for a couple of days," Tom "Bones" Malone said. "We went right downstairs to work."

In the filmed scene, Jake and Elwood walk into the wood-paneled lounge to find Murph singing a campy "Quando, Quando, Quando" behind an organ covered in red shag carpeting, playing to a near-empty room. Judy Belushi and Rosie Shuster portray cocktail waitresses in naughty-Santa dresses. Garish paintings of topless women and sailing ships adorn the walls.

The scene introduced Cropper and Dunn, "Bones" Malone, and drummer Willie "Too Big" Hall, who had replaced Steve Jordan before filming commenced. Murph ad-libbed Willie's nickname, "Too Big," on-camera, honoring the drummer's reputed penile endowment.

"We'll be back with the Magic Tones for the Armada Room's two-hour disco swing party after this short break," Murph intones at the set's close, as the filmmakers take another swipe at disco.

"Murph and the Magic Tones?" Jake sneers, joining the musicians around a table. "Look at you in those candy-ass monkey suits. And I thought I had it bad in Joliet."

"At least we got a change in clothes, sucker," Willie "Too Big" Hall snarls back. "You're wearing the same shit you had on three years ago."

"Jake ain't lying, though," Donald "Duck" Dunn counters, in a warm Memphis drawl. "We had a band powerful enough to turn goat piss into gasoline."

Landis reminded the musicians to be themselves, and not, God for-bid, to act. Willie Hall delivered his lines with real menace. The mere presence of Donald "Duck" Dunn, Steve "The Colonel" Cropper, and Matt "Guitar" Murphy on-screen guaranteed the film a modicum of immortality.

Landis revived the theme of class conflict that had suffused *Animal House* for a scene at Chez Paul, a stuffy white-tablecloth restaurant on Chicago's Magnificent Mile. The very essence of Midwestern aristocracy, the Chez Paul sat within a mansion built for the McCormicks, publishers of the *Tribune*.

Filmmakers had staged a bold stunt to announce the Brothers' arrival, set outside the actual restaurant. Elwood throws the speeding Bluesmobile into a 180-degree turn and slides sideways into a parking space. David Sosna rolled in a car carrier filled with several Blues-mobiles, expecting a few spectacular crashes before the stunt driver nailed the maneuver. But he threaded the Bluesmobile perfectly into the parking space on the first try. The crew broke into spontaneous applause.

"I've done this job for more than thirty years," Sosna recalled. "I haven't seen a crew applaud more than three times, if that. Ever. That's how astounding that stunt was."

After the stunt, around midnight, the crew broke for "lunch," which caterers served inside the Chez Paul dining room. Landis planned to film the interiors there. But as Sosna appraised the space in the harsh light of studio wattage, he recoiled. "It was a shithole": cracked wall-paper, peeling paint, a hundred little horrors cloaked by soft candle-light. Weeks later, the crew built a replica on the Universal lot.

Visually, the Chez Paul scene was "a departure from the way the rest of the movie looked," Stephen Katz said. "All the colors are kind of pastel and bubblegummy," the opposite of noir. In the filmed sequence, Jake and Elwood hope to persuade Alan "Mr. Fabulous" Rubin to quit his maître d' job and rejoin their band. When Elwood peers into the dining room through elegant French doors, elegant diners turn their heads as one to stare, interrupted from their meals by a street urchin.

Jake summons his best Shawnee Summer Theatre repartee: "Come, Elwood. Let us adjourn ourselves to the nearest table and overlook this establishment's board of fare." The boys claim an empty table and tuck linen napkins into their shirts. A snooty waiter arrives in reply to Jake's ear-shredding whistle: Paul Reubens, the man-child comedian who would shortly rise to fame as Pee-wee Herman. Jake orders five shrimp cocktails, reprising his antics in the hotel room on the night he met Lan-dis. Elwood tosses shrimps into Jake's mouth. The boys slurp hundred-dollar champagne. Jake turns to a prim upper-crust family, assumes a "gypsy" accent, and asks, "How much for the little girl?"

* * *

John and Dan spent downtime in a bungalow across from the sound-stage where Lon Chaney had performed in *The Phantom of the Opera*. John crawled under the stage and wrote his name on a wall with a caulking gun. He and Dan roamed the Universal lot in a golf cart. "We'd go up to the Frankenstein castle and crack open a couple of beers," Dan said.

Most of the musicians stayed at a hotel near the studio. One morning, they boarded a van to a soundstage to rehearse dance moves for the Ray Charles number. When the van arrived, the musicians poured out and met Dan, who greeted them with "Shhh. It's asleep." They found John snoring on the set.

"Belushi had been out partying all night long," Steve Cropper recalled. At dawn, "he found out what soundstage we were on, and he just went to sleep."

Brother Ray, notoriously mercurial, breezed through his scene in a Hollywood rebuild of Ray's Music Exchange. "I remember him laughing a lot and going to the little boy's room very frequently," Murphy Dunne said.

Few of the musicians were sober, and the horn section made creative use of the pawnshop's glass-topped display cases as Landis filmed. In one take, the musicians produced a dollar bill and pantomimed chopping it up and snorting it, "all for the amusement of the crew," Lou Marini recalled. In the next take, they repeated the routine with a price tag. In the third take, on a dare, "Alan Rubin pulls out a gram of coke and lays it out on the glass countertop, and we start to snort it," Tom Malone said. Landis spotted them. He yelled, "Cut!" and stormed up to the group and cried, "What the fuck are you guys doing?" One of the horns reminded the director that he had instructed them to act like musicians. A careful viewer can glimpse their antics in the background of the sequence as Charles negotiates with Jake and Murph.

In the filmed scene, Brother Ray sells the Brothers a beat-up keyboard, offering, "I'll throw in the black keys for free." Ray went along with a sight gag that played on his blindness, drawing a gun and firing warning shots at a boy who had crept into his store to shoplift a guitar.

In an early take, Charles went for the gun a bit too soon, before John and Murph could leap out of the way. "And the gun goes bang, bang, bang," Murph recalled. "And Landis says, 'Cut, cut, cut!'" Charles asked, "Did I miss my cue?" Landis replied, "Yes you did, Ray. Please take the gun away from Mr. Charles."

When the time came for Charles to play, he and the crew found that the Rhodes electric piano had lost power. There was no time to find a new cord, so Brother Ray performed the song with David Sosna kneeling beneath him, holding two strands of bare, live electrical wire against exposed metal tabs at the keyboard's base. Every time Charles stomped on the pedals, Sosna winced.

The scene would mark the on-screen debut of the full Blues Brothers band, dancing like pros and sounding like a Stax-Volt hit. In the editing room, George Folsey cut deftly back and forth between Ray's nimble performance and the impromptu dancers filmed on the Chicago street, an R. Crumb cartoon come to life. In one lovely shot, filmmakers caught the reflection of Brother Ray's hands on the keyboard in the lenses of his sunglasses.

After all the effort, "the studio didn't want the scene in the movie, wanted me to cut it way, way down," Folsey said. Some Universal executives deemed Ray Charles a faded icon. "They just didn't think modern audiences were gonna care." Landis and Folsey ignored the request.

On a Universal soundstage, the crew filmed a steam-bath sequence that tied together several other scenes leading up to the Blues Brothers' climactic gig in Chicago. Desperate to land a $5,000 gig, the entire band files into a steam room. In real life, Belushi loved to detox at the Tenth Street Baths in New York's East Village after a night of partying. Inside, Jake and Elwood corner a towel-clad promoter, played by singer Steve Lawrence in a cameo, and twist his arm into arranging the concert.

En route to the show, the Bluesmobile runs out of gas, triggering the service-station scene with Twiggy. The gas stop makes them late to the concert. Aware that police are pursuing, the Brothers park in a tunnel beneath a bridge, sneak into the amphitheater, and find Cab "Curtis" Calloway and the band keeping the stage warm for them.

A $5,000 gig required an elegant venue. The crew had shot exteriors in Chicago at South Shore Cultural Center, an old Mediterranean-revival structure that had once housed the South Shore Country Club, an organization that admitted neither Blacks nor Jews. For the concert itself, they considered the Aragon Ballroom, a brick fortress in the Uptown neighborhood on Chicago's North Side. When the shoot fell behind schedule, the crew moved the concert to the Hollywood Palladium, the art deco palace on Sunset Boulevard.

Chapter 25

It's Never Too Late to Mend

DAYS BEFORE the critical Hollywood Palladium shoot, at his desk inside the Black Tower, Sean Daniel received a call from Bob Weiss. "You'd better get down here."

John had been partying at someone's house in the Valley. A kid rode by on a skateboard. John asked if he could give it a try. He promptly fell, landing hard on his knee. When Sean Daniel arrived at the Universal bungalow, he found the star on his back, moaning in pain. "We have this momentous, gigantic, all singing, all dancing, cast-of-thousands concert sequence starting on Monday," Daniel recalled. "What the fuck are we gonna do? And the answer is, this is a gigantic production emergency. This has to get fixed."

It was Thanksgiving weekend. Daniel reasoned, "There is only one person who could call the doctors who are needed, get them to their office over the Thanksgiving holiday": Lew Wasserman, the studio boss. And the only person who could break the news to Wasserman was Daniel, "the guy he's been yelling at for months now."

Daniel padded into Wasserman's office and explained his dilemma. Wasserman telephoned one of the city's top orthopedists, who worked with the NFL. Daniel overheard snatches of tense conversation: "Listen, I know you're in the Springs, but I need you here."

The orthopedist examined Belushi. He "pulled the worst-looking shit out of his knee, put some other shit back in," Weiss said. The doctor fitted John with an Anderson knee stabler, a brace he could wear beneath his black suit.

The Palladium scene, shot in early December, demanded the usual concert calisthenics from John. Landis offered to swap in a stuntman; Belushi waved him off. Again, he would suck oxygen from a tank between shots to help catch his breath. Bob Tischler, the trusty sound engineer, wired the hall to record the crowd.

Once again, Stephen Katz arrived without working knowledge of the set. "I had drawings of it," he said. He "was lighting it theoretically," in his head.

"When we came there," Katz said, "we were supposed to shoot it in the next day or couple of days. The LA crew had prepped it with every generator in Hollywood," much like the Dixie Square mall. Katz filmed a screen test, Cab Calloway in a white tuxedo against an art deco bandstand and a starry skyline. "And it sucked. Cab's outfit, everything was wrong. The whites were overexposing." Landis had wanted Calloway in a snow-white tuxedo, "which was his signature in the thirties," he said, but pure white was hard to film.

"I went home and went to bed," Katz said. "I was so depressed. No one could find me. And then I woke up, and I said, 'I know what I have to do.' I went back, and I said, 'Tear it all down. We gotta start over.'"

Katz had been using a specific color filter, or gel, for all the blue hues in *The Blues Brothers*, imported from London at considerable expense. Just as he prepared to film the epic concert scene, he ran out of his prized blue gel. The cinematographer put the Palladium on hold while someone hand-delivered fresh blue gels from London. The crew worked through the night. "And I relit it, and I did a test, and it was perfect."

Like so many *Blues Brothers* scenes, the Palladium shoot fell a full day behind schedule. When the time came to film the final shots, the studio lacked extras to fill theater seats. Filmmakers ran a contest on a local rock radio station. The promotion yielded a crowd of mostly young, white fans. The crew recruited additional extras from a local unemployment office. "We wanted, you know, Black people," someone confided to a visiting reporter.

Many contest winners brought weed, and when the music started, they lit up. The plume of pot smoke triggered an aggressive response from the plainclothes police Universal had hired to keep order. Aggrieved patrons tore up the Palladium's bathrooms.

"Tension was rising," David Sosna recalled. "I asked the cop in charge if his guys could look the other way if people smoked dope in the bathroom," a less conspicuous compromise. "They agreed. I announced it to the crowd. They cheered like I was being elected president. The ruckus stopped."

The ruckus resumed as uniformed troopers filed into the hall, playing the officers who wait to arrest Jake and Elwood at the show's end. "These are real people, like yourselves," Landis counseled through a megaphone. "Not the police. You don't really see 'em. They're just here to be scary."

Landis didn't know what to expect from this crowd of random extras and contest winners when Cab Calloway took the stage to perform "Minnie the Moocher," his big hit from 1931, on a set magically transformed into a Depression-era dance hall.

Calloway himself wasn't so sure. He had stayed up late the night before, drinking with Steve Cropper and Donald Dunn. That morning, Morris Lyda recalled, "you could not find another more hungover group of guys, including Cab. I think he was not confident he was gonna be able to deliver."

Calloway strode out onstage, and his face cleaved into a radiant smile. And "he just broke into it, looked over to me, and nodded his hat," Murphy Dunne said. "And Cropper started the groove." Calloway brought the audience to life, chanting "Hidee hidee hidee hi, ho-de ho-de ho-de ho," as if the song still topped the charts. Jake and Elwood walked onstage to riotous cheers. Landis, speaking through his megaphone, instructed the extras to sit impassively when the band began to play: "You're not impressed at all. Who are these guys? From the CIA?"

When the Brothers hit the stage in the film, to a double-time arrangement of Otis Redding's "I Can't Turn You Loose," the crowd sits with arms crossed, unmoved. "We're so glad to see so many of you lovely people here tonight," Elwood intones, as the band cues

"Everybody Needs Somebody to Love," the Solomon Burke rave-up. "We would especially like to welcome all the representatives of Illinois's law enforcement community," he adds, as the camera cuts to backlit officers with rifles.

Jake and Elwood shimmy and shake, Belushi dancing on his bad knee. Their performance lifts the crowd to its feet. Midway through "Sweet Home Chicago," Jake and Elwood join hands and dance off the stage to elude their pursuers.

John faced perils offstage, as well. The knee injury had reignited his drug habit. Midway through the Palladium shoot, an armed man in a green suit arrived at the theater to collect money John owed him for drugs. Teamsters paid the debt and muscled him off the set. When Landis found out, he exploded.

On the evening of December 13, John and Dan attended the premiere of *1941*, Spielberg's madcap war comedy. The director had fled to Hawaii, fearing the worst. The Brothers rented a vintage automobile, donned formal wear, and headed out with their dates, John with Judy, Dan with Penny Marshall. They passed around a joint en route to the Cinerama Dome to calm nerves. The group arrived to "the most hostile audience I've ever seen in my life," Marshall said. "The whole movie, nothing. Silence."

Unable to leave, as honored guests, the foursome endured the picture, then retreated to their rented car and loosed a collective scream. At the post-premiere party, they sat with frozen smiles among shell-shocked studio executives, gamely supporting their absent director. One reviewer termed the film "Spielberg's Misguided Missile." Once again, critics singled out Belushi, but not for praise. "Belushi wears out his welcome early on," *Newsweek* opined. John feared the role might sink his career. Still, when Spielberg returned from Hawaii, John and Dan turned up at his house. "Fuck the critics," John roared. Spielberg was touched.

The next month, Penny Marshall talked Spielberg into stopping by John's thirty-first-birthday party in Coldwater Canyon. "Steven was quite depressed about *1941*, needless to say," she said. They arrived to find everyone wearing "little black buttons that Michael O'Donoghue had made that read, 'John Belushi: Born 1949, Died 1941.'"

John and Dan turned up at the height of the party with "a vintage Mercedes World War II German Army half-track personnel carrier," Dan said, borrowed from the Universal motor pool. The guard at the studio gate had spotted Belushi in the rig, cigarette in hand, feet up on the dash, and wordlessly waved them through.

Belushi made a pact with Landis to forgo, in the director's words, "anything that will fuck with your eyes" for six full days before shooting his climactic scene with Carrie Fisher inside an old pedestrian tunnel. The filmmakers had agreed that Jake would remove his dark glasses for his final appeal to the Mystery Woman. Workers built the tunnel on a Universal soundstage, using forced perspective, the passage behind the actors rendered in miniature.

In the filmed sequence, we learn that Jake has broken her heart by standing her up at their lavish wedding, which sounds, from her description, like a Belushi family event. "My uncle hired the best Romanian caterer in the state," she hisses through clenched teeth. "To obtain the seven limousines for the wedding party, my father used up his last favors with Mad Pete Trollo. So, for me, for my mother, my grandmother, my father, my uncle, and for the common good, I must now kill you and your brother."

To save his skin, Jake delivers an outrageous plea. "I ran outta gas. I had a flat tire. I didn't have enough money for cab fare. My tux didn't come back from the cleaners. An old friend came in from outta town. Someone stole my car. There was an earthquake, a terrible flood, locusts." He removes his glasses and arches his brow, revealing those impish, twinkling eyes.

"Oh Jake," Fisher coos. "Jake, honey."

Jake takes her in his arms in a Bogart-style kiss, then drops her to the muddy ground. "Let's go," he barks to Elwood, and they are off.

Winter had descended in Los Angeles. Temperatures dipped into the fifties as the crew gathered on the Universal lot to shoot a scene outside

Bob's Country Bunker. This sequence, too, had once been scheduled to film in Chicago. Now, cameras rolled at a cinder-block set near the lake where the mechanical *Jaws* shark startled tourists by day. The Cleaver residence from *Leave It to Beaver* lay beyond a hill. And the hill posed a problem: the script put Bob's Country Bunker in Kokomo, Indiana, which was flat. Landis tweaked the lights to hide the hills.

In the filmed scene, Jake steers the Bluesmobile across random countryside, heading to a nonexistent gig, having convinced the band he'd found one. He spots Bob's Country Bunker and hustles its owner into believing the Blues Brothers are that night's act, the Good Ole Boys. The resulting comedy of errors, shot separately on a Universal soundstage, inspires many memorable moments: the barkeep assuring Jake that the club embraces "country *and* western"; the band performing behind chicken wire in a hail of broken bottles; Jake and Elwood crooning "Stand By Your Man"; the band drinking $300 worth of beer. Dan had written the scene from interviews of the musicians, who shared stories from the road.

Landis stood offstage, "throwing bottles at us," Murphy Dunne said. "Boom, boom, boom. They're made of sugar. I think he was eating one."

John commanded the scene, trotting out an impressive Indiana hick accent and cracking a bullwhip onstage during the *Rawhide* number. But when the crew gathered outside to film the group departing the club under duress, John developed the yips, suddenly unable to remember his lines.

"We were freezing our asses off," Lou Marini said. "It's, like, two o'clock in the morning. Belushi does a take, and he fucks up the third to the last word. And he does another take, and he fucks up the tenth to the last word. And he works his way backward, and he finally fucks up the first word. The cumulative effect of all those bad takes, and us starting over and over again: we had a collective laugh, one of those soul-cleansing, weeping laughs. Everyone on the set was laughing."

In the chilly parking lot, the musicians debate their future with the Blues Brothers. Landis positioned a camera to capture Murphy Dunne's head beneath a blue neon cowboy hat. The Brothers emerge. Jake explains that the gig paid $200, and that they have drunk $300

worth of beer, and that the time has come to depart. The real Good
Ole Boys arrive, discover the ruse, and take off after the Bluesmobile.
In the subsequent chase scene, the Brothers speed past troopers Daniel
and Mount, named for the Universal executives. The troopers screech
onto the roadway and careen into the Winnebago carrying the Good
Ole Boys. All of this happens beneath a billboard advertising a fictional
movie called *See You Next Wednesday*. The title was a line lifted from *2001:
A Space Odyssey*. Landis had planted it in two of his prior films, *Schlock*
and *Kentucky Fried Movie*, as a recurring gag.

The Good Ole Boys shake themselves off and rejoin the chase. Later
in the film, Elwood spots their parked trailer outside the amphitheater
and glues the gas pedal to the floor. When the country-and-western
band piles back into the Winnebago after the Palladium show and sets
off after the Bluesmobile, the rig screeches out of control, flies off the
expressway, crashes through a barn, and lands in a lake. The filmed
scene cuts from a Chicagoland expressway to the Universal back lot,
where the lake sat along the route of the studio tram tours. To ensure a
safe landing for the Winnebago, crew workers cut the wooden periscope
off the top of a submarine they found submerged in the lake. Early the
next morning, carpenters reattached the periscope.

During a quiet moment in the Good Ole Boys shoot, outside Chicago,
Kaplan, the exhausted soundman, had crawled up onto the roof of a
truck on the set and fallen asleep. The truck served as an "insert car,"
carrying cameras and crew to film actors through the front windows of
other vehicles: in this case, the Good Ole Boys in their Winnebago. As
Kaplan slept, a stunt driver walked up to the truck and climbed in. He
would be towing the speeding Winnebago in the scene that showed the
trailer lurching out of control. Now, with Kaplan asleep on the roof,
the driver took the truck on a test run at full speed. The soundman
awakened and, realizing his predicament, screamed and pounded on
the roof, protests the driver never heard. When the driver completed
the run, he parked the truck, and the woozy soundman climbed down
from the roof.

Months later, Landis would hear that the studio planned to repur-
pose Bob's Country Bunker for use in a television show. The last thing

he wanted was for a *Blues Brothers* set to appear on television before his movie came out. Just before the television shoot, Landis and David Sosna returned to the set by night and broke the windows, rendering it unusable.

Fittingly, the final footage shot by the full *Blues Brothers* crew would supply the last scene in the film: the band, incarcerated at Joliet Prison, playing "Jailhouse Rock" for fellow inmates.

The movie's production was now scheduled to wrap on February 1, 1980. Well before that date, word had spread around the Hollywood press that *The Blues Brothers* "was another *Heaven's Gate*," Michael Cimino's $44 million disaster, Thom Mount recalled. Mount and Daniel knew *The Blues Brothers* was shaping up as a terrific film. Every time Lew Wasserman called Mount into his office and asked, "Are we gonna lose money on this?" Mount replied, "Of course not." Wasserman wasn't seeing the dailies, reels of raw footage screened after each day's shoot.

In January, the *Los Angeles Times* portrayed *The Blues Brothers* as "staggeringly over budget." Rival studios invoked the production as an off-the-rails exemplar. One dispatch claimed that "neither the studio nor director John Landis [has] any kind of real completion date in mind for the wayward comedy."

In that climate, the Universal bosses weren't about to let Landis and his crew stray a single day past February 1. Yet, when that day arrived, the crew had not yet completed the musical scene at Joliet Prison. "We needed, I think, one or two more days," Bob Weiss said. Weiss thought of the great Walter Matthau film *The Taking of Pelham One Two Three*. In that picture, Matthau faced a deadline to pay off bad guys before they started killing hostages. Matthau bluffed. He told the bad guys he had the money, even though he didn't, to buy time.

"I sent out a memo that said, 'Principal production is complete,'" Weiss recalled. It wasn't. "*The Blues Brothers* has commenced second unit production," he wrote to the Universal executives. The second unit looked a lot like the first unit: no one would know the difference. Weiss's bluff, he said, "enabled us to shoot the last two days" and finish the movie.

The film's penultimate scene ends in the assessor's office in Chicago with handcuffs clicking on the Blues Brothers' wrists, a hundred rifles pointed at their heads. Cut to the interior of the film's Joliet Prison, painstakingly re-created on the Universal lot, a pistachio-walled stage framed by a needlepoint-sampler-type design that reads, "It's never too late to mend."

Filmmakers had intended to shoot the film's denouement inside the actual prison, but Landis concluded the facility's dining hall wasn't large enough for the vast musical number he hoped to stage. The director had spotted the homespun message inside the prison and had studio artists make a replica on the Universal set.

In the filmed scene, the Brothers have traded their black suits for prison blues. The band begins to play. The inmates clang tin bowls. The first prisoner to climb on a table is Joe Walsh, the Eagles guitarist, in another cameo. This was another easy shoot for the musicians, pantomiming over a prerecorded track. Before the cameras rolled, a few of them had dropped acid.

By the close of the *Blues Brothers* production, sobriety ran in short supply. When studio executives watched the dailies from the musical numbers, they asked Stephen Katz, "Where are the close-ups?"

"Close-ups?" the cinematographer scoffed. "Have you seen their eyes?"

Chapter 26

The Black Tower

NO SOONER HAD FILMING WRAPPED on *The Blues Brothers* than Belushi set off on a walkabout. No one in his inner circle knew where he had gone. Loved ones sat fretfully by the phone, awaiting a call from him or, worse, a call about him. Three days later, he resurfaced, oblivious to the panic he had set off.

The episode sparked the first serious discussions among John's loved ones about some sort of intervention. Landis and others prodded Bernie Brillstein to stage a come-to-Jesus meeting with his mercurial client. John appeared one morning at Brillstein's corner office on Sunset Boulevard. He looked bad, and he smelled bad, as Brillstein divined when John leaned in for a hug.

"John," Brillstein said, "you've got to stop. You've got to get some help. You've got to get healthy."

"I can handle it," John replied. "I have the heart of a high school senior."

"You're going to kill yourself," Brillstein pressed. "You can't do this. You can't abuse yourself. You're going to put yourself out of show business."

John's eyes burned. He shut the office door.

"Look," he yelled. "I'm not paying you to be my best friend. I don't ask what you do after six o'clock. Don't ask me."

"You can't tell me not to love you," Brillstein pleaded. "I'm not talking about goddamn business. I'm talking about your life."

John cooled. They embraced again.

"You worry about your business," John said, "and I'll worry about mine." The intervention was over.

A rare image of Jake and Elwood without sunglasses surfaced in a February issue of the celebrity magazine *Us*. John and Dan posed whimsically with Jane Byrne, the Chicago mayor, and her daughter. The boys had lent the Byrnes their hats and shades. The mayor struck a Dillinger pose, hand cocked like a gun, a look marred by her strapless top. She apparently found the picture funny and authorized its release, but the image drew misogynist ridicule from male adversaries in city hall.

Mayor Byrne had allied herself publicly with *The Blues Brothers*, polarizing her enemies against the film. Landis miffed local press and politicians with closed sets and a near-total news blackout: only when the production paraded down Lake Shore Drive or dropped Pintos from the sky did the studio grudgingly concede facts to reporters. Belushi and Aykroyd had gone to considerable lengths to evade interviews.

The studio plotted to soften those hurts with a lavish Chicago premiere. Executives announced that *The Blues Brothers* would debut on June 18 at the four-thousand-seat Chicago Theatre downtown, followed by a live Blues Brothers concert. The evening would anchor a weeklong junket for out-of-town press, flown in for interviews, screenings, and perks.

On March 27, back in New York, John consulted the New York addiction specialist he had seen four years earlier. Again, the doctor told John to stop. "Patient very hostile," he wrote in his file, "alternately agitated and drowsy. Paranoid." The doctor told Judy that John "should be hospitalized for detoxification." John refused.

The next week, John traveled to Chicago to see his younger brother Jim perform in a play. Jim told John their grandmother, who now lived in California, was dying. Nena, the diminutive, English-challenged rock of the Belushi family, had endured three heart attacks. Jim broke down. "She's waiting for you," he pleaded.

"That's why I'm not going," John replied. "The longer I stay here, the longer she'll be alive." If Nena was hanging on for him, he reasoned, maybe he could prolong her life by staying away.

Judy telephoned from New York and urged John to see his dying grandmother. Still, he refused. She flew to Chicago and found him on a binge. "I told him I was going to California the next day, with or without him," she recalled. He relented.

After his three-picture, $1.85 million windfall from Universal in 1978, John had moved his parents and grandmother from Wheaton, Illinois, to a ten-acre ranch in the Cuyamaca Mountains, east of San Diego. For most of the prior decade, John had held his family at bay, lest he sink in their pit of need. Now, he had sufficient funds to pay college tuitions, to hire relatives and in-laws, and to float interest-free loans to distant Albanian cousins. Adam Belushi had grown up on a farm in the Albanian mountains. One of the few pastimes John and Adam shared was television westerns. Now, John had moved his family to a horse ranch.

John and Judy found Nena at a hospital near the new Belushi home-stead. The dying matriarch "lit up when she saw John," Judy said. "He dropped his sorrow and turned up the charm. He was cracking jokes, putting on a little show. Pretty soon he had Nena and the aunts and uncles in the room laughing and smiling. After a little of that, Nena fell asleep. John, sitting in a chair next to the bed, rested his head on her pillow and fell asleep, too."

John didn't look so good, and someone asked a doctor to look him over. John spoke frankly about his drug use. "You're killing yourself," the doctor told him.

Nena died the next day. John sprang to life. He arranged a lavish funeral at the Albanian Orthodox church in Chicago, flying in extended family and booking hotels and cars.

"John took care of everything that day," Jim Belushi recalled. "Nena was the heart, soul and conscience of our family, and so it was like we had lost a mother."

After the service, "we went to a banquet hall for a reception," Jim said. "I was standing to the side, talking to a couple of women, when all of the sudden the whole crowd shifted and looked to the center of the room, like someone had fallen or had a heart attack. I couldn't see, so I stood up on a chair to get a better look. There was John, in the middle of the banquet hall, one arm around the bishop and the other around the priest, sobbing like a baby."

In Hollywood, Universal executives decided to cancel the lavish Chicago *Blues Brothers* premiere. Recession had descended on the nation, and Ned Tanen worried about the optics of a weeklong press junket. Instead, cast and crew would host a quiet screening for Chicago politicians. The studio would donate money to local orphanages.

That meant one less controversy for the year's most controversial film. Press reports now put the final *Blues Brothers* budget as high as $35 or even $40 million, seven or eight times the $5 million first reported in *Variety*.

By April, John Landis and his editor, George Folsey, had assembled their first rough cut of *The Blues Brothers*. It came to "a little under three hours," Folsey recalled. They hosted a private viewing at the studio. Landis hoped to screen his action musical-comedy saga with a Broadway-style intermission, an indulgence more common to sweeping epics like *Ben-Hur* and *How the West Was Won*. He set the interlude just before dawn, inserting a fade-out just after Twiggy, Elwood's jilted date, gazes forlornly at her watch. The marathon screening ended with cheers and backslapping.

In May, the studio arranged an unadvertised *Blues Brothers* sneak preview at the Picwood, a postwar movie palace at LA's Westwood and Pico Boulevards, for studio executives and random Angelenos recruited from the streets to gauge their reactions. Landis didn't get the explosive response that had greeted *Animal House* at its first screening in Denver, but "basically, the movie played very well," George Folsey said.

"The early verdict on *The Blues Brothers Movie* is very positive," a Hollywood correspondent reported. "Which should make Universal execs in the studio's notorious Black Tower breathe easier."

"But, and it's a big 'but,'" the reporter hedged, "John Landis certainly has his work cut out for him before the film's June 18 opening date. For one thing, the film is too long." The reporter cited run-on scenes and excessive cameos.

As Weiss stood with Landis on Pico Boulevard after the screening, the producer glimpsed Ned Tanen rounding a corner down the block.

Tanen stopped, glared at Weiss, raised a hand, and made a scissoring motion with two fingers.

More screenings followed, tailored for theater owners and book-ers. "Fifty percent hated it," Landis told a reporter after a screening. "'Too many car crashes.' 'The plot doesn't make sense.' 'Too many nee-groes.'"

Lew Wasserman summoned Landis to the Black Tower. "We called it the Death Star," the director said of the Universal headquarters build-ing. "And there's Lew, sitting behind his desk, which is always immacu-late. And he says, 'John, do you know Mr. Mann?'" Ted Mann owned some of the top movie houses, including the Fox, Bruin, and National, all in Westwood. "And he's sitting there, older guy with an American flag lapel. I never sat down. I just stood."

Wasserman turned to Mann and asked him to tell Landis what he had just told Wasserman.

"Mr. Landis," Mann said, "I'm not gonna book your picture."

"May I ask why?"

"I don't want Blacks in Westwood."

Landis stood speechless. "Well," he said at length, "I respectfully disagree."

"Well," Mann repeated, "I don't want Blacks in Westwood, so I'm not booking your picture."

As Landis prepared to leave, Wasserman raised a hand and made a scissoring motion with two fingers.

"Whaddaya want me to cut, Lew?" Landis protested. He wasn't going to trim all the Black characters from the movie.

"Well, John," Wasserman replied, "we're gonna have trouble booking it, so we can't have a road show. You've gotta take the intermission out of there."

Racist theater owners said *The Blues Brothers* was too Black. Hipster journalists said the band was too white. Dan walked out of a screening and predicted, "The critics will gun us down."

"We talked about putting up a big billboard in Times Square for *The Blues Brothers*," Bob Weiss recalled. "Aykroyd didn't want to do it. He was nervous about the movie."

Landis and Folsey cut twenty minutes of footage, trimming the film's length to around two and a half hours. "We had another preview at the Picwood, and we had this beautiful seventy-millimeter print made," high-resolution film tailored for wide-screen epics, Landis said. "And based on that, we cut another ten or fifteen minutes, in a hurry."

Out went the gas-station explosion, one of the film's most audacious set pieces. Out went "Sink the Bismarck," a Johnny Horton number that Jake and Elwood performed at Bob's Country Bunker. Out went the scene at the aerosol factory where Elwood Blues worked, which set up another scene, still in the film, that showed Elwood spraying glue on the gas pedal to sabotage the Good Ole Boys. Out went precious seconds of "Boom Boom," the John Lee Hooker showcase. Out, too, went the intermission. Landis cut it after several "loud discussions" with Universal executives, recalled Sean Daniel, who reasoned that "this was not a movie whose energy should have been broken up in the middle."

After the final round of cuts and "an amazing, epic, bloody struggle," Daniel and his Universal colleagues felt they had "finally arrived at the right length for this movie."

Landis was heartsick. "The rhythm was gone," he said. The film felt "kind of choppy and abrupt in places. It wasn't before." Dan Aykroyd would never forgive the cuts to the John Lee Hooker number.

Even then, the film's length, two hours and thirteen minutes, meant fewer showings, especially at midnight on Fridays and Saturdays, a natural time slot for a Belushi picture. In the end, *The Blues Brothers* booked fewer than six hundred theaters for its opening week. The typical studio film opened on fourteen hundred screens.

In the May 28 issue of *Variety*, Ned Tanen announced the final production cost of *The Blues Brothers*: $27.5 million. The disclosure drew a mild rebuke from the industry journal, which noted that the studio had put the official budget at $20 million "as recently as March." Marketing and other studio costs pushed the full price tag to at least $32 million.

In lieu of a massive Chicago launch, Universal now planned a downsized press junket in New York starting Friday, June 13, with roughly two dozen reporters assembled for a screening and interviews with the principals.

In the June 12 issue of *Rolling Stone*, Dan and John announced a blockbuster Blues Brothers tour to support the film, starting in Chicago on June 27. John promised "a big-ass show."

Belushi's minders knew he would never make it through a national tour without a Secret Service–caliber bodyguard, someone to track his every move and break the supply chain that fed his habits. Help arrived in a tip from an unlikely source: Joe Walsh, the Eagles guitarist, who had substance issues of his own. Walsh put John in touch with Richard "Smokey" Wendell, an actual Secret Service agent who had graduated into higher-paid private security work. Walsh had hired Wendell to protect him from overzealous fans—and from himself. Now, he recommended the bodyguard to John. Bernie Brillstein negotiated a contract—$1,000 a week, plus expenses—for Wendell to live, eat, and travel with John until the tour's end. Walsh warned John: "You're not going to like him."

Wendell flew to New York on April 16 for a meeting at the Record Plant, where Walsh was helping John with a version of "Gimme Some Lovin'" for the *Blues Brothers* soundtrack. John arrived three hours late, his pockets stuffed with little cups of Häagen-Dazs. He passed them around and greeted Wendell.

John started work on the session. Minutes later, a well-dressed man entered the studio carrying an ornate walking cane and bottles of champagne, flanked by two glamorous women. John clearly knew him. The stranger disappeared into the bathroom, then returned. Wendell entered the bathroom. He found the packet of coke the dealer had concealed inside a paper-towel dispenser, pocketed it, and returned to the studio.

John went to the bathroom. He returned and approached the dealer. They talked furtively. "That's impossible," the dealer said. He slipped back to the bathroom and then returned, bewildered.

The three men played a high-stakes game of hide-and-seek, Wendell pocketing hundreds of dollars in cocaine. At length, he poured a cup of coffee and approached the dealer. "Look," he said, "we can do this all night long if you like, but it's going to be a lot more expensive for you than it is for me," he said, producing a packet from his pocket. "Now, if this were just Sweet'N Low . . ." he said, emptying the packet into his coffee. The dealer winced.

John huddled with the dealer. Then Wendell watched John wander around the studio and pick up a pack of Dunhills. He walked over to John. "Let me see the cigarettes," he instructed.

"What cigarettes?" John snapped. Wendell reached for the pack. John swung away. Neither man would release it. They tumbled to the floor, wrestling for the Dunhills. Wendell pried the package from John, arose, opened it, and found the stash within.

John turned to Joe Walsh, smiled, and said, "You're right. I'm not going to like him."

John and his new bodyguard retreated to an Italian restaurant. Wendell watched John consume antipasto, followed by spaghetti, ravioli, a meat course, and dessert. They repaired to the Blues Bar. On the way out, John tried to give Wendell the slip, instructing his driver to pull away before the bodyguard could climb in. Wendell chased the car down Hudson Street. It stopped. He opened the door and found John laughing. "I finally got you," he said.

"That depends on how you look at it," Wendell said. "Aren't we in the same car together?"

Back at the Belushi home, John gave Wendell a few instructions. "I don't go anywhere without Judy," he said. "Never leave her behind. Take care of her. She is very important to me. Remember that."

Wendell asked, "Why are you in this situation? Why do you do the Candyland?"

"It's the pressure," John said. "The demands, the hours. You need drugs to deal with everything the business puts on you. It's hard to be on for everyone all the time. And it makes me feel good."

Morris Lyda, who had served as John's driver and minder during the *Blues Brothers* shoot, reprised his role as road manager for the Blues Brothers band on the approaching tour. He arranged a session for John with a vocal coach, someone who helped performers learn "how to use your voice and not strain it." John had waved off an opening act, which meant he would have to sing for two straight hours a night, a much longer set than the band had played opening for Steve Martin.

John missed the appointment.

The band would have to pad its repertoire. John chose one of the new songs: "Guilty," a poignant composition by dark-humored singer-songwriter Randy Newman. The narrator gets high on whiskey and coke because he can't stand himself: "a whole lot of medicine . . . to pretend that I'm somebody else."

Chapter 27

A $30-Million Wreck

O N FRIDAY, JUNE 13, 1980, seventy-five reporters converged on the Plaza Hotel in New York for a two-day, $200,000 *Blues Brothers* preview. Most members of the visiting press were middle-aged men from flyover states.

Three hundred journalists, in all, filed into Cinerama II, the former Strand Theatre on Broadway at Forty-Seventh Street, for the Friday-night screening, joined by radio-contest winners and youths swept up from Times Square. The film opened to scattered laughter, befitting the austere setting and the Brothers' deadpan delivery. Then, the first musical number hit, and the crowd sprang to life, "stomping their feet to James Brown—who was present—or clapping their hands to Aretha Franklin," the *Los Angeles Times* reported. "They also ooh-ed and aah-ed one stunt after another, as though on a roller-coaster ride. And finally, about 1½ hours into the film, the audience broke into cheers for Belushi and Aykroyd" as the duo hit the Palladium stage.

"Afterwards, at the Plaza, the champagne flowed and the press dined on shrimp and roast beef." A scrum of New York critics "sat in a corner and talked mostly about how surprised they were to have enjoyed the film."

The next day, John and Dan flanked Landis at a Q-and-A session. Talk inevitably turned to the budget.

"I'll never apologize for spending money on entertainment," Landis said. He declared the movie "one of the biggest films ever made, even bigger than *Ben-Hur*." He invoked the great movie musicals, *The*

Wizard of Oz and *Singin' in the Rain*. Landis was on a roll. At one point, a reporter quipped, "Would you let the other two guys do a little more of the talking?"

The director had not yet turned thirty. He spent most of the day on the defensive, fending off graying reporters who seemed unwilling to take his film seriously. "I've been under attack for a year," he said, "and it's making me berserk." He produced a rubber band and shot it across the room.

"He's more like a kid playing with toys," one older reporter observed.

"Well, I'll tell you one thing," a colleague offered. "People my age won't be banging down the turnstiles. But my nineteen-year-old daughter can't wait to see the movie."

Landis and his stars returned to Chicago on Monday, June 16, for a quiet local premiere. They screened the film for crew and politicians in Norridge, an anonymous suburb. The audience included members of the Cook County Commission, the panel John Landis had circumvented with his visit to Sidney Korshak, the powerful lawyer.

When the film was over, two commissioners cornered Jane Byrne, the embattled mayor. Voices rose in anger. Landis heard one ask, "Do you think we're going to give permission to drive tanks on Daley Plaza? And land helicopters?" As long as I'm commissioner, he vowed, this picture will not be made.

"It happened months ago," the mayor scoffed, "and you didn't even notice."

On Friday, June 20, *The Blues Brothers* opened. Landis and company braced for the reviews.

They were dreadful.

"Mr. Belushi and Mr. Aykroyd have only about three funny scenes during the course of a long, bloated saga," Janet Maslin opined in the *New York Times*.

"A $30-MILLION WRECK, MINUS LAUGHS," the *Los Angeles Times* declared in its headline.

The *Washington Post* termed the film "a ponderous comic monstrosity."

Time called it "a demolition symphony that works with the cold efficiency of a Moog synthesizer gone sadistic."

Newsweek reported, "'The Blues Brothers' may be the most elaborate vanity production ever made."

With this film, critical appraisal did not break along generational lines: pretty much everyone hated it. "Exhausting overkill," Maslin's term, emerged as a theme, one that dovetailed with the established narrative of budgetary overrun.

"What did all that money buy?" Maslin asked. "Scores of car crashes. Too many extras. Overstaged dance numbers."

Even worse, to some reviewers, was the director's unthinkable decision to conceal the eyes of his stars behind impenetrable sunglasses. "Never, never, never should anyone, especially a performer with expressive eyes, be allowed the imbecilic drollery of concealing them from a motion picture audience," the *Washington Post* critic seethed.

Only the professional musicians escaped scorn. "The movie has two saving graces," *Newsweek* observed. "Aretha Franklin, playing a waitress who stops the show with a rocking rendition of 'Think,' and 72-year-old Cab Calloway, who tosses off 'Minnie the Moocher' with great aplomb."

Worst of all, some reviewers greeted *The Blues Brothers* as fundamentally racist. "People who love soul music and blues may have a little trouble accepting Aykroyd and Belushi as great performers in a movie that consigns the authentic greats to backup roles," David Denby wrote in *New York*. "Belushi and Aykroyd doubtless intended to pay homage to the great black performers who have inspired them, but the homage often comes close to insult and outright rip-off."

The only praise seemed to come from Chicago.

"'The Blues Brothers' is the Sherman tank of musicals," Roger Ebert wrote in the *Sun-Times*. "It's a big, raucous powerhouse that proves against all the odds that if you're loud enough, vulgar enough and have enough raw energy, you can make a steamroller into a musical, and vice-versa." Ebert awarded it three stars.

Gene Siskel in the *Tribune* went further, as he often did. "Take your pick," he wrote. "'The Blues Brothers' is the year's best film to date; one of the all-time great comedies; the best movie ever made in Chicago. All are true, and, boy, is that ever a surprise."

Siskel recapped the months of buzz about problems on the set, run-away budgets and the overfed egos of the two stars, "who apparently turned off a number of people during their stay here. Well, forget manners: 'The Blues Brothers' is a flat-out winner, from its opening eerie helicopter shot of the East Chicago steel mills at dawn to its concluding 120 mile-an-hour chase." With *The Blues Brothers*, Siskel concluded, John Landis "must be included in the ranks of important American directors."

To Landis, behind the comedy of *The Blues Brothers* lay the tragedy of Belushi's decline. "In *Animal House*," he would later recall, "he was there 100 percent for me and for himself. In *The Blues Brothers*, at the best moments, he's there 75 percent." You could see the best Belushi in the crackle of his delivery opposite Carrie Fisher in the tunnel, opposite Dan in the Chez Paul scene and brandishing the bullwhip at Bob's Country Bunker, and in most of the other LA footage. And you could see the diminished Belushi in some of the bleary Chicago scenes, stuffed up and somnambulant in Elwood's apartment, sleepwalking through the gas-station sequence. Maybe those dark glasses, so reviled by the critics, were a blessing. They hid John's sickness.

Landis didn't care about the critics. He trusted his instincts, and Dan's, in paying homage to the icons of rhythm and blues with a film that ultimately, inevitably, served as a vehicle for two white comedians. Universal would not have financed a Blues Brothers film that didn't star the Blues Brothers. The musical numbers hummed. The deadpan humor sizzled.

On June 24, Stephen Katz dashed off an exultant letter to his director.

Dear John,
I stood in line with the crowds Saturday night in San Francisco . . . the theatre was turning people away!

The audience laughed from the first frame to the last, applauded the music, the finale, and seemed to love it all. I'm sure they'll all be back for seconds!!

The print looked great, and I've never been in a theatre where the movie was so LOUD!

It made me proud to be a part of it all.

Then came the receipts. *The Blues Brothers* earned $4.9 million in its first weekend and $7.9 million in its first week, more than $1 million a day, a pace second only to *The Empire Strikes Back*. Landis's car-chase musical earned nearly $1 million that week in Chicago alone, where it played in only sixteen theaters.

"If the second weekend is better or equal to the first, nationally, it means we have a mega-hit," Landis told a reporter.

On Friday, June 27, the Blues Brothers' tour opened in Chicago. John cleaned up admirably. Smokey Wendell delivered an antidrug speech to the band, vowing, "If you're wired, you're fired." Eyes rolled.

Dan and John rewarded Gene Siskel for his four-star *Tribune* review with an exclusive interview at a corner table at the Pump Room, the celebrity magnet on Chicago's Gold Coast. Siskel wrote, "Belushi's fans scream phrases at him [that] he made famous on TV and in his films—'Toga! Toga!,' 'Food fight!,' 'Chizbugga! Chizbugga!'—while Aykroyd's groupies politely tell him, 'I really admire your work.' Belushi's fans think they know him; Aykroyd's fans are certain they don't."

Did John envy Dan's more manageable celebrity?

"I'm not envious of Danny," John said. "But I have real admiration for his writing skill and his intellect. Envy, no, but I wish I could be as good a writer as he is."

"But, John, you're just lazy," Dan cut in. "He's a good writer. He knows structure, he knows scripts, he knows comedy, he knows running order, he knows all those things."

"Dan, Dan, listen to me," John said. "We do different things well. In terms of getting the band together and motivating them, I'm better at that."

"Definitely."

"In terms of who calls the shots on the road and in the studio, I do that."

"My attitude," Dan resumed, "is that I've hooked up with a very big American star and that I'm in his workshop."

Paul "Shiv" Shaffer rejoined the Blues Brothers band for the tour, twenty-five shows in thirteen cities. His calendar was now clear, and

Belushi forgave him for defecting to Gilda Radner's camp a year earlier. John and Dan accepted no pay, diverting all ticket receipts to the
band. The tour opened, appropriately, at Poplar Creek in the Chicago
suburbs. The band played great, as it always did. Belushi still wasn't
much of a singer. On disc, his vocals sounded amateurish. In concert,
his showmanship prevailed. Reviewers wrestled with the paradox.

"Belushi's gravel-voiced singing is often off-key and usually more
growl than song," a *Sun-Times* reviewer opined, while Dan's harmonica
work "is workman-like at best." Yet, the critic termed the concert "one
of the most amazing shows I've ever seen," for the potent chemistry
between Belushi and his audience, a crowd dotted with black suits, white
shirts, and dark sunglasses.

The band traveled from Chicago to the Palladium in New York.
"There seems to be a critical consensus forming about the Blues Brothers," a *New York Times* reviewer wrote. "It is felt that as comedians they
aren't quite funny enough, and as live performers they simply don't live
up to their band, let alone to their soul inspirations." This critic dis-
agreed. "First, the Blues Brothers are by no means *that* bad. Mr. Belushi
has nothing to be deeply ashamed about, compared to a lot of white
people who try to sing Black popular music. And Mr. Aykroyd can play
functional harmonica and snap out the patter songs ('Riot in Cellblock
No. 9') handily enough. And that band *is* first-rate.

"Second, this sort of music depends in large measure on the projection of personality, and that the Blues Brothers have." Belushi could
cartwheel onto any stage and take command.

Warm reviews followed the band through Philadelphia to the Washington, DC, area, for a July 3 gig at Merriweather Post Pavilion.

"From the moment John Belushi first spiraled across the stage, heels
over head, until the final encore when the young crowd greeted 'Soul
Man' with tumultuous applause, the Blues Brothers sustained a level
of energy and excitement they never came close to achieving in their
recent movie," the *Washington Post* reviewer wrote. He termed the band
"the finest working in rhythm and blues today."

The tour traveled north to Saratoga Springs, New York, on Fourth of
July weekend. Smokey Wendell took John and Judy to his family farm

near Cooperstown. John fished, hunted, and gazed at the Ernie Banks plaque at the Baseball Hall of Fame: He loved Mr. Cub, like most Chicagoans. Wendell bought him an autographed Ernie Banks baseball. They watched a game. John turned to Wendell and said, "I'm at the home of baseball, eating a hot dog, watching a game. It can't get any better than this."

On Wednesday, July 9, Universal bought a full-page ad in *Variety*. Jake and Elwood danced beneath a banner that announced the film's box office receipts: $19 million in seventeen days. Landis had his megahit.

The forty-four-person Blues Brothers crew flew west to Cuyahoga Falls, Ohio, north to Detroit, and south to Memphis, traveling in a chartered Convair propeller plane that purportedly had once carried Elvis. On the trip south, the pilot had to fly around a giant thunderstorm. "As far as you could see out the window," Lou Marini recalled, "there was the storm. Then we get to Memphis. Everybody's wasted. And the next day, everybody went to the pool. And I remember saying to Steve Jordan, there was no way to swim in the pool because there were so many people in it."

Steve Jordan had rejoined the band on drums. Jordan was Black, and he was dating a white woman.

"You need some room?" Jordan asked. He and his girlfriend eased into the pool. "Within moments," Marini recalled, "two-thirds of the people who were in the pool got out of the pool."

The band flew to Houston, then to Dallas. After the July 13 show in Dallas, Wendell spotted some musicians passing cocaine around their hotel room.

"Give me some of that," John pleaded.

"Don't you listen to him," Wendell commanded. He grabbed the stash from the table. John reeled back, as if to throw a punch.

"Since when were you a quarterback?" Wendell smiled. "You got a football there?" John dropped his fist. "I don't believe I was going to hit you," John gasped. They exited the room together, tears streaming down John's face. "I'm sorry, so sorry, man."

Chapter 28

The 2,000 Pound Bee

THE BLUES BROTHERS BAND cartwheeled across the country. On July 15, they reached Red Rocks Amphitheatre in Colorado. Backstage, Blue Lou Marini introduced John to Sharif Khan, the great Pakistani Canadian squash champion. John took one look at Sharif and his family and said, "Jesus, they look like a bunch of fucking terrorists." After a moment of silence, the Khans burst into laughter—Belushi himself looked like a terrorist.

Judy Belushi couldn't remember seeing her husband in better shape. "There were a few nights when, after the concert, I went out with friends while John stayed in," she said. "That was different."

The nightly shows consumed John's energy. "That made him a different person," Smokey Wendell said. "The downtime, when nothing was going on, that's when he could get into trouble." When Wendell went out on an errand, John tagged along. "He would consciously take himself out of any situation where he was alone."

On July 16, *Variety* reported that *The Blues Brothers* had earned $25.7 million in twenty-four days, maintaining its blockbuster pace. The film would spend the rest of the summer fending off two other comedy smashes with shared DNA. One was *Airplane!*, the action-drama send-up conceived by the Kentucky Fried Theater troupe a half decade earlier. The filmmakers had persuaded Paramount to finance their parody. *Airplane!* opened a week after *The Blues Brothers* and matched its box-office tempo.

A month later, Orion Pictures rolled out *Caddyshack*, the second feature film from *National Lampoon*. Both *Airplane!* and *Caddyshack* had been made on modest seven-figure budgets. *Airplane!* reaped warm reviews. *Caddyshack* did not—critics winced at jokes about turds in swimming pools. Compared to *The Blues Brothers*, however, both films got off easy.

On Saturday, July 26, the Blues Brothers band opened a weeklong, valedictory stand at Universal Amphitheatre, where Bob Tischler would record a third Blues Brothers record. John's body remained clean, but he was losing his voice. He fell back on his cartwheels. Critics pounced. "Belushi's not bad," Robert Hilburn wrote in the *Los Angeles Times*, "just resoundingly mediocre."

The Blues Brothers band performed its final Universal show on August 1. No one knew it then, but John and Dan would not perform as the Blues Brothers again.

At the after-party, five patrons passed cocaine to John, slipping packets into the flapless pockets of his corduroy jacket, a gesture as common as a backslap in Hollywood circles of the era. John retreated to a bathroom. Wendell followed.

"C'mon," John pleaded. "Let me have a little."

Wendell stood firm. He was still on the clock.

"It's past midnight," John said. "You got your check."

After the after-party, John released Smokey Wendell from his duties, awarding him a $2,000 bonus and a ten-day vacation with his wife at the Hotel Bel-Air. Later that night, Wendell found John awake and afraid. They talked about fame.

"It gets worse as it gets better," John said. "You get caught up in this business, and the drugs are inevitable. They were here before me, and they will be here after me." John told Wendell he was frightened to be alone.

If things get bad, Wendell said, "Just call me, OK?"

The tour was over, but *The Blues Brothers* rolled on. On July 30, Universal took out a two-page spread in *Variety*. Jake and Elwood danced beside a message that read "$34,656,504" and, below that, "38 days."

The studio was already talking about a sequel. "Danny wants to pick up the action in the prison," where the first movie ended, Thom Mount told columnist Marilyn Beck.

John and Judy spent most of August in Europe. They stayed at a castle in Scotland, visited Michael O'Donoghue in southern France, and floated in gondolas through Venice. One afternoon, John took a call from Bernie Brillstein.

John put down the phone and turned to Judy. "Doug Kenney's dead," he said. She cried. They embraced. Kenney, vacationing in Hawaii, had fallen from a cliff—an accident, probably, although no one could rule out that he had jumped. (One *National Lampoon* colleague quipped that he had fallen while looking for a place to jump.) Kenney was thirty-three.

"I just feel terrible that we never made up," John said. Good-natured competition between *Blues Brothers* and *Caddyshack* had soured into petty rivalry. When Kenney had loaded his suitcases into a cab for a move to LA, John had refused to help.

"Those two guys had entered into that ever-faster spinning gyre of coke and who knows what else," said Rick Meyerowitz, the celebrated *National Lampoon* artist. He had once spent a blurry evening with the two men at Musso and Frank Grill in Hollywood, watching John eat minestrone with his hands.

In September, John prepared for his next film: a romantic comedy called *Continental Divide*, with Steven Spielberg as executive producer. Spielberg easily persuaded John to play the male lead, a crusty newspaper columnist modeled on Mike Royko, John's family friend. Universal offered John $850,000, his contracted rate. As director, the studio hired Michael Apted, fresh from the Loretta Lynn biopic *Coal Miner's Daughter*. The female lead went to Blair Brown, an auburn-haired beauty.

Though John remained relatively clean, his weight had ballooned to 245 pounds. He would need to slim down to play a romantic lead. Producers had considered Robert Redford, Robert De Niro, and Al Pacino for the part. Bernie Brillstein had lobbied hard for John, hoping to shed the Bluto image and rebrand him as a latter-day Spencer Tracy. To drop pounds, John enlisted Bill "Superfoot" Wallace, a full-contact karate champion who had worked with Elvis.

"We'd run a mile, do three sets of bench presses, three sets of curls, three sets of military presses, three sets of triceps extensions, and three sets of full incline sit-ups, every day. Plus, the martial arts and the boxing," Wallace said. "I put him on a hundred calories a meal. He'd yell at me, scream at me, call me all kinds of names. He lost forty-three pounds in, like, three months."

Rehearsals commenced in Los Angeles. John spent a day with Carrie Fisher, who had not yet tamed her own addictions. They drank sake on Sunset, then visited a private club above the Roxy. "I lost John for a second," Fisher remembered, "and then he came back over to me with this panicked look and said, 'Oh God, I just did some coke.'"

"John," Fisher said, "we can leave right now."

John gazed at her with raw fear in his eyes. "I can't."

John and Judy were due in Cañon City, Colorado, to film *Continental Divide*. Shortly before their departure, John became consumed by self-doubt. He met with the director, Sean Daniel, and Bernie Brillstein at Brillstein's home. "I can't do it," he begged, clearly terrified of playing a romantic lead. The others talked him down.

John also feared his recent lapse. He rehired Smokey Wendell to join Superfoot Wallace in his entourage. On location, John awoke daily at six to breakfast on puffed rice, black coffee, and cantaloupe. When enamored crewmen offered drugs, John waved them off.

"Every night after shooting wrapped, I'd go back to this little teeny motel where I was staying," Blair Brown said. "I'd be sitting in my room and I'd hear these little feet—John had little feet—just tap-tap-tapping by outside my window." Superfoot Wallace had John running laps around the motel. John and his trainer ran up and down mountain roads every night, "because that was the only time he had," Wallace said. "It was so dark, Smokey had to follow us in a car," headlights blazing, "so we could see where we were going."

John greeted a visitor to the set by pointing to his own face. "You know what these are?" he beamed. "Cheekbones."

To keep his mind and body busy, John required perpetual stimulation. Wendell imported a television, a drum kit, and a pinball machine.

In the film, John played a journalist sent off to the mountains to interview a bird-watcher, played by Brown. After a predictably rocky start, they fall in love.

"Every day we had to be helicoptered higher and higher," Brown said. One day, they happened upon some Belushi fans who had scaled a mountain, built an igloo, and camped out for two days to await the star. John climbed into the igloo to talk to them.

In mid-November, the *Continental Divide* crew finished work in the mountains and traveled to Chicago to shoot scenes on city streets and in the newsroom of the *Sun-Times*. No sooner had the plane landed than John made a beeline for the Blues Bar, still in business. Smokey Wendell resumed his hunter-gatherer routine, ferreting out cocaine hidden inside the potbellied stove. More often than not, John turned the drugs down.

John partied in Chicago, staying out late and regaining lost weight. But he never vanished completely, never wandered off on a walkabout. Fans treated him with more deference than in the *Animal House* years. Bluto now traveled with a champion kickboxer.

Among all the duties of the romantic lead, the love scene spooked John the most. He and Blair Brown shot the obligatory sequence on a closed set, naked beneath the sheets save for "little bitty underwear," Brown recalled.

"I don't think John had ever done a love scene before." He hadn't. "And he was clearly nervous about doing it. He just lay there in bed, trying to think up all the funny names for penis that he could: the Hose of Horror . . . Mr. Wiggly . . . We were weeping with laughter, it was so funny. It was just like watching a little kid stalling because he doesn't want to eat his vegetables."

At year's end, filming concluded on *Continental Divide*. After the customary wrap party, John reached into his pockets, produced several vials of cocaine, "and tossed them on the bed," Bernie Brillstein recalled. "That's how much had just been passed to him over the course of the evening by people trying to be his friend." John flushed them down the toilet.

The Belushis hosted a New Year's Eve party at their rented canyon home, joined by friends who were making their own bids for sobriety. One was John Candy, Dan's old Second City castmate. At midnight, they toasted with sparkling cider.

In December 1980, *Saturday Night Live* featured musical performances by Aretha Franklin and James Brown on consecutive weeks. Neither artist had done the show before, and both were riding high. Ray Charles played the Louisiana Superdome in November. Franklin sang for the Queen Mother at the London Palladium. *The Blues Brothers* had helped revive their careers, just as John and Dan had hoped, their mission from God fulfilled.

"As far as commercial interest in R & B is concerned, John helped get the ball rolling again," Brother Ray would say, a couple of years later. "Man, we owe him."

Dozens of journalists had condemned the Blues Brothers, first for covering Black music on disc and onstage, then for trotting out Black icons in a film that starred two white men. With the *Blues Brothers* film and soundtrack, "John Belushi and Dan Aykroyd have moved from the gratuitously racist to the merely patronizing—progress of a sort, I suppose," Dave Marsh fumed in *Rolling Stone*. "Using black people to betray and exploit themselves isn't exactly a noble endeavor."

The icons themselves seemed to disagree.

"The film was made with a lot of love and gave us all another chance," James Brown told *People* for a 1980 cover story. "I hate to admit it, but these young people never heard of me. They come to the movies and see James Brown and Aretha Franklin. If they like us, maybe they'll come hear us play."

They did. The Godfather went from half-empty rooms to packed houses. Franklin reaped a star on the Hollywood Walk of Fame.

"There's a moment when you're so in the pocket that your choices are America's choices," Mitch Glazer said. "That's the way it was with the

Blues Brothers. The blues were nowhere, but John liked them, decided that everyone should like them, and everyone did."

Perhaps no one gained so much currency from *The Blues Brothers* as Cab Calloway. "The effect on Cab's career was remarkable," writes biographer Alyn Shipton. Well past seventy, Cab found himself swamped with bookings like no time since his "Minnie the Moocher" heyday in the 1930s. He assembled a big band and hit the road.

In March 1981, Smokey Wendell told John he was ready to move on. John was between projects, enjoying the sand and surf and small-town vibe on Martha's Vineyard. Wendell had not intended to work as his personal assistant indefinitely.

"What are you talking about?" John snapped.

"Well, I think you're doing better now."

"You can't go," John said. "I don't want you to go, and I won't let you. I want you to stay."

"Well, that's not—"

"I'll pay you double."

"I'm flattered, but—"

"I'll buy you a house."

"That has nothing to do with it, John," Wendell said. "You're fine now. You kids have got your whole life ahead of you. You've got it all together."

Judy cut in. "Well, John, you know, if Smokey feels that he has to go, then, well, we can get by."

Wendell had learned a thing or two about Judy. "Whenever she's really nervous," he recalled, "she never looks directly at you. She sort of puts her head down and tilts it from side to side, with her hair falling down in her face a bit." She was doing that now.

"Judy," Wendell asked, "are you not comfortable with me going?"

"Well, Smokey," she dithered, still addressing the floor, "we're just, you know, used to having you here and, I mean, sure we're gonna miss you, but . . ." She stopped, looked Wendell straight in the eyes, and said, "No, I don't want you to go."

Wendell departed nonetheless, leaving John in the capable hands, and feet, of "Superfoot" Wallace.

Later that month, John went to see John Avildsen, the director who had won an Oscar for *Rocky*. Avildsen was going to direct a film adaptation of *Neighbors*, a satiric novel about suburban paranoia. The story featured a dull middle-class protagonist named Earl Keese and a boorish new neighbor whose vulgar family drives Earl to the brink.

Neighbors looked like the perfect vehicle for the next Aykroyd-Belushi collaboration. And Avildsen had a novel idea: "You should play Earl Keese," the boring, middle-aged victim.

"I think I'm the other guy," John replied. Belushi was The Thing That Wouldn't Leave. He should play Vic, the vulgar aggressor.

"You've played him," Avildsen said.

John said he would think about it.

Dan signed on. The friends agreed that switching roles sounded intriguing. Almost no one else involved in *Neighbors* much liked the idea, but Columbia Pictures would happily take Aykroyd and Belushi in any combination. The deal guaranteed John $1.25 million, his largest paycheck yet.

Rehearsals for *Neighbors* began on April 6. Some days later, John telephoned David Brown. Brown was producing *Neighbors* with partner Richard Zanuck, the team behind *Jaws*. John and Dan met with him at a restaurant in Greenwich Village, and John urged Brown to dump Avildsen as director. He wasn't funny. He wanted to shoot the scenes in order, like a play. He was too rigid. He wouldn't let John and Dan improvise. The producer wondered if John was projecting his self-doubts onto his director, and reminded him that Avildsen had won an Oscar. Brown politely declined.

Shooting began on April 20 on a Staten Island set. The arguments started that very day, John feuding with the director about his character's hair. Avildsen wanted Earl Keese to look middle-aged. He wanted more gray: John wanted less. Dan bleached his own hair blond and wore tinted contact lenses and a silver tooth to effect a punk-rock look.

John and Avildsen fought on. The production receptionist took to answering the phone, "General Hospital"—*Neighbors* had devolved into soap opera. A visiting reporter watched Belushi and Avildsen argue to the brink of a fistfight.

Without Wendell, John slipped back into the old, bad ways. Bill "Superfoot" Wallace remained by his side, leading him in daily workouts but no longer restricting his caloric intake. "I asked Avildsen, 'Do you want him thin?' 'No, I want him chubby,'" the director had replied.

When it came to drugs, Wallace wasn't sure he shared Wendell's broad mandate. He telephoned Bernie Brillstein.

"John's getting back into the shit," he said.

"Oh, no," Brillstein moaned.

"Do I have permission to keep it from him?"

Yes.

"Will you keep me from getting fired?"

Yes.

The next time Wallace saw John disappear into his *Neighbors* trailer with two female callers, he waited for the star to emerge and slipped inside.

"You're supplying John," Wallace told the strangers.

"Who the fuck are you?" one of them snapped.

Wallace found the drugs. "I'm the guy who just threw you off the set."

The women appealed to John. He raced over to Wallace. "What the fuck are you doing?"

"If I didn't care about you, I wouldn't care what you did," the kickboxer replied. "I love you like a brother."

John's eyes welled up. He embraced his new enforcer.

But John seethed at his director. Avildsen deliberated over every scene, polling people's opinions, hemming and hawing, qualities John took for weakness. "It was a matter of respect," Dan recalled. "John might disagree with you, but he'd work with you if he respected you."

One day, as Avildsen vacillated over where to place the cameras on a minor scene, John exploded: "OK, you motherfucker, you let me know when you're gonna shoot it." He stormed off the set.

John seemed to think the film belonged to him. He placed a midnight telephone call to John Landis. "Come do this movie," he pleaded.

"Wait," Landis replied. "Aren't you shooting now?"

"Yes."

"I can't do that. Are you fucking crazy?" Belushi replied with an expletive of his own and hung up.

The film progressed into bleary night shoots. Cocaine swirled around the set. One night, the crew waited on John for a scene that had Dan's character, Vic, fire a shotgun at Earl from a rooftop while clad in a frogman suit. After a lengthy delay, John stumbled out of his Winnebago, barely coherent. He mumbled something, then stumbled back in.

"He refused to come out of his trailer," Richard Zanuck recalled. "We had 150 people standing around waiting."

Zanuck entered John's trailer. "You've got to get out there," he pleaded, over the blare of teeth-rattling music.

"Not if that fucker is out there," John hissed.

"But John, he's the director."

"You direct the picture," John said.

"I don't want to direct the fucking picture." Zanuck felt like he was reasoning with a child.

"Well, let me direct it."

God, no.

"Let Danny direct it."

"Look," Zanuck said, "just go out there."

John staggered out. Half an hour later, he staggered back in.

The week progressed in similar fashion. At one point, Zanuck recalled, "we had two guys standing behind him, holding him up off-camera. You know, I mean that's the kind of shape he was in. He couldn't control it. And then no one could control him."

Dan coaxed John back to work. When the night shoots ended, John's binge subsided. Only a few weeks of production remained. "The only thing that got John through it without killing Avildsen or himself was the promise that we were to have two solid months on the Vineyard once shooting completed," Judy said. Filming ended on June 29.

The Belushis retreated to the island. John relaxed and recharged. He drove around in his black Jeep, stopping at Sandy's Fish & Chips for a fish burger, at Alley's General Store for the latest Conan comic, at

Tisbury Great Pond for oysters. The Belushis owned a prime stretch of private beach. John and Dan christened it Skull's Beach and required visitors to wear special skull-inscribed pins. They hosted mud parties, soaking in holes beneath the cliffs, letting the mud bake onto their skin. John would grab a driftwood club and run off down the beach like a giant clay monster, sneaking up on Dan and his date.

"Every single day of that summer was great," Dan said. "John and Judy would come over and wake us around eleven." The gang would drive over to a friend's clothing store, Take It Easy Baby, where John would work the register. "Then we'd go grab lunch somewhere, and then off to the beach for a swim and back to my place for a nap. James Taylor was there, Carly Simon. We had so many friends on the island.

". . . It was clear to everyone at that point that John had a problem, a physical problem, with cocaine. And all those hangers-on and folks that were constantly feeding him that stuff, they just weren't allowed."

One afternoon, Dan and John went out in one of the black Jeeps, with Dan behind the wheel. They reached the beach. They talked of fast cars, fast bikes, and death. Dan popped a cassette into the deck. A surf instrumental buzzed to life, the kind of rave-up John used to play with the Ravins.

"Wow!" John cried. "What is that?"

Dan identified it as "The 2,000 Pound Bee" by the Ventures, the '60s surf band.

John laughed: the name reminded him of the repellent bee sketches and the birth of the Blues Brothers. Soon, they were both howling. John and Dan were the 2,000 Pound Bees.

"You got to promise me something," Dan said, when they could speak again. "If I die before you do, you have to play this tape at my funeral." He broke up again. "Wouldn't it be great to lay this noisy, heavy tape on a church full of people?"

"Sure," John said. "And you do the same for me."

"Absolutely. Absolutely."

In September, John and Judy traveled to Amagansett, on New York's Long Island, for Lorne Michaels's wedding. He had finally divorced

Rosie Shuster and was marrying Susan Forristal, a model who had once dated Dan. Dan fled to the Yukon.

John arrived at the nuptials looking so haggard that Paul Simon intercepted him, cleaned him up, and helped him shave so he would look marginally presentable. John pulled it together for the ceremony, greeting the wedding couple in a woozy embrace. Michaels was touched. At the reception, John passed out on a lawn chair. Friends hoisted him, chair and all, and deposited him behind a hedge, out of sight.

Two days later, John and Dan attended a screening of *Neighbors* in a Broadway penthouse. John sat between the two producers. The mere presence of Avildsen, the hated director, put him in a foul mood. The film began, and John unleashed a running commentary of loud expletives: "No!" "Fuck!" "Shit!" The producers shushed him. John took to hitting the armrest, loudly, to punctuate his objections. In the latter frames, John amplified his protests with a shoe, reprising his Khrushchev sketch from junior high school. The screening ended in silence. Viewers scattered for the exits.

"That was one of those nights of hard, crashing reality, when you realize that all of the hard work you put in might have been wasted," Dan said.

John and Judy flew to Chicago in September for the premiere of *Continental Divide*. John led a *Rolling Stone* reporter on a tour of Old Town haunts. They wound up, of course, at the Blues Bar, where John hosted Steve Beshekas, the onetime West Compass Player, and Dan Payne, his high school drama teacher, the man who had steered him from football to footlights.

John stopped by Second City. The cast arranged for him to walk onstage as the troupe sat watching an episode of *Saturday Night Live*, a program that hadn't recovered from the recent departure of Lorne Michaels and the last of the original cast. At Belushi's entrance, the crowd leapt to its feet in an ecstatic cheer. Later in the set, John played rotund *Sun-Times* reviewer Roger Ebert in a parody of *Sneak Previews*, the dueling-critics show with Ebert and Gene Siskel of the *Tribune*. They delivered a scathing review of *Continental Divide*. "Belushi's a buffoon, not an actor," John lamented, summoning his best Ebert. The real Siskel sat in the audience, "almost in tears from laughter."

The sketch betrayed John's fears. He winced at the publicity attending *Continental Divide*. A reporter asked what he had worn during the love scene. No one would have posed that question to De Niro.

The film drew warm reviews. Siskel termed Belushi "adorable." Yet, once again, John's fans struggled to accept him as a serious actor. *Continental Divide* barely turned a profit.

"For John, it was a rejection," Sean Daniel said. "And, well, that wasn't good."

On October 3, Columbia held its first semi-public screenings of *Neighbors* for hundreds of Aykroyd-Belushi fans on the studio lot. The preview played to crickets. The studio plotted to release the film a week before Christmas in fifteen hundred theaters, a strategy that would fill seats and studio coffers before word of mouth could halt ticket sales.

One autumn weekend, Judy Belushi and Carly Simon shared a five-hour limousine ride from Martha's Vineyard to New York. They talked of drugs and infidelity. James Taylor had left Simon for another woman. John's indiscretions, by contrast, seemed more about flirting and drug taking than sex, let alone love. Judy said she couldn't see having children with John until he settled down, if he ever did. Simon wondered how much longer the Belushi marriage would survive.

John's musical obsession had moved on from blues to punk. He blasted the Dead Kennedys and the Sex Pistols. Dan saw John's new passion as a revival of his adolescent ardor for heavy metal.

"John gave me all his blues albums at one point, and it was really a drag," Mitch Glazer said. "He just said, 'I don't want to listen to this shit anymore.'"

John lobbied Columbia to populate the *Neighbors* soundtrack with the cacophonic stylings of Fear, a punk band he had befriended in LA. One day, he burst into a producers' meeting. "He was in terrible shape," Richard Zanuck recalled. "He was screaming and going on about the music and the score and how it was terrible and how much it sucked, and then he burst out again." Later, in a meeting with Columbia's music director, John ripped a phone from the wall and karate chopped a desk, a punk performance sans music.

John's antics sabotaged any chance of the studio taking his suggestions seriously. Still, Fear wasn't such an outrageous choice. *Neighbors* felt like a punk-rock film.

John lobbied *Saturday Night Live* more persuasively to hire Fear as the musical guest on Halloween, on the condition that Belushi make a cameo. Dozens of skinheads introduced slam dancing to a national audience in the segment, one of the strangest in *SNL* lore. Dick Ebersol had told the director to have a film standing by in case the musical segment devolved into chaos. Midway through Fear's performance, the director cued the film.

Neighbors opened on December 18, 1981. Patrons didn't much like it, just as the studio had predicted. But enough Blues Brothers fans came out to boost $6.4 million in ticket sales over the first weekend. *Neighbors* held on for a while before receipts tapered off. In the end, the film turned a profit.

"By this time," *Variety* opined, "audiences are ready to laugh at just about anything the former *Saturday Night Live* vets do."

Chapter 29

A Viking Funeral

I N LATE 1981, director Jay Sandrich searched for actors to appear in a romantic action-comedy called "Sweet Deception." The script had a California winemaker travel to New York for a competition, fall for a woman, and stumble into a diamond-smuggling ring, ultimately foiling the smugglers and winning the girl.

The male lead suited a modern Cary Grant. Sandrich wanted John Ritter of *Three's Company*, but the studios balked. Chevy Chase passed. Sandrich took a call from Michael Ovitz, the ascendant superagent. "What do you think of John Belushi?" he asked. Bernie Brillstein had hired Ovitz to negotiate film deals for John.

"Goodbye," Sandrich replied.

"No, no, wait," Ovitz said. "Look at *Continental Divide.*"

Sandrich attended a screening. He had heard about the drugs, but he liked what he saw. And Belushi was available; after *Neighbors*, he and Dan had agreed to each make a movie alone.

Michael Ovitz set up a meeting between John and Sandrich. He represented both men. John seemed drawn to the role. Sandrich spoke plainly: "If you're on drugs, then it's never going to work."

"I'm over that now," John replied. "I have to stay clean. If I don't, my wife is going to leave me."

Ovitz shopped "Sweet Deception" to the studios. Universal passed. Filmgoers hadn't warmed to John as romantic lead in *Continental Divide*. Why would they embrace him in "Sweet Deception"? Sean Daniel urged John to await a better script.

The film went to Paramount. On December 21, John met with the director and producers. He said he wanted to make the script funnier. He had enlisted Don Novello of *SNL* to work on a rewrite.

"Everyone involved in the project wanted something different," Novello remembered. "Sandrich," the director, "was expecting us just to 'polish' his lame script. John and I were under the impression that we had carte blanche to change it. . . . All Ovitz wanted was to sell this whole package to Paramount. What I didn't know then, and what I don't think John knew either, was that Michael Ovitz was representing every single person at the table and taking home a piece of everybody else's action."

That night, Novello and John attended a Christmas party thrown by Dick Blasucci. John's high school buddy had found work in Hollywood as a writer. Blasucci arranged to reunite the Ravins, who hadn't played together since 1967. They trotted out the old favorites "Louie Louie," "Gimme Some Lovin'," "Route 66," "Johnny B. Goode." The next night, the Ravins took the stage at the Central, a club on Sunset, joined by Derf Scratch, of the band Fear. The club's weekly open-mic night became another raucous Ravins reunion.

The next morning, John missed a breakfast meeting at Paramount. They proceeded without him, guaranteeing John $1.85 million for "Sweet Deception." Michael Ovitz negotiated a pay-or-play deal, which delivered John the money even if Paramount opted to make a different film.

John would need every penny. He was spending as much as $75,000 a month. His expenses included more than $15,000 in mortgage payments and rents on several properties, some of them occupied by relatives; $4,000 in medical insurance for him and Judy and several other Belushis and Jacklins; $4,000 in allowances to John's mother, father, sister, and brother Billy, and to Judy's parents; $1,500 to a high-end public-relations firm, to keep his excesses out of the news; and untold thousands in limousine rentals, restaurant tabs, and drug buys.

Not all of John's relatives celebrated his largesse. When John visited his father at the ten-acre ranch in the Cuyamaca Mountains, the one he had purchased for his parents, Adam Belushi griped that it could have been larger. "I thought you said it was gonna be like *Bonanza*."

At the month's end, John and Judy flew back to New York to celebrate the new year, their fifth wedding anniversary, and the improbable success of *Neighbors*. But John's poisonous rapport with the director and producers had soured him on the project. He glowered through obligatory interviews at the St. Regis Hotel.

"We're having a good time," Dan told a reporter from the *Boston Globe*, reaching an arm around his partner.

"Sure," John replied, staring straight ahead.

"It's been a helluva great ride," Dan said. "And we've just begun to fight."

"Fine," John deadpanned, gazing at the chandeliers. "Fine ride."

On January 8, John returned to Los Angeles, shadowed by Bill "Superfoot" Wallace. Judy remained in New York.

"I knew if I went with John to California, I could help keep him on track, but at the same time I couldn't keep playing the caretaker role," Judy remembered. "I didn't think it was good for John or myself in the long run." Judy was working on a new book. She was in therapy and explained the dilemma to her psychiatrist. He asked, "What are you afraid of?" She replied with the first thought that came to her: "I'm afraid that he'll die."

John settled into a suite at the Chateau Marmont to work on "Sweet Deception" with Don Novello. The studio expected a finished script by February 1.

Ensconced in Hollywood, John followed a Jekyll-and-Hyde routine. Superfoot Wallace minded him by day, driving him around the Los Angeles basin, leading him on three-mile runs along Santa Monica and Sunset Boulevards, stopping for sit-ups, pull-ups, dips, and stretches, checking in when they were apart. "Every couple of hours, I'd call him: 'Do you need anything?'" Wallace recalled. At night, John would disappear into his bungalow to work with Novello on the script until temptation lured him back out.

John stopped by the set of *Mork and Mindy*, Robin Williams's hit sitcom. The two comedians sat mesmerized through a performance by Jonathan Winters, who had been brought in as a character. Both men considered Winters a mentor. For once, John sat silent, shushing anyone else who dared to speak.

"Sweet Deception," with its flawed script, was hardly John's only option. Landis wanted him to play the lead in a biopic about showman P. T. Barnum. Louis Malle, the French auteur, wanted John and Dan to star in *Moon over Miami*, an artsy satire based on the Abscam public corruption scandal. They were in talks to appear on *SCTV*, Second City's response to *Saturday Night Live*. After three seasons of limited visibility, *SCTV* had been picked up by NBC just in time to supplant the flailing *SNL*. "It's the best show on TV," Dan told an interviewer.

Already, John was working with Dave Thomas on two ideas for *SCTV* sketches. One cast John as Napoleon, a character who had fascinated him since Second City days. The other was "a show-business sketch," Thomas recalled, "where Belushi would play a down-on-his-luck actor who'd had it all but was now 'box-office poison.' John loved that phrase."

On January 15, 1982, John stopped by Paramount to shoot a cameo for *Police Squad!*, a new show from the team behind *Airplane!* Producers had lined up a procession of guest stars to die on-screen at the start of each episode. Bob Weiss had signed on to produce. He suggested John appear as the victim of a mob hit, tossed in a river with cement boots. John had another idea: "Why don't you show me lying dead with a needle stuck in my arm?" It sounded a bit too real. They filmed the cement-boots scene instead, only to pull it from the finished episode when tragedy spoiled the joke.

That night, cast and crew gathered for the wrap party. The Ravins provided music. John was due at Mitch Glazer's wedding in New York the next day. He telephoned Glazer and begged off. Glazer was furious.

"You don't understand what's going on here," John pleaded. "You just don't understand."

"No, I don't."

Judy and Dan attended in John's stead. John placed a confessional call to Rhonda Coullet, one of Judy's best friends. "He was just so strung out. He wanted to be there for the wedding, wished he could be there, but felt like he couldn't face it, face Judy and all of us," she said. "He thought he was losing Judy. He thought she'd leave if he couldn't stay straight, and deep down he was afraid he'd never be able to."

Judy flew to Los Angeles on January 23. She could tell John's cocaine habit had spiked, but lecturing him about drugs never worked, so she ignored it.

John and Don Novello dined with Tommy Smothers of television's Smothers Brothers. Smothers taught them about wine making. He mentioned a fungus called botrytis, an affliction that adds intense sweetness to dessert wines and is known as "noble rot." Novello seized on the term as a new title for their film.

The screenwriters traveled to wine country, first alone and then with their wives, touring vineyards and procuring maps. The February 1 script deadline came and went. Judy grew increasingly alarmed at her husband's bingeing. They fought, and she begged him to return to New York to dry out. John insisted he stay and finish the script. "If I don't do this now, it will be too late," he said. "The work will be over in a few days."

Judy vowed to leave the next day: "I won't be a part of this anymore." Later that night, John came up to Judy and embraced her.

"I know why you're worried about me. I know I get crazy when I do this stuff," he said. "But I'm OK, honest I am."

Judy stammered. "John, I just feel . . ."

"I know what it is," John cut in. "I know what's worrying you. You think I'm doing heroin."

Judy exhaled a nervous laugh. "Well, no, I wasn't. Should I be?"

John confessed that he had taken heroin in the New York hospital after his knee injury, and that Dan had helped him beat the habit.

"I promise you I will never do heroin again. OK?" he said. He tugged at her chin with his hand. "Look me in the eye. Come on, I'm promising you." Judy began to cry. "Hey, now," John said, pulling her close. "Have I ever let you down on a promise?"

Judy returned to New York. With his wife absent, John favored the company of other glamorous women. On February 12, he attended the regular Friday-night movie hosted by Hugh Hefner at the Playboy Mansion. He found Lorne Michaels and Buck Henry there, and as the movie played, he entertained them by crawling up the aisle and stealing handfuls of popcorn from Hef's bowl.

Michaels had been John's boss. Now, he was between jobs, and Belushi was a big star. Still, Michaels pitied him.

"He was going on and on about *Noble Rot*. He seemed manic to me, on edge." He was snorting cocaine with abandon. "The old John was still there, the sweet, warm John. That guy was always there. But I thought, 'Oh, this is trouble.' I'd stopped thinking that John was trouble. He was just in trouble."

On Valentine's Day, John let himself into Steven Spielberg's home, raided his refrigerator, and left a note. He partied into the night with the Pretenders, who had played at UCLA. After midnight, he telephoned Judy from Chateau Marmont. "Chrissie Hynde has passed out," he said. "What should I do?" Call her road manager, Judy instructed coolly.

Two days later, John packed up and changed rooms at the Chateau. He settled into bungalow three, a two-bedroom suite with a private entrance.

Don Novello labored alone on the "Noble Rot" script, working through the weekend as his partner partied. On Sunday, February 21, John attended a fete at the home of Michael O'Donoghue and his new love, screenwriter Carol Caldwell. In mid-party, John pulled Caldwell aside and offered a pick-me-up. He produced bags of white powder, which she took to be cocaine, and laid out two lines. He snorted one, then fled into the bathroom and threw up. Caldwell asked, "What's the matter with you?"

"I've just been staying up too late."

"How much of this stuff are you doing?"

"Too much."

Caldwell herself soon felt sick. She collapsed on the bed. She later surmised John had given her heroin.

John returned to his bungalow at dawn.

"Where were you?" Novello asked.

"I was celebrating," John replied.

"What? That we got the script done?" That was rich. John had left Novello to finish the script by himself. John saw the look on Novello's face.

"I was celebrating for the both of us," he said, smiling.

Novello completed the script, which he considered a rough first draft. John delivered it to the printer. He chose a burgundy cover and instructed the typesetter to fit it on exactly 126 pages: two hours and change.

The writers had retooled "Noble Rot" as a screwball comedy à la *What's Up, Doc?*, the Barbra Streisand film about mixed-up luggage. John's character, heir to a wine fortune, flies to a convention in New York and accidentally grabs the wrong bag, filled with diamonds. A glamorous female seatmate takes his bag, filled with wine. He spends the balance of the film evading diamond smugglers, who labor to recover the jewels he has unwittingly purloined. The narrative builds to a climactic scene at the wine convention, straight out of the comedic playbook of the Kentucky Fried Theater founders, Jim Abrahams and David and Jerry Zucker.

"We had, like, the monks from the Christian Brothers, and the guys from Thunderbird wearing zoot suits, and the Mogen David guys were all, like, Hasidic Jews," Novello said. "We had Blue Nuns." The hero triumphs in the end, proving himself responsible after all. Novello knew the script needed work, but it felt light-years better than "Sweet Deception." Novello returned home to San Francisco. Copies of the script went out to the "Noble Rot" brain trust.

"It was terrible," Bernie Brillstein recalled. "Nothing was funny." He called Michael Ovitz, who agreed. They discussed how to tell John. Brillstein's phone rang; it was John. "I took a deep breath and told him the truth." They agreed to await the judgment of Michael Eisner, the studio head. Eisner hated it, too.

Jay Sandrich felt the script had devolved into, "basically, a car chase with a lot of very violent scenes"—a bloodier *Blues Brothers*. The director told John what he thought. John was crushed. "It delivered a terrible blow to his ego."

John returned to New York on February 23. He landed at the Blues Bar with Dan. Someone produced a bag of weed and a mound of blow. John and Dan rose and danced together, the Blues Brothers briefly reunited. After two a.m., Judy telephoned John at the bar. After the call, someone asked whether Judy had wanted to know when he was coming home. John arched an eyebrow: "My wife wants to know *if* I'm coming home." Before Dan departed, he walked up to John, punched him on the arm, and said, "Take it easy tonight and get home, OK?"

Two days later, John appeared at Mitch Glazer's door. He walked in, "put a huge pile of drugs on the coffee table and picked up the phone and just started screaming," terrorizing his manager and agent in California.

At the Blues Bar that night, John drank beers with Dan. John said he had fired Michael Ovitz, his agent. Dan scolded him: "It's only one script. Take a rest, let the business people handle it, go to the Vineyard, cool out."

No, John replied. He would return to Hollywood and duke it out. Do it by phone, Dan urged. "No," John said. "I got to meet with them. Got to go out there."

Glazer arrived at the Blues Bar. Dan departed. John went out on a coke run and returned. Hours passed. Glazer moved to leave. John begged him to stay. Then he told Glazer to take his car, so he and his new wife would get home safely. As the car drove off, Glazer peered out the back window and saw John. "He just stood there in the middle of the street, hands at his sides, and watched us drive away."

After daybreak Saturday, John returned to his Morton Street apartment and fell asleep. Hours later, he awoke, coughing up blood. Judy feared he might drop dead, then and there. John felt her eyes on him. "What? What is it? What is that look?"

"It's a look of concern, John. I don't know how you can do this to yourself."

"Oh, so I do it to myself?" he said, coughing.

"Yes, you do it to yourself. You know it's the coke. It's this last week in LA. Your body can't take the abuse."

"Oh, is that so?" he yelled, removing his pajama top and hurling it on the bed. "What are you saying? I'm out of control?"

"Yes!"

"I'm out of control?!" John cried again. Was it a question, or a statement? Judy couldn't tell. John stomped out and slammed the door.

John resolved to return to Los Angeles the next day. Judy and Dan begged him to stay. John partied into the night. Judy tagged along. After four in the morning, the mood darkened, and Judy wanted to leave.

"I wanted John to come home with me," she said. "He wanted to stay out. He walked me to a cab and, even though I was angry, kissed me goodnight. As the cab pulled off, I turned, expecting to see him walking back into the club or talking with someone. But he was just leaning against the building, watching me pull away. He looked exhausted." Judy waved goodbye.

John spent the day at the Tenth Street Baths, then caught an afternoon flight to LA, never returning home to Judy.

The next day, Monday, March 1, John met with Michael Eisner at bungalow three. Eisner wanted to talk John out of "Noble Rot." "The script was horrible, completely unintelligible and non-producible," Eisner recalled. "He had maps on the floor of the wine country. As if maps of the wine country had anything to do with a script that didn't work." Eisner lobbied John to star in a different film, *Joy of Sex*, adapted from the legendary manual.

"*Joy of Sex* wasn't any funnier than 'Noble Rot,' but it was faster and cheaper and easier to produce and market by Christmas," Don Novello said. "Michael Eisner wanted John Belushi in a Christmas movie. It didn't matter what it was."

Neither man convinced the other, but John said he would look at the *Joy of Sex* script. As Eisner left, John asked for his telephone number. He found a red pen and wrote it on the bungalow wall.

The next evening around nine, John met with Eisner and Jeffrey Katzenberg, Eisner's lieutenant, at On the Rox, a Hollywood VIP club. "Lined up in front of him on the bar were three, five, six Big Macs," Eisner recalled. John entertained the executives by acting out scenes from "Noble Rot." Then he turned serious. "You know," he told the executives, "if you don't do 'Noble Rot,' I'm going to get my lawyers, Jacoby and Meyers, after you." That was a joke: Jacoby and Meyers was a personal-injury law firm that blanketed TV stations with ads.

By ten p.m., Katzenberg was gone and Eisner and his wife were heading out. John dragged them back in: "You got to see this." On a big screen inside the club, NBC was airing a *Saturday Night Live* repeat. There was Belushi, raging about drugs on "Weekend Update."

"Why am I up here wasting my valuable time telling you this? To tell you the truth, I'd rather be out smoking hash on the streets! I could be out smoking hash on the streets, but nooooooo." The audience cheered. Eisner smiled. The couple went out to their car. Jane Eisner turned to her husband and said, "I feel as though I've just seen *Sunset Boulevard*." No, no, he said. John was hot. Living in the past, maybe, but still very much in the game. "Look at how funny he was."

"*Sunset Boulevard*," Jane Eisner repeated. "I'm telling you. We just saw it."

At dawn on Thursday, March 4, John telephoned Judy in New York. She was barely awake. He apologized for not returning home before his LA flight. He said he had to stay for one more meeting. "You wouldn't believe what they want me to do with this *Joy of Sex* script," he said. One scene had him in a diaper. He told Judy he loved her.

John was still doing daily workouts with Bill Wallace, his driver, minder, and babysitter. But not today. Wallace was getting divorced and had to fly to Memphis to sign papers. He coordinated with Bernie Brillstein, both men fearing what might happen to an unsupervised Belushi. "I flew out first thing in the morning," Wallace said. "I flew back that night."

Dan arrived at the business office he and John shared in New York. He was working on a new script about ghosts in Manhattan. It could be the next Aykroyd-Belushi project. He checked the phone messages and heard John's slurred voice. "He was fucked up, and he was hurting. I'd never heard him that bad before. I thought, I'm going to finish this paragraph, and then I'm going to get on a plane and get the fuck out there."

John stopped by Brillstein's office. The manager pushed the *Joy of Sex* script: John needed a hit, and they mustn't fuck up the Paramount deal. He and Novello could continue to polish "Noble Rot." John seemed placated but also distracted. He told Brillstein he needed $1,500 in cash to buy a vintage guitar.

"I'm not going to give you money," Brillstein said. "You'll use it on drugs."

"Am I here?" John protested. "Am I OK?"

Dan telephoned Brillstein, who handed the receiver to John. "John, c'mon man, you gotta come home," Dan pleaded. "I'm writing something great for us here that's gonna solve everything. But you've gotta come back." Dan had an offer from a navy captain: two weeks out at sea, just the two of them, to dry out, unwind, and plan their next move. OK, John replied. He would take a red-eye home.

Dan wasn't sure John would follow through. He and Judy reached out to Smokey Wendell, John's beloved enforcer, asking if he could fly out and bring him home.

"I can go tonight," Wendell said.

"Well," Judy considered, "I should let John know you're coming." Wendell agreed to depart the next day.

Dan closed up the business office and walked over to Judy's house to talk about John.

"I may have to put myself on the line," Judy said. "If he doesn't come home soon, I'm going to move out." At some point, she had to take care of herself.

Dan understood. He sometimes felt married to John. In their creative relationship, Dan played the responsible one, cleaning up John's messes and doing most of the work. Dan would see that Wendell or Superfoot Wallace or someone got him on a plane. "We'll handcuff him, if necessary," Dan joked. They parted at midnight.

John spent most of the evening at On the Rox. He jammed with Johnny Rivers, the pop singer of "Secret Agent Man" fame. At eleven, another *SNL* rerun came on the big screen, from the week John had spent in the hospital with the knee injury. A head shot of John appeared on-screen above the caption ". . . in happier times."

In the early hours of March 5, Robin Williams dropped by bungalow three. The suite reeked of excess: empty wine bottles, pizza boxes, dirty laundry, random maps, script pages, drug paraphernalia, and a retinue of seedy characters. John offered Williams cocaine. John sat back down and nodded off.

"Are you OK?" Williams asked.

"Yeah," John said, reviving. "Took a couple of 'ludes."

Williams eased out of the bungalow. Robert De Niro arrived. John offered him coke. John was hosting a pair of seedy companions, one of them Cathy Smith, a rock 'n' roll groupie and singer from Canada whose tempestuous romance with Gordon Lightfoot had inspired his hit song "Sundown." Now, she was dealing drugs to support a heroin habit. De Niro and the other guest departed. That left John with Cathy Smith.

"Do you want me to leave?" Smith asked.

"No, stick around," John replied. "Can you get some more coke?"

Not at this hour, she said. "You haven't had any sleep for days. Why don't you go to sleep?"

John produced some of his remaining coke. Smith mixed it with heroin, a concoction known as a speedball, one shot for her, one for him. She delivered the injections. They took showers and settled into John's bed. She made a tentative sexual overture. He rebuffed it. He said he felt cold. She told him to get under the covers and turned up the heat.

Smith went off to write a letter. After a time, she returned to John's bed and asked if he was hungry. He waved her off.

She left, then returned again. John was coughing and wheezing. "John, are you all right?"

"Yeah," he said. "What's wrong?"

"You don't sound right. Do you want a glass of water?"

She brought him water. He told her his lungs were congested. She said she would go out to find food.

"Don't leave," John said. She called room service and ordered coffee and toast. She checked on John again, found him snoring, cleaned up the paraphernalia, and left bungalow three. It was 10:15 a.m.

Around noon, Bill "Superfoot" Wallace arrived, returned from his brutal one-day trip to Memphis. He had a typewriter and a tape recorder for John. Wallace knocked, got no answer, and let himself in. A stifling heat assaulted him. Peering into the back bedroom, Wallace thought he saw John sleeping in the bed, but he did not hear the characteristic snore. With mounting alarm, he walked to the bed, shook John's shoulder, and said, "John, time to get up." He was late for a meeting at Paramount.

John lay in a fetal ball, a pillow over his head. Wallace shook him. Nothing. He pulled the pillow away. John's lips looked purple, and his tongue protruded. He flipped John onto his back.

"I jumped on the bed, clamped my mouth over his, and started giving him CPR," Wallace said. "I pounded on his chest, breathed, pounded, breathed. He still didn't move." Tears welling in his eyes, Wallace cried, "You dumb son of a bitch," over and over.

Wallace telephoned Bernie Brillstein. "I'm having trouble waking John up," he said. Someone in Brillstein's office telephoned paramedics, who arrived around 12:30.

At 12:45, paramedics pronounced John Belushi dead.

Brillstein telephoned Dan at the office. "Danny, sit down," he instructed. "Now, listen to me. We have no time for overreaction. John is dead." Dan listened in stunned silence. "You have to leave your office now. Go directly to Judy's house, so she doesn't hear it on the radio. You have to tell her."

"Yes," Dan replied mechanically.

Dan raced down Fifth Avenue, then angled toward Morton Street. "I knew if I stopped for a second, I would lose it," he recalled. He reached the Belushi apartment and let himself in. He took the stairs three at a time. He found Judy.

"He started to say something," Judy remembered, "but stopped and just stood there, running his hand over the top of his head."

"I . . . I don't know how to tell you this," he said. "I don't know what to say."

Judy's mind flooded with images: a car crash, a plane crash. She rose and moved toward him.

"Danny, what is it? Has John been hurt?"

"No, honey," he replied, voice softening, shaking his head. "He's dead."

The words hit her like a slap. "No!" she cried, reeling backward, clutching her head, squeezing her eyes shut.

"We always knew something like this would happen." Dan spoke through tears, pacing the floor, rambling about Bill Wallace and needles and heroin.

Judy collapsed onto a couch, then rolled to the floor. "Danny was still talking, still pacing, and he sounded so far away. I stood up, went over and hugged him. . . . He felt cold and stiff. I felt cold and stiff."

Dan telephoned John Landis. "We lost him," Dan said. Landis called Sean Daniel. "Meet me in John's office. Now," he instructed. Landis and Daniel gathered at the office John kept on the Universal lot. They searched the space, looking for drugs, paraphernalia, anything incriminating. They found nothing.

Around two p.m., Cathy Smith returned to the Chateau in John's rented red Mercedes, driving the wrong way up an exit road. She encountered a policeman. "I'm just returning John's car," she said.

"John who?"

"John Belushi."

Police cuffed her and led her away.

Obituary writers hedged on the Belushi legacy.

"He came and went like a comet," Tom Shales wrote in the *Washington Post*. "He could not be casually encountered; he will not be casually forgotten."

The *New York Times* tucked the obituary on page ten, hailing John as the "rotund comedian" of television's *Saturday Night Live*, burying his film career. Few in the entertainment industry regarded either *The Blues Brothers* or *Animal House* as an important work.

"He descended on an unsuspecting nation out of nowhere, with the impact of a bowling ball dropped into a vat of Jell-O," *Newsweek* reflected, "one of those rare characters who can capture the spirit of an age—in his case, an age somewhere between 8½ and 11."

Bernie Brillstein traveled to bungalow three at the Chateau Marmont and cleaned it out. "The scene was not only depressing," he said, "it was depraved. I couldn't believe John had lived there."

Thoughts turned to burial. In the previous summer, John and Judy had driven past a small cemetery on Martha's Vineyard. "When I die," Judy said, "I'd like to be buried here." John rested his hand atop hers, grinned, and replied, "I think I'd like a Viking funeral."

Agnes Belushi telephoned. She and Judy spoke of arrangements. "It's all up to you, honey," Agnes said. "What should we do?"

"We're going to Martha's Vineyard for a Viking funeral."

"Viking funeral? What do you mean?"

"Well, we'll have a boat, a pyre built, and we put John on that and it's pulled out to sea and set on fire . . ."

"Nooooo," Agnes wailed. "You can't burn him. He'll go to hell!"

Judy's mind raced. John probably hadn't been serious about the Viking funeral. Another time, he had said he wanted to be interred in a tomb, like Lenin. They settled on a traditional service.

That night, Bill Wallace arrived at the Belushi home. He sat on the edge of Judy's bed and clasped her hands. "I want to say something to you, and I want you to listen," he said. "That girl didn't mean a thing to John." The mystery woman, now in police custody, was all over the news. "John loved you, and that girl was just there for drugs. You know that, don't you?" Judy's eyes teared up. "I know that, Bill," she said, nodding.

A corporate jet carried John's body to the Vineyard. The crew laid the body bag across two seats. Brillstein sat across from it. "It was the worst seven and a half hours of my life," he said.

The March 9 service played out to "an odd mix of people," Harold Ramis said: "the folks from the early days, the Hollywood friends, the hangers-on, the people who were just there to be seen, and an army of press, both on the ground and circling in helicopters above." Journalists had rented every available car. A snowstorm loomed.

Judy had John dressed in his punk-rock boots, green army pants, jacket, and tie. Lorne Michaels filed past the body and quipped, "I've seen him look worse." Dan slipped a pack of cigarettes and some hundred-dollar bills into John's pocket. Agnes Belushi threw herself onto her son's lifeless body. An Albanian Orthodox minister conducted the service, mostly in Albanian, inside a New England Congregational church to an audience of about one hundred relatives and friends.

After the service, Dan donned a Chicago police jacket, climbed on his Harley, and led the mourners to Abel Hill Cemetery. "That's where they bury all the whalers, the Indians, the smugglers and the pirates," he reflected, "so it was a good place for John." He gunned the motor, hoping John would hear.

Harold Ramis delivered a eulogy, recounting the time John wore little cardboard wings to play an angel in a Second City sketch. James Taylor sang "That Lonesome Road," raising his voice indignantly when a paparazzi helicopter settled loudly overhead. A gentle snow descended as mourners lowered John's body into the ground. John's head faced east, in the Orthodox tradition.

A reception followed, but most out-of-town guests flew out ahead of the gathering storm. "I drove to this private airstrip with a couple executives from a record label," Bernie Brillstein said. "Passing the cemetery where we'd just buried John, in the back seat of the car, they were doing lines of cocaine."

Dan went home. "The house was completely empty, and I was all by myself," he said. "The clouds were low, and the snow was coming down heavy now, big, fat, white powdery flakes of it. That's when I really broke down for the first time. I just fell to my knees and wept."

At sunset, a few friends gathered at the Belushi home. Dan led an impromptu honor guard in a twenty-one-gun salute. Before the final shot, Dan lowered his rifle and cried, "This one's for you, Johnny." His voice echoed into the night.

On the morning of March 11 in New York, a procession of limousines left Morton Street for a circuitous journey to the Cathedral of St. John the Divine, on Amsterdam Avenue near Columbia University, for a noon memorial. A somber crowd had gathered outside the Belushi home. The procession of mourners drove downtown to Tribeca and the Blues Bar, then up to the Blues Brothers' business office, then on past 30 Rock, through Central Park, and into Morningside Heights to the cathedral.

A bishop introduced Jim Belushi to an audience of one thousand. Jim tugged on his belt, a habit he shared with his late brother, and gazed around the Gothic nave. "This is a beautiful hall," he said. "I can't help but think that John would have loved to play this room. I can see him doing somersaults down the aisle," he said, evoking the church scene from *The Blues Brothers*.

Paul Shaffer and ace saxophonist Tom Scott played "For a Dancer," the Jackson Browne song, and Rhonda Coullet sang: "You were always dancing in and out of view / I must've thought you'd always be around."

Dan walked up the center aisle to the pulpit, wearing a dark suit and horn-rimmed glasses.

"I wrote many things for and with John," Dan said. "I know this is one assignment he'd rather I didn't have to take on. Although I had a close, head to head, arm to arm, working relationship with John, that proximity never affected the fact that from the moment I met him, through all the work, I remained his number-one fan. He was a brilliant performer, writer, tactician, business strategist and, most importantly, he was the only man I could dance with."

Dan's talk turned to drugs. "In some cases, real greatness gives license for real indulgence, whether it's as a reward, as therapy, or as sanctuary. For as hard as John worked, there had to be an additional illicit thrill to make the effort all worthwhile.

"John was a nighthawk, true, but he was not an immoral individual. He was a good man, a kind man, a warm man, a hot man." Dan paused. "What we are talking about here is a good man, and," leaning into the mic, "a bad boy."

Dan told of the summer day on the Vineyard when he had played "The 2,000 Pound Bee" on the tape deck, and the two friends had promised "that we'd force it upon a church full of people at the time of our respective deaths. Whomever went first."

Dan leaned over and produced a tape deck. He planted it beside the microphone. "So here it is, for the King Bee." He cued the song. At first, the audience sat in stunned silence. A few titters broke out. Laughter filled the room. When the song faded, Dan lowered the machine back into his knapsack. "So there, Johnny," he said.

Judy had a skull and bones carved across the top of John's tombstone. The inscription was something John had told Don Novello one night at the Chateau Marmont.

"What do you want on your tombstone?" John had asked.

"Why would you ask a question like that?" Novello had protested.

John was serious. "I want 'I may be gone, but Rock and Roll lives on.'"

Epilogue

WITH BELUSHI'S DEATH, the television generation grew up a little bit. "The theory was that you couldn't get physically addicted to cocaine," Roger Ebert recalled, months later, "but as George Carlin once explained, 'The way cocaine makes you feel is like having some more cocaine.'"

Young Hollywood grew up some more in the summer of 1982, when a helicopter spun into the Santa Clara River, killing three actors, two of them children, on a film set. The crash came during a predawn shoot for *Twilight Zone: The Movie*, with John Landis directing. Forty years later, the *Twilight Zone* accident endures as the worst on-set disaster in Hollywood history.

"Have you heard the latest joke?" Dan asked Gene Siskel of the *Tribune* that summer. "The joke is, 'What's blue and sings alone?' The answer is, 'Dan Aykroyd.'"

Hollywood had come to view Dan as half of a comedy team. For his career to thrive, Dan would have to make it on his own. In the spring of 1983, Universal released *Doctor Detroit*, casting Dan as a mild-mannered professor who masquerades as a mobster to rescue some call girls from certain doom. Ticket sales would tell whether Dan could carry a film.

Doctor Detroit bombed. On the brighter side, Dan married Donna Dixon, one of his costars.

Dan's deliverance arrived a month later, with the release of *Trading Places*, the new John Landis comedy.

After *The Blues Brothers*, Landis had traveled to England to shoot *An American Werewolf in London*, from the horror-comedy script he had carried around for a decade. *Werewolf* opened in the summer of 1981. Once again, Landis scored a box-office smash but reaped indifferent reviews. He proceeded to Philadelphia to shoot *Trading Places*, persuading Paramount to cast Dan opposite the ascendant Eddie Murphy.

With *Trading Places*, Landis and Dan had another hit, a sweet holiday story about a snooty broker (Dan) and a street hustler (Murphy) whose circumstances are suddenly reversed.

Still, in 1983, conventional wisdom held that none of the celebrated *SNL* alumni had done much with their subsequent careers.

That premise informed *Wired*, a Belushi biography that appeared in 1984. Judy Belushi had approached Bob Woodward of the *Washington Post*, a fellow Wheaton native, to investigate John's death. Nearly two hundred pages of the 423-page narrative covered the blurry months after John had finished *Neighbors*, his final film. The book's focus was addiction rather than artistry.

"I think they hoped I'd find he'd been kidnapped and forced to take drugs," Woodward reflected.

That summer, Dan's film career hit a bittersweet peak. Columbia released *Ghostbusters*, his ghosts-in-Manhattan comedy. Dan had been writing dialogue for John's character when the telephone rang with news of his demise.

John's part went to Bill Murray. Denied his costar in corporeal form, Dan cast John as a ghost named Slimer. Ivan Reitman directed. Released in June 1984, *Ghostbusters* delivered a massive critical and commercial hit, positing the phrase "Who you gonna call?" at the center of popular culture.

In the critical mindset of the time, *Ghostbusters* marked the first unqualified success of the post-*SNL* era. Bill Murray and Harold Ramis had made *Caddyshack*, and Ramis and Chevy Chase had made *National Lampoon's Vacation*, and Dan and John had made *The Blues Brothers*, and they had been hits. But critics had panned them all.

In the summer of 1985, Aretha Franklin released *Who's Zoomin' Who?*, an album that capped a stirring comeback. Arista Records had signed Franklin partly on the strength of her turn in *The Blues Brothers*. She spent the next five years climbing the charts. *Zoomin'* became her first platinum studio album.

Later that year, Warner Brothers released *Spies Like Us*, another script Dan had conceived for him and John. Cowritten with Dave Thomas and directed by Landis, *Spies Like Us* paid gentle homage to the *Road* movies of Crosby and Hope. Chevy Chase stepped in as costar. Critics mostly hated it, but filmgoers mostly loved it. A year later, Orion and Home Box Office released *Three Amigos*, another film once slated to star Dan and John. Into the void stepped Chase, Steve Martin, and Martin Short, with Landis at the helm. *Three Amigos* did better with the critics, not so well with the public.

In the autumn of 1986, a judge sentenced Cathy Smith to three years in prison for involuntary manslaughter in the death of John Belushi. Widow Judy sat in the front row of the courtroom.

Later that year, Dan reunited the Blues Brothers band to perform at the opening of a Hard Rock Café in Dallas. Dan had struck up a friendship with Hard Rock cofounder Isaac Tigrett, whose London-based chain had not yet descended into cliché. Dan became an investor. After that, he recalled, "every time we opened a Hard Rock Café, the Blues Brothers band came together." Sam Moore of Sam and Dave stood in for John. In years to come, Sam would give way to Jim Belushi and, later, to John Goodman, the *Roseanne* everyman.

In 1989, John Lee Hooker released *The Healer*, an album of collaborations with the likes of Carlos Santana and Bonnie Raitt, capping his own decade-long comeback. The record reached sixty-two on the *Billboard 200* album chart, the highest mark of Hooker's career.

The next year, Judy Belushi released a memoir, *Samurai Widow*, recounting the tumultuous months after her husband's death. Judy portrayed a sweeter, more meditative Belushi than the talented train wreck in *Wired*. She said she had forgiven Robin Williams and Robert De Niro, neither of whom had called with condolences. She had even forgiven Cathy Smith.

In the autumn of 1992, Dan and Isaac Tigrett launched a new restaurant brand, House of Blues, in Harvard Square. The next year, Dan debuted a syndicated *House of Blues Radio Hour*, spinning roots music as Elwood Blues.

One weekend in 1996, James Brown joined the new Blues Brothers in opening a House of Blues in Chicago. Landis flew in and announced he was penning a *Blues Brothers* sequel.

The studio had considered a second *Blues Brothers* film in the heady days that followed the release of the first. It never came together. "There was not a sequel reflex in those days, the way it exists now," Bob Weiss said. "The original was expensive, and a headache for some of the studio folks." Gradually, the titular Brothers became distracted by other projects. Two years passed, Belushi died, and the sequel died with him. More than a decade later, Aykroyd and Landis revived it.

Blues Brothers 2000 opened in 1998, with Dan returning as Elwood Blues and John Goodman replacing the absent Belushi. Aretha Franklin and James Brown returned, joined by Wilson Pickett and B.B. King, who had missed the first film. In the sequel, Elwood emerges from prison after serving time for his misdeeds, learns of his brother's death, and sets about getting the band back together—again—while eluding a new army of pursuers. Critics responded with benevolent indifference.

"*Blues Brothers 2000* isn't anywhere close to the landmark its predecessor was," wrote James Berardinelli, one of a new generation of critics working in a new medium, the blog.

Landmark? Yes. Sometime over the previous eighteen years, *The Blues Brothers* had ascended from maligned hit to cult classic to Important Film.

Hollywood history brims with rehabilitation stories of films that critics had panned upon their release. By and large, those works fall outside the critically respected genres of drama and literary comedy: they are horror films, such as Stanley Kubrick's *The Shining* (1980) and John Carpenter's *The Thing* (1982); lowbrow comedies, like *Caddyshack* and Amy Heckerling's *Fast Times at Ridgemont High* (1982); and science-fiction pulp, like Ridley Scott's *Alien* (1979) and *Blade Runner* (1982). In each case, filmgoers defied the critics, either at the box office or later in videotape and DVD rentals and midnight-movie revivals. At length, pop-cultural reappraisal inspired critical reappraisal, and all the films emerged as genre classics.

"It happens, and it happens a lot with comedies," said Fionnuala Halligan, top reviewer at the British film magazine *Screen International*, who counts *The Blues Brothers* among her favorite comedies. Studios live in perpetual fear that critics won't "get" their comedies, "which is why distributors prefer critics to see films with an audience instead of by themselves in screening rooms with no atmosphere. You can also say that critics aren't really renowned for their sense of humor."

In June 1980, David Ansen of *Newsweek* called *The Blues Brothers* a "desperately unfunny $30 million youth-exploitation flick," and Janet Maslin of the *New York Times* termed it "exhausting overkill." Upon rereading their reviews, forty-odd years later, Ansen reflected, "I knew it wasn't favorable but didn't remember just how scathing it was," while Maslin observed that the film "obviously had more staying power than I gave it credit for."

The critics of 1980 pounced on *The Blues Brothers*, stirred to righteous fury over a film that seemed to embody everything wrong with Hollywood at the end of the 1970s: overspending, overindulgence, overkill. Four decades later, in an era of $350 million, galaxy-shredding comicbook superhero films, the $27.5 million budget and cartoonish mayhem of *The Blues Brothers* look positively quaint.

The critical currency of *The Blues Brothers* rose alongside the stature of its stars. By the new millennium, critics and historians recognized *Saturday Night Live* as one of television's great achievements and the Belushi-Aykroyd ensemble as its greatest cast. Lorne Michaels left *SNL* in 1980, but he returned in 1985 and seeded artistic revival, restoring the program as a cultural and comedic force. As *SNL* matured into a late-night institution, the program's Carter-era cast ascended into Rushmore-size legend, almost beyond criticism's reach, this despite many weak sketches and uneven episodes. (A 1979 entry, hosted by a septuagenarian Milton Berle, may stand as the nadir.)

Bill Murray, Chevy Chase, and Dan Aykroyd helped their own case, remaining busy in Hollywood and delivering the occasional gem:

Murray with standout roles in *Ghostbusters* and especially *Groundhog Day*, an ingenious déjà vu farce directed by Harold Ramis; Chase with *Caddyshack* and the *Vacation* films; Aykroyd with *Ghostbusters* and classier stuff, such as roles in the 1989 Oscar winner *Driving Miss Daisy* and the 1992 biopic *Chaplin*. Belushi was gone but not forgotten.

The Blues Brothers gained further gravitas as arguably the finest work of John Landis, whose oeuvre established him as one of America's great comedic directors, notwithstanding the *Twilight Zone* tragedy. Starting with *The Kentucky Fried Movie* in 1977, Landis had delivered a string of comedy hits that aged into critical favorites, perennial picks on millennial lists of Hollywood's greatest comedies.

The Blues Brothers endures as a big, noisy, noir valentine to the city of Chicago. Landis and his crazy car-crash musical ushered in a golden age of cinema filmed in the city and its suburbs: Robert Redford's *Ordinary People* in 1980; *Vacation* and the Tom Cruise showcase *Risky Business* in 1983; the John Hughes mid-1980s comedy classics *Sixteen Candles*, *The Breakfast Club*, *Ferris Bueller's Day Off*, and *Planes, Trains and Automobiles*; Brian De Palma's *The Untouchables* in 1987; the Christmas farce *Home Alone* in 1990; the *SNL* spin-off *Wayne's World* in 1992; and the Harrison Ford smash *The Fugitive* in 1993. But no film inhabited the Windy City quite like *The Blues Brothers*.

"Chicago is like *Ferris Bueller's Day Off* if you're rich," one South Side musician recently observed, "and it's like *The Blues Brothers* if you're poor."

Finally, *The Blues Brothers* earned immortality as a priceless artifact of American music. The Brothers and their director didn't know it in 1979, but their paper-thin *SNL* spin-off, their one-joke skit turned big-budget film, would stand as perhaps the finest cinematic showcase for five of the greatest musical artists of the century. In a 2008 survey of pop music's great singers, *Rolling Stone* would list James Brown tenth, Ray Charles second, and Aretha Franklin first. Footage of their *Blues Brothers* performances loomed ever larger in popular culture after their deaths, Charles in 2004, Brown in 2006, Franklin in 2018. YouTube videos of Franklin's and Charles's performances each claim more than twenty million views. History would remember John Lee Hooker, who died in

2001, as one of the great postwar blues artists. Cab Calloway, who died in 1994, had dominated an earlier era in popular music, surpassed only by Duke Ellington. Had the Duke remained alive in 1979, John Landis probably would have approached him for a role in *The Blues Brothers.*

Around the time of *Blues Brothers 2000,* someone at the FBI telephoned Universal Studios. A mystery print of *The Blues Brothers* had surfaced on eBay, the online auction site. The feds seized it. Universal screened it. Landis saw it. He beheld a glorious, seventy-millimeter print of *The Blues Brothers,* the one he had previewed at the Picwood in 1980, shortly before the film's release. A theater employee had stored it in his garage. "It was about twenty minutes longer than the theatrical one," Landis said, before the final, brutal cuts. Landis supervised work on a *Blues Brothers* extended edition, restoring seventeen glorious minutes of lost footage for release in 1999. The gas-station explosion was back in.

But the original, nearly three-hour "road-show" cut of *The Blues Brothers* would never be seen again. For an earlier home-video release of the film, Universal had invited Landis to restore lost footage. He and Bob Weiss discovered that someone at the studio had dumped the missing scenes, replacing the film in the Universal vaults with footage from a 1980s sitcom, *The New Leave It to Beaver.*

In the summer of 2003, a movie house in Melbourne, Australia, held its last Friday-night screening of *The Blues Brothers,* ending a continuous weekly run that had stretched for twenty years. Hundreds of fans over the decades had filed into the Valhalla Cinema, later rechristened the Westgarth, arriving in costume as Jake or Elwood or the Penguin or one of the Nazis, a ritual that invoked the participatory spirit of *The Rocky Horror Picture Show.*

On April Fool's Day in 2004, Dan and Judy gathered with Jim Belushi and famous friends to unveil John Belushi's star on the Hollywood Walk of Fame. Judy and Jim had petitioned for the star ten years earlier. In the intervening decade, Belushi's currency had risen, and the committee's objections over the manner of his death had softened.

"Whoever John was, however he passed away, whatever he did, it doesn't really matter," Jim said at the ceremony. "He was funny."

Dan added simply, "He was my partner and my best friend."

In 2005, *The Blues Brothers* turned twenty-five. In a sweeping retrospective, the *Chicago Sun-Times* declared that the film had "embraced Chicago as no other film has, before or since." *The Blues Brothers* had "become part of the culture," broadcast hundreds of times a day on television stations in forty-five countries.

In 2010, the Catholic Church declared *The Blues Brothers* a "Catholic classic," one of a dozen films recommended for viewing by the flock, a list that included *The Ten Commandments* and *It's a Wonderful Life*. A mission from God, indeed.

In 2013, *Vanity Fair* published a sprawling oral history of *The Blues Brothers*, declaring it Universal's "greatest farce."

In 2015, with the fortieth anniversary of *Saturday Night Live* approaching, *Rolling Stone* published a ranking of every performer the program had employed, 145 names. Dan came in fifth, just ahead of Bill Murray. "Of the original greats," the magazine opined, "Aykroyd is the least imitated—just because nobody else can do what he did." The top spot went to Belushi, "the first rock & roll star of comedy."

That year, the Writers Guild named *The Blues Brothers* to its list of 101 funniest screenplays, placing it alongside several other films hatched from the Second City/*Lampoon*/*SNL* brain trust. Few, if any, had been hailed as comedy classics upon their release. The list included three other John Landis films, *Animal House, Trading Places*, and *Coming to America*; two other *National Lampoon* films, *Caddyshack* and *Vacation*; *Groundhog Day*; *Stripes*, an earlier Ramis-Murray collaboration; *This Is Spinal Tap*, the brilliant rockumentary parody that delivered real celebrity, at last, to Christopher Guest; *Planes, Trains and Automobiles*, with John Candy in his finest role; *Mean Girls*, a 2004 showcase for several latter-day *SNL* talents, scripted by Tina Fey; and *Ghostbusters*.

As an overall artistic work, *The Blues Brothers* surely ranked among the greatest of those films. On the Internet Movie Database, only *Groundhog Day* boasts a higher rating, 8.0 out of 10, versus *Blues Brothers*' 7.9.

And none of the other films had Aretha Franklin.

In 2020, the Library of Congress inducted *The Blues Brothers* into its National Film Registry, flagging it as a work of historical, cultural, or aesthetic significance, marked for preservation. The congressional library had previously recognized *Animal House, Groundhog Day, Spinal Tap, Ghostbusters,* and *Michael Jackson's Thriller,* an epic music video that Landis had directed in 1983.

One July weekend in 2022, eleven thousand Italians gathered to watch an outdoor screening of *The Blues Brothers* on the Piazza Maggiore in Bologna, with John Landis as honored guest. *The Blues Brothers* had been one of the first big films to earn more overseas ($58 million) than in the United States ($57 million), $115 million in all.

The next month, five thousand fans watched Dan and Jim Belushi perform with the Blues Brothers band at Old Joliet Prison in the inaugural Blues Brothers Con, short for convention. Patrons lined up to purchase memorabilia at the same counter where Jake Blues had once collected his broken digital watch and used prophylactic. In a photograph from the event, captured by a *Chicago Tribune* photographer, Dan gazed out at the crowd with the same beatific smile he had worn as he watched John Lee Hooker sing "Boom Boom" on Maxwell Street, his crazy blues dream made manifest.

Acknowledgments

THIS PROJECT BEGAN as a stack of bootlegged VHS tapes on a bookshelf in my father's home, which lay a mile west of 1060 West Addison: Wrigley Field. I amassed the collection in high school and screened the films for my friends, over and over, in the early 1980s. I copied a few dozen movies in all. Five were John Landis films: *The Kentucky Fried Movie, Animal House, An American Werewolf in London, Trading Places*, and *The Blues Brothers*.

I telephoned Landis in September 2020, out of the blue. I was finishing a biography of B.B. King, and I wanted to know why B.B. wasn't in *The Blues Brothers*. Landis told me. So began the conversation that led to this book.

Landis deserves special thanks. So do several other sources who spoke to me many times over many months as I assembled the manuscript. They include *Blues Brothers* producer Robert K. Weiss, assistant director David Sosna, and cinematographer Stephen Katz; Sean Daniel and Thom Mount, the young Universal executives behind that film and *Animal House*; and Joe Flaherty, the Second City legend, who performed with both Aykroyd and Belushi. I also want to thank the Blues Brothers Band: you guys tell a great story.

Thank you to all the other artists and friends who spoke to me, often multiple times, about Dan and John and their film. The list includes, from Belushi's childhood, Will Greene, Juanita Payne, Jeff Moffat, Chris and Craig Sautter, Cathy Shields, George Karwoski, Michael Blasucci, Mark Carlson, John Owens, Tom Stansfield, Peggy Gentry, Paul Carney, and Bob Haeger; from Shawnee Summer Theatre, Mark Kurlansky, Vic Caroli, and Giz Heyden; from John's Second City days, Roberta Maguire, Jim Fisher, Eugenie Ross-Leming, Warren Leming,

Judy Morgan, Paul Flaherty, and Peter Elbling; from John's *National Lampoon* tenure, Michael Simmons, Sean Kelly, Rhonda Coullet, Janis Hirsch, Beverly Emmons, Brian McConnachie, Laila Nabulsi, Bob Tischler, Amy Ephron, and Rick Meyerowitz; from Aykroyd's childhood, Aykroyd himself, as well as Paul Shaffer, Dave Thomas, Howard Shore, Gary O'Dwyer, Gordon Flagler, Geoff Winter, Lauren Drewery, Marcus O'Hara, Gay Hauser, Deirdre Bowen, Elizabeth Hanna, William Lane, Stu Gillard, and Andrew Alexander; from the *SNL* days, Rosie Shuster, Tom Schiller, Alan Zweibel, and Bill Boggs; from the *Animal House* shoot, Katherine Wooten, Peter Riegert, Jamie Widdoes, Curtis Salgado, and Robert Cray; from the *Blues Brothers* era, Steve Cropper, Tom Malone, Mitch Glazer, Lou Marini, Murphy Dunne, George Folsey, Michael Chinich, Morris Lyda, Mark Hogan, Fran Roy, Dennis Wolff, and William Kaplan; from the post–*Blues Brothers* era, Smokey Wendell, Gary Deeb, Tim Kazurinsky, Bruce Jarchow, Bill Wallace, Don Novello, Michael Eisner, and Bob Woodward; and for the epilogue, Fionnuala Halligan, David Ansen, and Janet Maslin.

Many people helped me find archival clippings, photographs, and sources, including Kelly Leonard at Second City, Marline Al Koura at St. Patrick's High School, Carrie Bowie at Pius X High School, Christina Chenard and Amarpreet Vaid at Carleton University, Veronica Norris at the Wheaton Public Library, Carol Taverner at ACTRA, Cathy Jaeger at Wheaton Warrenville South High School, Nalini Singh and Larry Alford at the University of Toronto libraries, Erin Sidwell at the Library of Congress, Genevieve Maxwell at the Academy of Motion Picture Arts and Sciences, and Mirabella Johnson, a journalism student at Northwestern University.

Dan Aykroyd and Judy Belushi supported my work throughout and, I suspect, gave a crucial thumbs-up to friends who weren't sure whether to talk to me. Thank you both.

George Gibson at Grove Atlantic has now edited three of my books. He is a superb wordsmith and a real gentleman, and I hope he never tires of me. This is also my third book with Deborah Grosvenor, a marvelous literary agent and a formidable editor in her own right. Emily Burns at Grove is working tirelessly on the photo insert as I write this.

John Mark Boling will be working tirelessly on publicity when you read it, after Amy Hughes completes a flawless copyedit. They're real pros.

Lastly, and mostly, thank you, Sophie. Remember the night Otis Clay made me profess my love to you in front of the crowd at Rosa's on Armitage? A scary moment, yes . . . and one of the proudest moments of my life.

Notes

Prologue

adjusted his thin: Bob Woodward, *Wired: The Short Life and Fast Times of John Belushi* (New York: Simon & Schuster, 1984), 139.

"Danny knows this": Judith Belushi Pisano and Tanner Colby, *Belushi* (New York: Rugged Land, 2005), 152.

Chapter 1: *Cheesebooger*

would corral customers: Jim Belushi, "Bad Santa," *Chicago Sun-Times*, December 18, 2012; Mike Royko, "My Belushi Pals," *Chicago Sun-Times*, March 7, 1982. Jim recalled the brother's name as Paul, but Royko remembered him as Pete, and US Census records favor the columnist.

"almost didn't let me": Judith Belushi Pisano and Tanner Colby, *Belushi* (New York: Rugged Land, 2005), 16.

"was like a little man": Pisano and Colby, *Belushi*, 17.

"Everyone thought it was": Judy Jacklin Belushi, *Samurai Widow* (New York: Carroll & Graf, 1990), 244.

The city's white head count: William Voegeli, "The Truth about White Flight," *City Journal*, Autumn 2020.

"We weren't literally": Will Greene, author interview, August 17, 2021.

"A lot of people": Juanita Payne, author interview, August 5, 2021.

"Mrs. Moffat": Jeff Moffat, author interview, August 23, 2021.

"You've gotta meet": Chris Sautter, author interview, December 10, 2021.

"John played comedy": Pisano and Colby, *Belushi*, 18.

"John could do all": Pisano and Colby, *Belushi*, 18.

"When the teacher": Sautter, author interview.

"He never mimicked": Pisano and Colby, *Belushi*, 18.

"Just laugh": Bob Woodward, *Wired: The Short Life and Fast Times of John Belushi* (New York: Simon & Schuster, 1984), 43.

"Number one": Woodward, *Wired*, 43.

"And here comes": George Karwoski, author interview, August 20, 2021.

"Mr. and Mrs. Belushi": Pisano and Colby, *Belushi*, 18.

"He connected with everyone": Sautter, author interview by email, August 31, 2021.

"The place had thick": Royko, "My Belushi Pals."

"One night we were": Pisano and Colby, *Belushi*, 19.

thought they were brothers: Michael Blasucci, author interview, August 9, 2021.

They pressed one hundred: Woodward, *Wired*, 38; Blasucci, author interview.

"He didn't like": Peter Carlson, "Belushi," *People*, March 22, 1982.

"One-fifth for wrestling": Woodward, *Wired*, 34–35.

"That's where John got": Payne, author interview.

"And we needed Kelley": Tom Stansfield, author interview, November 3, 2021.

"I'll take care of it": Pisano and Colby, *Belushi*, 18.

"He's gonna throw": Stansfield, author interview.

"All right, campers": Karwoski, author interview.

"Hey, listen": Pisano and Colby, *Belushi*, 23.

"hands stuffed": These passages draw from Pisano and Colby, *Belushi*, 20; Belushi, *Samurai Widow*, 31; and Marianne Partridge, ed., *"Rolling Stone" Visits Saturday Night Live* (New York: Rolling Stone Press, 1979), 96.

"Good at sports": R. J. Cutler (dir.), *Belushi*, Showtime Documentary Films, 2020.

A photograph: Stan Becker, "MSU Institute Trains Teens in Communications Skills," *Lansing (MI) State Journal*, July 24, 1966.

"These are white-bread": Karwoski, author interview.

"He was fast": Bob Haeger, author interview, September 2, 2021.

"Most of the activity": Pisano and Colby, *Belushi*, 21.

"He got his bell": Stephanie Nolasco, "Jim Belushi Explains How Medical Marijuana Could Have Helped Save His Brother John Belushi's Life," *Fox News*, August 19, 2020; https://www.foxnews.com/entertainment/jim-belushi -medical-marijuana-john-belushi-growing-belushi; Jeff Ragovin (host), "Jim Belushi, Founder, Belushi's Farm," *Alchemy*, podcast, April 13, 2020, https: //vimeo.com/407142723.

"Whenever John walked": Pisano and Colby, *Belushi*, 19.

"somewhat serious": Haeger, author interview. Band name draws from Cutler, *Belushi*.

"She's the one": Payne, author interview.

"And there was something": Belushi, *Samurai Widow*, 156–57.

Chapter 2: Rantoul Rag

"I'm not sure": This scene draws from Bob Woodward, *Wired: The Short Life and Fast Times of John Belushi* (New York: Simon & Schuster, 1984), 35–37; and Judith Belushi Pisano and Tanner Colby, *Belushi* (New York: Rugged Land, 2005), 24–27.

He dismounted: Mark Kurlansky, author interview, August 3, 2021.

"Well, John had": Vic Caroli, author interview, August 2, 2021.

"I can't believe it here": Judy Jacklin Belushi, *Samurai Widow* (New York: Carroll & Graf, 1990), 231.

"Strangely enough": Kurlansky, author interview.

"He wasn't very big": Caroli, author interview.

"He'd have somebody": Kurlansky, author interview.

"Some special word": "The Shawnee Review," *Linton (IN) Daily Citizen*, July 6, 1967.

"Well, I guess": Belushi, *Samurai Widow*, 233–34; R. J. Cutler (dir.), *Belushi*, Showtime Documentary Films, 2020.

"It's not about you": Caroli, author interview, December 10, 2021.

"I just couldn't believe": Pisano and Colby, *Belushi*, 27.

"You know, Caroli": Caroli, author interview, December 10, 2021.

"You should leave": Belushi, *Samurai Widow*, 157.

"The Albanian?": Woodward, *Wired*, 39.

They crafted scenes: Donna McCrohan, *The Second City: A Backstage History of Comedy's Hottest Troupe* (New York: Perigee Books, 1987), 25.

a Second City primer: William Leonard, "Second City Revue Opens in New Playhouse," *Chicago Tribune*, August 3, 1967.

"This, this is what": Pisano and Colby, *Belushi*, 27; Cutler, *Belushi*.

"Dear Judy": Cutler, *Belushi*.

"Democracy is no good": Belushi, *Samurai Widow*, 158, 241.

"One night at a drive-in": Belushi, *Samurai Widow*, 159.

"I'll give you": Woodward, *Wired*, 40–41.

"On payday": Pisano and Colby, *Belushi*, 31.

"A bluegrass band": Warren Leming, author interview, August 4, 2021.

"huge crowds on TV": Pisano and Colby, *Belushi*, 29.

"I can't believe": This scene draws from Juanita Payne, author interview; and Woodward, *Wired*, 41.

An auction listing: "Auction Sale," classified ad, *Chicago Tribune*, June 7, 1970.

"It had a coat-hanger": Pisano and Colby, *Belushi*, 31.

"Look": Pisano and Colby, *Belushi*, 31; Woodward, *Wired*, 42–43.

"actually ran away": Cutler, *Belushi*.

"John started fooling around": Pisano and Colby, *Belushi*, 32.

"Most of the sketches": Pisano and Colby, *Belushi*, 32.

"I'll come see you": Belushi, *Samurai Widow*, 160–61.

"You've only been": Belushi, *Samurai Widow*, 242.

"We had no money": Pisano and Colby, *Belushi*, 33.

"Whatever you decide": Belushi, *Samurai Widow*, 162–64.

"definitely not fit": Pisano and Colby, *Belushi*, 36–37.

"There'd be a table": Pisano and Colby, *Belushi*, 37.

"He had a leather": Roberta Maguire, author interview, August 13, 2021.

Chapter 3: The Next Generation

"We don't need": This scene draws from Judith Belushi Pisano and Tanner Colby, *Belushi* (New York: Rugged Land, 2005), 43; Sheldon Patinkin, *The Second City: Backstage at the World's Greatest Comedy Theater* (Naperville, IL: Sourcebooks, 2000), 91; and Donna McCrohan, *The Second City: A Backstage History of Comedy's Hottest Troupe* (New York: Perigee Books, 1987), 173.

"We were drawing": Jim Fisher, author interview, August 31, 2021.

"made a difference": Judy Morgan, author interview, August 19, 2021.

natural roles: This characterization draws from Sam Wasson, *Improv Nation: How We Made a Great American Art* (New York: Houghton Mifflin Harcourt, 2017), 144; and Jim Fisher, author interview.

"Remember when": William Leonard, "Sweet Simplicity at Second City," *Chicago Tribune*, March 5, 1970.

were probably thinking: Sahlins and Sloane never seem to have acknowledged replacing Ramis with Belushi, but Ramis certainly felt supplanted when he returned to the ensemble after his sabbatical.

Sahlins generally auditioned: Bob Woodward, *Wired: The Short Life and Fast Times of John Belushi* (New York: Simon & Schuster, 1984), 46–48.

At twenty-two: Contrary to legend, Belushi was not the youngest performer ever hired to the main Second City cast. The theater had employed actors as young as eighteen.

He went off: This passage draws from Woodward, *Wired*, 48; and Pisano and Colby, *Belushi*, 43.

"Belwish?": Pisano and Colby, *Belushi*, 44.

"Something about him": Fisher, author interview.

"We'd get an idea": Joe Flaherty, author interview, November 17, 2021.

"Why don't you use": Roberta Maguire, author interview.

"a medley": Max Norris, "Second City Darts Pin Pope, Politics and Life in General to the Wall," *Sacramento Bee*, May 14, 1971.

"We'd be down": Maguire, author interview.

"We would take questions": Joe Flaherty, author interview, November 17, 2021.

"She was always dressed": Maguire, author interview by email, August 21, 2021.

"He would just eat": Eugenie Ross-Leming, author interview, August 8, 2021.

"I started hearing": Joe Flaherty, author interview, November 17, 2021.

"this red flying helmet": Fisher, author interview.

"We all have": Sydney J. Harris, "A Second City Winner!" *Chicago Daily News*, October 29, 1971.

"And what he was saying": Paul Flaherty, author interview, November 2, 2021.

"This is me": Fisher, author interview.

"I carry that article": Woodward, *Wired*, 50–51.

a round of flirting: Paul Flaherty, author interview, December 22, 2021.

"I think there were": McCrohan, *Second City*, 168–69.

"Hey, I've gotta": This scene draws from Ross-Leming, author interview; and Pisano and Colby, *Belushi*, 45–46.

"I don't give a damn": Woodward, *Wired*, 54–55.

"Judy had a practical": Paul Flaherty, author interview, December 22, 2022.

"If you don't like": Paul Flaherty, author interview by email, November 5, 2021.

"You're high": Fisher and Joe Flaherty, November 17, 2021, author interviews.

"And he was noticeably": Paul Flaherty, author interview, December 22, 2021.

"It was amazing": This passage draws from Pisano and Colby, *Belushi*, 51; and Ross-Leming, author interview.

"That heavy-metal": Ross-Leming, author interview.

"Mr. and Mrs. Jacklin": This passage draws from Woodward, *Wired*, 52; and Pisano and Colby, *Belushi*, 52.

"My work's better": Joe Flaherty, author interview, March 10, 2022.

"Del," John said: Mitchell Glazer and Timothy White, "John Belushi: Made in America," *Rolling Stone*, April 29, 1982.

He bought a bicycle: Gene Siskel, "The Blues Brothers," *Chicago Tribune*, June 29, 1980.

Back at the theater: This scene draws from Pisano and Colby, *Belushi*, 49; an original Second City videotape supplied by Jim Fisher; and Fisher, Ross-Leming, and Morgan, author interviews. Memories conflict: Morgan recalled the funeral sketch evolving from an audience suggestion rather than an actual funeral outing.

the best-known sketch: A few years later, Jim Fisher recalled in an author interview, "the writers from *The Mary Tyler Moore Show* went to see a Second City touring company that did the funeral. They saw the scene; they saw the reaction." In the fall of 1975, *Mary Tyler Moore* (CBS) would broadcast "Chuckles Bites the Dust." The premise: prim television newswoman Mary Richards struggles to stifle laughter at the funeral of a clown stomped to death by an elephant. "Chuckles" would endure as one of television's most celebrated sitcom episodes.

"I coulda been": Marshall Rosenthal, "Stamped with His Own Brando," *Chicago Daily News*, April 15, 1972.

"Boy, John": This scene draws from Joe Flaherty, author interview, November 17, 2021; and Pisano and Colby, *Belushi*, 55.

Peter told John: Peter Elbling, author interview by email, August 5, 2021.

Chapter 4: Freud, Marx, Engels, and Jung

"had little more": "Nightmare in the Catskills," *New York Times*, August 18, 1969.

"If there was anything": Judith Belushi Pisano and Tanner Colby, *Belushi* (New York: Rugged Land, 2005), 55, 59.

"The tape contained": Pisano and Colby, *Belushi*, 59.

"Our mission that night": This scene draws from Joe Flaherty (November 17, 2021), and Eugenie Ross-Leming (December 25, 2021), author interviews.

"John inserted himself": Pisano and Colby, *Belushi*, 60. Not all agreed that the night belonged to John. Jim Fisher, for one, believed Tony Hendra was there to audition the entire cast, not Belushi alone. John appalled him by hogging the stage. Fisher recalled that Hendra went backstage after the show and announced to the troupe that *National Lampoon* needed someone who played bass. "And I said, 'I only play the one-string washtub bass.' And then he talked to John, who lied and said he played the bass. And then John went to Eugenie, who played the bass, and said, 'Could you teach me to play the bass?'" Jim Fisher, author interview, December 24, 2021.

"Come on back": This passage draws from Bob Woodward, *Wired: The Short Life and Fast Times of John Belushi* (New York: Simon & Schuster, 1984), 59; and Pisano and Colby, *Belushi*, 60.

"had a very sad": Pisano and Colby, *Belushi*, 60.

"There wasn't a feeling": Pisano and Colby, *Belushi*, 61–62.

"was a stickler": Michael Simmons, author interview, January 27, 2022.

"the rock 'n' roll generation": Anne Beatts, interview by Jim McKairnes, Television Academy Foundation, May 7, 2009.

"I've gotta leave": This scene draws from Pisano and Colby, *Belushi*, 63; and Matty Simmons, *If You Don't Buy This Book We'll Kill This Dog* (New York: Barricade Books, 1994), 97–98.

"The audience never": This scene draws from Pisano and Colby, *Belushi*, 63; Woodward, *Wired*, 61; and Simmons, *If You Don't*, 98–99.

"'Lemmings' Fails Early": Mel Gussow, "'Lemmings' Fails Early, Recovers Later," *New York Times*, January 26, 1973.

"Friendly and self-effacing": Douglass Watt, "'Lemmings' Is a Wow at Village Gate," *New York Daily News*, January 27, 1973.

"invaluable": Edith Oliver, "Wait for It, Wait for It," *New Yorker*, February 3, 1973.

The show grossed: Ellin Stein, *That's Not Funny, That's Sick: "The National Lampoon" and the Comedy Insurgents Who Captured the Mainstream* (New York: W. W. Norton, 2013), 123.

"was sort of like": Michael Simmons, author interview.

"That left him": Pisano and Colby, *Belushi*, 71.

John fell: Pisano and Colby, *Belushi*, 70.

"Everybody did a hit": Michael Simmons, author interview.

"Right over there": Woodward, *Wired*, 63.

"It was incredibly dangerous": Pisano and Colby, *Belushi*, 71.

"You guys are": This passage draws from Pisano and Colby, *Belushi*, 72; and Michael Simmons and Sean Kelly (March 4, 2022) author interviews. Whether Matty Simmons followed through on the threat is a matter of dispute. Tony Hendra recalled that Matty ordered him to fire John. Hendra refused: John was irreplaceable. Matty remembered differently: he never asked anyone to fire John.

"and see if there was": Kelly, author interview.

"I was always": Rhonda Coullet, author interview, January 19, 2022.

"Oh.": Pisano and Colby, *Belushi*, 74. Some accounts place this scene at Chevy Chase's office at *Saturday Night Live*, a few years later. This narrative favors Chevy's own recollection.

Chapter 5: Welcome Back: The Death Penalty

"Would you like": Janis Hirsch, author interview, January 12, 2022.

an abrupt "no": Judith Belushi Pisano and Tanner Colby, *Belushi* (New York: Rugged Land, 2005), 79.

Roughly sixty: Les Brown, "2 Radio Networks Turn to the Past," *New York Times*, October 30, 1973. Syndication figures from *Broadcasting*, May 6, 1974.

"It seemed like": Sean Kelly, author interview.

They impishly neglected: Brian McConnachie, author interview, January 11, 2022.

On Easter Sunday: Matty Simmons, *If You Don't Buy This Book We'll Kill This Dog* (New York: Barricade Books, 1994), 128; Pisano and Colby, *Belushi*, 80–81.

Nearly two hundred: Matty Simmons later claimed six hundred stations carried the show. But *Lampoon*'s own advertising in the spring of 1974 reported that 162 stations carried the program. A piece in *Broadcasting* two months later put the figure at 185.

John traveled to Toronto: Many conflicting dates have been given for John's arrival in Toronto. John could not have visited the Old Fire Hall before 1974, when Second City opened there. He did not visit in early 1974, because Aykroyd was not there. A scarf and sweater would not seem necessary in summer. Thus, an autumn date seems likely. The timing of Wayne Cochran's residency at El Mocambo narrows the date to September.

"We were backstage": Dan Aykroyd, interview by Marc Maron, *WTF with Marc Maron*, podcast, March 23, 2020, http://www.wtfpod.com/podcast/episode-1108-dan-aykroyd; Helena de Bertodano, "The Man Who Thinks He's a Ghost," *Ottawa Citizen*, October 20, 2000.

Chapter 6: Change for a Quarter

The family lived: Dan Aykroyd, author interview, December 9, 2022.

"My mother would send": Dan Aykroyd, interview by Marc Maron, *WTF with Marc Maron*, podcast, March 23, 2020, http://www.wtfpod.com/podcast/episode-1108-dan-aykroyd.

"Even then": Donna McCrohan, *The Second City: A Backstage History of Comedy's Hottest Troupe* (New York: Perigee Books, 1987), 191.

At a school assembly: Peter Robb, "Dan Aykroyd: It's All about McNamara's Band and the Ottawa Little Theatre," *Ottawa Citizen*, May 23, 2014.

"I was running around": Peter Swet, "Just Give This Man Some Hard Work," *News and Observer* (Raleigh, NC), February 23, 1992.

"gave me a sense": Robb, "Dan Aykroyd."

"We deserved it": Marianne Partridge, ed., *"Rolling Stone" Visits Saturday Night Live* (New York: Rolling Stone Press, 1979), 121.

"Well, Dan": Aykroyd, Maron interview; "Dan Aykroyd," *The Big Interview with Dan Rather*, AXS TV, season 6, episode 16, aired November 13, 2018.

"We were up": Gary O'Dwyer, author interview, August 23, 2021.

"Abandon ship!": O'Dwyer, author interview.

"He made a lot": Gordon Flagler, author interview by email, January 11, 2022.

"To the fun": O'Dwyer, author interview.

"throwing hamburgers": Dan Aykroyd, "The Holiday That Changed Me," *Daily Telegraph* (London), November 13, 2021.

"We were supposed": Partridge, *"Rolling Stone" Visits*, 122.

"There was always": Aykroyd, *Big Interview with Dan Rather*.

"I worked all kinds": Swet, "Hard Work."

"We had to walk": Geoff Winter, author interview, August 19, 2021.

After one impression: Christopher Guly, "Our Danny Boy," *Ottawa Magazine*, April 1991.

"I came back": This scene draws from "Dan Aykroyd, Still Full of the 'Blues,'" interview by Terry Gross, *Fresh Air*, NPR, November 22, 2004, https://freshairarchive.org/segments/dan-aykroyd-still-full-blues; and Roger Gatchet, "Interview and Review: The Blues Brothers," *Austin Sound*, May 18, 2007.

"this whole underworld": Partridge, *"Rolling Stone" Visits*, 122.

Aykroyd, author interview: Aykroyd, Gross interview; Gatchet, "Interview and Review"; "Dan Aykroyd Is Excited for Blues Brothers Con," interview by Bob Sirott, WGN Radio 720, Chicago, August 9, 2022, https://wgnradio.com/bob-sirott/dan-aykroyd-is-excited-for-the-blues-brothers-convention/.

"The most notorious": Lauren Drewery, author interview by email, June 20, 2022.

"You're not going": Aykroyd, author interview.

"a full-inch videotape": Aykroyd, Maron interview.

Chapter 7: The Great Canadian Humour Test

"It was kind of": Howard Shore, author interview, March 2, 2022.

They formed a stand-up: Pomerantz said Michaels called him just after he finished law school (he graduated in 1965).

On the day: Dan Aykroyd, interview by Marc Maron, *WTF with Marc Maron*, podcast, March 23, 2020, http://www.wtfpod.com/podcast/episode-1108-dan-aykroyd.

"We played in the": Dan Aykroyd, author interview.

"they were sons": Marcus O'Hara, author interview, May 23, 2022.

His ultimate fantasy: Rosie Shuster, author interview, May 15, 2023. The observation actually came from her brother.

"as a prankster": William Lane, author interview by email, August 17, 2021.

"Turkish underground character": Gay Hauser, author interview, August 31, 2021.

"And there might be": Elizabeth Hanna, author interview, August 19, 2021.

"I wondered how": Lauren Drewery, author interview by email.

"The best job": Marianne Partridge, ed., *"Rolling Stone" Visits Saturday Night Live* (New York: Rolling Stone Press, 1979), 123.

"Danny and I": Dave Thomas, *SCTV: Behind the Scenes* (Toronto: McClelland & Stewart, 1996), 13.

"They were like": Marcus O'Hara, author interview.

"It involved singing": Stu Gillard, author interview, September 1, 2021.

"They arranged": Sheldon Patinkin, *The Second City: Backstage at the World's Greatest Comedy Theater* (Naperville, IL: Sourcebooks, 2000), 92.

"the mind of a calculator": This scene draws from Donna McCrohan, *The Second City: A Backstage History of Comedy's Hottest Troupe* (New York: Perigee Books, 1987), 190–91; and Joe Flaherty, author interview, November 17, 2021.

"in a welter": Herbert Whittaker, "Second City Shows Best in Polished Routines, *Globe and Mail* (Toronto), June 12, 1973; Urjo Kareda, "Second City: Watch It Grow and Explode," *Toronto Star*, June 12, 1973.

Only one thing: Joe Flaherty, author interview, November 17, 2021.

"If Valri came out": Joe Flaherty, author interview, March 10, 2022.

"Street-car drivers": Roger Gatchet, "Interview and Review: The Blues Brothers," *Austin Sound*, May 18, 2007.

"greasy hair": Sam Wasson, *Improv Nation: How We Made a Great American Art* (New York: Houghton Mifflin Harcourt, 2017), 203–4.

"We were hugging": Patinkin, *Second City*, 97.

"License me the rights": Andrew Alexander, author interview by email, April 30, 2023.

"You'd go down": Dan Aykroyd, interview by Cabral Richards, *Cabbie Presents*, podcast, June 28, 2019, https://podcasts.apple.com/ca/podcast/149-dan-aykroyd/id506577876?i=1000443042990.

"There was a change": Dave Thomas, author interview, February 25, 2022.

"Over two hundred.": Thomas, *SCTV*, 18.

"Now that I've got": Dan Aykroyd, author interview.

Scanning the daily papers: A reasonably thorough search of newspaper records from that summer turned up no story about Illinois politicians attempting to tax parochial schools. Yet, Aykroyd clearly remembered reading one.

Chapter 8: You're the Pits

"Your mind is going": Dave Thomas, author interview.

"I knew that this": Judith Belushi Pisano and Tanner Colby, *Belushi* (New York: Rugged Land, 2005), xi.

"What is this?": This scene draws from Dan Aykroyd, author interview; "Dan Aykroyd, Still Full of the 'Blues,'" interview by Terry Gross, *Fresh Air*, NPR, November 22, 2004, https://freshairarchive.org/segments/dan-aykroyd-still -full-blues; Amy Longsdorf, "Back in 'Blues,'" *Morning Call* (Allentown, PA), February 6, 1998; and Ned Zeman, "Soul Men: The Making of *The Blues Brothers*," *Vanity Fair*, January 2013.

"You could call it": Shore doesn't recall saying this, but he defers to Aykroyd's account. Shore, author interview.

"was making more money": Pisano and Colby, *Belushi*, 84.

One by one: This scene draws from Joe Flaherty, author interview, November 17, 2021; and Gilda Radner, interview by Jeffrey Sweet, in Sweet, *Something Wonderful Right Away: An Oral History of the Second City and the Compass Players* (New York: Avon Books, 1978). Radner recalled getting the call after her return from her Second City residency in Chicago in the summer of 1974.

"We did a parody": Brian McConnachie, author interview.

"Somebody's father": Janis Hirsch, author interview.

"And there's all these": This scene draws from Bob Woodward, *Wired: The Short Life and Fast Times of John Belushi* (New York: Simon & Schuster, 1984); and Dan Aykroyd, interview by Marc Maron, *WTF with Marc Maron*, podcast, March 23, 2020, http://www.wtfpod.com/podcast/episode-1108-dan-aykroyd.

"very gay": This scene draws from Hirsh, author interview; and Pisano and Colby, *Belushi*, 87.

"one of the most": Pisano and Colby, *Belushi*, 92.

"Do not carry": Simmons, author interview.

"Actually": Mel Gussow, "Stage: A New 'Lampoon,'" *New York Times*, March 3, 1975.

"Brian, he's got": Pisano and Colby, *Belushi*, 93.

"for the greater part": Matty Simmons, *If You Don't Buy This Book We'll Kill This Dog* (New York: Barricade Books, 1994), 138.

Chapter 9: Saturday Night

"about something that isn't": This scene draws from Dick Ebersol, interview by Dan Pasternack, Television Academy Foundation, June 23 and 24, 2000; Dick Ebersol, *From Saturday Night to Sunday Night: My Forty Years of Laughter, Tears, and Touchdowns in TV* (New York: Simon & Schuster, 2022), 58–59; and Tom Shales and James Andrew Miller, *Live from New York: An Uncensored History of "Saturday Night Live"* (New York: Little, Brown, 2002), 17–18.

"If you're that funny": Shales and Miller, *Live from New York*, 15.

"Are you crazy?": Doug Hill and Jeff Weingrad, *Saturday Night: A Backstage History of "Saturday Night Live"* (New York: Vintage Books, 1986), 38.

"Lily used to use": Ellin Stein, *That's Not Funny, That's Sick: "The National Lampoon" and the Comedy Insurgents Who Captured the Mainstream* (New York: W. W. Norton, 2013), 214.

"I felt that American": Sam Wasson, *Improv Nation: How We Made a Great American Art* (New York: Houghton Mifflin Harcourt, 2017), 215.

"I would like": Hill and Weingrad, *Saturday Night*, 31.

The network suits: Hill and Weingrad, *Saturday Night*, 41–44.

"brought out these mushrooms": Tom Schiller, author interview, April 27, 2022.

"So the network": Hill and Weingrad, *Saturday Night*, 53.

"very, very young": Ebersol, Television Academy interview.

"Do you think": Dave Thomas, author interview.

On a hiatus: Dan Aykroyd, interview by Marc Maron, *WTF with Marc Maron*, podcast, March 23, 2020, http://www.wtfpod.com/podcast/episode-1108-dan-aykroyd.

The big hire: Hill and Weingrad, *Saturday Night*, 55.

"sort of dominated": Judith Belushi Pisano and Tanner Colby, *Belushi* (New York: Rugged Land, 2005), 97.

"Television is crap.": This scene, through Belushi's exclamation "I blew it," draws from Shales and Miller, *Live from New York*, 33–34; Bob Woodward, *Wired: The Short Life and Fast Times of John Belushi* (New York: Simon & Schuster, 1984), 71–72; and Hill and Weingrad, *Saturday Night*, 70.

"just another": Carll Tucker, "John Belushi: He Who Laughs First," *Village Voice*, July 28, 1975.

"A sad odor": Hill and Weingrad, *Saturday Night*, 71.

"I've been waiting": Hill and Weingrad, *Saturday Night*, 71–72.

"There was a station": R. J. Cutler (dir.), *Belushi*, Showtime Documentary Films, 2020.

"Somebody better hire": Schiller, author interview, April 27, 2022.

"John will be trouble": Shales and Miller, *Live from New York*, 35.

"beginning of our dreams": Brad Steuernagel (dir.), "The SCTV Guide to Showbiz," YouTube video, posted by GooseOD, July 3, 2021, https://www.youtube.com/watch?v=iGPCHzH1TGA.

"we're talking about": Joe Flaherty, author interviews, November 17, 2021.

"They were sort of": David Sheff, "Playboy Interview: Dan Aykroyd," *Playboy*, August 1993.

"Who's to say": Judy Jacklin Belushi, *Samurai Widow* (New York: Carroll & Graf, 1990), 125.

John appeared: "Saturday Night Live Screen Test John Belushi," YouTube video, posted by The Deano Frank Channel, January 25, 2019, https://www.youtube.com/watch?v=o5AhA_Xps4Q.

Dan appeared: "Saturday Night Live—Screen Test—Dan Aykroyd," YouTube video, posted by The Deano Frank Channel, March 18, 2018, https://www.youtube.com/watch?v=F08wjo9ZYSs.

a viewing party: This scene draws from Hill and Weingrad, *Saturday Night*, 74; and Shales and Miller, *Live from New York*, 83–84.

"Everyone in the cast": Pisano and Colby, *Belushi*, 98.

"stormed off": Pisano and Colby, *Belushi*, 98.

Chapter 10: I'm a King Bee

"Would you sign": This scene draws from Bob Woodward, *Wired: The Short Life and Fast Times of John Belushi* (New York: Simon & Schuster, 1984), 74; Doug Hill and

Jeff Weingrad, *Saturday Night: A Backstage History of "Saturday Night Live"* (New York: Vintage Books, 1986), 88–89; and Tom Shales and James Andrew Miller, *Live from New York: An Uncensored History of "Saturday Night Live"* (New York: Little, Brown, 2002), 49–50.

"If this sketch": Dan Aykroyd, interview by Dan Dunn, *What We're Drinking with Dan Dunn*, podcast, August 20, 2020, https://podcasts.apple.com/us /podcast/79-vodka-with-dan-aykroyd/id1469002731?i=1000488664420.

"our generation's": Martin Short, *I Must Say: My Life as a Humble Comedy Legend* (New York: HarperCollins, 2014), 99.

"The reaction": Woodward, *Wired*, 76.

A few papers: Reviews appeared in the October 13 editions of the respective papers.

"Even an offbeat": John J. O'Connor, "TV: Simon and Garfunkel Reunion on NBC's 'Saturday Night,'" *New York Times*, October 20, 1975.

"like puppy dogs": Hill and Weingrad, *Saturday Night*, 96.

Dan and John crashed in: This scene draws from Woodward, *Wired*, 79–80; and Hill and Weingrad, *Saturday Night*, 96–97.

"NBC's *Saturday Night*": Tom Shales, "Zingers on 'Saturday Night,'" *Washington Post*, November 8, 1975.

"getting the most": Woodward, *Wired*, 81.

"For however long": John J. O'Connor, "TV View: Sprightly Mix Brightens NBC's 'Saturday Night,'" *New York Times*, November 30, 1975.

"the only new": Dick Adler, "Saturday Is for Laughing," *Los Angeles Times*, December 12, 1975.

"Hey, it's the bee!": Woodward, *Wired*, 83–85.

"And heeeere's": Jeff Greenfield, "He's Chevy Chase and You're Not, and He's TV's Hot New Comedy Star," *New York*, December 22, 1975.

"I gotta do that": Judith Belushi Pisano and Tanner Colby, *Belushi* (New York: Rugged Land, 2005), 101; Tom Schiller, author interview, June 24, 2022.

"had been the top banana": This quote and Glazer's below draw from R. J. Cutler (dir.), *Belushi*, Showtime Documentary Films, 2020.

"You want see": Woodward, *Wired*, 81–82.

"I'd like to meet": This scene draws from Woodward, *Wired*, 87–88; and David Michaelis, *The Best of Friends: Profiles of Extraordinary Friendships* (New York: William Morrow, 1983), 281–83.

John caught up: Woodward, *Wired*, 88.

"and everything stopped": Buck Henry, interview by Jenni Matz, Television Academy Foundation, February 26, 2009.

"Do you want to do": Shales and Miller, *Live from New York*, 66.

"and it was an instant": This scene draws from Howard Shore, Paul Shaffer, and Dan Aykroyd, author interviews; Paul Shaffer, interview by Dan Pasternack, Television Academy Foundation, June 24, 2009; and Shales and Miller, *Live from New York*, 116.

"Why can't one": Marianne Partridge, ed., *"Rolling Stone" Visits Saturday Night Live* (New York: Rolling Stone Press, 1979), 41.

"Fuck Lorne": Paul Shaffer with David Ritz, *We'll Be Here for the Rest of Our Lives: A Swingin' Show-Biz Saga* (New York: Flying Dolphin, 2009), 176–77.

Chapter 11: Bass-o-Matic

In the Monday meetings: Descriptions of the *SNL* routine draw primarily from Doug Hill and Jeff Weingrad, *Saturday Night: A Backstage History of "Saturday Night Live"* (New York: Vintage Books, 1986), 120–26.

"A clothesline": Laraine Newman, interview by Amy Harrington, Television Academy Foundation, March 20, 2013; Laraine Newman, *May You Live in Interesting Times* (n.p.: Audible Originals, 2021).

"There were dirty clothes": Hill and Weingrad, *Saturday Night*, 236.

"It was like being": R. J. Cutler (dir.), *Belushi*, Showtime Documentary Films, 2020.

"When they were working": Tom Schiller, author interview, June 24, 2022.

"I think an unconscious": Judy Jacklin Belushi, *Samurai Widow* (New York: Carroll & Graf, 1990), 107.

"And he was just": Jane Curtin, interview by Jenni Matz, Television Academy Foundation, May 28, 2015.

"When we had our": Schiller, author interview, April 27, 2022.

"So, they have the cocaine": Tom Shales and James Andrew Miller, *Live from New York: An Uncensored History of "Saturday Night Live"* (New York: Little, Brown, 2002), 82–83.

"spent an afternoon": Tom Shales, "Viewpoint," *Los Angeles Times*, September 30, 1979.

"Aunt Helen": Dan Aykroyd, interview by Marc Maron, *WTF with Marc Maron*, podcast, March 23, 2020, http://www.wtfpod.com/podcast/episode-1108-dan-aykroyd.

twenty-two million Americans: In fact, *Saturday Night* drew roughly 7.5 million viewers a week in season one, according to Hill and Weingrad, *Saturday Night*, 307.

Watching his scene: Bob Woodward, author interview, December 12, 2022.

He told O'Donoghue: This scene draws from Judith Belushi Pisano and Tanner Colby, *Belushi* (New York: Rugged Land, 2005), 105; and Bob Woodward, *Wired: The Short Life and Fast Times of John Belushi* (New York: Simon & Schuster, 1984), 97–98.

Chapter 12: Albanian Oak

"a little birthday party": Bernie Brillstein with David Rensin, *Where Did I Go Right? You're No One in Hollywood Unless Someone Wants You Dead* (New York: Little, Brown, 1999), 153–54.

"We drank a lot": This scene draws from Tom Shales and James Andrew Miller, *Live from New York: An Uncensored History of "Saturday Night Live"* (New York: Little, Brown, 2002), 93–94; Bob Woodward, *Wired: The Short Life and Fast Times of John Belushi* (New York: Simon & Schuster, 1984), 99–100; and Alan Zweibel, author interview, May 3, 2022.

"To get a motor": Woodward, *Wired*, 100–1.

"Nobody can stomach": Marianne Partridge, ed., *"Rolling Stone" Visits Saturday Night Live* (New York: Rolling Stone Press, 1979), 25–45.

"most visible comic": Tom Shales, "Chevy Chase: So Long to 'Saturday Night'?," *Washington Post*, August 27, 1976.

"Chevy was ready": Doug Hill and Jeff Weingrad, *Saturday Night: A Backstage History of "Saturday Night Live"* (New York: Vintage Books, 1986), 224.

"No, I don't": Ben Fong-Torres, "Joe Cocker Gets a Little Help," *Rolling Stone*, November 18, 1976.

"It just didn't feel": Judith Belushi Pisano and Tanner Colby, *Belushi* (New York: Rugged Land, 2005), 110.

"Henry gamely remained": Buck Henry, interview by Jenni Matz, Television Academy Foundation, February 26, 2009.

"John used to love": Pisano and Colby, *Belushi*, 107–8; Dan Aykroyd and John Belushi, "New South Burn," *Rolling Stone*, January 13, 1977.

"to babysit Belushi": This scene draws from Dick Ebersol, interview by Dan Pasternack, Television Academy Foundation, June 23 and 24, 2000; and Alan Zweibel, author interview, September 29, 2022.

"would sleep all day": Pisano and Colby, *Belushi*, 113.

"You don't know": Woodward, *Wired*, 103–4.

"All of us get": Tom Shales, "Chevy's Gone, but 'Saturday Night' Lives," *Washington Post*, November 17, 1976.

"I give so much pleasure": Woodward, *Wired*, 104–5.

"Oh God, I'll tell": Laraine Newman, *May You Live in Interesting Times* (n.p.: Audible Originals, 2021).

"Everyone had been": Pisano and Colby, *Belushi*, 111–12.

"Judy had given": Rosie Shuster, author interview.

Chapter 13: Night of the Seven Fires

"He showed up": Judith Belushi Pisano and Tanner Colby, *Belushi* (New York: Rugged Land, 2005), 115.

"I heard you tell": Pisano and Colby, *Belushi*, 115.

"No, John": Bob Woodward, *Wired: The Short Life and Fast Times of John Belushi* (New York: Simon & Schuster, 1984), 109–110.

"He was really fucked up": This scene draws from Judith Belushi Pisano and Tanner Colby, *Belushi* (New York: Rugged Land, 2005), 117; and Tom Shales and James Andrew Miller, *Live from New York: An Uncensored History of "Saturday Night Live"* (New York: Little, Brown, 2002), 104. In an alternate telling, John was playing a samurai.

"On morphine and Demerol": This scene draws from Judy Jacklin Belushi, *Samurai Widow* (New York: Carroll & Graf, 1990), 176; and Jann Wenner, *Like a Rolling Stone: A Memoir* (New York: Little, Brown, 2022), 222.

He later confessed: This scene draws from Woodward, *Wired*, 111; and Belushi, *Samurai Widow*, 50–51.

"About three months ago": Mitchell Glazer, "Saturday Night's All Right for Fighting," *Crawdaddy*, June 1977.

"Quite often": Clifford Terry, "The Swaggering Wit of John Belushi," *Chicago Tribune*, May 14, 1978.

"The episode won an Emmy." The sketch was written by Dan Aykroyd and called "Ask President Carter."

"He was mad": Shuster, author interview.

Fist-size holes: Doug Hill and Jeff Weingrad, *Saturday Night: A Backstage History of "Saturday Night Live"* (New York: Vintage Books, 1986), 242.

"If you're not going": This scene draws from Woodward, *Wired*, 113; and David Michaelis, *The Best of Friends: Profiles of Extraordinary Friendships* (New York: William Morrow, 1983), 289–90.

"Who's on the show": This scene draws from Bill Boggs, author interview, July 10, 2022; Angela Barbuti, "An Interview with a Quintessential New York Interviewer, *Our Town* (New York), November 28, 2021; Marianne Partridge, ed., *"Rolling Stone" Visits Saturday Night Live* (New York: Rolling Stone Press, 1979), 93; Random Notes, *Rolling Stone*, June 2, 1977; and "Michael O'Donoghue/John Belushi—Interview 1977," Reelin' in the Years Productions, YouTube video, posted by ReelinInTheYears66, August 14, 2019, https://www.youtube.com/watch?v=ou8yAcuqnmg.

Some days later: Judy Jacklin Belushi, *Samurai Widow* (New York: Carroll & Graf, 1990), 51.

"would make an entrance": This scene draws from Wenner, *Like a Rolling Stone*, advance reader copy, 227–28; and Mitchell Glazer and Timothy White, "John Belushi: Made in America," *Rolling Stone*, April 29, 1982.

"It was too personal": Pisano and Colby, *Belushi*, 132.

"Let me help you": Josh Karp, *A Futile and Stupid Gesture: How Doug Kenney and "National Lampoon" Changed Comedy Forever* (Chicago: Chicago Review Press, 2006), 278.

"You can't leave": Matty Simmons, *If You Don't Buy This Book We'll Kill This Dog* (New York: Barricade Books, 1994), 141.

"At the center": Chris Nashawaty, *Caddyshack: The Making of a Hollywood Cinderella Story* (New York: Flatiron Books, 2018), 77.

"What? What is it?": Pisano and Colby, *Belushi*, 133.

"It was funny": Nashawaty, *Caddyshack*, 78.

"I was a huge fan": Thom Mount, author interview, May 27, 2022.

"I hate this treatment": Matty Simmons, *Fat, Drunk, and Stupid: The Inside Story behind the Making of "Animal House"* (New York: St. Martin's Press, 2012), 46. Matty reported the figure in various writings as $2.5 million and $3 million, but Sean Daniel (June 10, 2022), in an author interview, distinctly recalled a $2 million budget.

"It's hilarious": Sean Daniel, author interview, June 10, 2022.

Chapter 14: Schlock

"We lived in a middle-class": John Landis, author interview, May 23, 2022.

"It was my first": Gregg Kilday, "Film-Maker, 23, Throws Scare into the Monster Biz," *Los Angeles Times*, December 13, 1973.

"I was never diagnosed": Landis, author interview, May 23, 2022.

"In the sixties": Landis, author interview, May 23, 2022.

"Who are you looking": Katherine Wooten, author interview, March 17, 2023.

"Sight gags and tits": Thom Mount, author interview, May 27, 2022.

"It was the funniest": Chris Nashawaty, *Caddyshack: The Making of a Hollywood Cinderella Story* (New York: Flatiron Books, 2018), 83.

"We can't film that": Sean Daniel, author interview.

"He was an outsider": Nashawaty, *Caddyshack*, 84.

"I remember Doug": Nashawaty, *Caddyshack*, 80.

"Jesus": Bob Woodward, *Wired: The Short Life and Fast Times of John Belushi* (New York: Simon & Schuster, 1984), 117.

John burst in: Judith Belushi Pisano and Tanner Colby, *Belushi* (New York: Rugged Land, 2005), 134.

"And then he got": Landis, author interview, May 23, 2022; Sean Daniel, author interview.

"They can't do it": Woodward, *Wired*, 119.

"You do it": This passage draws from Woodward, *Wired,* 119; and Landis, author interview, May 23, 2022.

"What the hell": Woodward, *Wired*, 120.

"I got to get out": This scene draws from Woodward, *Wired*, 120–23.

Chapter 15: Little Chocolate Donuts

Dan wanted to write alone: David Michaelis, *The Best of Friends: Profiles of Extraordinary Friendships* (New York: William Morrow, 1983), 290.

"It's sort of like": Tom Shales, "'Saturday Night': A Show the Peacock Can Crow About," *Washington Post*, September 28, 1977.

"For the first time": Doug Hill and Jeff Weingrad, *Saturday Night: A Backstage History of "Saturday Night Live"* (New York: Vintage Books, 1986), 274.

"By the end of": Judith Belushi Pisano and Tanner Colby, *Belushi* (New York: Rugged Land, 2005), 122–23.

"I am Beelzebub": Hill and Weingrad, *Saturday Night*, 243.

"Who the fuck is": Sean Daniel, author interview, June 10, 2022.

"Two million dollars": Daniel, author interview, June 10, 2022.

"That's him!": Pisano and Colby, *Belushi*, 134.

"a week of rehearsals": Peter Riegert, author interview, May 27, 2022.

"You Hollywood fags": This scene draws from Pisano and Colby, *Belushi*, 135–36; and Jamie Widdoes, author interview, June 7, 2022.

"Why are you always": Lee Grant, "John Belushi, All-Media Man," *Los Angeles Times*, May 31, 1978.

"I had worked with": Thom Mount, author interview, May 27, 2022.

"Come here": Bob Woodward, *Wired: The Short Life and Fast Times of John Belushi* (New York: Simon & Schuster, 1984), 126.

"never did a drug": Stephen Katz, author interview, July 2, 2022.

"John was a fun": Riegert, author interview.

"He would yell": Widdoes, author interview.

"What is that?": John Landis, author interview, June 3, 2023.

"It's perfect for": Riegert, author interview.

Salgado felt a tug: This scene draws from Curtis Salgado, author interviews, November 30 and December 27, 2022; Robert Cray, author interview by email, September 11, 2022; and interviews with Salgado in *Blues Blast*, May 17, 2018, *Statesman-Journal* (Salem, OR), December 9, 2004, *Columbian* (Vancouver, WA), June 18, 1987, and *Louder Sound*, August 13, 2016.

"To Frank.": Pisano and Colby, *Belushi*, 144.

"magnificent tirade": Hill and Weingrad, *Saturday Night*, 285–86.

"I like the fat guy": Pisano and Colby, *Belushi*, 150.

"This was their regular": Widdoes, author interview.

"If I ever put": Steve Cropper, author interview, August 31, 2022.

"John asked me": Don Novello, author interview, June 30, 2022.

"And I'm sure Billy": Tom Shales and James Andrew Miller, *Live from New York: An Uncensored History of "Saturday Night Live"* (New York: Little, Brown, 2002), 118–19.

"I don't want to do": Clifford Terry, "The Swaggering Wit of John Belushi," *Chicago Tribune*, May 14, 1978.

Minutes before the show: This scene draws from Nick De Semelyn, *Wild and Crazy Guys: How the Comedy Mavericks of the '80s Changed Hollywood Forever* (New York: Crown Archetype, 2019), xi–xiii; Shales and Miller, *Live from New York*, 118–122; Hill and Weingrad, *Saturday Night*, 255–57.

Tom Schiller recruited John: Tom Schiller, author interview, April 27, 2022.

"Hello there, Thing": Marianne Partridge, ed., *"Rolling Stone" Visits Saturday Night Live* (New York: Rolling Stone Press, 1979), 115–16.

Chapter 16: Joliet Jake

"What he was doing": Judith Belushi Pisano and Tanner Colby, *Belushi* (New York: Rugged Land, 2005), 149.

"Why don't you warm": Pisano and Colby, *Belushi*, 151.

"straight from Lenny Bruce": Dan Aykroyd, author interview.

"two ne'er-do-well": Tom Malone, author interview by email, July 13, 2022.

"We thought it would": Tarpley Hitt, "Dan Aykroyd on How Cocaine Fueled 'The Blues Brothers' and Aretha Franklin's Iconic Performance," *Daily Beast*, July 4, 2020.

"We're wasting our time": Malone and Howard Shore, author interviews; research by Brad Robinson of *The Not Ready for Prime Time Podcast*.

"the only time": Pisano and Colby, *Belushi*, 152.

"You got any blow?": Malone, author interview, July 15, 2022.

"I've tried doing drugs": Bob Woodward, *Wired: The Short Life and Fast Times of John Belushi* (New York: Simon & Schuster, 1984), 143.

"about how great": Pisano and Colby, *Belushi*, 153.

"That's not gonna fly": Pisano and Colby, *Belushi*, 153.

"birdseed": Bernie Brillstein with David Rensin, *Where Did I Go Right? You're No One in Hollywood Unless Someone Wants You Dead* (New York: Little, Brown, 1999), 163.

"You can't have John": Aykroyd, author interview.

"You can't do this": This scene draws from Aykroyd, author interview; Pisano and Colby, *Belushi,* 154; and Henry Schipper, "Blues Go Platinum: Brief Case Full of Rip-offs," *Berkeley Barb*, March 15, 1979.

"There was a big": Peter Riegert, author interview. This scene draws from Sean Daniel, Thom Mount, and John Landis, author interviews.

"You couldn't hear": Sean Daniel, author interview, June 16, 2022.

"How did it go?": John Landis, author interview, June 3, 2023.

"John, I love you": Mount, author interview, May 27, 2022; Woodward, *Wired*, 144; and Josh Karp, *A Futile and Stupid Gesture: How Doug Kenney and "National Lampoon" Changed Comedy Forever* (Chicago: Chicago Review Press, 2006), 312.

"At its best": Janet Maslin, "Screen: 'Animal House,'" *New York Times*, July 28, 1978.

"stodgy"; "offers little": Rex Reed, *New York Daily News*, July 28, 1978; Harry Themal, *Sunday News Journal* (Wilmington, DE), July 30, 1978.

"terribly funny"; "vulgar, raunchy": Gene Siskel, "In 'Animal House,' Life Is a Fun, Fraternizing Riot," *Chicago Tribune*, August 25, 1978; Roger Ebert, "National Lampoon's Animal House," RogerEbert.com, https://www.rogerebert.com /reviews/national-lampoons-animal-house-1978.

"Belushi is due": Bob Greene, "John Belushi Isn't a Complacent 'Animal,'" *Chicago Tribune*, August 22, 1978.

"Chicago loved the movie": Sean Daniel, author interview, June 16, 2022.

"We want you": This scene draws from Paul Shaffer with David Ritz, *We'll Be Here for the Rest of Our Lives: A Swingin' Show-Biz Saga* (New York: Flying Dolphin, 2009), 178; and Pisano and Colby, *Belushi*, 155.

"Hi, I'm John": This scene draws from Colin McEnroe, "Newly-Minted Blues Brother Playing with Shaboo All-Stars," *Hartford (CT) Courant*, February 22, 1980; and Pisano and Colby, *Belushi*, 155–56.

"The business meeting": This scene draws from Tom Malone, author interviews, July 15, 2022; and Pisano and Colby, *Belushi*, 156.

John made some phone calls: Steve Cropper, author interview.

"I've seen it three times": Marianne Partridge, ed., *"Rolling Stone" Visits Saturday Night Live* (New York: Rolling Stone Press, 1979), 99.

"Sounds like a movie": Sean Daniel, author interview, June 16, 2022; Pisano and Colby, *Belushi*, 182.

"Wait'll Wasserman hears this": Ned Zeman, "Soul Men: The Making of *The Blues Brothers*," *Vanity Fair*, January 2013; Sean Daniel, author interview, May 11, 2023.

"was nothing against": Brillstein, *Where Did I Go Right?*, 162.

"OK, here's the problem": Thom Mount (June 29, 2022), Sean Daniel (May 11, 2023), author interviews.

"We were looking at": Pisano and Colby, *Belushi*, 161.

"It was like date night": Mitchell Glazer, author interview, June 24, 2022; Cropper, author interview.

"At the beginning": Pisano and Colby, *Belushi*, 161.

"There was something": Lou Marini, author interview, July 8, 2022.

"threw ideas around": Pisano and Colby, *Belushi*, 161–62.

"They'll hate you": Woodward, *Wired*, 145.

"The glasses are crucial": Mitchell Glazer, "The Legend of Jake and Elwood," *Crawdaddy*, December 1978.

"I learned one thing": Landis, author interview, July 22, 2022.

"I want a chili dog": Glazer, "Legend."

Chapter 17: Briefcase Full of Blues

"And I'm out there": Lou Marini, author interview, July 8, 2022.

After the set: Mitchell Glazer, "The Legend of Jake and Elwood," *Crawdaddy*, December 1978.

"But I didn't have": Glazer, author interview.

"a lively": Robert Hilburn, "Martin's Zany Group Therapy," *Los Angeles Times*, September 11, 1978.

Agnes Belushi beamed: Bob Woodward, *Wired: The Short Life and Fast Times of John Belushi* (New York: Simon & Schuster, 1984), 147.

"make it down": Paul Shaffer, author interview, June 29, 2022.

"It is a smog-brown": This scene draws from Glazer, "Legend"; and Glazer, author interview.

"I can't turn down": Woodward, *Wired*, 149–50.

Only Mick Jagger: Doug Hill and Jeff Weingrad, *Saturday Night: A Backstage History of "Saturday Night Live"* (New York: Vintage Books, 1986), 332.

The band tried: Hill and Weingrad, *Saturday Night*, 333.

"I've encouraged them": Tony Schwartz, "'Saturday Night' Fever," *Newsweek*, February 26, 1979.

"Danny used to do": Rosie Shuster, author interview.

"I'll go out for": Woodward, *Wired*, 153.

"Then it took us": Judith Belushi Pisano and Tanner Colby, *Belushi* (New York: Rugged Land, 2005), 169.

"Get that fucking thing": Dave Hirshey, "The Blues Brothers," *New York Daily News*, January 14, 1979.

Briefcase Full of Blues: John chose the title, repurposing a lyric he had misheard in an Elton John spoof on a *National Lampoon* album; Paul Shaffer had actually sung "briefcase full of loot."

"Everyone was completely loaded": Pisano and Colby, *Belushi*, 189.

"Get me the Jenkins file": Pisano and Colby, *Belushi*, 169.

"Disco was on its": Pisano and Colby, *Belushi*, 162.

"were so good": Bob Tischler, author interview, July 22, 2022.

"their genius lies": Timothy White, "The Blues Brothers' Funky Family Reunion," *Rolling Stone*, January 25, 1979; Robert Christgau, "Blues Brothers: *Briefcase Full of Blues* [Atlantic 1978]," RobertChristgau.com, n.d., https://www.robertchristgau.com/get_album.php?id=6432.

"Can white comedians": Tom Popson, "The Blues Brothers," *Chicago Tribune*, January 21, 1979.

"the only thing": Dave Marsh, "Sam & Dave: A Dose of the Real Thing," *Rolling Stone*, May 3, 1979.

"we've got the Blues Brothers": William K. Knoedelseder Jr., "Blues Brothers: No. 1 And That's No Joke," *Washington Post*, February 5, 1979; Lynn Van Matre, "'Briefcase' a hit, but empty," *Chicago Tribune*, February 18, 1979.

"Musically, it was obvious": Henry Schipper, "Blues Go Platinum: Brief Case Full of Rip-offs," *Berkeley Barb*, March 15, 1979.

"was demanding parity": Hill and Weingrad, *Saturday Night*, 339.

"One day he called me": Pisano and Colby, *Belushi*, 173.

Following a familiar pattern: This scene draws from Woodward, *Wired*, 155–56; and Michael Dare, "The Life and Death of Captain Preemo," blog post, January 11, 2009, BartCop Entertainment, http://suprmchaos.com/bcEnt-MichaelDare.index.html.

"You can do this": Woodward, *Wired*, 159.

"This movie has no": Curtis Salgado, author interview, December 27, 2022.

"And there's a thousand": Dave Thomas, author interview, February 25, 2022.

While shooting a scene: Laurent Bouzereau (dir.), *The Making of "1941,"* Universal Pictures, 1996.

"basically took the trip": This scene draws from Bob Weiss, author interview, July 7, 2022; and Giulia D'Agnolo Vallan, *John Landis* (Milwaukie, OR: M Press, 2008), 222.

"We play ourselves": This scene draws from Marianne Partridge, ed., *"Rolling Stone" Visits Saturday Night Live* (New York: Rolling Stone Press, 1979), 103–13; and Mikal Gilmore, "Saturday Night's Soul Fever," *Rolling Stone*, November 2, 1978.

"Without a script": Thom Mount, author interview, June 29, 2022.

"God": Woodward, *Wired*, 162.

Chapter 18: The Phone Book

"differently—not every day": Bob Woodward, *Wired: The Short Life and Fast Times of John Belushi* (New York: Simon & Schuster, 1984), 163.

"totally out of it": This scene draws from Tom Shales and James Andrew Miller, *Live from New York: An Uncensored History of "Saturday Night Live"* (New York: Little, Brown, 2002); Judith Belushi Pisano and Tanner Colby, *Belushi* (New York: Rugged Land, 2005); Woodward, *Wired*; and Doug Hill and Jeff Weingrad, *Saturday Night: A Backstage History of "Saturday Night Live"* (New York: Vintage Books, 1986).

"I wrote a lot of it": Dan Aykroyd, author interview.

"What's the most": Paul Shaffer with David Ritz, *We'll Be Here for the Rest of Our Lives: A Swingin' Show-Biz Saga* (New York: Flying Dolphin, 2009), 185.

"I really didn't know": Pisano and Colby, *Belushi*, 183.

"was really kind of": This scene, through Ned Tanen's *Close Encounters* quote, draws from Giulia D'Agnolo Vallan, *John Landis* (Milwaukie, OR: M Press, 2008), 73–74; and Sean Daniel, Thom Mount, and John Landis (July 22, 2022), author interviews.

"We didn't want": Charles Schreger, "The Pizza Comes Full Circle," *Los Angeles Times*, February 7, 1979.

"Sure": Landis, author interview, July 22, 2022.

"Be on your property": Bob Weiss, author interviews, July 7 and July 26, 2022.

"It was classic Aykroyd": Daniel, author interview, June 16, 2022.

"The characters were": Thom Mount, author interview, June 29, 2022.

"cast and crew": This scene draws from Woodward, *Wired*; Pisano and Colby, 167, *Belushi*; and R. J. Cutler (dir.), *Belushi*, Showtime Documentary Films, 2020.

"I think probably": Tom Shales, "Live and Passionate, It's 'Saturday Night,'" *Washington Post*, May 31, 1979.

"Whatever Belushi decides": George Maksian, "Busy Belushi May Drop 'Live,'" *New York Daily News*, June 13, 1979.

"You're not doing": This scene draws from Paul Shaffer (June 29, 2022), Bob Tischler (July 22, 2022), and Murphy Dunne (July 18, 2022), author interviews; Bernie Brillstein with David Rensin, *Where Did I Go Right? You're No One in Hollywood Unless Someone Wants You Dead* (New York: Little, Brown, 1999), 182–83; and from Hill and Weingrad, *Saturday Night*, 338–41.

Problem solved: Brillstein said Belushi called Murphy Dunne, but Dunne says Landis offered him the job.

"And we started": Stephen Katz, author interview, July 2 and August 13, 2022.

"hurt the comedy": This passage draws from Katz, George Folsey (June 30, 2022), and John Landis, author interviews.

"When we first laid": Eleanor Ringel, "Landis Isn't Singin' the Blues," *Atlanta Constitution*, July 3, 1980; this passage also draws from production documents provided by Stephen Katz.

"told us in no": David Sosna, author interview, July 24, 2022.

"in the neighborhood": "Landis to Direct 'Blues Brothers' for Universal," *Variety*, March 14, 1979.

"everybody was nervous": Weiss, author interview, July 26, 2022.

"because you can't": Landis (July 22, 2022) and Aykroyd, author interviews. Oddly enough, Illinois legislators hatched just such a scheme in the spring of 1979, shortly after Aykroyd completed his script. Critics pounced, and the measure died.

Chapter 19: The Mission from God

"recognize these veteran": Dan Aykroyd, author interview.

"And he was lovely": John Landis, author interview, July 22, 2022.

"You know: John Belushi": Mitchell Glazer and Timothy White, "John Belushi: Made in America," *Rolling Stone*, April 29, 1982.

"Danny's ideas": Landis, author interview, July 22, 2022.

"As you will read": John Landis, letter to Cab Calloway, June 8, 1979.

The timing seemed calculated: Chris Nashawaty, *Caddyshack: The Making of a Hollywood Cinderella Story* (New York: Flatiron Books, 2018), 127–28.

the contest would turn: Bob Woodward, *Wired: The Short Life and Fast Times of John Belushi* (New York: Simon & Schuster, 1984), 190.

"He's much more alive": Woodward, *Wired*, 170.

"There wasn't an official": Christopher Borrelli, "Remembering 'Blues Brothers' 30 years later," *Chicago Tribune*, June 16, 2010.

"I was given his": Bob Weiss, author interview, July 26, 2022.

"I thought he looked sick": This scene draws from Weiss, Landis, Sean Daniel, and Thom Mount, author interviews; Borrelli, "Remembering"; and Judith Belushi Pisano and Tanner Colby, *Belushi* (New York: Rugged Land, 2005), 183–84. Landis felt sure that he, not Belushi, had addressed the mayor, while Weiss believed he had done the talking. This account favors the mayor's own recollections.

"Mr. Belushi!": Woodward, *Wired*, 171.

"All he did is": Pisano and Colby, *Belushi*, 185.

"Don't give him": Woodward, *Wired*, 1; and Weiss, author interview, August 14, 2022.

On the night of July 12: This scene draws from Paul Dickson, *Bill Veeck: America's Greatest Maverick* (London: Walker Books, 2012).

"One of our intentions": Eleanor Ringel, "Landis Isn't Singin' the Blues," *Atlanta Constitution*, July 3, 1980.

"The trip was supposed": This scene draws from Pisano and Colby, *Belushi*, 184; Doug Hill and Jeff Weingrad, *Saturday Night: A Backstage History of "Saturday Night Live"* (New York: Vintage Books, 1986), 311–12; and Shuster, author interview.

Chapter 20: Sweet Home Chicago

"stabbings on consecutive": Sosna, author interview, July 24, 2022.

"Shut up and show": Sosna, author interview, July 24, 2022.

"control of the freeway": Sosna, author interview by email, February 18, 2023.

"The resulting traffic jam": This scene draws from Diane Amann, "Blues are all over, Brother," *Chicago Tribune*, July 23, 1979; and Bob Weidrich, "This scene was no ordinary stunt," *Chicago Tribune*, July 25, 1979.

"brought braille music": Bob Tischler, author interview, July 22, 2022.

"She was sitting": Lou Marini, author interview, July 8, 2022.

"It was like letting": This passage draws from John Landis, Tischler, Marini, and Michael Chinich (July 20, 2022), author interviews; and John Landis, "'Blues Brothers' Director John Landis Remembers Aretha Franklin," *Hollywood Reporter*, August 17, 2018.

"He had to be": Bob Weiss, author interview, July 26, 2022.

"They knew what we": Pisano and Colby, *Belushi*, 187.

"There were times": Pisano and Colby, *Belushi*, 185.

"It was glorious": Murphy Dunne, author interview, July 18, 2022.

"an impassable mass": Rick Kogan, "70,000 Open ChicagoFest," *Chicago Sun-Times*, August 4, 1979.

"There was a whole": Sosna, author interview, August 11, 2022.

"We didn't have": Stephen Katz, author interview by email, July 30, 2022.

"as we knew": Landis, author interview by email, May 22, 2023.

"And the boys": Katz, author interview, July 2, 2022.

Chapter 21: The Blues Bar

"if anyone fucks up": David Standish, "On the Set with the Blues Brothers," *Oui*, August 1980.

"There are shoots": Katherine Wooten, author interview.

"hit with such": Morris Lyda, author interview, August 26, 2022.

"They had shot": George Folsey, author interview, June 30, 2022.

"All of a sudden": Mark Hogan, author interview, June 27, 2022.

"You can't really tell": David Sosna, author interview, July 24, 2022.

"Playing ChicagoFest": This scene draws from Lynn Emmerman, "Blues Brothers take a dive for privacy's sake," *Chicago Tribune*, August 9, 1979.

"Drinks for everybody!": Judith Belushi Pisano and Tanner Colby, *Belushi* (New York: Rugged Land, 2005), 186.

"give them the scoop": Stephen Katz, author interview, July 2, 2022.

"Is this guy": Bob Weiss, author interview, August 14, 2022.

"Cocaine was a currency": Tarpley Hitt, "Dan Aykroyd on How Cocaine Fueled 'The Blues Brothers' and Aretha Franklin's Iconic Performance," *Daily Beast*, July 4, 2020.

"who was The Man": Malone, author interview, July 15, 2022; Sosna, author interview, July 24, 2022.

"He was like a kid": Don Novello, author interview, June 30, 2022.

"Jesus Christ, kid": Pisano and Colby, *Belushi*, 188.

"We hired hot": Mount, author interview, June 29, 2022.

"He sounds like": Lyda, author interview.

"What about Carrie?": John Landis, author interview, July 22, 2022.

"They're different": Bob Woodward, *Wired: The Short Life and Fast Times of John Belushi* (New York: Simon & Schuster, 1984), 18.

"some kid had got": Lyda, author interview.

"John, should you be": This passage draws from Pisano and Colby, *Belushi*, 189–90.

"spaced out": Katz, author interview, August 4, 2022.

"like Dante's Inferno": Landis, author interview by email, August 5, 2022; Sosna, author interview, July 24, 2022.

"What did those guys": Landis, author interview, February 28, 2023.

"paid big money": Dennis Wolff, author interview, August 5, 2022.

"bleached out": Katz, author interview by email, February 25, 2023.

"The warden's holding": William B. Kaplan, author interview, March 20, 2023.

Chapter 22: Get Off of That Picasso

"I want nothing more": Doug Hill and Jeff Weingrad, *Saturday Night: A Backstage History of "Saturday Night Live"* (New York: Vintage Books, 1986), 343. In an alternate telling, Michaels learned of Aykroyd's departure in July, before the *People* article appeared. Tom Shales and James Andrew Miller, *Live from New York: An Uncensored History of "Saturday Night Live"* (New York: Little, Brown, 2002), 169.

"nothing planned": George Maksian, "Curses! 'Live' May Lose Aykroyd," *New York Daily News*, August 31, 1979.

"the press won't be": Bob Woodward, *Wired: The Short Life and Fast Times of John Belushi* (New York: Simon & Schuster, 1984), 172.

"Not only did it go": Bob Weiss, author interview, July 7, 2022.

"I don't think": David Sosna, author interview by email, February 27, 2023.

"dinky little car": John Landis, author interview, February 28, 2023. Five years later, the *Kentucky Fried Movie* gang would execute the ultimate Pinto gag in their film *Top Secret!*, when a German military truck gently taps the back fender of a red Pinto, and it explodes.

"and he wanted": Landis, author interview, June 5, 2023; Andy Tarnoff, "Blues Bros. 'Illinois Nazi' Lives in Milwaukee, Is Pro Santa, Holds Black Belt," *OnMilwaukee*, February 16, 2018, https://onmilwaukee.com/articles/schuldt-blues-brothers.

"He hit the ramp": This passage draws from Chris Foran, "Our Back Pages: When Blues Brothers crashed Milwaukee," *Milwaukee Journal Sentinel*, August 23, 2016; and Weiss, author interview, July 7, 2022.

"The thing about miniatures": Weiss, author interview, July 7, 2022.

"That was the last": Sosna, author interview, June 21, 2022.

"didn't find it funny": Landis, author interview, July 22, 2022.

"I get the invariable": Weiss, author interview, March 22, 2023.

"I said, 'Fuck it'": Stephen Katz, author interview, July 2, 2022.

The Daley Plaza shoot: Some details in this passage are drawn from Dave Newbart, *The Blues Brothers* retrospective, *Chicago Sun-Times*, June 20, 2005, and Christopher Borrelli, "Remembering 'Blues Brothers' 30 years later," *Chicago Tribune*, June 16, 2010.

"Get off of that": Landis, author interview by email, February 7, 2023.

"is now expected": This passage draws from Marilyn Beck, "Brando's ex-wife reveals all in book," *News-Pilot* (San Pedro, CA), September 18, 1979; Todd McCarthy, "U.S. Pic Budgets into Megabuck Era, *Variety*, August 29, 1979; and Weiss, Landis, and George Folsey, author interviews. Memories differ on which news item caught the producer's eye, but the five-column *Variety* headline seems the likely candidate.

"It's too late": Print ad for *The Blues Brothers*, *Variety*, September 5, 1979.

"It was quite famous": Sean Daniel, author interview, June 30, 2022.

"We had always intended": This passage draws from Landis, author interview, February 28, 2023; and Chris Nashawaty, *Caddyshack: The Making of a Hollywood Cinderella Story* (New York: Flatiron Books, 2018), 105.

"I want to speak": Sosna, author interview, July 24, 2022.

"the teamsters": This passage draws from Sosna, author interview, June 21, 2022.

"going 110 mph": This scene draws from Sosna, Landis, and Katz, author interviews; and Eleanor Ringel, "Landis Isn't Singin' the Blues," *Atlanta Constitution*, July 3, 1980.

"Those were my trains": Sosna, author interview, June 21, 2022.

Chapter 23: The Pinto Drop

"They had to contact": David Sosna, author interview, June 21, 2022.

"Production commenced on September 10": David Fusaro, "'Blues Brothers' – on location in Harvey," *Harvey Star Tribune*, September 23, 1979.

"It was a cold night": This passage draws from Dan Aykroyd, interview by Greg Hill, *The Greg Hill Show*, podcast, November 8, 2019, https://omny.fm/shows/the-greg-hill-show/ghs-guest-dan-aykroyd-joins-the-show-discussing-hi; Darren Weale, "The Story Of The Blues Brothers," *Louder Sound*, August 13, 2016; Jason Ingolfsland, "That Time John Belushi Randomly Disappeared From The Blues Brothers Set," *CinemaBlend*, November 15, 2020; and Morris Lyda, author interview.

The Bluesmobile crashed in: John Landis said the woman in the red top was "where she was supposed to be." David Sosna wasn't so sure: "Another six inches and she would've been injured." Landis, author interview, June 7, 2023; Sosna, author interview, June 12, 2023.

"like a mall was lit": Katz, author interview, July 2, 2022.

"I get to the meeting": Weiss, author interview, July 26, 2022. Some details drawn from Dave Newbart, *The Blues Brothers* retrospective, *Chicago Sun-Times*, June 20, 2005.

"And he and I": Landis, author interview, July 22, 2022.

"You couldn't ask Landis": Weiss, author interview, July 26, 2022.

"a big fucking deal": Sosna, author interview, July 24, 2022.

"an 18-inch-high": This passage draws from Abe Peck, "Movies," *Chicago Sun-Times*, June 8, 1980; and Jack Zink, "Blues Brothers propels Landis to big leagues," *Fort Lauderdale News*, June 29, 1980.

"pope-a-mania": Weiss, author interview, July 7, 2022.

"You didn't want": Sean Daniel, author interview, June 30, 2022.

"I don't think": Weiss, author interview, July 7, 2022.

"we needed a dance": Dan Aykroyd, author interview.

"What's curious about this": David Standish, "On the Set with the Blues Brothers," *Oui*, August 1980. This scene also draws from Landis and Katherine Wooten, author interviews.

"We have to go back": Sosna, author interview, June 21, 2022.

"He was a very": Folsey, author interview, June 30, 2022.

William B. Kaplan, author interview, March 18, 2023: "Looking for Belushi," Random Notes, *Rolling Stone*, December 13, 1979.

"They just drove down": Sosna, author interview, June 21, 2022, and February 23, 2023. Further details drawn from Dave Newbart, *The Blues Brothers* retrospective, *Chicago Sun-Times*, June 20, 2005.

"We left Chicago late": Lyda, author interview; Landis, author interview, February 3, 2021; Bob Woodward, *Wired: The Short Life and Fast Times of John Belushi* (New York: Simon & Schuster, 1984), 19–22.

"Are we clear": Sosna, author interview, August 11, 2022.

"Both times": Landis, author interview, July 22, 2022.

Chapter 24: Have You Seen the Light?

"That day": Stephen Katz, author interview, July 2, 2022.

"They expected me": This scene draws from David Sosna (July 24, 2022), Dan Aykroyd, Bob Tischler (July 22, 2022), and Katz (July 2, 2022), author interviews.

"makes a racial point": R. J. Smith, *The One: The Life and Music of James Brown* (New York: Gotham, 2012), 328.

"We were told": Sosna, author interview, June 21, 2022.

"She wasn't sure": David Ritz, *Respect: The Life of Aretha Franklin* (New York: Little, Brown, 2014), 320–21.

"I didn't know": Kevin Polowy, "'The Blues Brothers' at 40," *Yahoo Entertainment*, June 25, 2020.

"The lunch counter": Lou Marini, author interview, July 8, 2022; John Landis, author interview, June 10, 2023.

"But it didn't work": William B. Kaplan, author interview, March 18, 2023.

"But she pulled through": John Landis, "'Blues Brothers' Director John Landis Remembers Aretha Franklin," *Hollywood Reporter*, August 17, 2018.

"I like you": Sosna, author interview, June 21, 2022.

John cleaned up: Bob Woodward, *Wired: The Short Life and Fast Times of John Belushi* (New York: Simon & Schuster, 1984), 22–23.

"a thousand-foot": Author interview on background, 2023. A second crew member confirmed the film-can scheme and said the contents were probably earmarked for several customers, not Belushi alone. Author interview on background, June 2023.

"You can't tell": This scene draws from John Landis, author interview, June 10, 2023; Pisano and Colby, *Belushi*, 198; and David Sosna, author interview, February 12, 2023.

"The picture is only": Marilyn Beck, "'Blues' May Sing a Song of Big Profits," *News-Pilot* (San Pedro, CA), November 10, 1979.

"I'm uncomfortable with": George Folsey, author interview, June 30, 2022.

"We stayed there": Malone, author interview, August 16, 2022.

"I've done this job": Sosna, author interview by email, February 11, 2023.

"a departure from": Katz, author interview, August 13, 2022; Sosna, interview by email, February 12, 2023.

"We'd go up": This passage draws from Steve Cropper, author interview; and Judith Belushi Pisano and Tanner Colby, *Belushi* (New York: Rugged Land, 2005), 196.

"I remember him laughing": This scene draws from Dunne, Marini, Sosna, Katz, and Malone, author interviews.

"the studio didn't": Folsey, author interview, July 4, 2022.

Chapter 25: It's Never Too Late to Mend

"You'd better get": This scene draws from Sean Daniel (July 25, 2022) and Bob Weiss (August 14, 2022), author interviews; Judith Belushi Pisano and Tanner Colby, *Belushi* (New York: Rugged Land, 2005), 197; and Ned Zeman, "Soul Men: The Making of *The Blues Brothers*," *Vanity Fair*, January 2013.

"I had drawings": Stephen Katz, author interview, July 2, 2022.

"We wanted": This scene draws from Katz, Steve Cropper, Morris Lyda, David Sosna, John Landis, and Murphy Dunne, author interviews; and David Standish, "On the Set with the Blues Brothers," *Oui*, August 1980. Sosna clearly recalled a last-minute radio appeal to fill theater seats; Daniel and Landis said the contest would have been planned in advance. Daniel and Landis also rejected the *Oui* reporter's account of the crew recruiting extras from an unemployment office.

"the most hostile": This scene draws from Bob Woodward, *Wired: The Short Life and Fast Times of John Belushi* (New York: Simon & Schuster, 1984), 173–74; Pisano and Colby, *Belushi*, 191; and David Ansen, "Spielberg's Misguided Missile," *Newsweek*, December 17, 1979.

"Steven was quite": This scene draws from Pisano and Colby, *Belushi*, 192; and "Random Notes," *Rolling Stone*, March 20, 1980.

"anything that will": Judith Belushi Pisano and Tanner Colby, *Belushi* (New York: Rugged Land, 2005), 196.

"throwing bottles": Dunne, author interview, July 18, 2022; Lou Marini, author interview, July 8, 2022.

"I hadn't slept": William B. Kaplan, author interview, March 20, 2023; David Sosna, author interview, June 21, 2022.

"another *Heaven's Gate*": Thom Mount, author interview, June 29, 2022.

"staggeringly over budget": This passage draws from Ellen Farley, "Comic Duo Gets High on Fame," *Los Angeles Times*, January 6, 1980; and Bill Royce, "Hollywood's recent disaster epics have been casualties," *Baltimore Evening Sun*, January 18, 1980.

"We needed, I think": Weiss, author interview, July 7, 2022.

"Close-ups?": Katz, author interview, August 4, 2022.

Chapter 26: The Black Tower

"you've got to stop": Bob Woodward, *Wired: The Short Life and Fast Times of John Belushi* (New York: Simon & Schuster, 1984), 24–25.

A rare image: This passage draws from Alan D. Mutter, "Blues pix put Byrne photog out of picture," *Chicago Sun-Times*, February 9, 1980; and "Mayor Takes Negative View of Photo," *Los Angeles Times*, February 10, 1980.

"Patient very hostile": Woodward, *Wired*, 25.

"She's waiting": This scene, through Nena's funeral, draws from Judith Belushi Pisano and Tanner Colby, *Belushi* (New York: Rugged Land, 2005), 198–99.

"a little under": This passage draws from George Folsey (August 27, 2022) and John Landis (August 30, 2022), author interviews.

"the early verdict": Bill Royce, "Sneak Preview: 3 Films Pass First Hurdle," *Austin American-Statesman*, May 18, 1980; Bob Weiss, author interview, March 22, 2023.

"Too many car crashes": Abe Peck, "The Blues Brothers Ask the $32 Million Question," *Rolling Stone*, August 7, 1980.

"We called it": Landis, author interview, August 30, 2022.

Weiss, author interviews: Aykroyd quote comes from Peck, "The Blues Brothers Ask."

"We had another preview": Landis, David Sosna, Folsey, Daniel, Aykroyd, and Weiss, author interviews. The director recalled that the second Picwood screening was the version later released on Blu-ray with a 2:28 running time, incorporating most of the footage from that screening, but not all of it

"as recently as March": "U's 'Blues Bros.' Hits $27,500,500; Cancel Chi Hoopla," *Variety*, May 28, 1980.

"a big-ass show": Random Notes, *Rolling Stone*, June 12, 1980.

"You're not going to": This scene draws from Smokey Wendell, author interview, September 30, 2022; Woodward, *Wired*, 28–31; and Pisano and Colby, *Belushi*, 202–3.

"how to use": Morris Lyda, author interview.

Chapter 27: A $30-Million Wreck

"stomping their feet": Clarke Taylor, "Friday Night Live at 'Blues' Press Junket," *Los Angeles Times*, June 22, 1980.

"It happened months ago": This scene draws from John Landis, author interview, July 22, 2022; and Christopher Borrelli, "Remembering 'Blues Brothers' 30 years later," *Chicago Tribune,* June 16, 2010.

"Mr. Belushi": Critical appraisals draw from reviews in the *New York Times, Chicago Tribune, Chicago Sun-Times,* and *Los Angeles Times* of June 20, 1980; *Washington Post* of June 21; *Newsweek* and *New York* of June 30; and *Time* of July 7.

"Take your pick": Had the film come out a few years later, Siskel and Ebert might have celebrated it together in their dueling-critics television show *At the Movies,* which would debut in 1982.

"he was there 100 percent": Kevin Polowy, "'The Blues Brothers' at 40," *Yahoo Entertainment,* June 25, 2020.

"Dear John": Stephen Katz, letter to John Landis, June 24, 1980.

"If the second weekend": Eleanor Ringel, "Landis Isn't Singin' the Blues," *Atlanta Constitution,* July 3, 1980.

"If you're wired": Smokey Wendell, author interview, September 30, 2022.

"Belushi's fans": Gene Siskel, "The Blues Brothers," *Chicago Tribune,* June 29, 1980.

"Belushi's gravel-voiced": Rick Kogan, "Belushi, Aykroyd Bring Bluesy Fun to Poplar Creek," *Chicago Sun-Times,* June 30, 1980.

"There seems to be": John Rockwell, "Soul: The Blues Brothers," *New York Times,* July 3, 1980.

"From the moment": Mike Joyce, "In Concert," *Washington Post,* July 4, 1980.

"I'm at the home": Wendell, author interview, September 30, 2022.

"As far as you could": Lou Marini, author interview, August 24, 2022.

"Give me some": This scene draws from Bob Woodward, *Wired: The Short Life and Fast Times of John Belushi* (New York: Simon & Schuster, 1984), 184; and Wendell, author interview.

Chapter 28: The 2,000 Pound Bee

"Jesus, they look": Lou Marini, author interview, August 24, 2022.

"There were a few": Comments from Judy Belushi and Smokey Wendell in this passage draw from Judith Belushi Pisano and Tanner Colby, *Belushi* (New York: Rugged Land, 2005), 208.

"Belushi's not bad": Robert Hilburn, "The Blues Brothers Get Goofy," *Los Angeles Times,* July 28, 1980.

"C'mon": This passage draws from Bob Woodward, *Wired: The Short Life and Fast Times of John Belushi* (New York: Simon & Schuster, 1984), 189; and Smokey Wendell, author interview.

"$34,656,504": *The Blues Brothers,* print ad, *Variety,* July 30, 1980.

"Danny wants to": Marilyn Beck, "A 'Blues Brothers' sequel?," *Akron (OH) Beacon Journal,* July 29, 1980.

"I just feel terrible": Woodward, *Wired,* 190–91; and Pisano and Colby, *Belushi,* 213; Rick Meyerowitz, author interview by email, May 2, 2023.

"We'd run a mile": This passage draws from Bill Wallace, author interview, September 15, 2022; and Pisano and Colby, *Belushi,* 218.

"I lost John": Pisano and Colby, *Belushi,* 218.

"I can't do it": Woodward, *Wired,* 193.

"Every night": This scene draws from Wallace and Wendell, author interviews; Pisano and Colby, *Belushi,* 220–24; and Woodward, *Wired,* 196.

"little bitty underwear": This scene draws from Pisano and Colby, *Belushi,* 227.

"and tossed them": Pisano and Colby, *Belushi,* 228.

"As far as commercial": Mitchell Glazer and Timothy White, "John Belushi: Made in America," *Rolling Stone,* April 29, 1982.

"Using black people": Dave Marsh, "The Blues Brothers Original Soundtrack," review, *Rolling Stone,* September 4, 1980.

"The film was": David Sheff, "Comedy's Great White Hopes," *People,* August 4, 1980.

"There's a moment": Pisano and Colby, *Belushi,* 242.

"The effect on Cab's": Alyn Shipton, *Hi-De-Ho: The Life of Cab Calloway* (Oxford: Oxford University Press, 2010), 225.

"What are you talking": Pisano and Colby, *Belushi,* 229; Wendell, author interview.

"You should play": Woodward, *Wired,* 208. Other sources said John and Dan thought of flipping roles.

The producer wondered: Woodward, *Wired,* 213–14.

The arguments started: This passage draws from Woodward, *Wired*; Pisano and Colby, *Belushi*; and Wallace, author interview.

"John's getting back": Woodward, *Wired,* 219.

"OK, you motherfucker": Pisano and Colby, *Belushi,* 236. This scene, through the end of filming, draws from Pisano and Colby, *Belushi*; R. J. Cutler (dir.), *Belushi,* Showtime Documentary Films, 2020; and Woodward, *Wired*.

"Come do this movie.": Woodward, *Wired,* 220.

"He refused to come": Woodward, *Wired,* 221.

"The only thing": Pisano and Colby, *Belushi,* 237–38.

The Belushis retreated: Woodward, *Wired,* 227–28.

"Every single day": Pisano and Colby, *Belushi,* 240.

"Wow!": Woodward, *Wired,* 230–31.

John arrived: Woodward, *Wired,* 237–38.

The mere presence: This scene draws from Woodward, *Wired,* 238–39; and Pisano and Colby, *Belushi,* 242.

"Belushi's a buffoon": This scene draws from Aaron Gold, "Tower Ticker," *Chicago Tribune,* September 18, 1981; Donna McCrohan, *The Second City: A Backstage History of Comedy's Hottest Troupe* (New York: Perigee Books, 1987), 110; and Lewis Grossberger, "Belushi," *Rolling Stone,* January 21, 1982.

"adorable": Gene Siskel, "'Divide' Conquers with Belushi, Charm," *Chicago Tribune,* September 18, 1981.

"it was a rejection": Pisano and Colby, *Belushi,* 241.

One autumn weekend: Woodward, *Wired,* 268–69; Cutler, *Belushi*.

"John gave me": Cutler, *Belushi*.

"He was in terrible": Pisano and Colby, *Belushi,* 242.

Dick Ebersol had told: Tom Shales and James Andrew Miller, *Live from New York: An Uncensored History of "Saturday Night Live"* (New York: Little, Brown, 2002), 243–44.

"By this time": "Neighbors," *Variety,* December 16, 1981.

Chapter 29: A Viking Funeral

"What do you think": This passage draws from Bob Woodward, *Wired: The Short Life and Fast Times of John Belushi* (New York: Simon & Schuster, 1984), 272–73; and Judith Belushi Pisano and Tanner Colby, *Belushi* (New York: Rugged Land, 2005), 248–49.

"Everyone involved": Pisano and Colby, *Belushi*, 249.

That night: Woodward, *Wired*, 289–90. The accounting of Belushi's expenses also draws from *Wired*.

"I thought you said": Author interview on background, 2022.

"We're having a good": Michael Blowen, "Meet the Me Generation's Laurel and Hardy," *Boston Globe*, January 7, 1982.

"I knew if I went": Pisano and Colby, *Belushi*, 249.

"Every couple of hours": Bill Wallace, author interview.

"It's the best show": Joe Baltake, "Aykroyd's Appeal Is Element of Surprise," *Cincinnati Enquirer*, January 5, 1982.

"Why don't you show": Dave Thomas, author interview by email, September 14, 2022; Pisano and Colby, *Belushi*, 250.

"You don't understand": Pisano and Colby, *Belushi,* 251.

"If I don't": Judy Jacklin Belushi, *Samurai Widow* (New York: Carroll & Graf, 1990), 50–52.

"He was going on": Pisano and Colby, *Belushi*, 252.

"Chrissie Hynde": Woodward, *Wired*, 312.

"What's the matter": Pisano and Colby, *Belushi*, 252.

"Where were you?": Don Novello, author interview, September 16, 2022.

"We had, like": Novello, author interview, September 16, 2022; Bernie Brillstein with David Rensin, *Where Did I Go Right? You're No One in Hollywood Unless Someone Wants You Dead* (New York: Little, Brown, 1999), 204.

"basically, a car chase": Pisano and Colby, *Belushi*, 254.

"My wife wants": Woodward, *Wired*, 335–36.

"put a huge pile": This scene draws from Woodward, *Wired*, 342; and Pisano and Colby, *Belushi*, 254–55.

"What? What is it?": Belushi, *Samurai Widow*, 16; Gene Siskel, "Dan Aykroyd: 'We Knew It Wouldn't Last,'" *Chicago Tribune*, July 29, 1982.

"I wanted John": Pisano and Colby, *Belushi*, 255.

"The script was horrible": Michael Eisner, author interview, October 11, 2022.

"*Joy of Sex* wasn't": Pisano and Colby, *Belushi*, 256; Novello, author interview.

"Lined up in front": This scene draws from Eisner, author interview; and Woodward, *Wired*, 369–71.

"You wouldn't believe": Pisano and Colby, *Belushi*, 256–57.

"I flew out": Wallace, author interview.

"He was fucked up": This scene draws from Brillstein, *Where Did I Go Right?*; Woodward, *Wired*; Pisano and Colby, *Belushi*; and Eisner, author interview. Brillstein recalled Michael Eisner joining the meeting; Eisner did not.

"I can go tonight": Smokey Wendell, author interview.

"I may have to": Woodward, *Wired*, 387–88.

"in happier times": Woodward, *Wired*, 393–94.

"Are you OK?": This scene draws from Woodward, *Wired*, 398–401.

"are you all right?": Woodward, *Wired*, 401.

"John, time to get up": This scene draws from Pisano and Colby, *Belushi*, 259–61; Brillstein, *Where Did I Go Right?*, 206–10; and Wallace, author interview.

"I knew if I stopped": This scene, and Aykroyd's meeting with Judy Belushi, draws from Pisano and Colby, *Belushi*, 261; and Belushi, *Samurai Widow*, 4–5.

"John who?": The scenes at Universal and at Cathy Smith's arrest draw from John Landis, author interview, June 11, 2023; Woodward, *Wired*, 408; and Pisano and Colby, *Belushi*, 261.

Obituary writers: Obituary references draw from the *Washington Post* and *New York Times* of March 6, 1982; and Newsweek of March 15, 1982.

"The scene was not": Brillstein, *Where Did I Go Right?*, 209.

"When I die": Belushi, *Samurai Widow*, 11–12.

"I want to say": Belushi, *Samurai Widow*, 26.

"an odd mix": The funeral scene draws from Pisano and Colby, *Belushi*; Belushi, *Samurai Widow*; Larry Stammer and Boris Yaro, "Signs of Drug Use on Belushi Body Reported," *Los Angeles Times*, March 10, 1982; and Peter Carlson, "John Belushi, 1949–1982," *Newsweek*, March 22, 1982.

"This is a beautiful": The memorial scene draws from Belushi, *Samurai Widow*, 53–59; and Peter W. Kaplan, "Belushi, Exit Laughing," *Washington Post*, March 12, 1982.

"What do you want": Novello, author interview.

Epilogue

"The theory was": Roger Ebert, "Belushi: The Curtain Fell a Year Ago," *Philadelphia Daily News*, March 5, 1983.

"Have you heard": Gene Siskel, "Dan Aykroyd: 'We Knew It Wouldn't Last,'" *Chicago Tribune*, July 29, 1982.

"I think they hoped": Bob Woodward, author interview.

"every time we opened": David Sheff, "Playboy Interview: Dan Aykroyd," *Playboy*, August 1993.

"There was not": Bob Weiss, author interview, April 4, 2023.

"*Blues Brothers 2000*": James Berardinelli, "Blues Brothers 2000, The," *ReelViews*, blog post, n.d., https://www.reelviews.net/reelviews/blues-brothers-2000 -the.

"It happens": Fionnuala Halligan, author interview by email, March 15, 2023.

"I knew it"; "obviously had": David Ansen, author interview by email, March 1, 2023; Janet Maslin, author interview by email, March 16 and 17, 2023.

Lorne Michaels left: That is not to discount the contributions of Eddie Murphy, now regarded as perhaps the greatest *SNL* performer of them all, though hampered by uneven casts and material.

"Chicago is like": Leonard Pierce, "*The Blues Brothers* Is a Wild Ride through 1970s Chicago," *Jacobin*, March 3, 2023, https://jacobin.com/2023/03 /the-blues-brothers-1970s-chicago-working-class-black-musicians.

cinematic showcase: "100 Greatest Artists," *Rolling Stone*, December 3, 2010, https://www.rollingstone.com/music/music-lists/100-greatest -artists-147446/; "100 Greatest Singers of All Time (2008)," *Rolling Stone*,

November 27, 2008, https://www.rollingstone.com/music/music-lists/100
-greatest-singers-of-all-time-147019/.

"It was about twenty": John Landis, author interview, August 30, 2022.

"Whoever John was": This scene draws from William Wan, "John Belushi Gets a
Star on Walk of Fame," *Los Angeles Times*, April 2, 2004; and Chris Jones, "With
Hollywood star, memories of Belushi will twinkle again," *Chicago Tribune*, April
2, 2004.

"embraced Chicago": Dave Newbart, "They 'Were on a Mission from God,'" *Chicago
Sun-Times*, June 20, 2005.

"Catholic classic": Eric J. Lyman, "Vatican Endorses 'The Blues Brothers,'" *Reuters*,
June 17, 2010.

"greatest farce": Ned Zeman, "Soul Men: The Making of *The Blues Brothers*," *Vanity
Fair*, January 2013.

"Of the original greats": Rob Sheffield, "'Saturday Night Live': 145 Cast Members
Ranked," *Rolling Stone*, February 11, 2015, https://www.rollingstone.com
/tv-movies/tv-movie-lists/saturday-night-live-all-145-cast-members-ranked
-146340.

Index

ABC-Paramount label, 208
acid (drug), 40, 43, 234
acoustic country blues, 211
"Adopt Belushi for Christmas Contest" sketch, 131
Airplane! (movie), 299, 300
Airport parody, 145
Alda, Alan, 22
Alexander, Andrew, 76, 81
All in the Family (TV show), 105
All-Star Dead Band (parody), 52
All You Need Is Cash (mockumentary), 237
Allen, Steve, 137
American Hot Wax (movie), 184
An American Werewolf in London (movie), 145,
    331–332
angel dust (drug), 41–42
Animal House (movie)
    cast for, 145–148, 152
    concept of, 152
    cost of, 183
    Delta House, 146–147, 152
    earnings, 183, 184, 186
    film shoot, 151–156, 158
    origin of, 139, 141
    premiere, 171
    reviews, 171–172
Anka, Paul, 98
Anne of the Thousand Days (drama), 20
Ansen, David, 335
Apocalypse Now (movie), 257
Apted, Michael, 301
Arista Records, 332
Arkin, Alan, 22
Arledge, Roone, 98, 100
Asner, Ed, 22
Atlantic Records, 167, 169, 176, 207, 208
Australia, *Blues Brothers* movie in, 337
Avildsen, John, 306–308, 310
Aykroyd, Dan: personal
    acting classes, 65
    adolescence, 65–71, 80
    after John's death, 331
    blues music, 70–72, 83, 84, 311
    Bromfield, Valri, 70, 72, 73
    Carleton University, 74, 77
    childhood, 63–65

death of John, 325–326, 328, 329
drugs, 75, 88
family of origin, 63
father, 64, 65
harmonica, 71, 72, 114, 297
high school, 65–69, 70, 72
impressionist in childhood, 63–65, 67, 70
marriage to Donna Dixon, 331
music in teen years, 70–72
personality, 66, 74
as prankster, 74
talked down partygoer locked in bathroom,
    135–136
teen rebellion, 68–69
Tourette syndrome, 64, 70
Aykroyd, Dan: professional
    advertising spot writing and acting, 94–95
    after John's death, 331–332, 335–336
    Animal House, 147
    Blues Bar, 187
    Blues Brothers movie costar, 203
    Blues Brothers movie script, 194–195, 196,
        198–199, 200, 205, 212
    Bromfield and, 73–74, 76, 77
    as collaborator with John, 136–137, 296, 306
    Doctor Detroit, 331
    early career, 74–83
    505 Club, 79, 88, 186
    friendship with John, 85–87, 99, 124–125, 138,
        163, 164, 238, 271, 309
    Ghostbusters, 332, 336
    Hard Rock Cafe and restaurant businesses,
        333
    House of Blues Radio Hour, 334
    meeting Belushi, 84–85
    music, 70–71
    performance for Beatles, 123–124
    road trips with John, 111–112, 127–128
    Saturday Night, 97, 98, 99, 103, 104, 107, 108,
        134–139, 150–151
    Saturday Night audition, 99–100
    at *Saturday Night Live*, 158–164
    at Second City, 61–62, 78, 81, 94, 98–99
    Spies Like Us, 333
    Trading Places, 331, 332
    writing partnership with John, 198

Aykroyd, Lorraine (mother), 63, 65
Aykroyd, Peter (brother), 63, 79
Aykroyd, Samuel Augustus (great-grandfather), 63
Aykroyd, Samuel Cuthbert Peter Hugh "Pete"
    (father), 63, 65, 68

"'B' Movie Box Car Blues" (song), 189
"Bad Boy" (song), 8
"Bad Girls" (song), 216
Barnes, Howard, 9
Baxter, Father Paul, 67, 263
Beach Boys special, 123, 124
Beard, Henry, 46, 52
Beatles, *Saturday Night* and, 121
Beatts, Anne, 50, 60, 93–94, 101, 117, 136, 185
Beck, Marilyn, 268, 301
"Bee Hospital" sketch, 104, 105, 106
Belushi, Adam (father), 1, 4, 5, 6, 7, 10, 17, 24,
    25–26, 181, 285, 314
Belushi, Agnes (mother), 2, 5–10, 26, 36, 181, 285,
    314, 327
Belushi, Anastassios (grandfather), 1, 2
Belushi, Jim (brother), 2, 4, 14, 25–26, 37, 55,
    284, 285, 328, 337
Belushi, John: personal
    birth, 2
    burial, 326
    childhood, 2–7
    college years, 21–24, 25, 26, 28, 29
    craving female attention, 39
    death, 325
    debate and, 13, 15
    drugs and alcohol, 15, 18–19, 20, 23, 27, 28,
        40–41, 43, 48, 54, 118, 123–124, 127–129,
        133, 134–136, 137–138, 149, 154, 165, 168,
        169, 174, 178, 189, 193, 196, 197, 213, 216,
        231, 232–233, 237–238, 252–253, 260–262,
        267, 271, 274, 277, 283–284, 285, 289–290,
        296, 297–298, 300, 302, 307, 308, 309, 310,
        311–312, 316–324
    ethnic stigma and, 6
    expenses while successful, 314
    fatal drug overdose, 324–325
    fires in bed from cigarettes, 128
    first drug overdose, 261, 262
    funeral, 326–329
    health, 197, 201, 231, 232, 250, 262, 283, 285,
        301–302, 310, 320
    high school, 7–15, 18
    impressionist in childhood, 5, 6
    knee injury, 274
    legacy, 326
    marriage to Judy, 132
    military service, 28
    moves out of family home, 25
    obituary, 326
    overweight, 301–302
    parents, perspective on, 26
        personality, 10, 50
        schooling, 4
        theater and, 13, 15, 18–19
        thirtieth birthday, 196, 197
        tombstone, 329
        wife. *See* Belushi, Judy; Jacklin, Judy
        Woodward biography of, 332
Belushi, John: professional
    Animal House, 147, 148, 153–154
    bees and, 104, 105, 106, 109, 113, 114, 125, 309
    Blues Bar, 187
    Chevy Chase and, 109, 111, 125, 127
    as collaborator with Dan, 136–137, 296, 306
    Continental Divide, 301–303, 310, 311, 313
    desire to act, 21
    drag characters, 187, 192
    at Ebersol home, 128
    friendship with Dan, 85–87, 99, 124–125, 138,
        163, 164, 238, 271, 309
    Goin' South, 149, 150, 151
    impressions, 19
    injured in *Saturday Night* college show,
        135–136
    Joe Cocker impression, 27, 35, 45, 48, 50, 52,
        106, 111, 113–114, 123, 126, 158
    Joy of Sex, 321
    knee injury, 274–276
    legacy, 326
    Lemmings, 47–57
    love scene in *Continental Divide*, 303
    meeting Aykroyd, 84–85
    name change, 34
    National Lampoon Radio Hour, 58–61, 78, 83,
        85, 118
    National Lampoon stage show, 87–88, 89, 109
    Neighbors, 306–308, 310, 311, 312
    1941 (movie), 182, 186, 192–193, 257, 277–278
    Noble Rot (movie idea), 317, 318, 321, 322
    obituary, 326
    performance for Beatles, 123–124
    public memorial, 328
    Ravins band, 8, 9, 85, 158, 314, 316
    road trips with Dan, 111–112, 127–128
    at *Saturday Night*, 98, 101–131, 150–151
    Saturday Night audition, 95–96, 97
    Saturday Night contract, 101, 102
    at *Saturday Night Live*, 150–151, 153, 158–164,
        197–198
    SCTV sketches, 316
    Second City, 33–45, 118
    Second City appearance as alumnus, 310
    Second City Toronto touring company, 61–62
    star on Hollywood Walk of Fame, 337
    "Sweet Deception" (comedy), 313–316
    in Toronto, 84
    TV, opinion of, 95, 96
    West Compass Players, 26, 27, 29–30, 33, 34
    writing partnership with Dan, 198

Belushi, Judy (wife)
  John and drugs, 134, 149, 169, 213, 216, 233,
    261, 315, 317–324
  John's death, 325–326
  John's star on Hollywood Walk of Fame, 337
  life with John, 202, 218, 238, 267, 285, 297–
    298, 299, 301, 304, 308–309, 310, 311, 315
  memoir Samurai Widow, 333
  role in Blues Brothers movie, 269
  See also Jacklin, Judy
Belushi, Marian (sister), 2, 4, 7
Belushi, Pete (uncle), 2, 7
Belushi, Vasilo "Nena" (grandmother), 2, 5, 8, 14,
    284–286
Belushi bottle, 168
Berardinelli, James, 334
Bergen, Candice, 107, 108, 112, 129–131, 267
Bernstein, Elmer, 171
Beshekas, Steve, 26, 34, 223, 310
Bible skit, 37, 78
Billy Goat Tavern (Chicago), 161
Bixby, Bill, 142
Black Top Vamps (group), 74
Blasucci, Dick, 8, 314
Blasucci, Michael, 8, 9
blind detective skit, 60
blues (music), 70, 83, 84, 165, 166
Blues Bar, 187, 223, 230, 236, 303, 310, 319, 320
Blues Brothers 2000 (movie), 334
Blues Brothers albums, 170, 188, 190–191, 300
Blues Brothers band
  about, xii–xiii, 85, 114, 158, 164, 165–167,
    173–175, 202
  business office, 190
  Chicago tour, 296–297
  debut, 114, 160
  Jake and Elwood Blues, xi, 160, 167, 175, 179
  Los Angeles shows, 178–182, 188, 203, 300
  New York tour, 297
  reunion after John's death, 333
  reviews, 296, 297
  San Francisco show, 195–196
  on Saturday Night Live, 188–189
  tours, 297–298, 299
  Universal Amphitheatre performance, 177,
    178–182, 203, 300
Blues Brothers Con, 339
Blues Brothers movie, 207–235
  about, 175, 180, 191
  after John's death, 334–336, 337, 338–339
  Australian showings, 337
  box office receipts, 298
  budget, 221, 225, 254, 256, 257, 258, 286,
    292–293
  Chicago premiere, 293
  cost of, 221, 251, 288
  cuts to please critics and studio, 287–288
  director, 199, 293

"Disco Sucks" slogan, 217
Dixie Square mall, 220–221, 252–254
drugs and, 231–232, 234, 271, 276
early versions of movie from editing stage, 337
earnings, 296, 298, 299, 300, 339
filming crew, 203
follow-up film, 334
immortality, 336, 337
location scouts, 220–221
Los Angeles shoot, 263–273, 274–276,
    278–280, 295
Milwaukee shoot, 238–240
movie launch, 288–289
Nazis in, 246–247, 255
papal visit to Chicago and, 256
permission to shoot in Chicago, 213–214, 254
Pinto, 239, 240–241, 255–256
plot, 195, 200, 205–206, 239, 282
premiere, 284, 286, 293
preview in New York, 292
producer, 199
production details, 203–205, 275
racism and, 287, 294, 304
recent accolades, 337–339
recent overseas showing, 339
recent rehabilitation, 334–336
reviews, 292, 293–294
sadistic nun sketch, 67
schedule, 268, 275
script, 194–195, 196, 198–199, 200, 205, 212,
    268
shooting the film, 213–215, 219–235, 238–250,
    251–262, 263–281
star singers in, 207–212
working title "Joliet Jake," 196
Bluesmobile, 221, 225, 227, 239, 241, 253, 270,
    272, 279, 280
Bob's Country Bunker sketch, 279, 280, 288, 295
Boggs, Bill, 137–138
"Boogie Chillen'" (song), 211
"Boom Boom" (song), 227, 288, 339
Bored of the Rings (parody), 46
bouillabaisse sketch, 120
Boyd, William Beaty, 152
Brando, Marlon
  Belushi impression, 36, 44, 48, 112
  group therapy session sketch, 112–113
Brenner, David, 137
Brezhnev, Leonid, Aykroyd impersonation, 136
"Brian's Nightmare" sketch, 124
Briefcase Full of Blues (album), 188, 189, 196
Brillstein, Bernie, 102, 123, 148, 169, 170, 171,
    175, 181, 182, 186, 202, 203, 231, 238, 244,
    283, 289, 301, 302, 303, 307, 313, 319,
    322–323, 325, 327, 328
Britton, Layne "Shotgun," 232
Bromfield, Valri, 70, 72, 73, 78, 79, 81, 92, 94, 101
brothel scene, Blues Brothers movie, 268

Brown, Blair, 301–303
Brown, David, 306
Brown, James, 144, 209–210, 211, 217, 220, 244, 264, 267, 304, 334, 336
Browne, Jackson, 180, 259
Buckley, William F., Flaherty's impression, 36
Bullitt (film), 206
Burnett, Carol, sketches about, 92
Burton, Richard, 144
Butterfield, Paul, 70, 160
Byrne, Jane, 213, 224, 230, 248, 254, 293

Caddyshack (comedy farce), 212, 213, 237, 300, 301, 332, 338
Caesar, Sid, 93
Calloway, Cab, 166, 210, 211, 212, 217, 244, 272, 275, 276, 294, 305, 337
Camp Concentration sketch, 11, 12
The Canadian Show 1 or, Upper U.S.A. (revue), 61
Candy, John, 61, 81, 82, 94, 98, 193, 223, 304, 338
cannabis. *See* marijuana
Cannibal Girls (comedy), 89, 141
capital punishment skit, 60–61, 89
Capote, Truman, Belushi impression, 36, 48
Carlin, George, 91, 100, 103, 105, 331
Carlson, Mark, 11–12
The Carol Burnett Show (TV show), 95
Caroli, Vic, 18, 19, 20–21
Carson, Johnny, 90
Carter, Jimmy, Aykroyd impression, 130, 135, 150, 215
Cavett, Dick, 38
"Chain of Fools" (song), 207
Chaka Khan (singer), 264
Chambers, John, 144
Chapman, Graham, 47
Charles, Ray, 70, 147, 208–209, 222, 244, 257–258, 271–272, 304, 336
Chase, Cornelius "Chevy"
    about, 47, 49, 50, 51, 52, 56, 57, 95, 97, 118, 313
    after John's death, 333, 335–336
    Caddyshack, 212
    Gerald Ford stunts, 109, 120, 130
    "Jaws II" sketch, 107–108
    job interview sketch, 110
    John and, 109, 111, 125, 127, 185
    leaves *Saturday Night*, 126
    National Lampoon's Vacation, 332, 338
    Saturday Night, 104, 107–108, 109, 110, 119, 125, 126
    Saturday Night Live, 161–162
    Spies Like Us, 333
    Three Amigos, 333
    "Weekend Update," 104, 106, 108, 109, 119, 126, 134, 151
Checkers Records, 167
Chess Records, 167
Chez Paul scene, *Blues Brothers* movie, 269–271, 295

Chicago
    ChicagoFest, 215, 224, 230
    Comiskey Park, 217
    Dixie Square mall, 220–221, 252–254
    Great Migration and, 3
    papal visit to, 256
    postwar suburbanization and white flight, 3
    shooting *Blues Brothers* movie in, 213–215, 219–235, 241–250, 251–262, 273
    South Shore Country Club, 273
Child, Julia, Belushi sketch, 192
Christgau, Robert, 191
Christmas episodes (Candice Bergen), 112, 129–131
CinemaScope, 204
Cleaver, Ward, 33
Cleese, John, 47
Cleveland, James, 264
Close, Del, 43–44
Close Encounters of the Third Kind (movie), 182
Coca, Imogene, 93
cocaine, 54, 119, 123, 128, 129, 168, 178, 193, 197, 213, 216, 231, 233, 237, 261–262, 267, 271, 289–290, 300, 302, 303, 308, 309, 317, 318, 319, 320, 324, 331
Cochran, Wayne, 85
Cocker, Joe
    about, 180
    Belushi's impression, 27, 35, 45, 48, 50, 52, 106, 111, 113–114, 123, 126, 158
    at *Lemmings* show, 53
    Saturday Night appearance, 126
"Cold Sweat" (song), 209
"Colorado" (song), 50
Comiskey Park, 217
commercial parodies, 104, 105, 120, 159
Compass Players (theater ensemble), 22
Coneheads, 134
Connors, Jimmy, 100
consumer protection spoof, 130–131
Continental Divide (movie), 301–303, 310, 311, 313
Coppola, Francis Ford, 187
Cosell, Howard, 98
Coullet, Rhonda, 56, 316, 329
Crawdaddy (rock zine), 111, 180
Cray, Robert, 156
Cray Band, 167
Crayhawks (band), 156
Cropper, Steve, 160, 174, 176, 189, 191, 269, 271, 276
Crystal, Billy, 101
Curtin, Jane, 97, 98, 104, 106, 118, 130, 151, 160, 161, 167, 198

Dahl, Steve, 217
Dale (drug dealer), 87
Daley, John, Belushi impression, 26
Daley, Richard J., 213, 215

Dangerfield, Rodney, 212–213
Daniel, Sean, 141, 145, 152, 171, 172, 175, 199,
    200, 244, 256–257, 274, 280, 281, 288, 302,
    311, 313
Davis, Tom, 100, 119, 159, 168
"A Day in the Life of the School" sketch, 67
De Niro, Robert, 324, 333
Dead String Quartet, 112
death penalty skit, 60–61, 89
Decline, Ron (character), 237
Deeb, Gary, 105
Delta blues, 210
Delta House, 146–147, 152, 171
Denby, David, 294
DePalma, Brian, 213
Diamond, Neil, 190
"Disco Demolition Night," 217
disco music, 216–217
Dixon, Donna, 331
Doctor Detroit (movie), 331
Donen, Stanley, 204
"Don't Look Back in Anger" (film), 162
Doyle-Murray, Brian, 34
Dr. Al Kazali (graffiti character), 74
Dr. John (musician), 160
Dr. Psychedelic, 41
Dr. Zonk and the Zunkins (children's show), 95
drag characters, Belushi and, 187, 192
Drewery, Lauren, 75–76
"Drown in My Own Tears" (song), 208
drugs
    Aykroyd and, 75
    Belushi and, 15, 18–19, 20, 23, 27–28, 40–41,
        54, 118, 123–124, 127–129, 133, 134–136,
        137–138, 149, 154, 165, 168, 169, 174, 178,
        189, 193, 196, 197, 213, 216, 231, 232–233,
        237–238, 252–253, 260–262, 267, 271, 274,
        277, 283–284, 285, 289–290, 296, 297–298,
        300, 302, 307, 308, 309, 310, 311–312,
        316–324
    Belushi bottle, 168
    Blues Brothers movie shoot, 231–232, 234, 271,
        276, 282
    Carrie Fisher and, 233
    at filming of 1941, 193
    at Goin' South shooting, 149
    Rolling Stones and, 183
    at Saturday Night, 118–119
    at Second City, 32, 43
Dunn, Donald "Duck," 160, 174, 176, 191, 230,
    269, 276
Dunne, Murphy, 203, 224

Eagles (band), 259, 289
Ebersol, Duncan "Dick," 90, 92, 94, 95, 96, 98, 101,
    102, 104–105, 108, 109, 119, 128
Ebert, Roger, 172, 294, 310, 331
Eisner, Jane, 322

Eisner, Michael, 319, 321
ejection seat sketch, 82
Elbling, Peter, 45, 47–49
Elwood Blues (character), xi, 160, 188, 191, 195,
    206, 225, 228, 238–242, 259, 265, 268, 269,
    270, 272, 276, 277, 280, 283, 288, 298, 334
    See also Blues Brothers movie
Ertegun, Ahmet, 169
"Everybody Needs Somebody to Love" (song),
    223, 277

Father Sarducci (character), 159
Fear (punk band), 311, 312
"Feeling' Alright" sketch, 126
Ferlinghetti, Lawrence, 74
Festrunk brothers sketch, 150–151, 167
The Final Days (Woodward & Bernstein), 121
Fisher, Carrie, 187, 189, 233–234, 254, 278, 295, 302
Fisher, Jim, 32, 33, 35
"A Fistful of Yen" (parody), 141
Five Du-Tones (soul-vocal group), 258
505 Club, 79, 88, 186
Flaherty, Joe, 32–38, 40–41, 61, 78, 79, 80, 81, 85,
    88, 98–99, 112, 193
Flaherty, Paul, 38, 40, 42, 43, 49
"Flip, Flop and Fly" (song), 160
folk-blues revival, 211
Folsey, George, Jr., 203, 227–228, 229–230, 259,
    268, 272, 286
"For a Dancer" (song), 329
Ford, Gerald, 109, 120, 121, 130
Forristal, Susan, 310
43rd Parallel (revue), 43
"fourth wall," 22, 103, 106, 125, 156
Franken, Al, 100, 119, 159, 197
Franklin, Aretha, 207, 211, 212, 217, 222, 244,
    264, 265–267, 294, 304, 332–333, 334, 336
Franklin, Cecil, 265
The French Connection (movie), 248
"Freshman Year" (story), 139
From the Second City (revue), 22
Furst, Stephen, 158

Garvin, Fred (character), 198
George the Thief, 74
"Georgia on My Mind" (song), 208
Ghostbusters, 332, 336
Gibson, Henry, 247, 255
Gilda Radner, Live from New York (album), 192,
    202, 237
Gillard, Stu, 77
"Gimme Some Lovin'" (song), 223, 289, 314
"The Girl from Ipanema" (song), 243
"Girl, You Turn Me On" (song), 100
Glazer, Mitch, 111, 134–135, 160, 176, 180,
    181–182, 186, 304–305, 316, 320
Global Village (theater), 76
Glover, Elwood, 195

Gods (Land), 74
Godspell (show), 77, 78, 81
Goin' South (movie), 149, 150, 151
Good Ole Boys, 280, 288
Goodman, John, 333, 334
Gordon, Brian, 65
Gordy, Berry, 70
Gougeon, Hélène, 120
Gould, Elliott, 112, 122
Grateful Dead, 187
Great Migration, 3
Greed (game show), 77
Greenberg, Jerry, 169
Greene, Will, 3
grossest date sketch, 39
Groundhog Day (movie), 336
Groundlings (improv group), 92
Guest, Christopher, 47, 49–50, 51, 52, 53, 56, 92, 98, 134
"Guilty" (song), 291
Guitar Slim (musician), 157

Hackman, Gene, 248
Haeger, Bob, 13, 15
Hall, Willie "Too Big," 269
"Hallelujah I Love Her So" (song), 208
Halligan, Fionnuala, 335
hallucinogens, 40–41
Hanks, Tom, 104
Hanna, Elizabeth, 75
"hard light," 204
Hard Rock Café, 333
harmonica, 71, 72, 114, 188, 227, 297
Harris, Barbara, 22
Harris, Sydney J., 38
Harris, Wynonnie, 166
Harryhausen, Ray, 143
The Hart and Lorne Terrific Hour (TV series), 73, 91
Harvard Lampoon, 46
Harvey (drama), 20
Hauser, Gay, 74, 75
The Healer (album), 333
Heaven's Gate (movie), 281
Hefner, Hugh, 181, 317
Hello Dali (revue), 81
Helm, Levon, 160
Hendra, Tony, 47–49, 54, 55, 56, 95–96
Henry, Buck, 113, 126, 317
Hermans, Pee-wee, 270
heroin, 134, 138, 317, 318, 324
"Hey Bartender" (song), 157, 166, 167
High School Yearbook (parody), 140
"Highway Toes" (song), 50
Hilburn, Robert, 180–181, 300
Hirsch, Janis, 58–59, 86, 87
Hogan, Mark, 230
Hollywood Walk of Fame, 337
Holstein, Ed, 44

"The Honeydripper" (song), 210
Hooker, John Lee, 165, 210–211, 227, 228, 288, 333, 336–337, 339
Hope, Bob, 181
Horton, Big Walter, 223, 227
Horton, Johnny, 288
"Hot Stuff" (song), 216
"Hotel" (skit), 78
House of Blues (restaurant brand), 333
House of Blues Radio Hour, 334
"Howard Shore and His All-Bee Band," 113
Howlin' Wolf (musician), 211
Hutton, Lauren, 193
Hynde, Chrissie, 318

I Am Curious (Maple) (TV special), 73
"I Can't Turn You Loose" (song), 179, 276
"I Don't Know" (song), 157, 168
"I Dreamed of a Hill-Billy Heaven" (song), 15
"I Gave My Love a Cherry" (song), 155
"I Got Everything I Need Almost" (song), 189
"I Got You (I Feel Good)" (song), 209
"I'm a King Bee" (song), 113, 114
improvisation, first rule, 35
improvisational theater, 22, 79
The Incredible Shrinking Woman (film), 199
Insana, Tino, 26, 34, 37
Italy, *Blues Brothers* movie showing, 339
"I've Got a Woman" (song), 208

"Jackie Christ, Superstar" sketch, 51, 52
Jacklin, Judy
    about, 86, 100
    alcohol, 15, 23
    Blues Brothers, 177–178
    college years, 27, 29
    doing drugs, 15, 23–24, 27–28, 54
    John and drugs, 128, 131, 134, 149, 169
    John at *Lemmings*, 48, 49, 54, 55
    John at Second City, 40, 42–43, 56
    marriage to John, 132
    married years. *See* Belushi, Judy
    ongoing relationship with John, 86, 100, 117, 128, 131, 132
    pregnancy, 28
    working at *Lemmings*, 51
    working at *National Lampoon*, 58, 59, 117
    youth, 12–13, 14, 15, 18, 20, 21, 23, 39, 86
Jacklin, Rob, 24–25, 132, 314
Jackson, Kate, 198
Jacobs, Paul, 49, 50, 52
Jagger, Mick, 180, 183
"Jailhouse Rock" (song), 223
Jake Blues (character), xi, 20, 160, 167, 175, 179, 188, 191, 195, 205, 206, 214, 225, 235, 241–242, 265, 266, 268, 269, 272, 276, 277, 278, 279, 283, 288, 298
    See also Blues Brothers movie

James, Cleophus (character), 264–265
James, Skip (musician), 211
"Jaws II" sketch, 107–108
Jaws (movie), 182
Joel, Billy, 190
John Loves Mary (comedy), 20
John Paul II (pope), 256
Johnson, Luther "Guitar Junior," 223, 227
Johnson, Robert, 211
Joliet Correctional Center, 235–237, 281, 339
Jones, Calvin "Fuzz," 227
Jordan, Steve, 173, 180, 298
Joy of Sex (movie), 321
"The Jumpin' Jive" (song), 210
Justice Is Done or, Oh, Calcolidge! (revue), 33

Kaplan, William B., 229, 267, 280
Karwoski, George, 5–6, 13
Katz, Stephen, 203, 224, 225, 226, 231, 234, 235, 249,
    251–252, 259, 263, 264, 270, 275, 282, 295
Katzenberg, Jeffrey, 321
Kaufman, Andy, 104, 106
Kazurinsky, Tim, 215–216
Keese, Earl (character), 306
Kelly, Sean, 52, 56, 60
Kelly's Heroes (comedy), 145
Kennedy-era toga party sketch, 155
Kenney, Doug, 46, 89, 139, 148, 213, 247, 301
Kentucky Fried Movie, 141–142, 145, 194, 247, 248,
    336
Kentucky Fried Theater (comedy troupe), 91, 92,
    142, 145, 299
Khan, Sharif, 299
Khrushchev, Nikita, Belushi impression, 6
Kidder, Margot, 198
King, B.B., 211, 258, 334, 341
"King Tut" (musical number), 168
Kirshner, Don, Shaffer impression of, xi, xiii
Klein, Allen, 237
Klenfer, Michael, 169–170
Koch, Ed, 184
Korshak, Sidney, 214, 293
Krenitsky, Karen, 190
Kurlansky, Mark, 19

La Diva (album), 207
Landis, John
    about, 196, 254–255, 316, 331–332, 338
    after John's death, 331–332, 336
    An American Werewolf in London, 331–332
    Animal House, 142, 145, 147, 151–152, 154–156,
        158, 171, 174, 178
    Belushi and, 185, 261, 267, 283
    bio, 143–145
    Blues Brothers movie, 199, 200, 201, 203,
        204–205, 206, 207–208, 209, 212, 213, 222,
        225, 227, 230, 233, 235, 237, 238, 241, 242,
        243, 246, 248–249, 252, 258, 259–260, 261,
        263, 265, 266, 267, 268, 269, 272, 276, 277,
        279, 280, 281, 282, 283, 286, 287, 292–293,
        295, 336
    John's death, 326
    marriage, 178
    Neighbors movie, 307–308
    Trading Places, 331, 332
Landis, Marshall, 143, 201
Landis, Shirley, 143
Lane, William, 74
"Lasser Orgy Girls" sketch, 139
Lawrence of Arabia skit, 59
Lazenby, George, 142
Leming, Warren, 24, 26, 36
Lemmings (album), 56
Lemmings (show), 45, 47–57
"Lemmings Lament" (song), 50
Leonard, William, 33
Lettow, Al, 13
Levy, Eugene, 61, 77, 80, 81, 82, 94, 194
Lipowitz, Lorne David. *See* Michaels, Lorne
"Listen to Me Now" (song), 9
Little, Rich, 93
Little Richard (singer), 209
Live at the Apollo (album), 209
Lloyd, John, 220, 221, 268
Lone Star Café, 211
"Lonely at the Bottom" (song), 50
Long, Brady, 69, 75
Long, Tommy, 19, 21
Los Angeles
    Blues Brothers band at Universal
        Amphitheatre, 178–182, 188, 203
    Blues Brothers movie shoot, 263–273, 274–276,
        278–280, 295
"Louie Louie" (song), 49, 171, 314
Lowry, Lynn, 18
Lunney, Leonard, 65, 66
Lyda, Morris, 228–229, 232–233, 252, 260, 290

Mabon, Willie, 168
Maguire, Roberta, 29, 33, 35, 36
Malle, Louis, 316
Malone, Tom, 165–166, 168, 171, 174, 269
Manilow, Barry, 190
Mann, Ted, 287
marijuana, 23, 27, 28, 40, 75, 87, 88, 118, 123, 138,
    154, 276, 277, 319
Marini, Lou, 171, 180, 222, 265, 266, 271, 298, 299
Marsh, Dave, 191, 304
Marshall, Penny, 128, 234, 277
Martin, Andrea, 76, 94
Martin, Steve, 91, 104, 150, 167, 168, 333
Mary Stigmata, Sister (character), 198, 205, 263
The Mary Tyler Moore Show, Radner parody of,
    87–88
Maslin, Janet, 171–172, 293, 294, 335
May, Elaine, 22

McClinton, Delbert, 189
McConnachie, Brian, 86
McGill, Bruce, 153
McNamara, Robert, 238
McQueen, Steve, 254
Mean Girls (movie), 338
Meat Loaf (singer), 89
Meatballs (movie), 184, 237
"Megadeath" (song), 52
mescaline, 40–41, 54–55
Metcalf, Mark, 153
Meyerowitz, Rick, 301
Michaels, Lorne
    about, xii, 72, 128, 136, 142, 151, 164, 184, 189,
        197, 317, 327
    on Belushi, 188, 327
    Gilda Radner album, 192, 202, 237
    1941 (movie), 201
    Saturday Night Live film, 175
    Saturday Night show, 91–101, 109, 123, 134–135,
        138, 159, 183, 202, 238, 335
    wedding, 309–310
Miller, Chris, 139
"Minnie the Moocher" (song), 210, 212, 276, 294
"Moby!" (parody), 86
Modern Sounds in Country and Western Music
    (album), 208
Moffat, Jeff, 4
Moment by Moment (film), 199
"Money (That's What I Want)" (song), 158
Monty Python's Flying Circus, 91
Moon over Miami (movie), 316
Mooney, Paul, 109
"moonwalk," 210
Moore, Sam, 71, 333
Morgan, Judy, 32, 33, 44
Morris, Garrett, 95, 161, 184, 188
Mount, Thom, 140–141, 146, 152, 154, 171, 175,
    186, 196, 200, 201, 280, 281, 301
Mountain Men sketch, 15
movies, rehabilitation stories of, 334–335
Muddy Waters, 211, 228
Muddy Waters (band), 71
Murphy, Eddie, 332
Murphy, Matt "Guitar," 173, 174, 176, 189, 208,
    212, 265, 266, 268, 269
Murray, Bill
    about, 61, 82, 88, 89, 97, 98, 185
    after John's death, 332, 335–336
    Caddyshack, 212, 332
    Ghostbusters, 332, 336
    Groundhog Day, 336
    Meatballs, 184, 237
    Prime Time Players, 98
    Saturday Night, 133–134, 135, 161, 187
Murray, Brian
    National Lampoon Radio Hour, 60, 88
    National Lampoon Show, 89

Prime Time Players, 98
Saturday Night, 133
Saturday Night Live, 159
Second City, 32, 33, 34, 36, 61, 78
Second City Toronto, 78, 80
mushrooms (hallucinogens), 40, 93, 123

Nadoolman, Deborah, 145, 153, 178, 254–255
National Lampoon (magazine), 46, 49, 56, 58
National Lampoon Radio Hour, 58–61, 78, 83
    Aykroyd and, 87
    final show, 89
    High School Yearbook parody, 140
    John at, 58–61, 78, 83, 85, 118
    stage show (Philadelphia), 87–88, 89, 109
    touring company, 85
National Lampoon Show, 89, 95
National Lampoon's Animal House (film). *See Animal
    House*
National Lampoon's Vacation (movie), 332, 338
Nazis, in *Blues Brothers* movie, 246–247, 255
NBC (TV network), 90, 123, 124, 316
Neidermeyer, Douglas C., 153
Neighbors (movie), 306–308, 310, 311, 312
Nelson, Willie, 160
Nessen, Ron, 120
"New Dad Insurance" (parody), 103
Newhart, Bob, 4
Newman, Laraine, 92, 95, 106, 116, 118, 120, 129,
    134, 184
Newman, Randy, 291
The Next Generation (revue), 32
Nichols, Mike, 22
Nicholson, Jack, 148, 149, 180
"Night of the Seven Fires" (script), 140–141
1941 (movie), 182, 186, 192–193, 257, 277–278
Nixon, Richard, Aykroyd impression, 82, 121
Noble Rot (movie idea), 31, 317, 318, 322
Not Ready for Prime Time Players, xi, 100, 105,
    111
Novello, Don, 159, 161, 314, 317–319, 321, 322,
    329

O'Connor, John, 105, 108
O'Donoghue, Michael, 47, 58–60, 93–94, 95, 97,
    107, 109, 112, 117, 119, 122, 133, 138, 237,
    301, 318
O'Dwyer, Gary, 66
O'Flaherty, Joe, 34
O'Hara, Catherine, 61, 81, 82, 94, 129
O'Hara, Marcus, 74, 76, 79, 80
Old Fire Hall, 81
Old Joliet Prison, 235–237, 281, 339
"The Old Landmark" (song), 264
Omega House, 146, 152
opium, 233
The Original Disco Man (album), 210
O'Toole, Peter, Belushi impression, 59

Ottawa Little Theatre, 75
Ovitz, Michael, 313, 314, 319, 320
Oz, Frank, 235

"Papa's Got a Brand New Bag" (song), 209
Paramount Pictures, 254, 314, 316, 332
Pardo, Don, 103
Payne, Dan, 15, 16–18, 20, 21, 310
Payne, Juanita, 4, 9, 15, 20
Peckinpah, Sam, tribute to, 107
Penniman, Richard, 209
Perkins, Pinetop, 227
peyote, 40
Pickett, Wilson, 207, 334
The Pickle (vaudeville act), 77
Pl*yb*y (parody), 46
Place, Mary Kay, 160
Planes, Trains and Automobiles (movie), 338
Playten, Alice, 49, 52, 53
"Please, Please, Please" (song), 209
Plimpton, George, 46
Police Squad! (show), 316
Pomerantz, Hart, 72, 73, 91
Pomus, Doc, 170, 171
"Positively Wall Street" (song), 50
pot. See marijuana
Prater, Dave, 71
Prime Time Players, 98, 100
Pryor, Richard, Saturday Night, 90–91, 109–110
punk (music), 311
Purify, James and Bobby, 165

Quaaludes, 54, 118, 123, 129, 174, 323

racism, Blues Brothers movie, 287, 294, 304
Radcliffe, Rosemary, 77, 81
Radio Hour. See National Lampoon Radio Hour
Radio Ranch, 58, 86
Radner, Gilda
    about, 61, 62, 77, 82, 184
    Aykroyd and, 76, 129
    John and, 118
    LP album, 192, 202, 237
    Michaels and, 192
    National Lampoon Show, 89
    National Lampoon stage show, 87–88, 89
    Saturday Night, 94, 96, 104, 151, 198
    Second City Toronto, 78, 79, 81
Ramis, Harold, 33, 39, 43, 45, 61, 78, 85–86, 88,
    89, 126, 139, 140, 146, 147, 153, 213, 237,
    247, 327, 332
Rantoul Rag, 28, 29
Ravins (band), 8, 9, 85, 158, 314, 316
Ray the Green Beret, 74
RCO All-Stars (band), 160, 177
Redding, Otis, 207
Reed, Rex, 172
Rehner, Adrian, 16–18, 20

Reiner, Rob, 105–107
Reitman, Ivan, 77, 88, 89, 139–141, 237, 332
"Respect" (song), 207, 212
The Return of the Blues Brothers (script), 200
Reubens, Paul, 270
"Rhoda Tyler Moore" (skit), 87–88
rhythm-and-blues music, 71, 164, 165, 206, 207,
    304
Richards, Keith, 183, 187, 197
Riegert, Peter, 154, 156, 170
"Ring My Bell" (song), 216
Ritter, John, 313
Rivers, Joan, 22
Robertson, Cliff, 45
Robillard, Duke, 170, 191–192
Robinson, Ray Charles, 208
rock 'n' roll, 50, 216
rock stars, dress, 165
"Rocket 88" (song), 166
Rolling Stones, 183, 267
Ronstadt, Linda, 91, 180
Roomful of Blues (band), 170, 191
Rosenthal, Marshall, 44
Ross, Diana, 207
Ross-Leming, Eugenie, 36, 39–40, 41–42, 48
Rowan & Martin's Laugh-In (TV show), 73
Royce, Rose (disco group), 211–212
Rubin, Alan, 173, 177, 271
Rutles (band), 237

Sahlins, Bernie, 32, 33, 35, 40, 41, 61, 81, 193
Salgado, Curtis, 156–157, 158, 160, 164, 167, 193,
    194
Sam and Dave (musicians), 157, 165, 333
"Samurai Delicatessen" sketch, 113
samurai sketch, 110–111, 112, 126, 134
Samurai Widow (Judy Belushi), 333
Sandrich, Jay, 313, 319
Saturday Night Live (ABC show), xi, xii–xiii, 98,
    100
Saturday Night Live (film), 175
Saturday Night/Saturday Night Live (NBC show),
    90–122
    "Adopt Belushi for Christmas Contest," 131
    after John's death, 335
    auditions for, 96–97, 100
    Beatles and, 121
    Belushi bee sketch, 104, 105, 106
    Brando group therapy session sketch, 112–113
    "Brian's Nightmare" sketch, 124
    Candice Bergen at, 107, 108
    the Cave, 116–117
    Christmas episodes, 112, 129–131
    college shows, 132–134
    concept of, 95
    consumer protection spoof, 130
    creation of, 93–101
    Dead String Quartet, 112

debut, 100, 103
drug use at, 118–119
earnings, 185
Emmy awards, 122
fake commercials, 104, 105, 120, 159
female colleagues as artistic equals, 118
generational divide in response to, 105
"Howard Shore and His All-Bee Band," 113
"Jaws II" sketch, 107–108
job interview sketch, 110
King Tut episode, 183
Michaels and, 335
planning, 92–93
premiere, 103–104
Pryor at, 90–91
recent rankings of performers, 338
Reiner at, 105–107
return to live broadcast (1977), 150–151
reviews of, 105, 108, 109
"Samurai Delicatessen," 113
samurai sketch, 110–111, 112, 126, 134
season one, 103–123
season two, 126–139
season three, 183
season four, 183–185, 202
season five, 238
set of, 103
Simon and Garfunkel tunes, 105
as *SNL*, 150–151, 157–164, 167–168
weatherman sketch, 119
"Weekend Update," 104, 106, 108, 109, 119,
    126, 134, 151, 167–168
work week, 115–116
See also Blues Brothers band
Saturday Night with Howard Cosell, 98, 100, 118,
    133, 139
Sautter, Chris, 4, 5, 6
Schiller, Tom, 93, 97, 110, 119, 162
Schlock (film), 145
Schlosser, Herb, 90–92
Schoenstein, Donald "Boon," 153
Scott-Heron, Bill, 109
SCTV, 316
Second City (improv troupe)
    about, 32
    bible skit, 37, 78
    California operation, 94
    The Canadian Show 1 or, Upper U.S.A. (revue),
        61
    Chicago and Toronto companies trading
        places (1974), 82, 84
    drug use and, 32, 43
    43rd Parallel (revue), 43
    funeral scene, 44, 78
    Hello Dali (revue), 81
    history of, 21–22
    "Hotel" (skit), 78
    John at, 35–45, 118

John's appearance as alumnus, 215–216, 310
John's audition performance for *Lemmings*, 48
Justice Is Done or, Oh, Calcolidge! (revue), 33
The Next Generation (revue), 32
    profanity at, 39–40
    Sergio Mendes parody, 48
    Toronto touring company, 32, 61–62, 77–80,
        81, 84, 94
    We're Gonna Be All Right sketch, 81
Second City Television, 193
Second City Toronto, 32, 61–62, 77–80, 81, 84, 94
See You Next Wednesday (fictional movie), 280
Seidenberg, Sid, 211
Servants of the People (Ferlinghetti), 74
The 7th Voyage of Sinbad (fantasy epic), 143
Shaffer, Paul, xi–xii, xiii, 77, 113, 114, 130, 167,
    173, 174, 179, 181, 192, 198, 202, 203, 223,
    296–297, 329
Shales, Tom, 108, 120, 125, 129, 202
Shatner, William, Aykroyd impression, 78, 122
Shawnee Summer Theatre, 17–21
"She Came In through the Bathroom Window"
    (song), 27
"She Caught the Katy" (song), 223
The Shining (movie), 257
Shipton, Alyn, 305
"Shootin' up the highway on the road map of my
    wrist" (song), 50
Shore, Howard, 73, 85, 104, 113, 114, 165, 202
Short, Martin, 76, 77, 81, 333
Shuster, Rosie, 73, 94, 117, 126, 131, 136, 189, 198,
    218, 269, 310
Silverman, Fred, 198
Simmons, Matty, 49, 51, 52, 53, 58–60, 61, 89, 101,
    139–141, 171
Simmons, Michael, 40, 54, 88
Simon, Carly, 53, 169, 310
Simon, Paul, 189
Sinatra, Frank, 98
Singin' in the Rain (song), 204
"Sink the Bismarck" (song), 288
Siskel, Gene, 172, 294–295, 296, 310
Sister Mary Stigmata (character), 198, 205, 263
Sloane, Joyce, 32, 33–34, 78
Smith, Cathy, 324, 326, 333
Smith, R.J., 265
Smith, Willie "Big Eyes," 227
Smokey and the Bandit (film), 206
Smothers Brothers, 318
Sneak Joint (bar), 223
Snow-White and Rose-Red (drama), 75
Sosna, David, 203, 204, 220, 221, 222, 224–225,
    230, 234, 235, 239, 248, 249, 250, 251, 255,
    259, 260, 265, 267, 270, 276, 281
"Soul Man" (song), 157, 177, 188, 191
South Shore Country Club, 273
Southern California Community Choir, 264
speed (drug), 40

speedball (drugs), 324
Spielberg, Steven, 111, 174, 182, 191, 192, 194,
    244, 301, 318
Spies Like Us (movie), 333
St. Pius X Preparatory (Ottawa), 66
"Stand By Your Man" (song), 279
Stansfield, Tom, 4, 10
Star Trek, O'Donoghue and, 122
Star Wars (movie), 182
steam-bath sequence, *Blues Brothers* movie, 272
Stevens, George, 144
Stewart, Rod, 190
stormy Weather (film), 210
Streisand, Barbra, 190
Summer, Donna, 216
Sutherland, Donald, 142, 145, 152
"Sweet Deception" (comedy), 313–316
"Sweet Home Chicago" (song), 223

The Taking of Pelham One Two Three (movie), 281
Tanen, Ned, 140–141, 145, 152, 171, 175, 199, 257,
    268, 286–287
Taylor, Elizabeth, Belushi parody, 187
Taylor, James, 53, 169, 232, 310, 327
"That's Armageddon" (film), 142
Themal, Harry, 172
"Theodoric of York, Medieval Barber" sketch,
    167
Thigh, Brian (character), 237
"The Thing That Wouldn't Leave" (skit), 163
"Think" (song), 212, 222, 266, 294
This Is Spinal Tap (parody), 338
Thomas, Dave, 77, 81, 84, 94–95, 194, 316, 333
Thomas, Dylan, 55
Three Amigos (movie), 333
Throne of Blood (movie), 181
Tigrett, Isaac, 333
Tippecanoe and Déjà Vu (revue), 78
Tischler, Bob, 58, 86, 164, 190–191, 202, 222,
    264, 300
Titters (book), 117
Today Makes Me Nervous (TV special), 73
Tomlin, Lily, 91–92, 126, 199
Top Hat and the Downtowners (musical act), 72
The Towering Inferno (movie), 145
Trading Places (movie), 331, 332, 338
"Tutti Frutti" (song), 209
"The 2,000 Pound Bee" (song), 309

ultra-wide lenses, 204
Universal Life Coffee House, 29
Universal Studios, 213, 268, 286, 287, 301, 313,
    331, 337
University of Illinois at Chicago Circle, 29

Veeck, Bill, 217
Veeck, Mike, 217
Vietnamese Baby Book (O'Donoghue story), 47
Virgin Mary skit, 37, 78

Waiting for Godot skit, 59
Wallace, Bill "Superfoot," 302, 306, 307, 315, 322,
    323, 324–325, 327
Wallach, Eli, Belushi impression, 148–149
Walsh, Joe, 289
Ward, Anita, 216
Warner Brothers, 333
Wasserman, Lew, 171, 257, 274, 281, 287
Waters, Muddy, 211, 228
weatherman sketch, 119
"Weekend Update" sketch, 104, 106, 108, 109,
    119, 126, 134, 151, 167–168
Weiss, Bob, 194, 195, 199, 200, 214, 216, 223, 224,
    231, 232, 235, 238, 239, 243, 244, 254, 255,
    256, 257, 274, 281, 286, 287, 316, 337
"Welcome Back: The Death Penalty" (skit),
    60–61, 89
Wendell, Richard "Smokey," 289–290, 296,
    297–298, 300, 302, 303, 305–306, 323
Wenner, Jann, 125, 127, 138
We're Gonna Be All Right sketch, 81
West Compass Players (troupe), 26, 27, 29–30,
    33, 34
"What'd I Say" (song), 208
What's Up, Doc? (comedy), 319
Wheaton (IL), 3–4
White, Timothy, 195
Who's Zoomin' Who? (album), 332, 333
Widdoes, Jamie, 153, 155
wide-angle films, 204
Wilderness Road (band), 24, 41, 42
Williams, Robin, 315, 323–324, 333
Wilson, Brian, 124
Wilson, Dave, 93
Winkler, Henry, 180
Winters, Jonathan, 4, 5, 315
Wired (Woodward), 332
Wood, Ron, 267
"Woodshuck Festival, Three Days of Peace, Love,
    and Death" (parody), 47
Woodstock parody (*National Lampoon*), 47, 50–51
Woodward, Bob, 121, 332
Wooten, Katherine "Boots," 145, 228

Young, Charles M., 174
Your Show of Shoes (NBC), 92–93, 108
"You're the Pits" (parody song), 87

Zanuck, Richard, 306, 308, 311–312